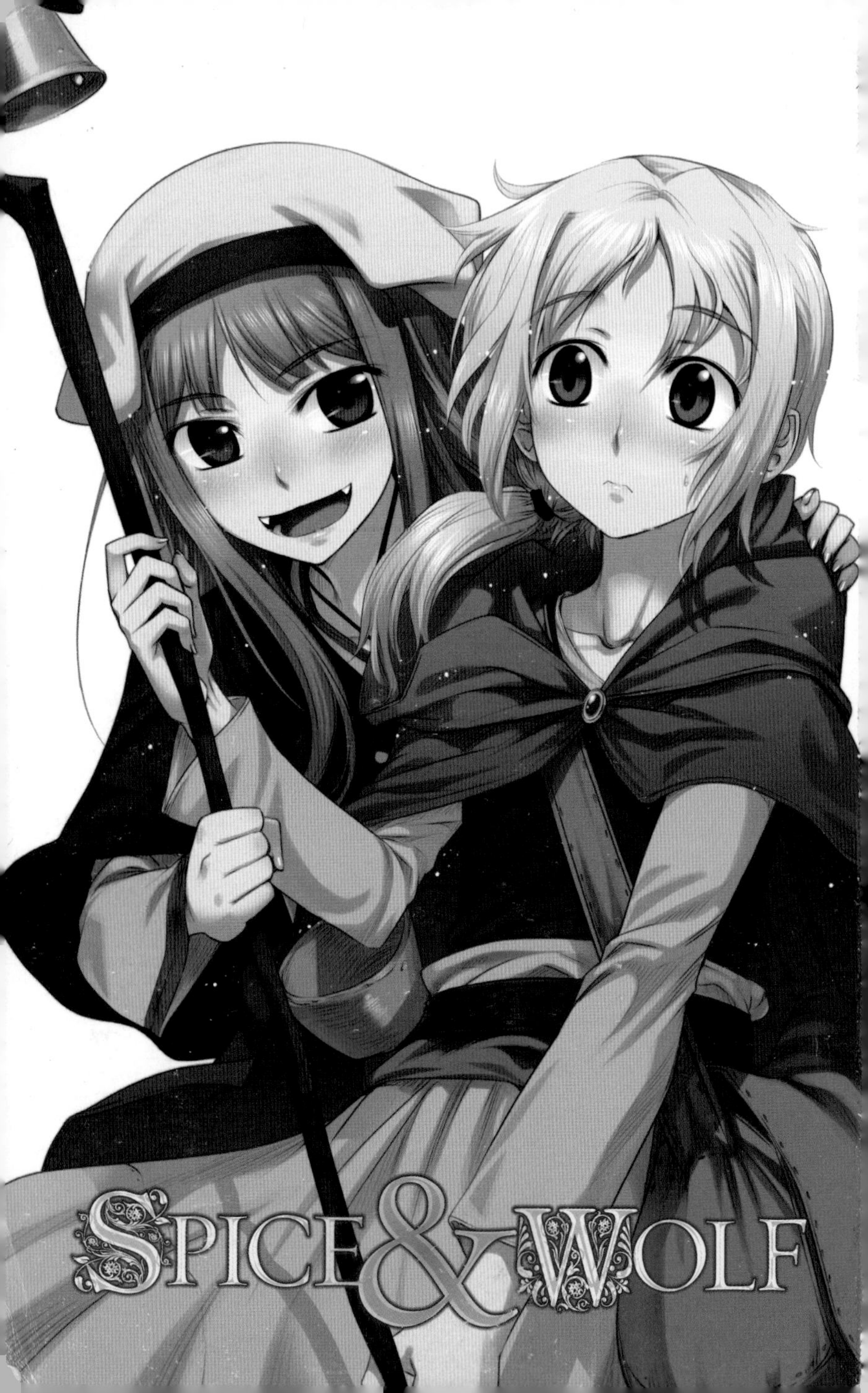
SPICE&WOLF

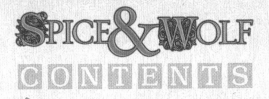

SPICE & WOLF

CONTENTS

Chapter 19 3

Chapter 20 31

Chapter 21 61

Chapter 22 87

Chapter 23 119

Chapter 24 153

Bonus Track 177

Outline

On the way to the Church city of Ruvinheigen, Lawrence the traveling merchant and Holo, the wolf-god of the harvest (in her human form), stop in the town of Poroson to turn their cargo of pepper into coin. The cunning master of a trading company there tries to swindle them, but Holo sees through the ruse...

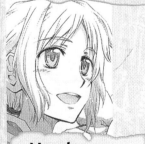

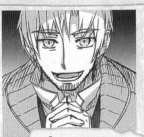

Norah
A talented young shepherdess employed by the Church in Ruvinheigen.

Lawrence
A traveling merchant journeying north to bring Holo to her homeland of Yoitsu.

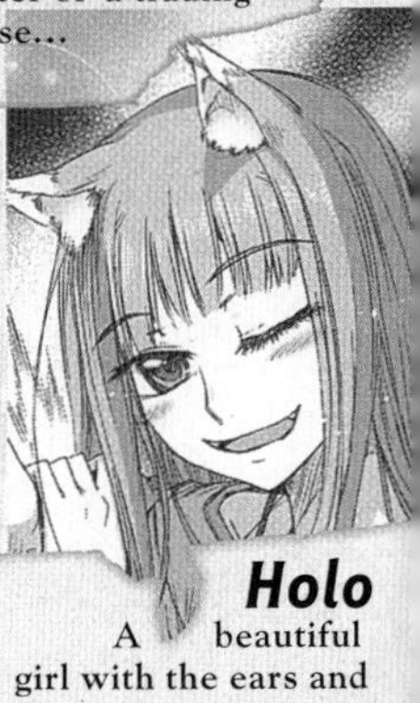

Holo
A beautiful girl with the ears and tail of a wolf. Her true form is that of the wolf-god of the harvest.

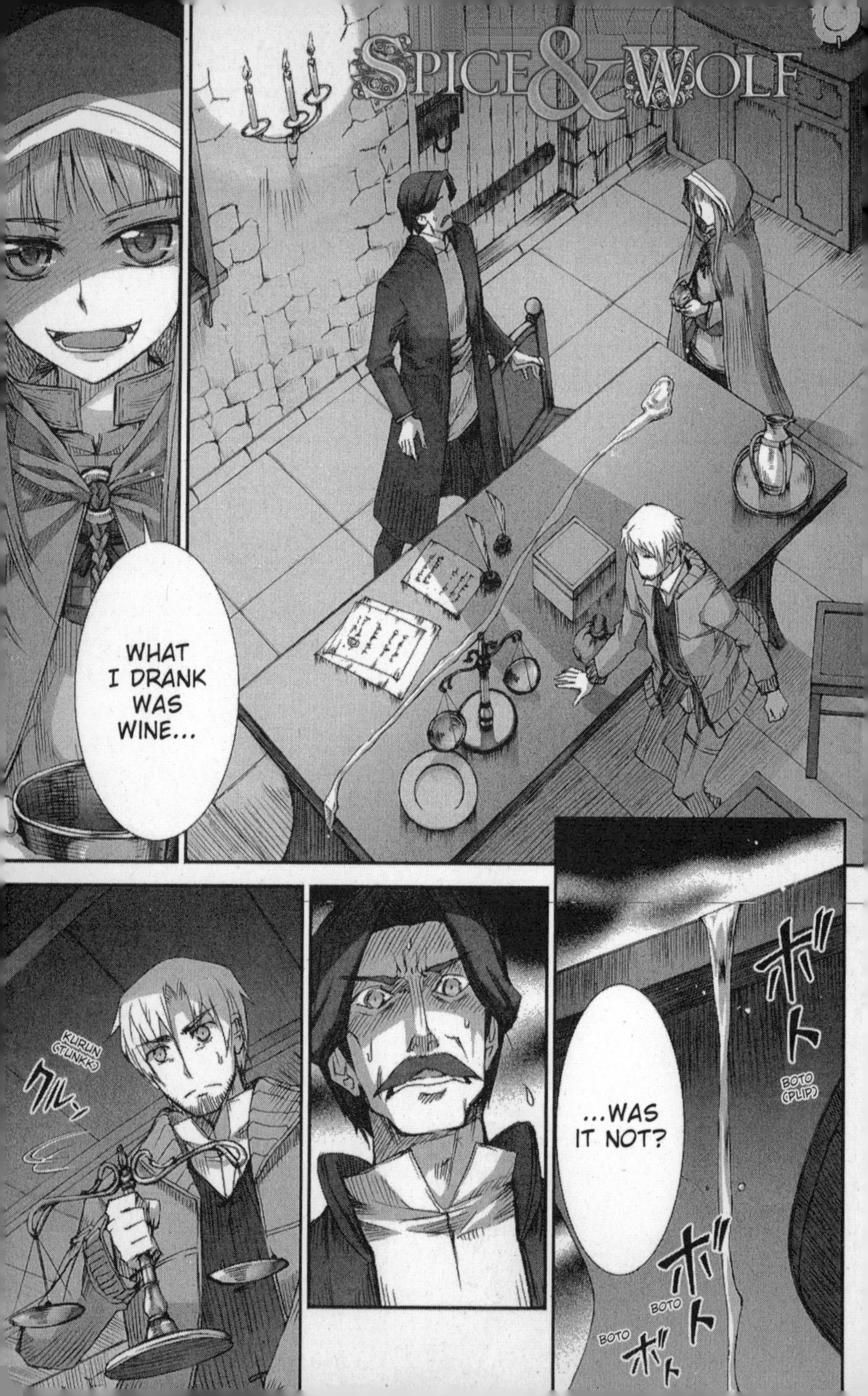
SPICE & WOLF
WHAT I DRANK WAS WINE...
ボト
BOTO (PLIP)
...WAS IT NOT?
ボト
BOTO
ボト
BOTO
クルン
KURUN (TUNKK)

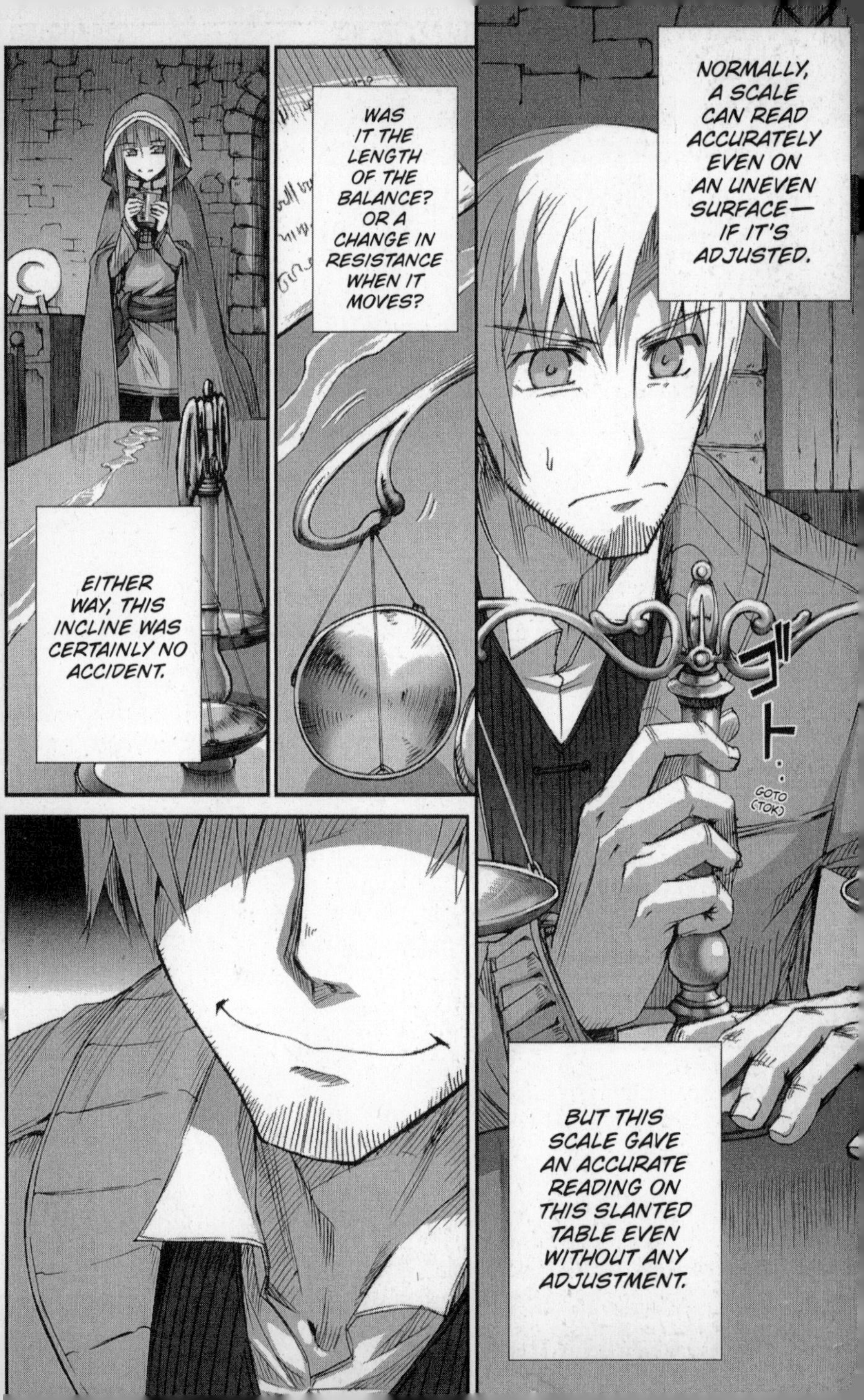
NORMALLY, A SCALE CAN READ ACCURATELY EVEN ON AN UNEVEN SURFACE—IF IT'S ADJUSTED.
ゴト
GOTO (TOK)
BUT THIS SCALE GAVE AN ACCURATE READING ON THIS SLANTED TABLE EVEN WITHOUT ANY ADJUSTMENT.
WAS IT THE LENGTH OF THE BALANCE? OR A CHANGE IN RESISTANCE WHEN IT MOVES?
EITHER WAY, THIS INCLINE WAS CERTAINLY NO ACCIDENT.

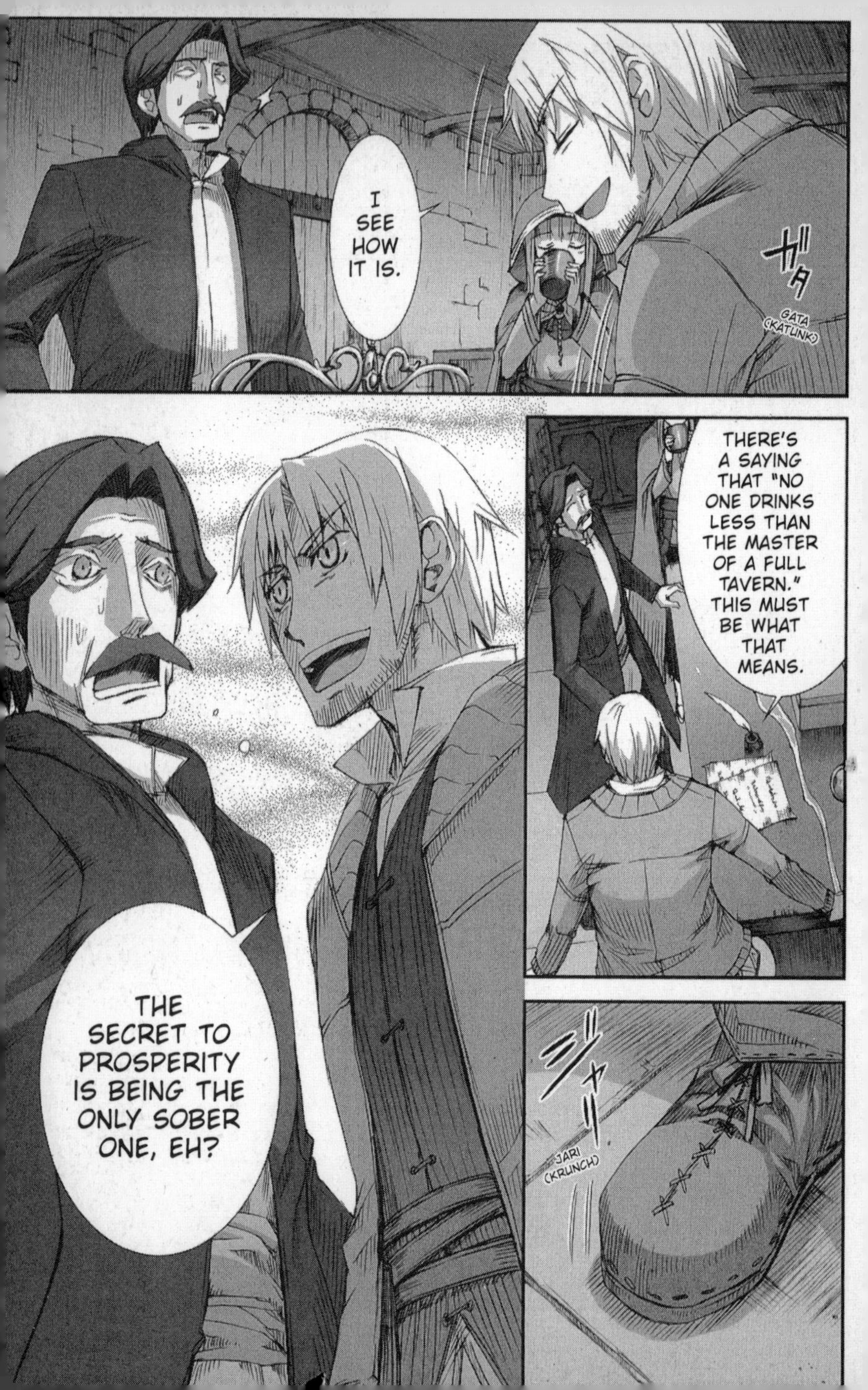

ガタ
GATA (KATUNK)
I SEE HOW IT IS.
THERE'S A SAYING THAT "NO ONE DRINKS LESS THAN THE MASTER OF A FULL TAVERN." THIS MUST BE WHAT THAT MEANS.
THE SECRET TO PROSPERITY IS BEING THE ONLY SOBER ONE, EH?
ジャリ
JARI (KRUNCH)

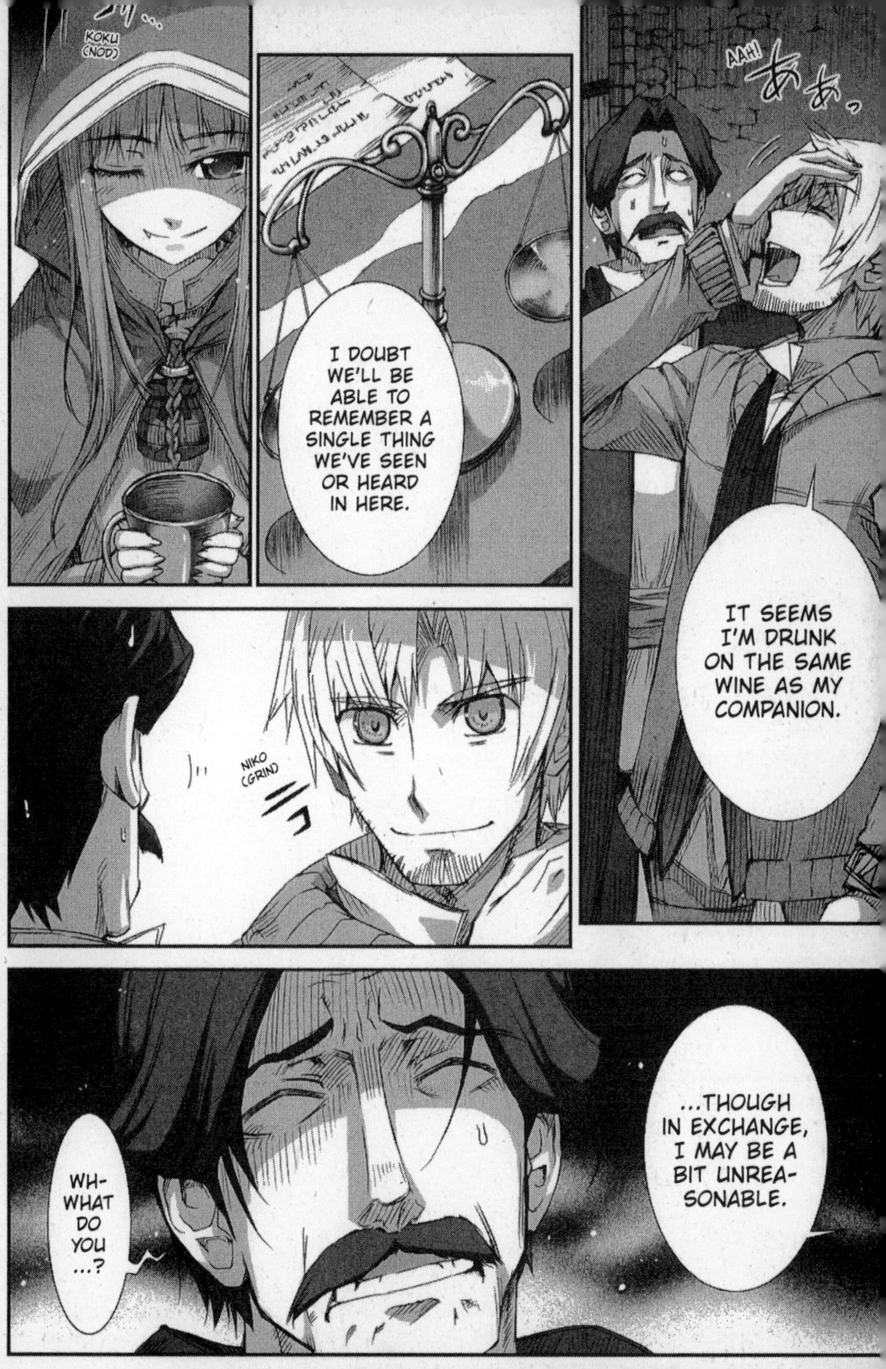
AAH!
あぁっ
IT SEEMS I'M DRUNK ON THE SAME WINE AS MY COMPANION.
I DOUBT WE'LL BE ABLE TO REMEMBER A SINGLE THING WE'VE SEEN OR HEARD IN HERE.
KOKU (NOD)
NIKO (GRIN)
...THOUGH IN EXCHANGE, I MAY BE A BIT UNREASONABLE.
WH-WHAT DO YOU ...?

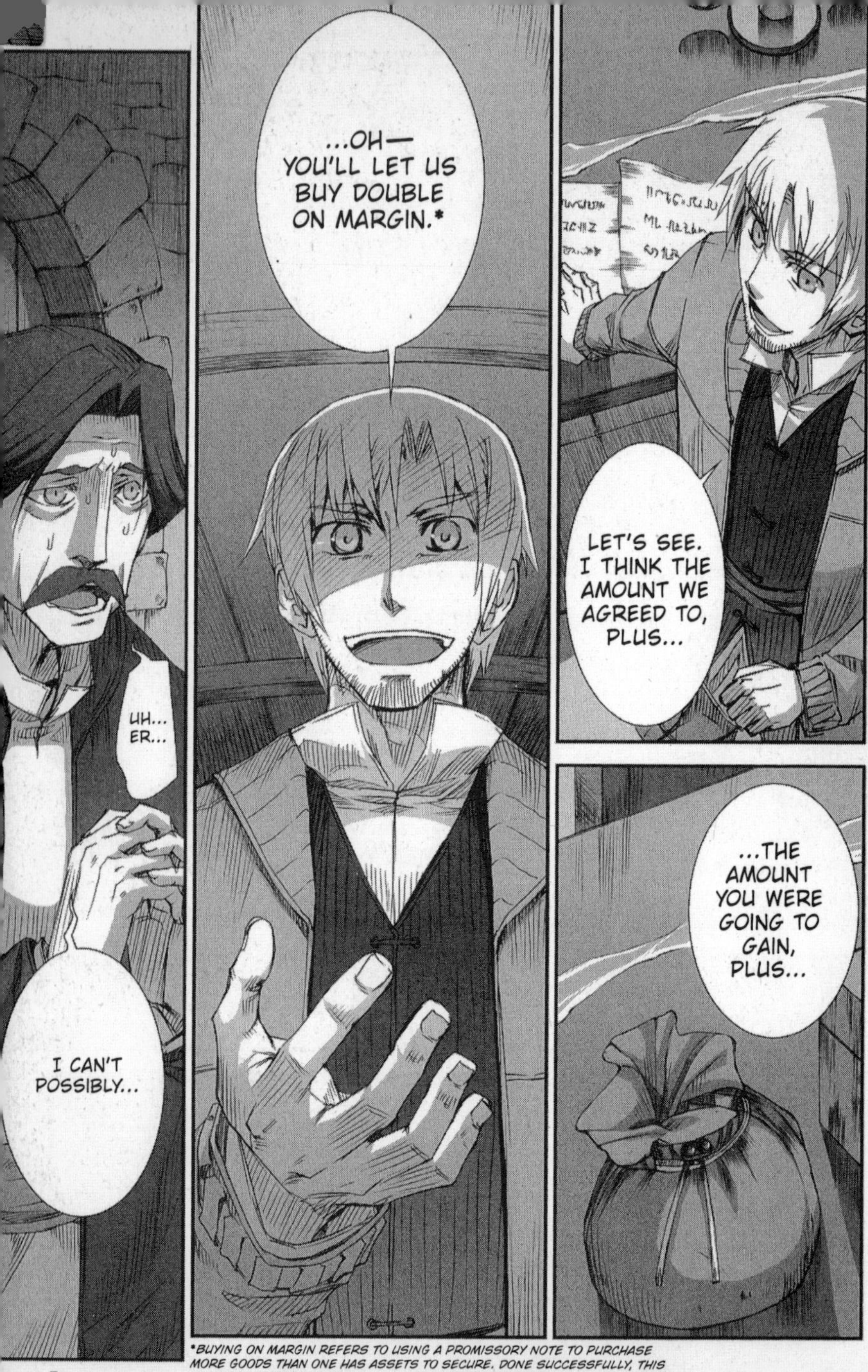
LET'S SEE. I THINK THE AMOUNT WE AGREED TO, PLUS...
...THE AMOUNT YOU WERE GOING TO GAIN, PLUS...
...OH— YOU'LL LET US BUY DOUBLE ON MARGIN.*
UH... ER...
I CAN'T POSSIBLY...

*BUYING ON MARGIN REFERS TO USING A PROMISSORY NOTE TO PURCHASE MORE GOODS THAN ONE HAS ASSETS TO SECURE. DONE SUCCESSFULLY, THIS ALLOWS A MERCHANT TO REALIZE A GREATER-THAN-USUAL AMOUNT OF PROFIT.

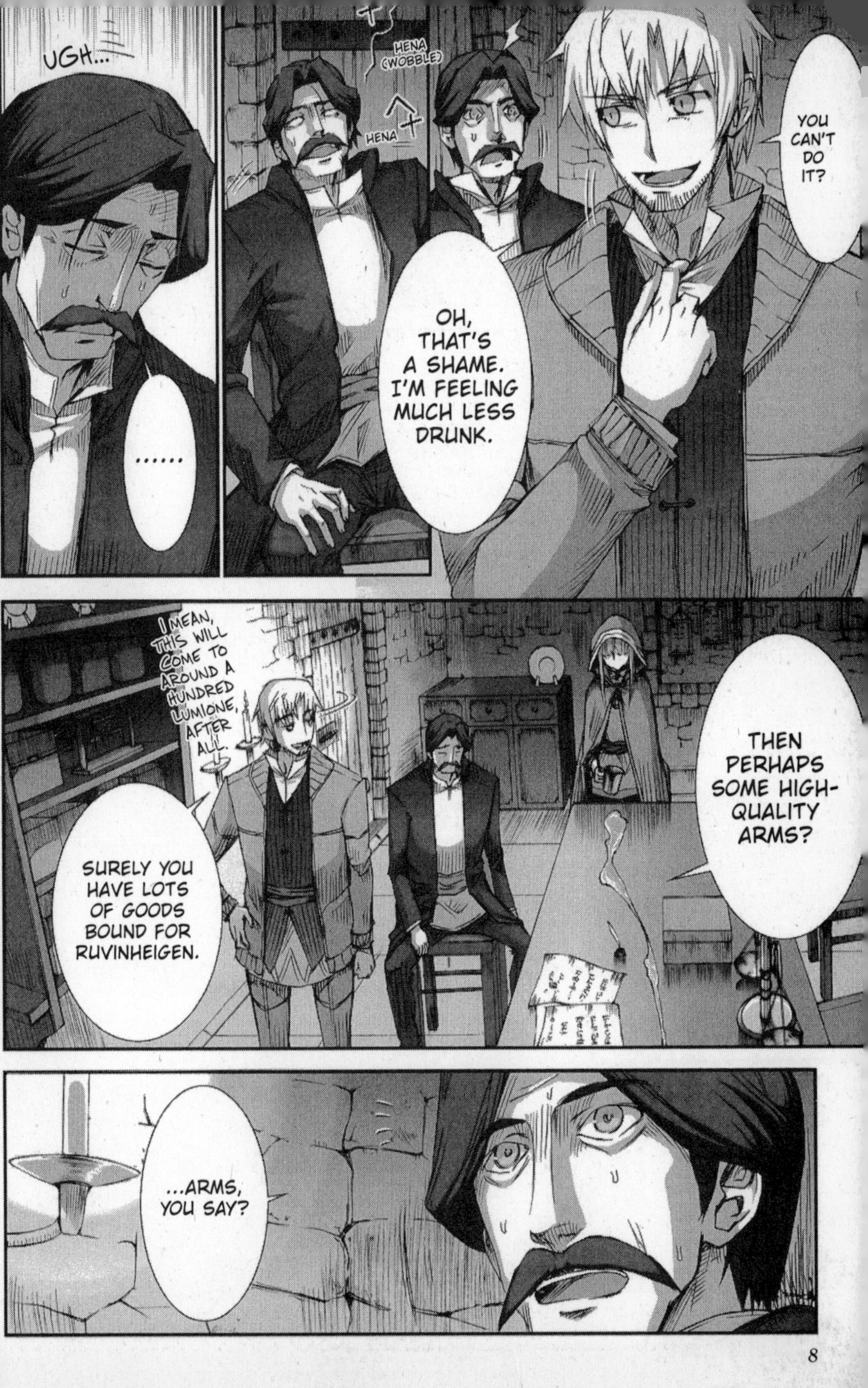
YOU CAN'T DO IT?
HENA (WOBBLE)
HENA
OH, THAT'S A SHAME. I'M FEELING MUCH LESS DRUNK.
UGH...
......
THEN PERHAPS SOME HIGH-QUALITY ARMS?
I MEAN, THIS WILL COME TO AROUND A HUNDRED LUMIONE, AFTER ALL.
SURELY YOU HAVE LOTS OF GOODS BOUND FOR RUVINHEIGEN.
...ARMS, YOU SAY?

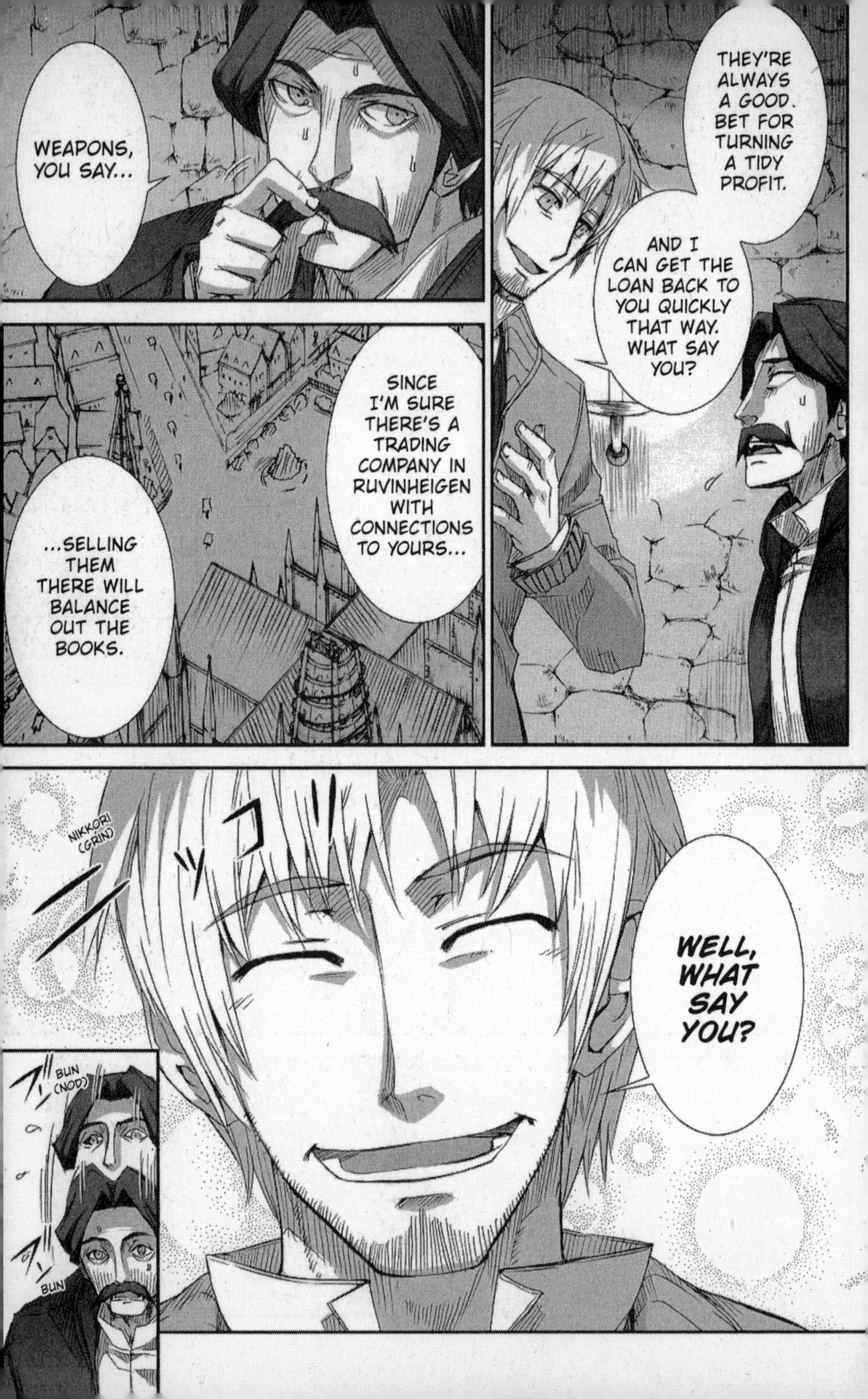
THEY'RE ALWAYS A GOOD BET FOR TURNING A TIDY PROFIT.
AND I CAN GET THE LOAN BACK TO YOU QUICKLY THAT WAY. WHAT SAY YOU?
WEAPONS, YOU SAY...
SINCE I'M SURE THERE'S A TRADING COMPANY IN RUVINHEIGEN WITH CONNECTIONS TO YOURS...
...SELLING THEM THERE WILL BALANCE OUT THE BOOKS.
WELL, WHAT SAY YOU?
NIKKORI (GRIN)
BUN (NOD)
BUN

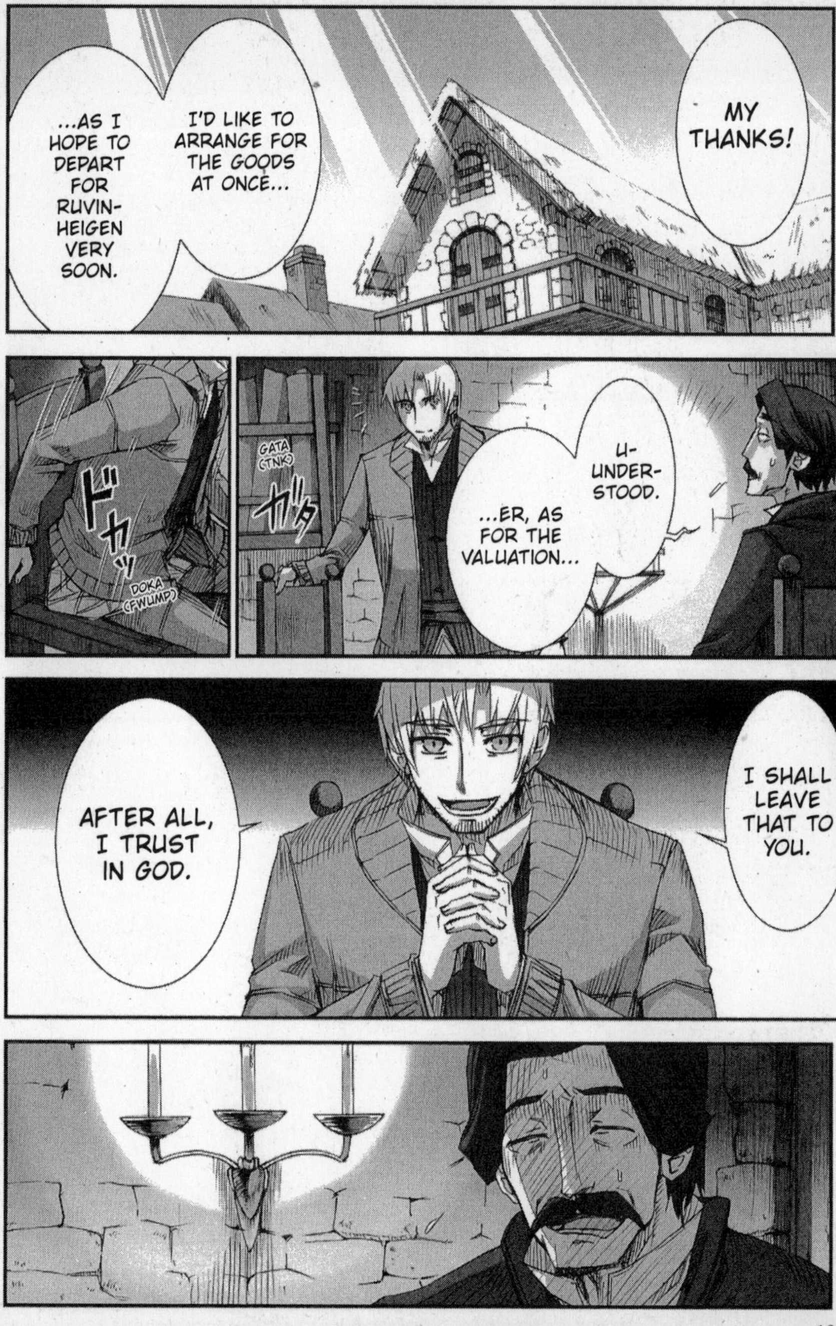
MY THANKS!
I'D LIKE TO ARRANGE FOR THE GOODS AT ONCE...
...AS I HOPE TO DEPART FOR RUVINHEIGEN VERY SOON.
U-UNDERSTOOD.
...ER, AS FOR THE VALUATION...
ガタ
GATA (TNK)
ドカッ
DOKA (FWUMP)
I SHALL LEAVE THAT TO YOU.
AFTER ALL, I TRUST IN GOD.

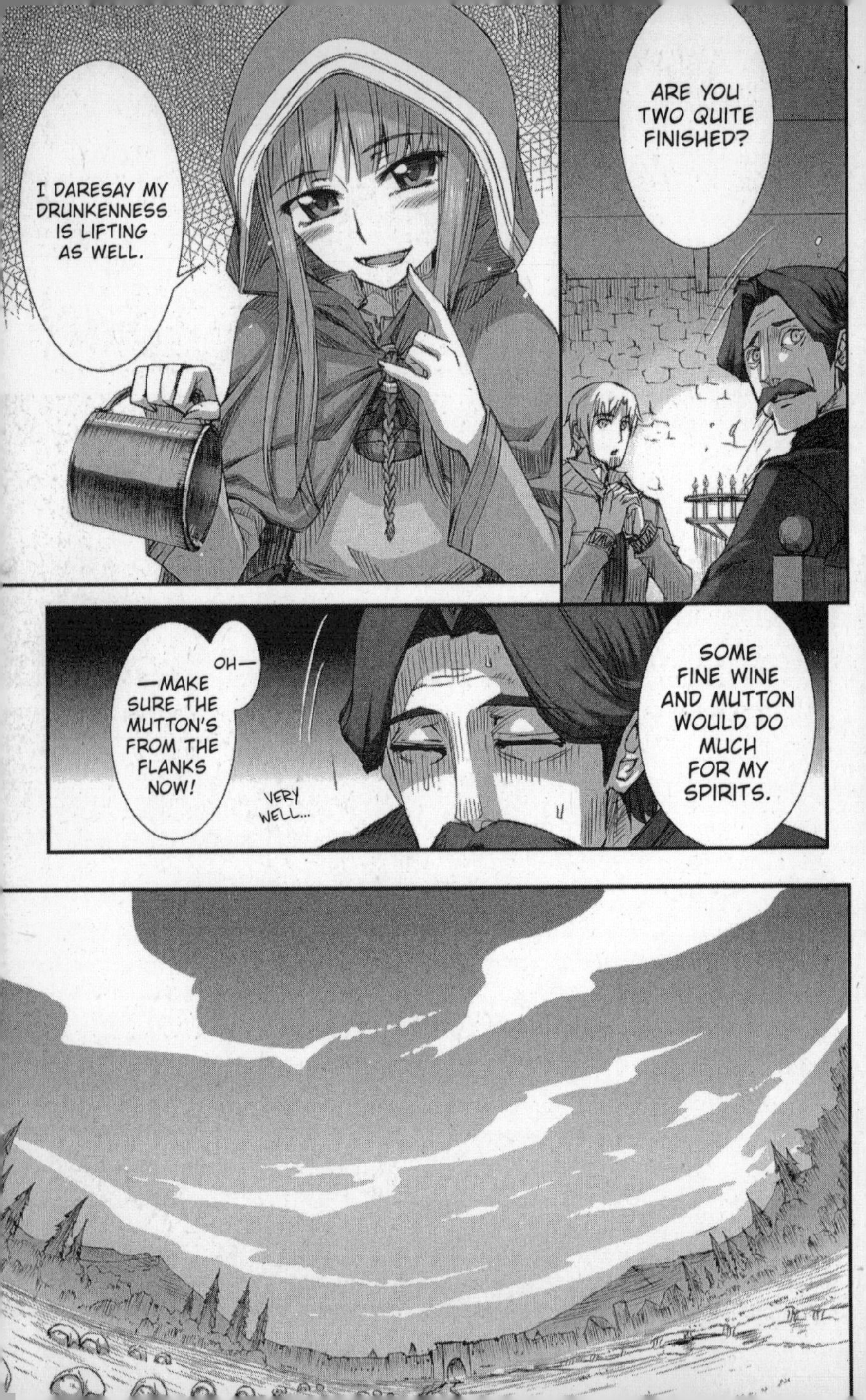
ARE YOU TWO QUITE FINISHED?
I DARESAY MY DRUNKENNESS IS LIFTING AS WELL.
SOME FINE WINE AND MUTTON WOULD DO MUCH FOR MY SPIRITS.
VERY WELL...
OH—
—MAKE SURE THE MUTTON'S FROM THE FLANKS NOW!

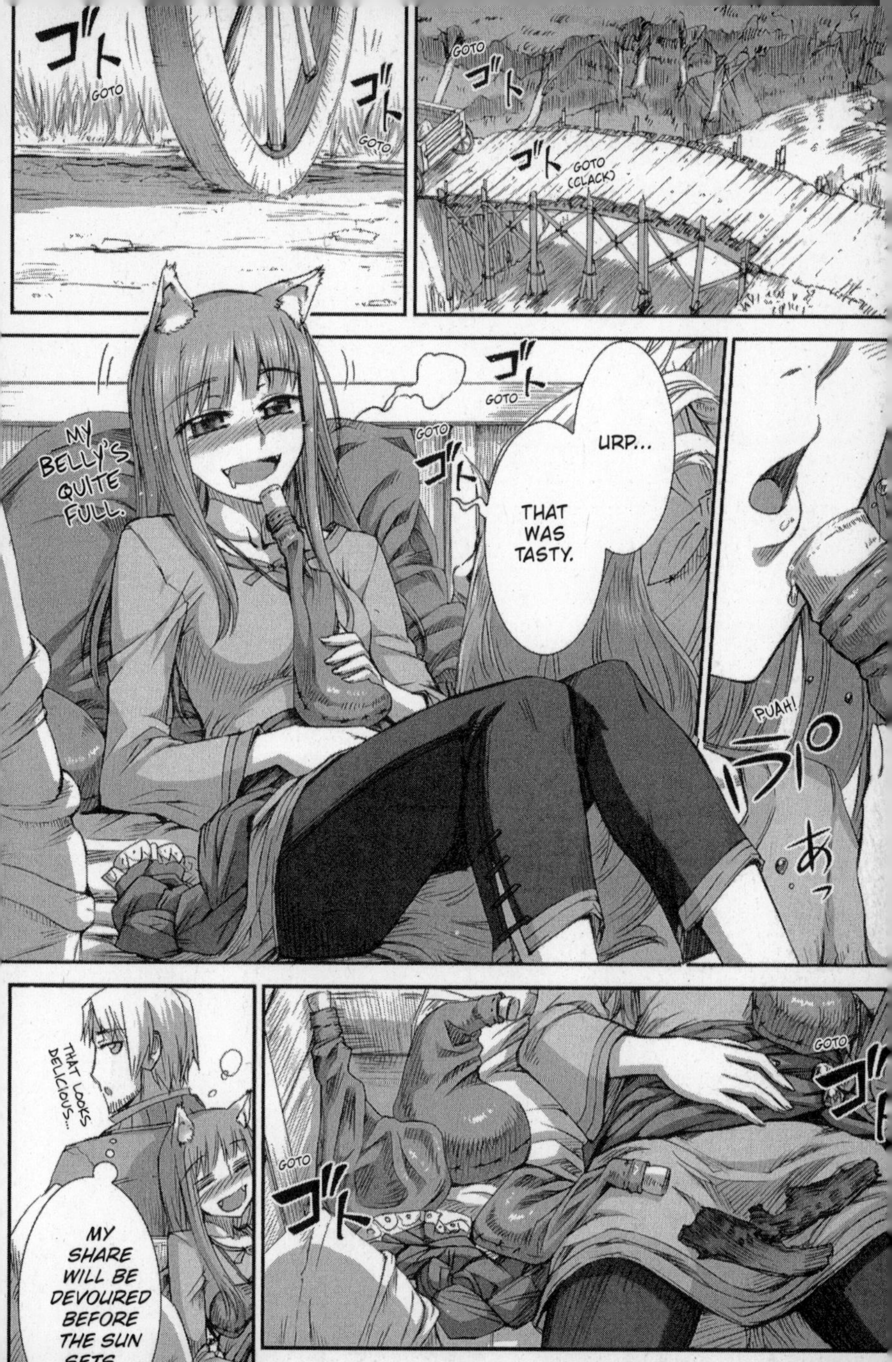
GOTO
ゴト
GOTO
(CLACK)
ゴト
ゴト
GOTO
ゴト
GOTO
PUAH!
ぷあっ
GOTO
ゴト
URP...
THAT WAS TASTY.
GOTO
ゴト
MY BELLY'S QUITE FULL.
GOTO
ゴト
GOTO
ゴト
THAT LOOKS DELICIOUS...
MY SHARE WILL BE DEVOURED BEFORE THE SUN SETS...

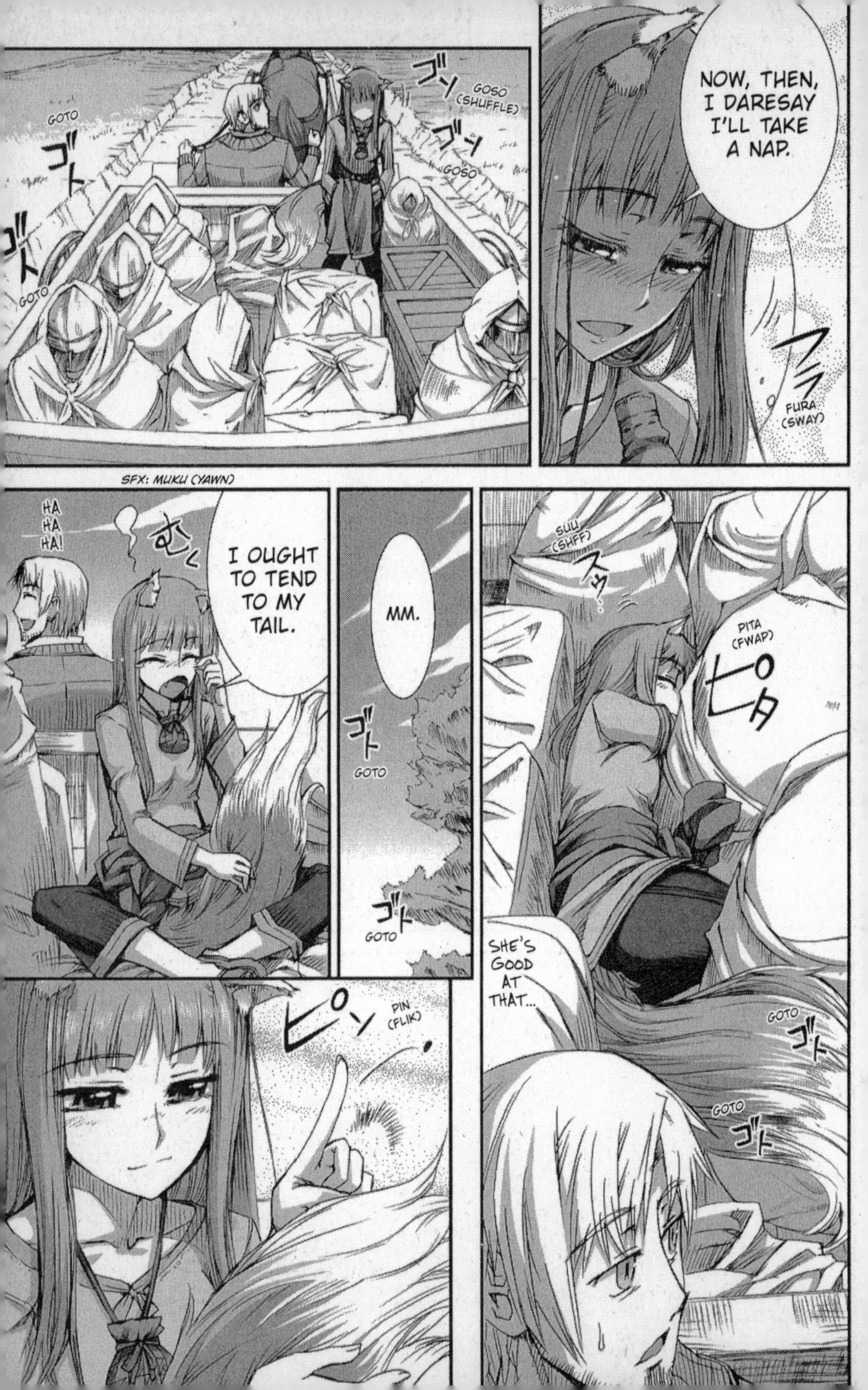
NOW, THEN, I DARESAY I'LL TAKE A NAP.
FURA (SWAY)
GOSO (SHUFFLE)
GOSO
GOTO
GOTO
SFX: MUKU (YAWN)
SUU (SHFF)
PITA (FWAP)
SHE'S GOOD AT THAT...
GOTO
GOTO
MM.
GOTO
GOTO
I OUGHT TO TEND TO MY TAIL.
HA HA HA!
PIN (FLIK)

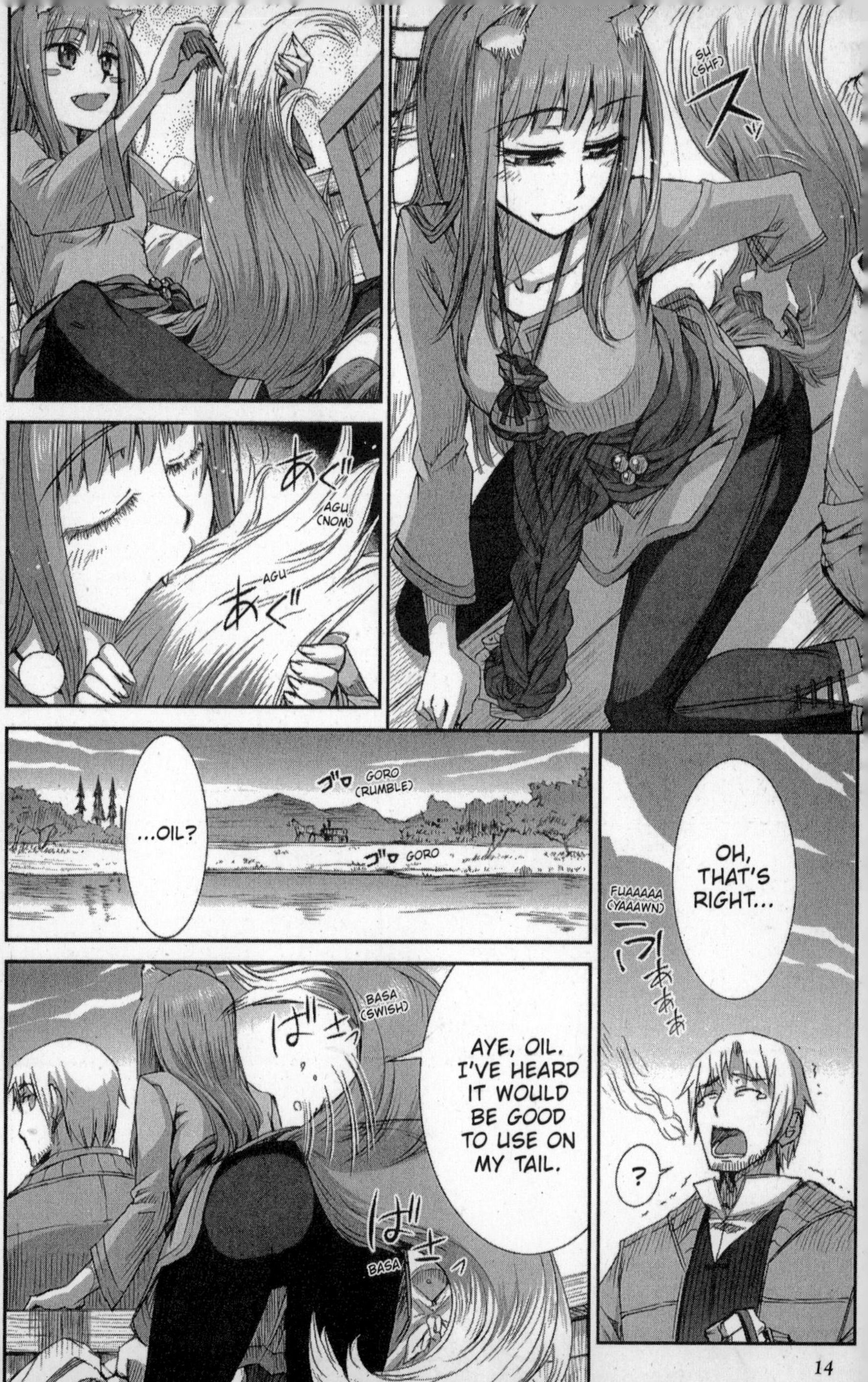
SU (SHF)
ス
あぐ
AGU (NOM)
AGU
あぐ
OH, THAT'S RIGHT...
FUAAAAAA (YAAAWN)
ふあぁぁ
...OIL?
ゴロ GORO (RUMBLE)
ゴロ GORO
?
AYE, OIL. I'VE HEARD IT WOULD BE GOOD TO USE ON MY TAIL.
BASA (SWISH)
ばさ
ばさ
BASA

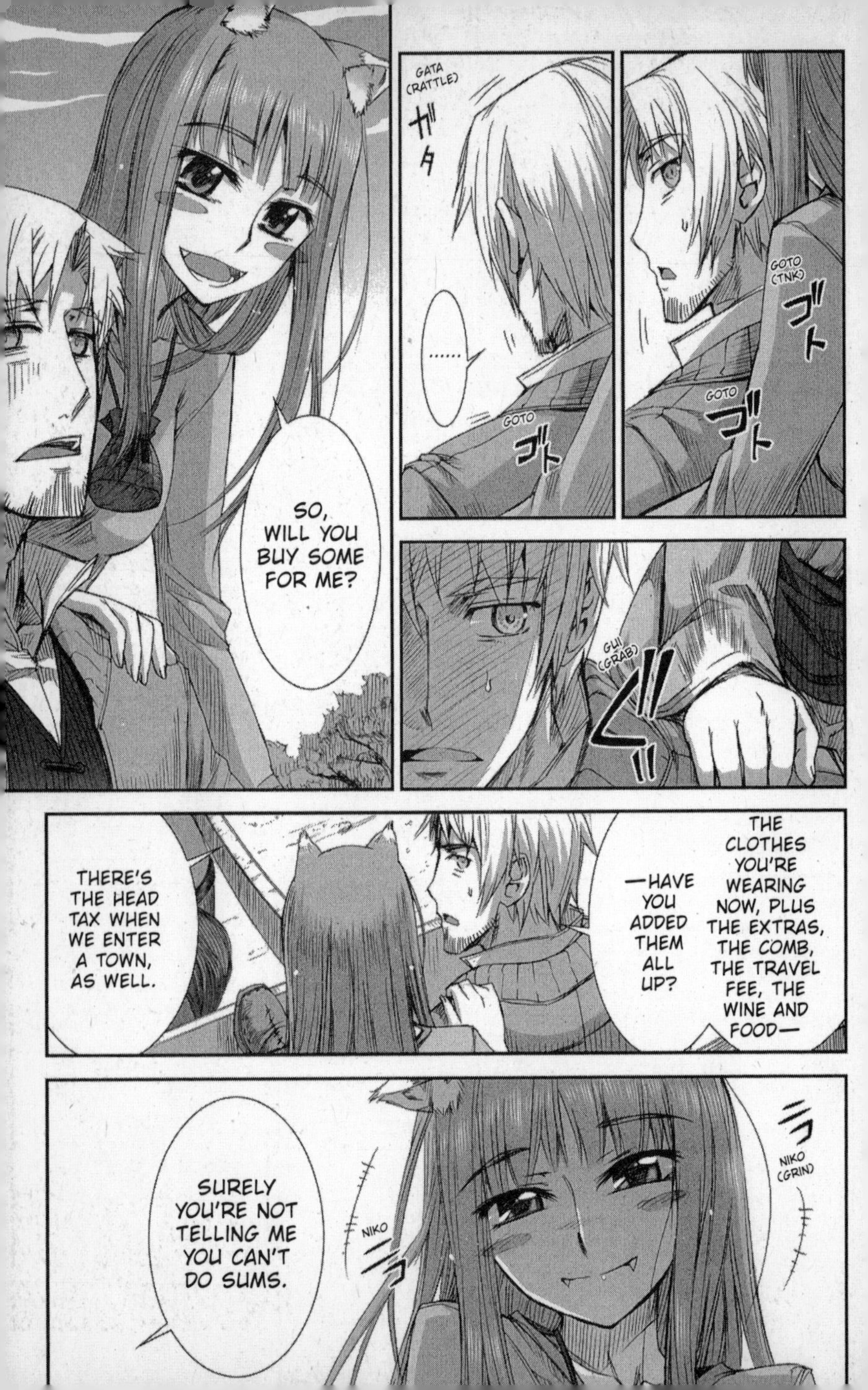
GOTO (TNK)
ゴト
GOTO
ゴト
GATA (RATTLE)
ガタ
......
GOTO
ゴト
GUI (GRAB)
ぐい
SO, WILL YOU BUY SOME FOR ME?
THE CLOTHES YOU'RE WEARING NOW, PLUS THE EXTRAS, THE COMB, THE TRAVEL FEE, THE WINE AND FOOD—
—HAVE YOU ADDED THEM ALL UP?
THERE'S THE HEAD TAX WHEN WE ENTER A TOWN, AS WELL.
NIKO (GRIN)
ニコ
SURELY YOU'RE NOT TELLING ME YOU CAN'T DO SUMS.
NIKO
ニコ

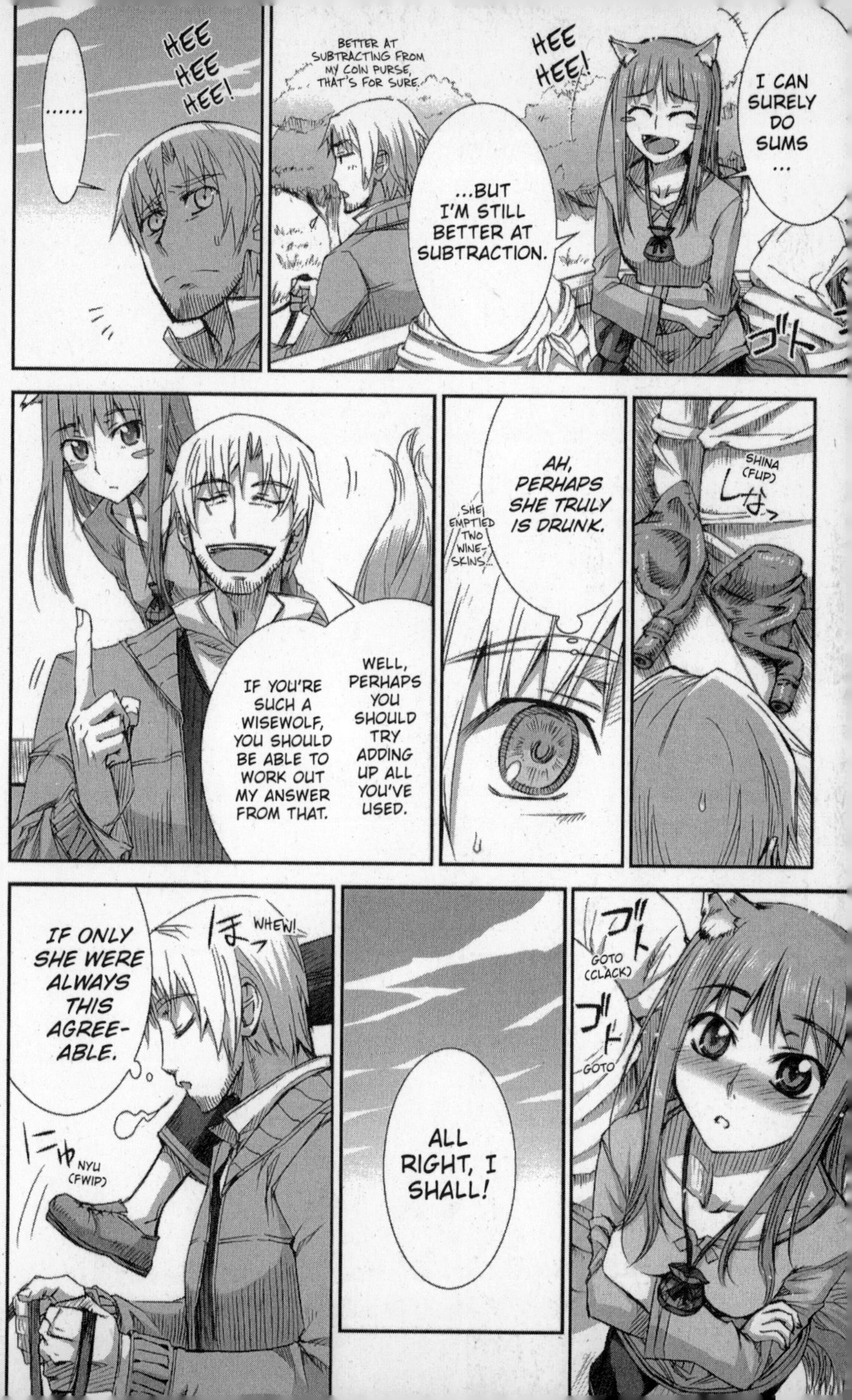
ゴト
I CAN SURELY DO SUMS...
HEE HEE!
...BUT I'M STILL BETTER AT SUBTRACTION.
BETTER AT SUBTRACTING FROM MY COIN PURSE, THAT'S FOR SURE.
HEE HEE HEE!
......
しなっ
SHINA (FUP)
AH, PERHAPS SHE TRULY IS DRUNK.
SHE EMPTIED TWO WINE-SKINS...
WELL, PERHAPS YOU SHOULD TRY ADDING UP ALL YOU'VE USED.
IF YOU'RE SUCH A WISEWOLF, YOU SHOULD BE ABLE TO WORK OUT MY ANSWER FROM THAT.
ゴト
GOTO (CLACK)
ゴト
GOTO
ALL RIGHT, I SHALL!
ほっ
WHEW!
IF ONLY SHE WERE ALWAYS THIS AGREE-ABLE.
にゅ
NYU (FWIP)

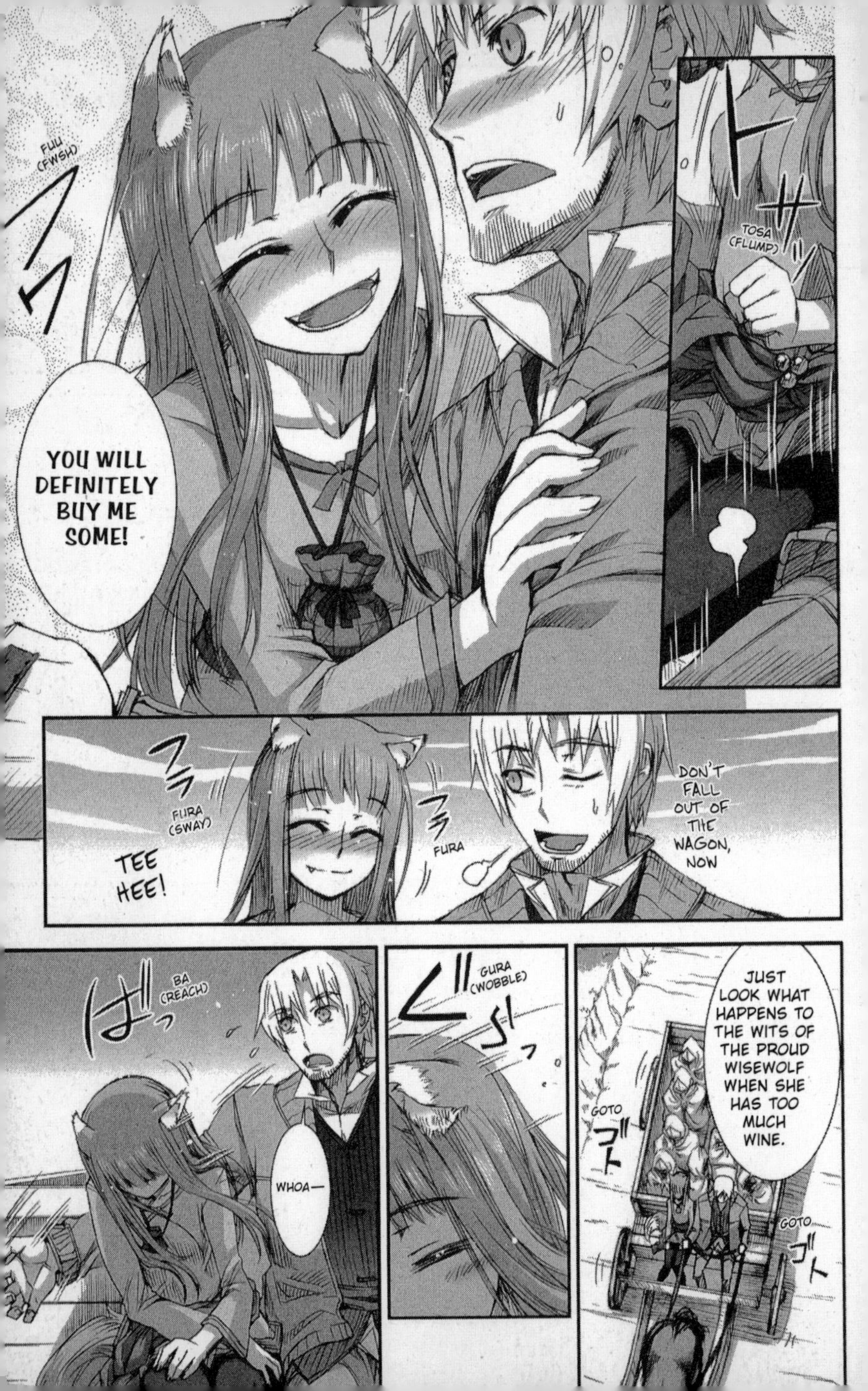
TOSA (FLUMP)
FUU (FWSH)
YOU WILL DEFINITELY BUY ME SOME!
DON'T FALL OUT OF THE WAGON, NOW
FURA
FURA (SWAY)
TEE HEE!
JUST LOOK WHAT HAPPENS TO THE WITS OF THE PROUD WISEWOLF WHEN SHE HAS TOO MUCH WINE.
GOTO
GOTO
GURA (WOBBLE)
BA (REACH)
WHOA—

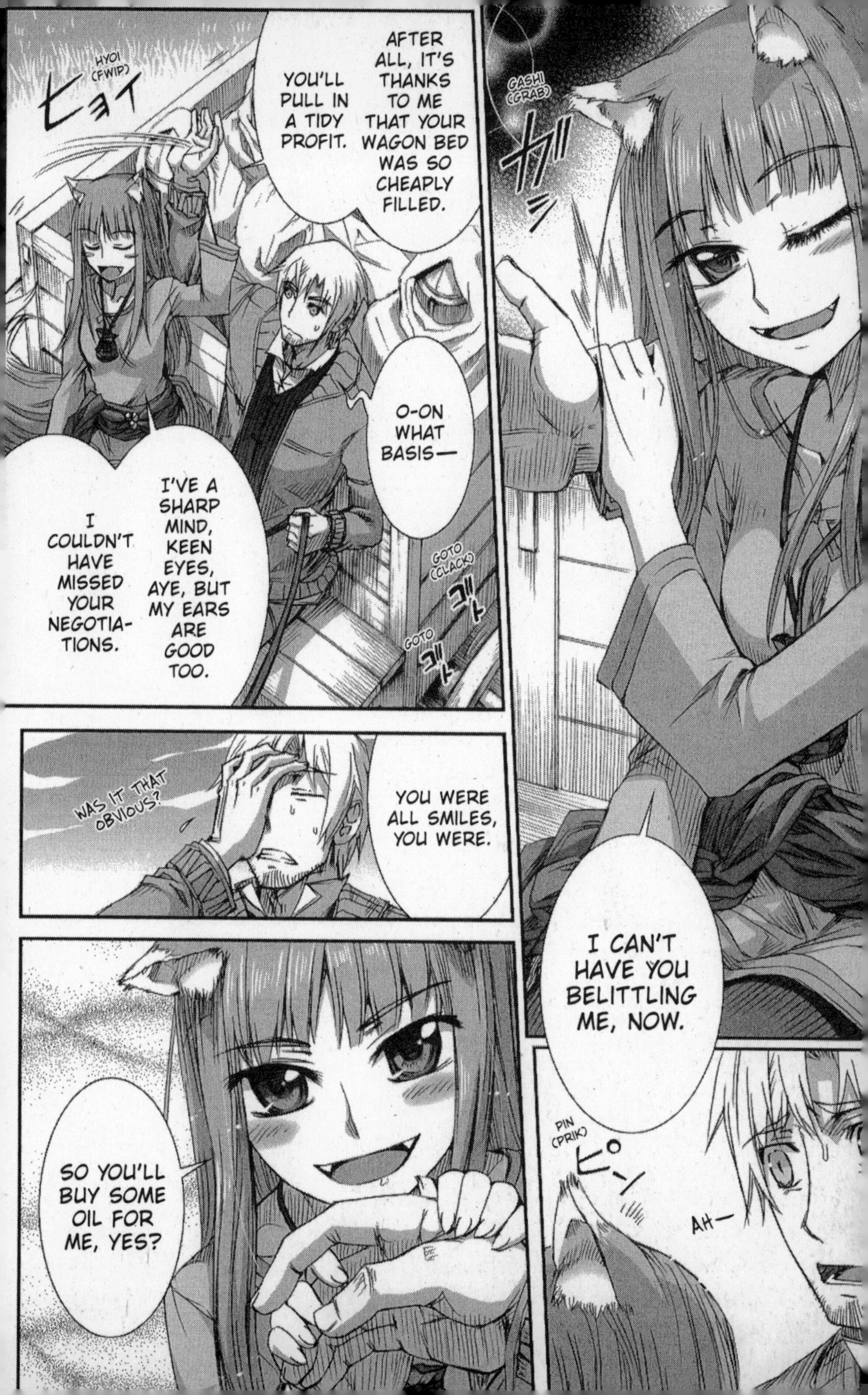
GASHI (GRAB)
ガシ
I CAN'T HAVE YOU BELITTLING ME, NOW.
HYOI (FWIP)
ヒョイ
AFTER ALL, IT'S THANKS TO ME THAT YOUR WAGON BED WAS SO CHEAPLY FILLED.
YOU'LL PULL IN A TIDY PROFIT.
O-ON WHAT BASIS—
I'VE A SHARP MIND, KEEN EYES, AYE, BUT MY EARS ARE GOOD TOO.
I COULDN'T HAVE MISSED YOUR NEGOTIATIONS.
GOTO (CLACK)
ゴト
GOTO
ゴト
YOU WERE ALL SMILES, YOU WERE.
WAS IT THAT OBVIOUS?
PIN (PRIK)
ピー
AH—
SO YOU'LL BUY SOME OIL FOR ME, YES?

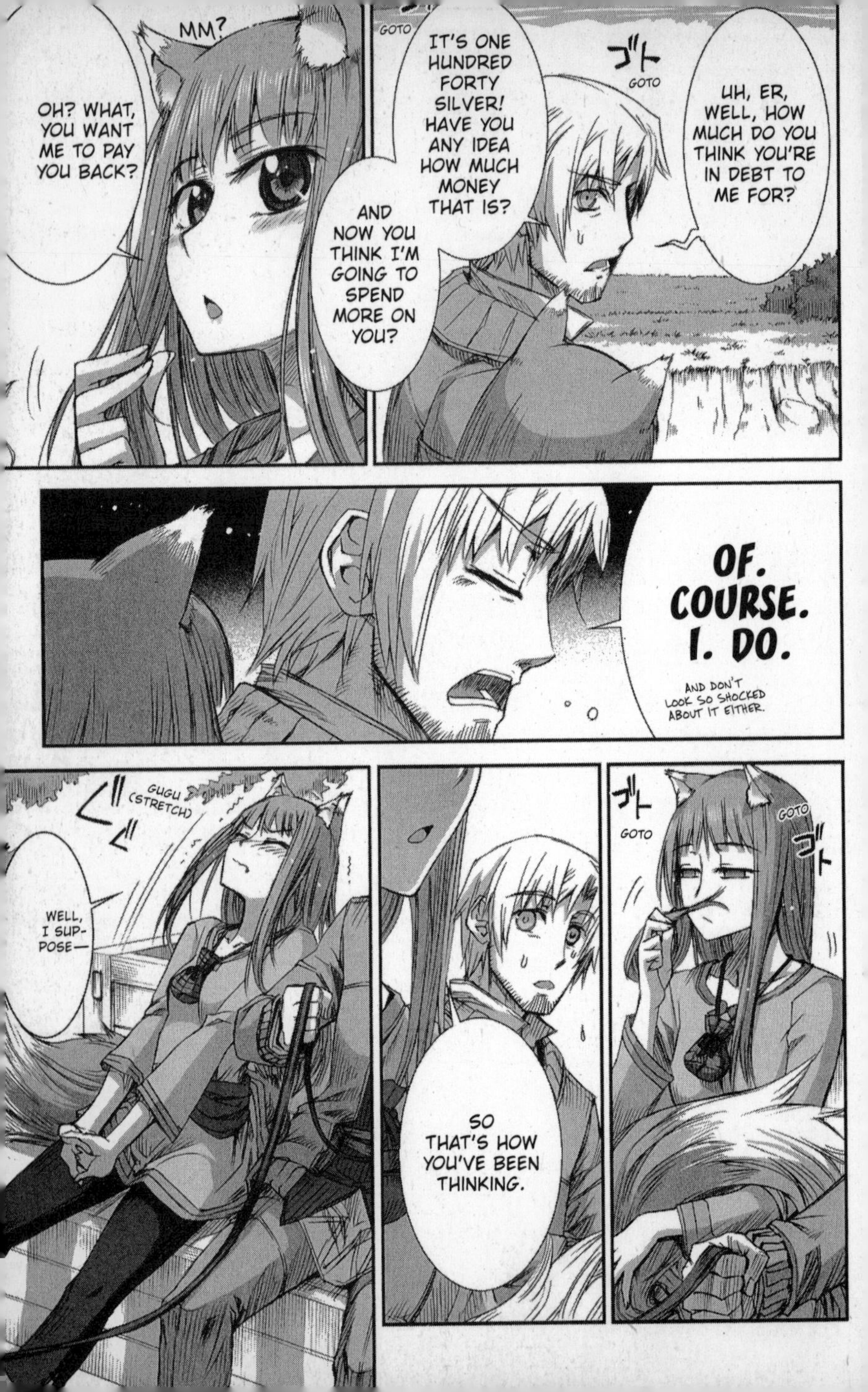
ゴト
GOTO
UH, ER, WELL, HOW MUCH DO YOU THINK YOU'RE IN DEBT TO ME FOR?
GOTO
IT'S ONE HUNDRED FORTY SILVER! HAVE YOU ANY IDEA HOW MUCH MONEY THAT IS?
AND NOW YOU THINK I'M GOING TO SPEND MORE ON YOU?
MM?
OH? WHAT, YOU WANT ME TO PAY YOU BACK?
OF. COURSE. I. DO.
AND DON'T LOOK SO SHOCKED ABOUT IT EITHER.
GOTO
ゴト
ゴト
GOTO
SO THAT'S HOW YOU'VE BEEN THINKING.
ぐぐ
GUGU (STRETCH)
WELL, I SUP-POSE—

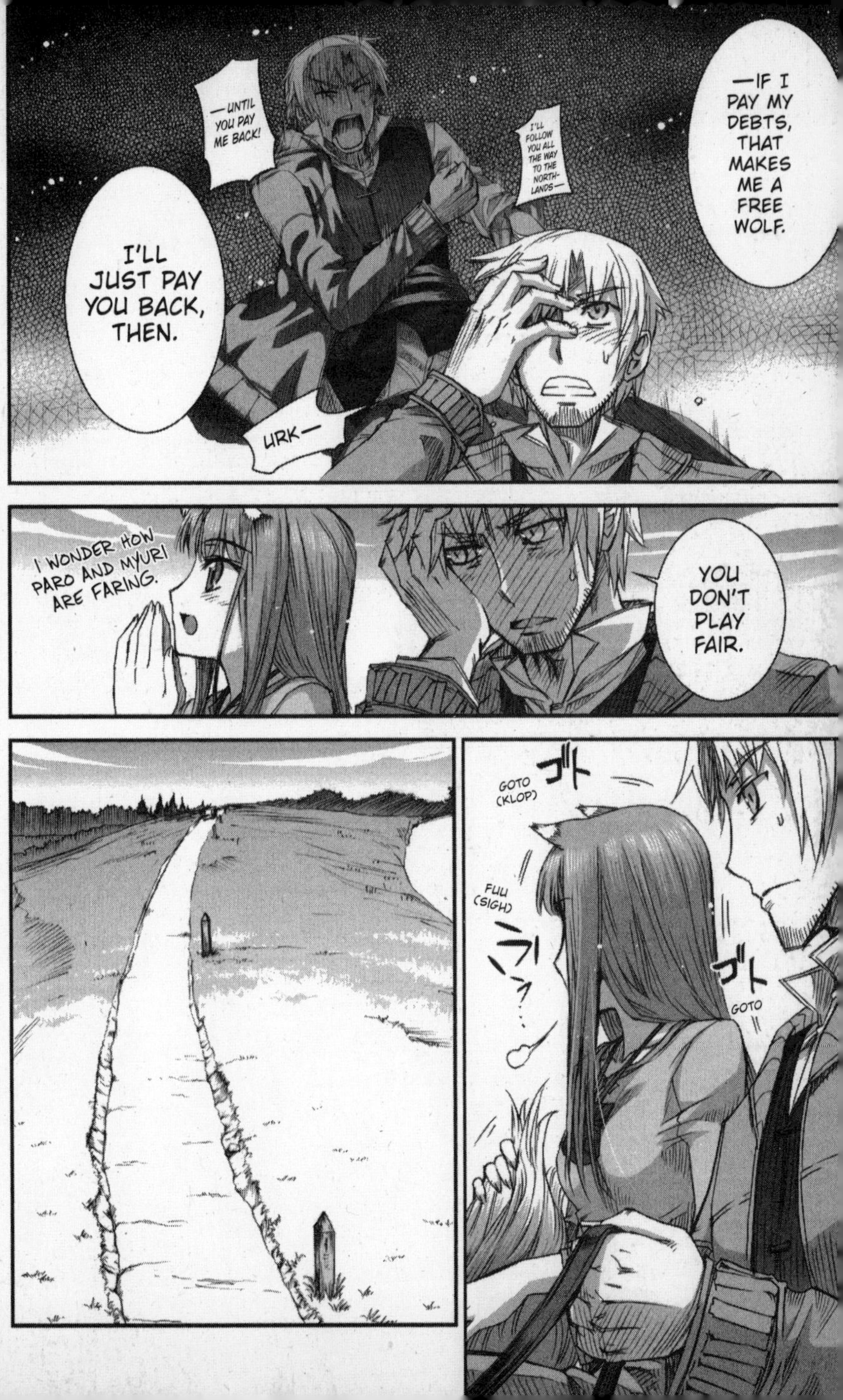
—IF I PAY MY DEBTS, THAT MAKES ME A FREE WOLF.
I'LL FOLLOW YOU ALL THE WAY TO THE NORTH-LANDS—
—UNTIL YOU PAY ME BACK!
I'LL JUST PAY YOU BACK, THEN.
URK—
YOU DON'T PLAY FAIR.
I WONDER HOW PARO AND MYURI ARE FARING.
ゴト
GOTO (KLOP)
FUU (SIGH)
ゴト
GOTO

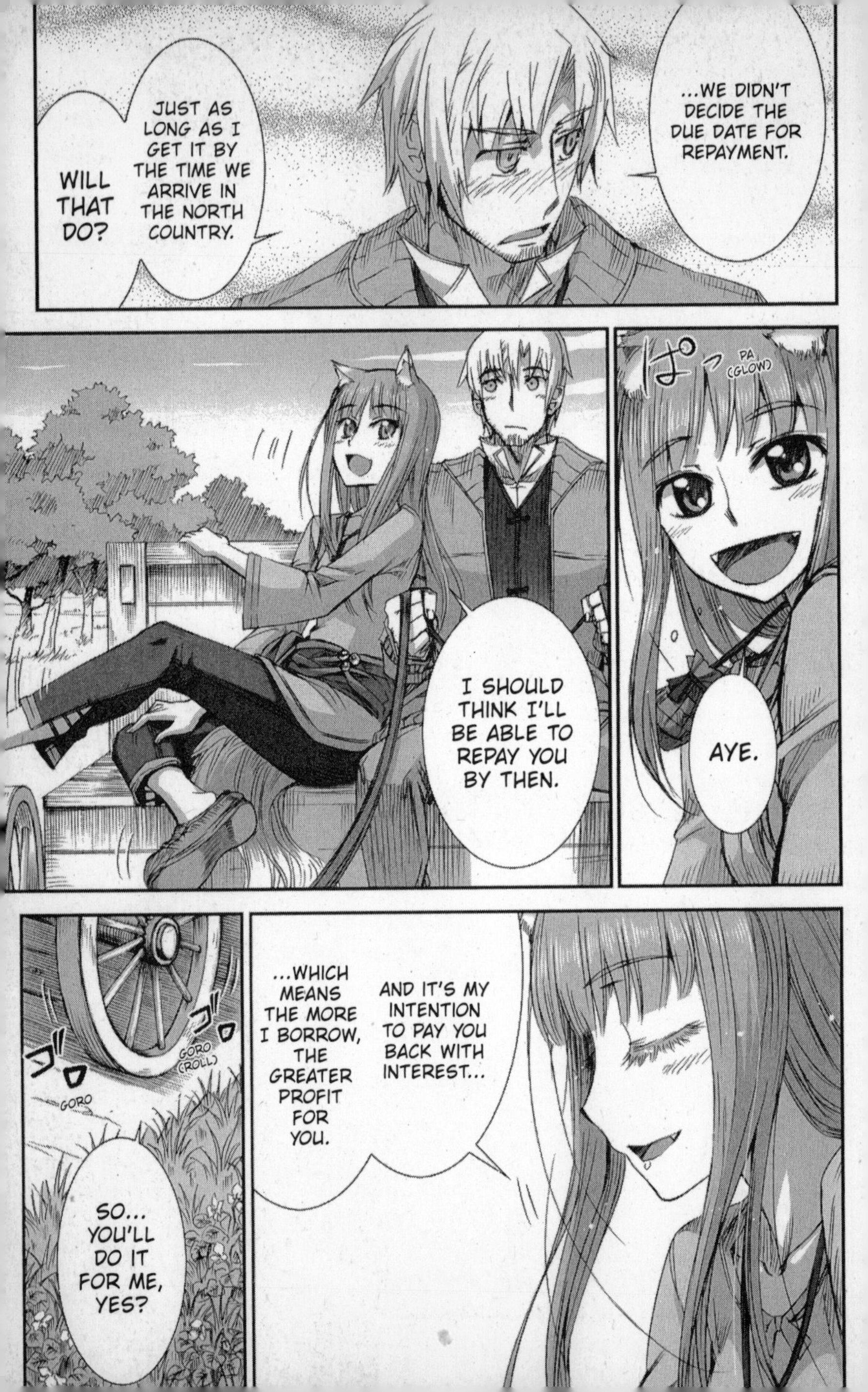
...WE DIDN'T DECIDE THE DUE DATE FOR REPAYMENT.
JUST AS LONG AS I GET IT BY THE TIME WE ARRIVE IN THE NORTH COUNTRY.
WILL THAT DO?
ぱっ
PA (GLOW)
AYE.
I SHOULD THINK I'LL BE ABLE TO REPAY YOU BY THEN.
AND IT'S MY INTENTION TO PAY YOU BACK WITH INTEREST...
...WHICH MEANS THE MORE I BORROW, THE GREATER PROFIT FOR YOU.
ゴロ
GORO (ROLL)
ゴロ
GORO
SO... YOU'LL DO IT FOR ME, YES?

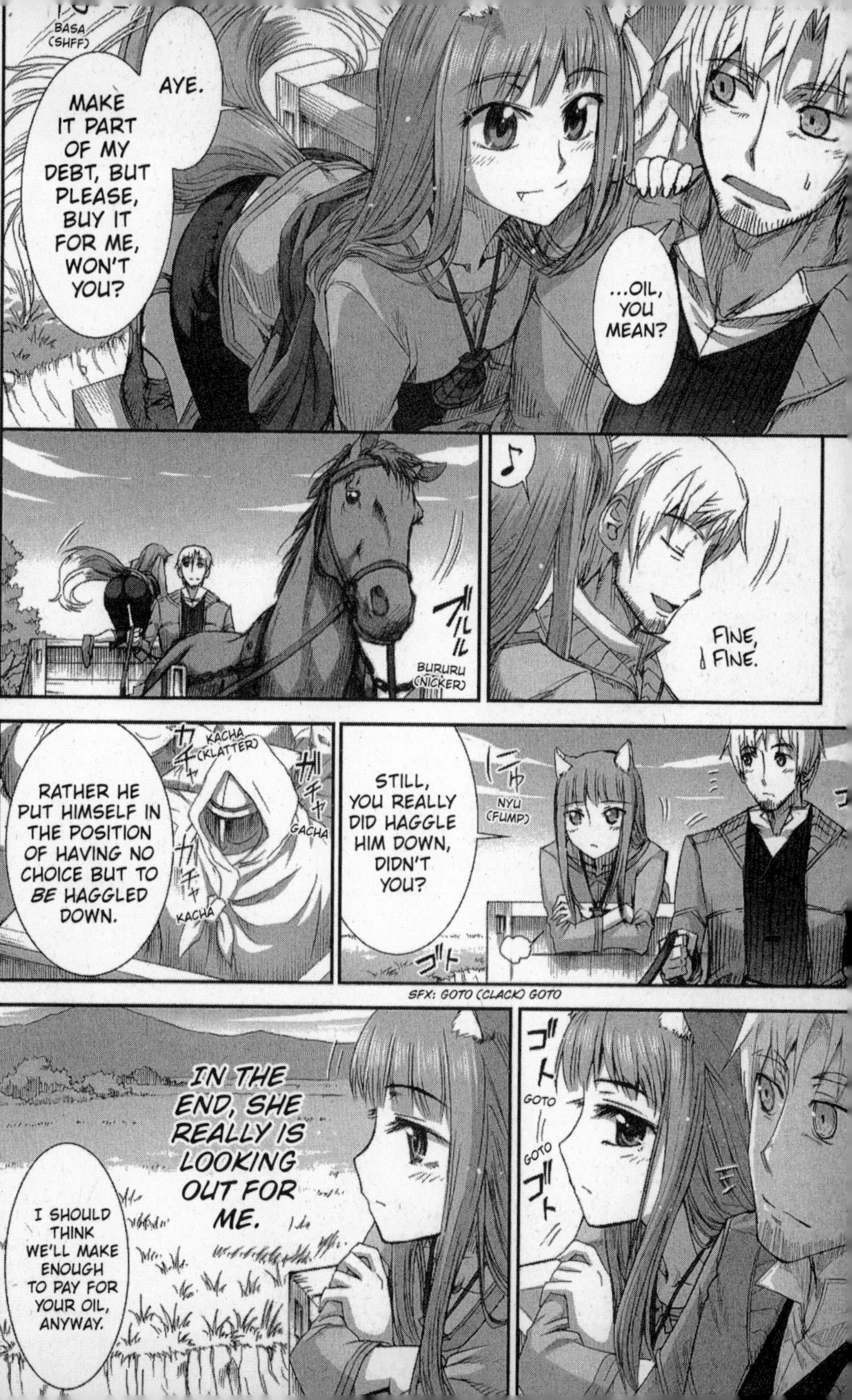
...OIL, YOU MEAN?
AYE.
MAKE IT PART OF MY DEBT, BUT PLEASE, BUY IT FOR ME, WON'T YOU?
BASA (SHFF)
♪
FINE, FINE.
BURURU (NICKER)
STILL, YOU REALLY DID HAGGLE HIM DOWN, DIDN'T YOU?
NYU (FUMP)
KACHA (KLATTER)
GACHA
KACHA
RATHER HE PUT HIMSELF IN THE POSITION OF HAVING NO CHOICE BUT TO BE HAGGLED DOWN.
SFX: GOTO (CLACK) GOTO
GOTO
GOTO
IN THE END, SHE REALLY IS LOOKING OUT FOR ME.
I SHOULD THINK WE'LL MAKE ENOUGH TO PAY FOR YOUR OIL, ANYWAY.

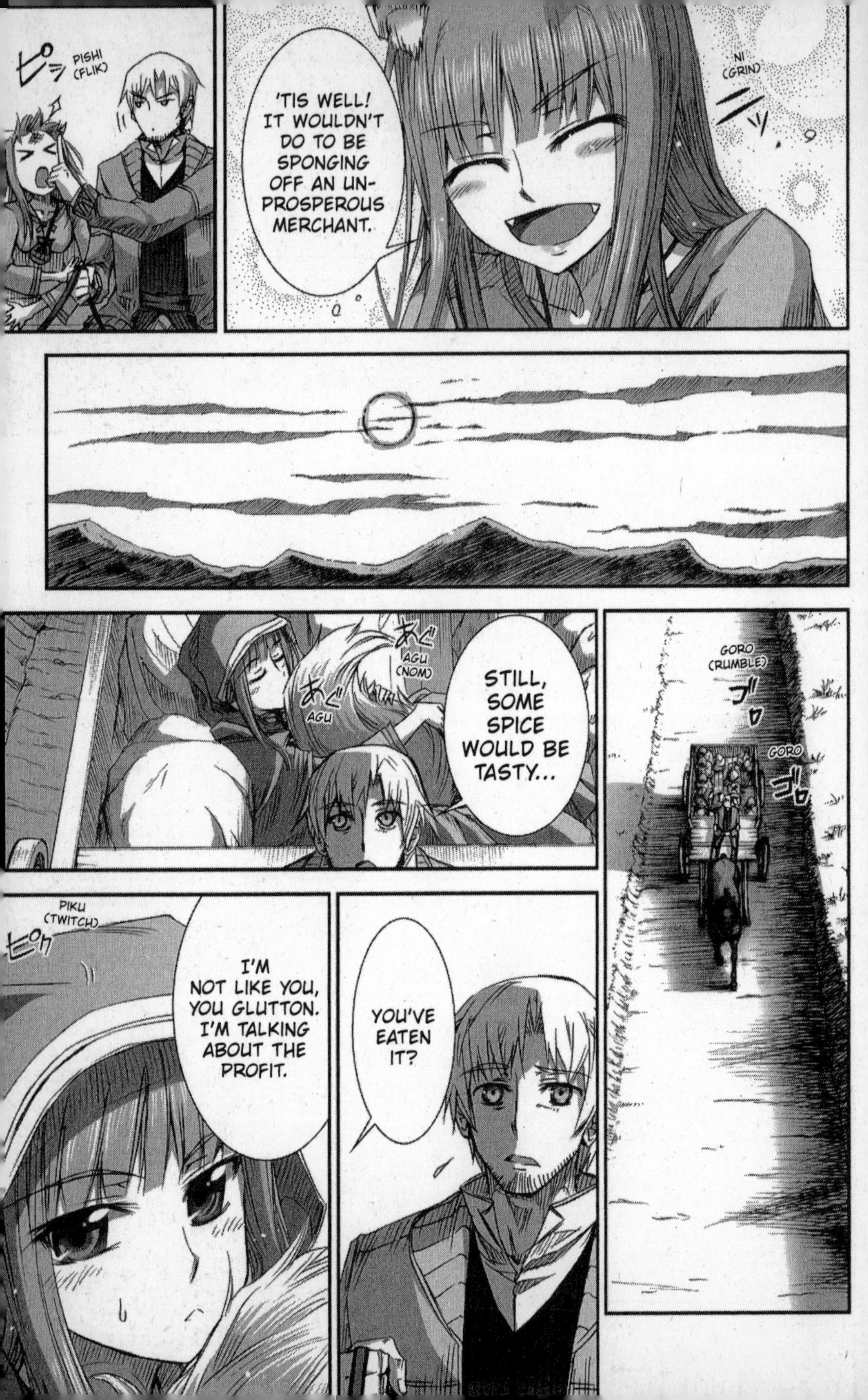
NI (GRIN)
'TIS WELL! IT WOULDN'T DO TO BE SPONGING OFF AN UN-PROSPEROUS MERCHANT.
PISHI (FLIK)
GORO (RUMBLE)
GORO
AGU (NOM)
AGU
STILL, SOME SPICE WOULD BE TASTY...
YOU'VE EATEN IT?
PIKU (TWITCH)
I'M NOT LIKE YOU, YOU GLUTTON. I'M TALKING ABOUT THE PROFIT.

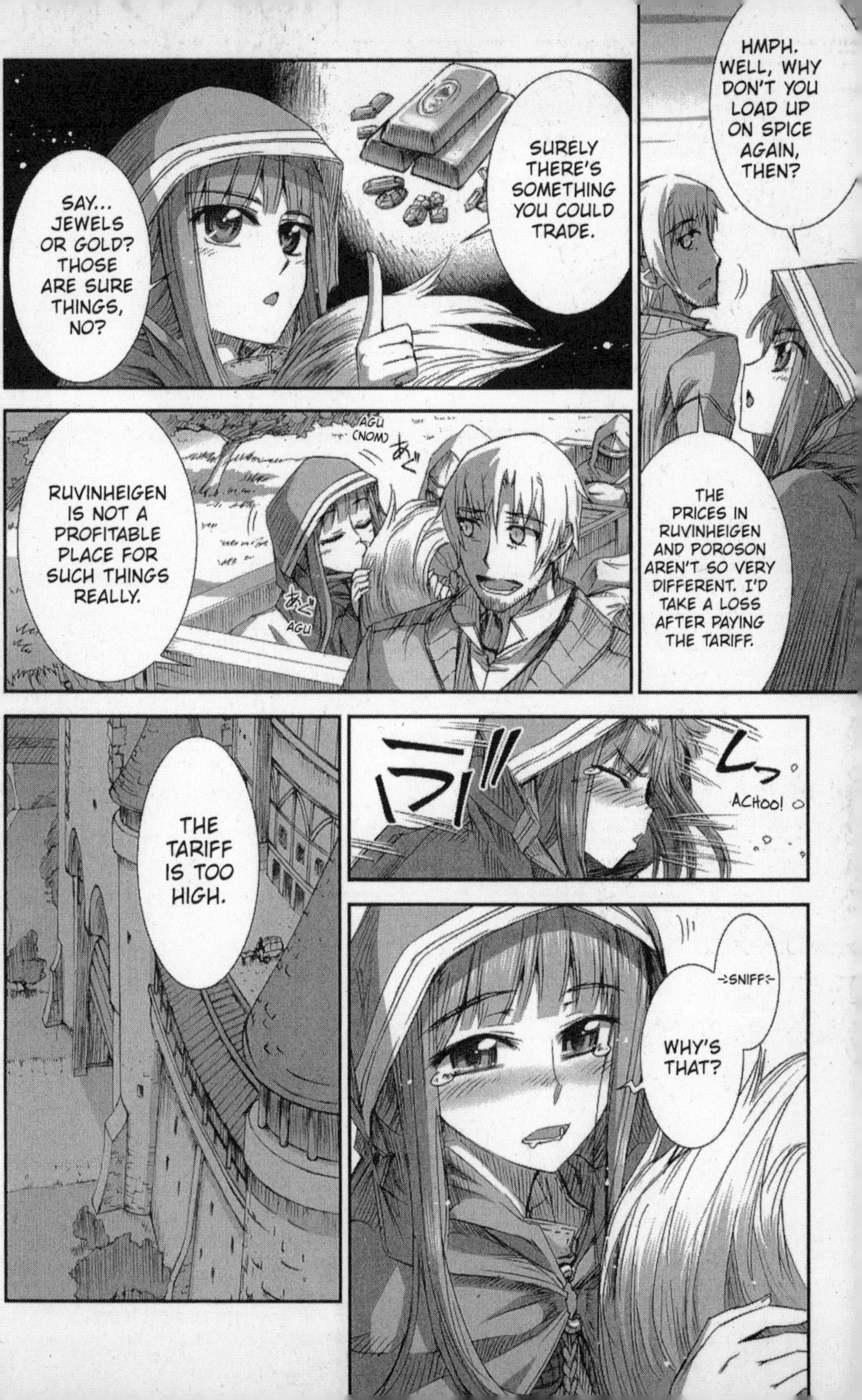
HMPH. WELL, WHY DON'T YOU LOAD UP ON SPICE AGAIN, THEN?
THE PRICES IN RUVINHEIGEN AND POROSON AREN'T SO VERY DIFFERENT. I'D TAKE A LOSS AFTER PAYING THE TARIFF.
SURELY THERE'S SOMETHING YOU COULD TRADE.
SAY... JEWELS OR GOLD? THOSE ARE SURE THINGS, NO?
AGU (NOM) あぐ
RUVINHEIGEN IS NOT A PROFITABLE PLACE FOR SUCH THINGS REALLY.
あぐ AGU
ACHOO!
SNIFF
WHY'S THAT?
THE TARIFF IS TOO HIGH.

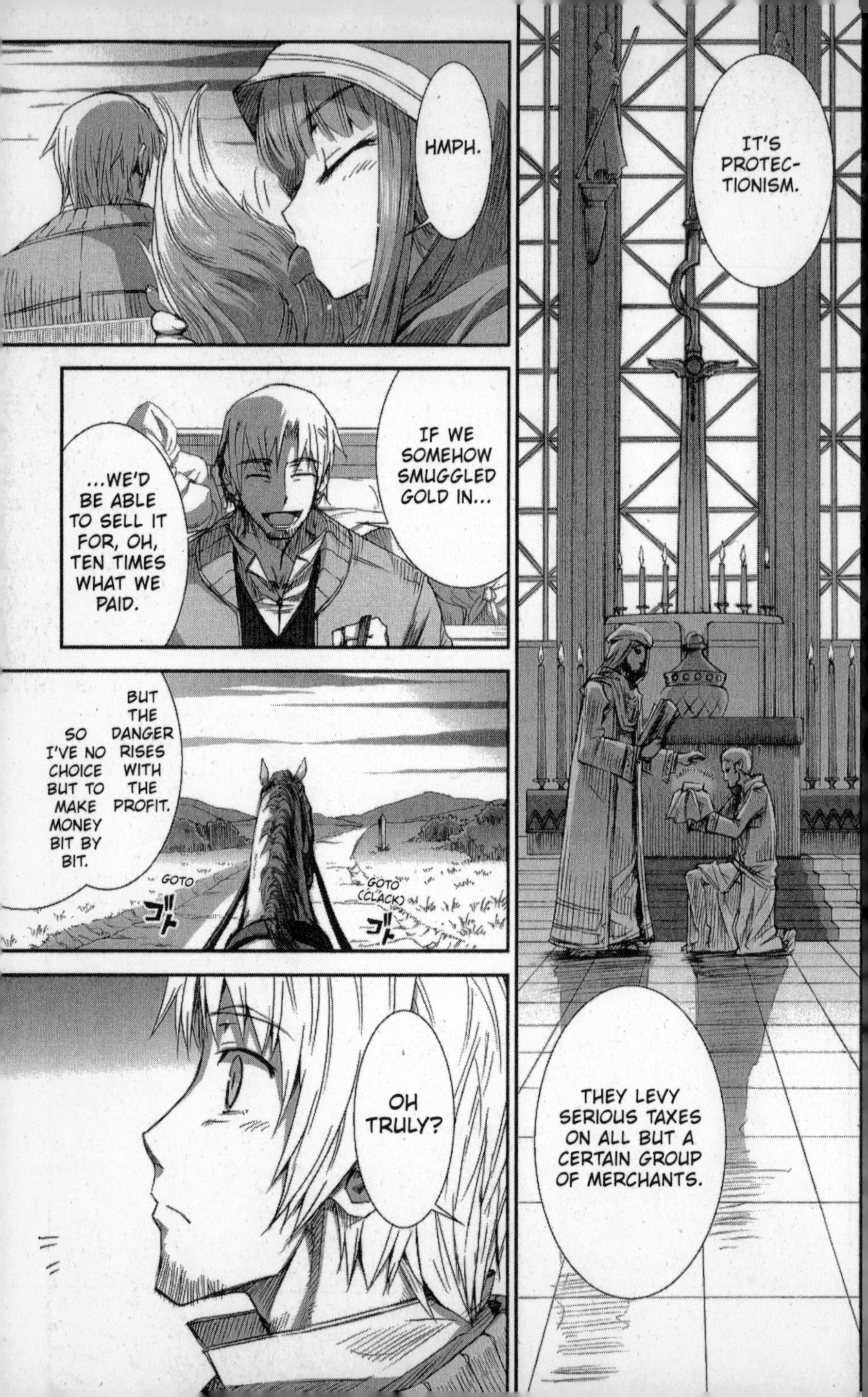
IT'S PROTECTIONISM.
THEY LEVY SERIOUS TAXES ON ALL BUT A CERTAIN GROUP OF MERCHANTS.
HMPH.
IF WE SOMEHOW SMUGGLED GOLD IN...
...WE'D BE ABLE TO SELL IT FOR, OH, TEN TIMES WHAT WE PAID.
BUT THE DANGER RISES WITH THE PROFIT.
SO I'VE NO CHOICE BUT TO MAKE MONEY BIT BY BIT.
GOTO (CLACK)
ゴト
GOTO
ゴト
OH TRULY?

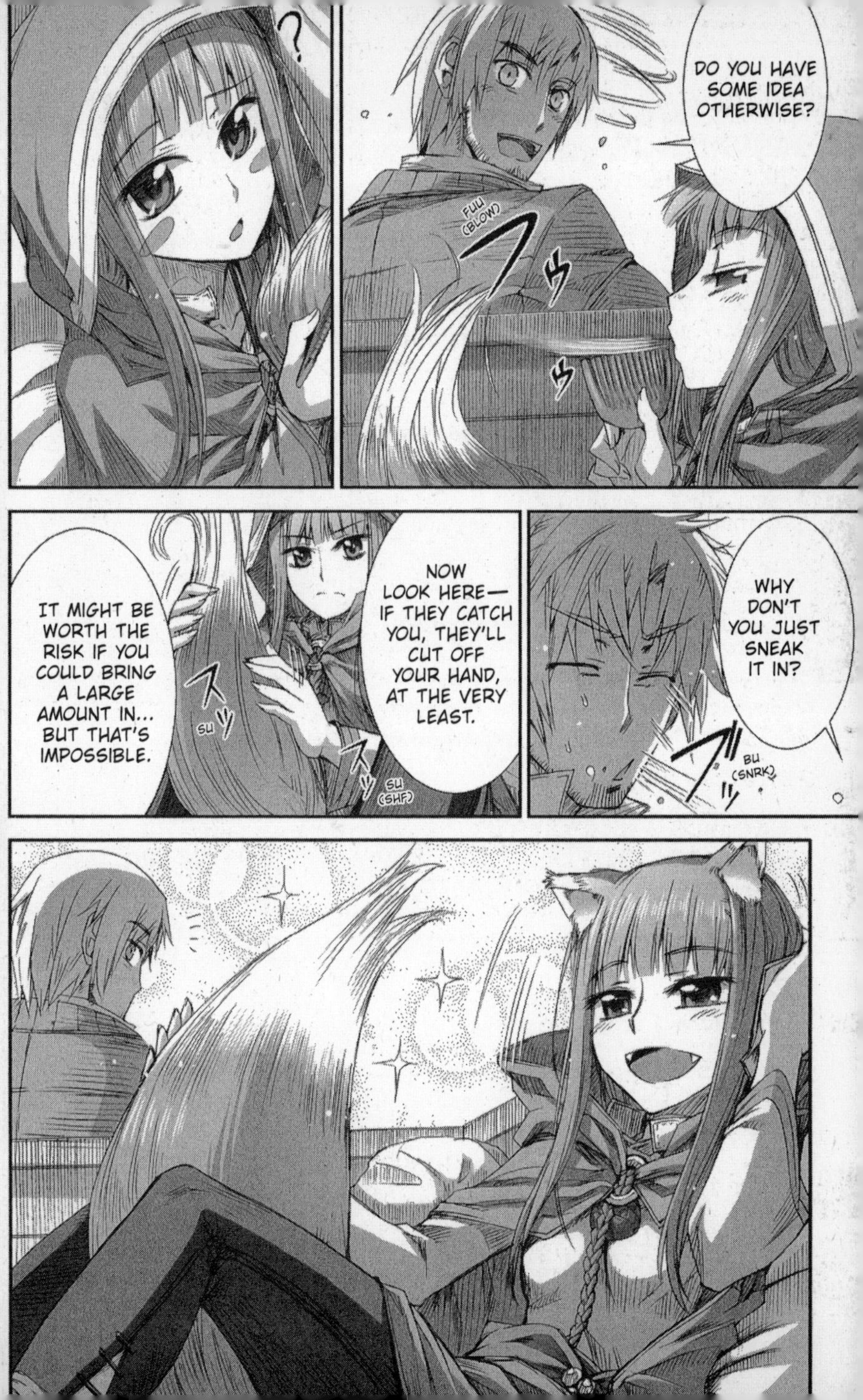
DO YOU HAVE SOME IDEA OTHERWISE?
FUU (BLOW)
?
WHY DON'T YOU JUST SNEAK IT IN?
BU (SNRK)
NOW LOOK HERE— IF THEY CATCH YOU, THEY'LL CUT OFF YOUR HAND, AT THE VERY LEAST.
SU (SHF)
IT MIGHT BE WORTH THE RISK IF YOU COULD BRING A LARGE AMOUNT IN... BUT THAT'S IMPOSSIBLE.
SU

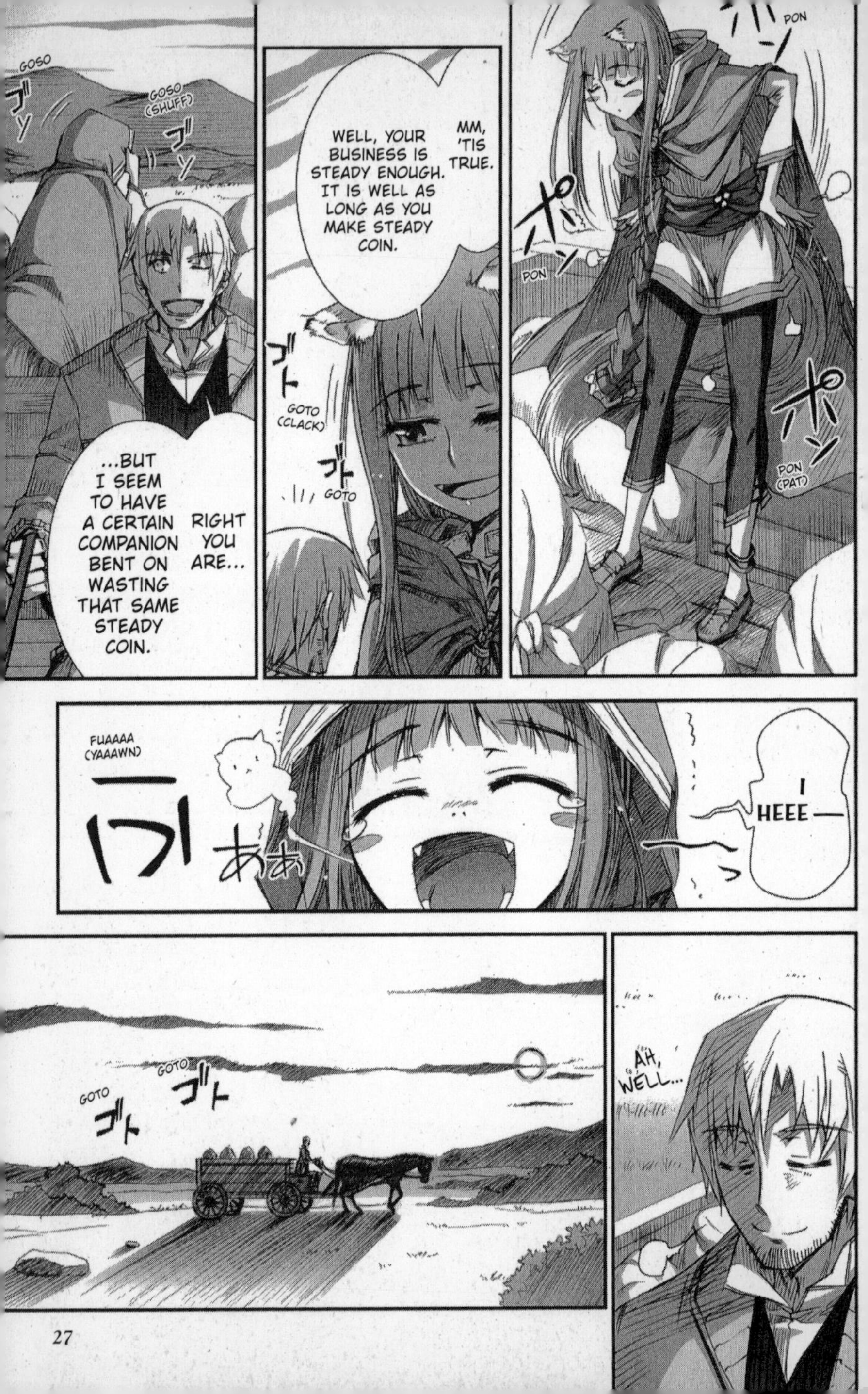
PON
PON
PON (PAT)
MM, 'TIS TRUE.
WELL, YOUR BUSINESS IS STEADY ENOUGH. IT IS WELL AS LONG AS YOU MAKE STEADY COIN.
GOTO (CLACK)
GOTO
GOSO
GOSO (SHUFF)
RIGHT YOU ARE...
...BUT I SEEM TO HAVE A CERTAIN COMPANION BENT ON WASTING THAT SAME STEADY COIN.
I HEEE—
FUAAAA (YAAAWN)
AH, WELL...
GOTO
GOTO

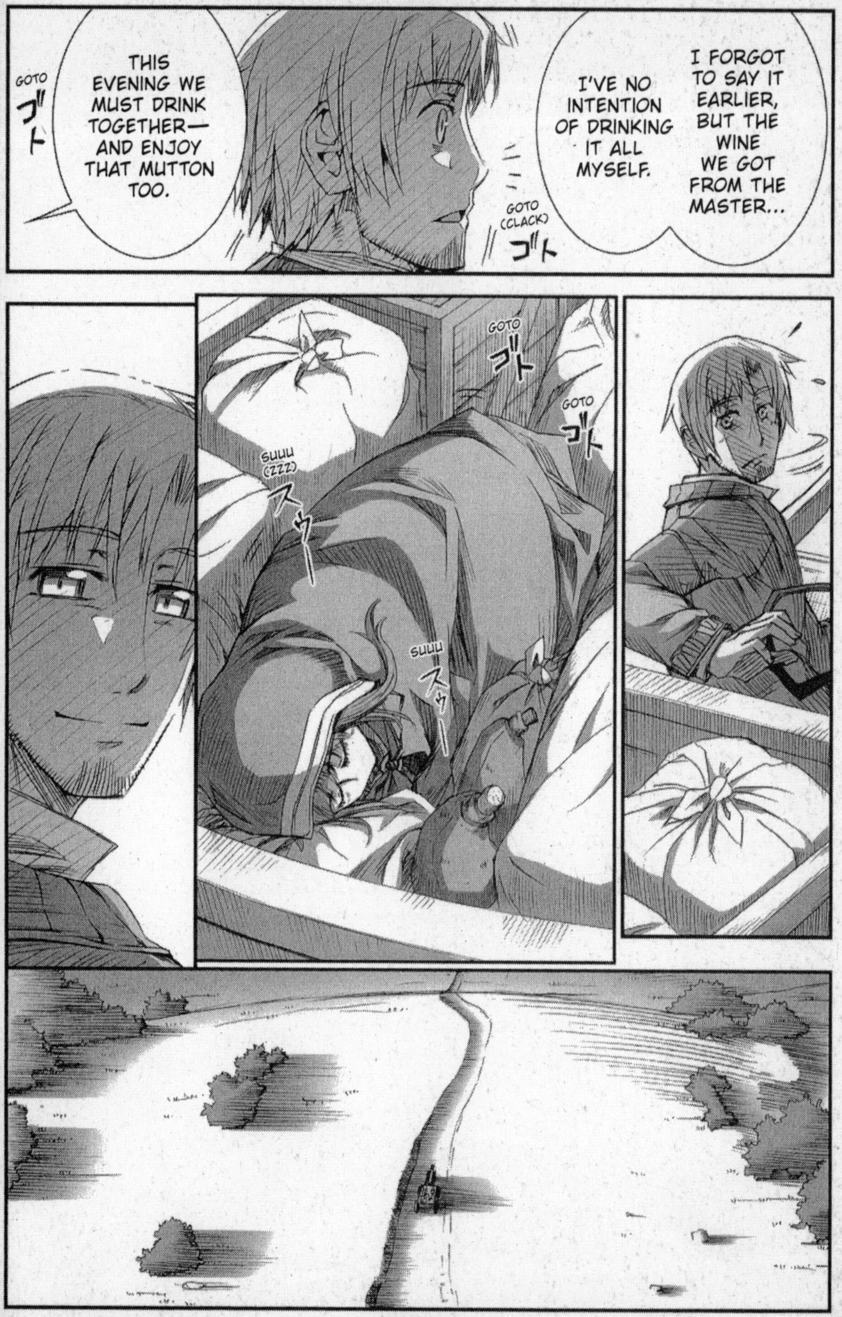
I FORGOT TO SAY IT EARLIER, BUT THE WINE WE GOT FROM THE MASTER...
I'VE NO INTENTION OF DRINKING IT ALL MYSELF.
GOTO (CLACK)
ゴト
THIS EVENING WE MUST DRINK TOGETHER—AND ENJOY THAT MUTTON TOO.
GOTO
ゴト
GOTO
ゴト
GOTO
ゴト
SUUU (ZZZ)
スゥー
SUUU
スゥー

SPICE & WOLF

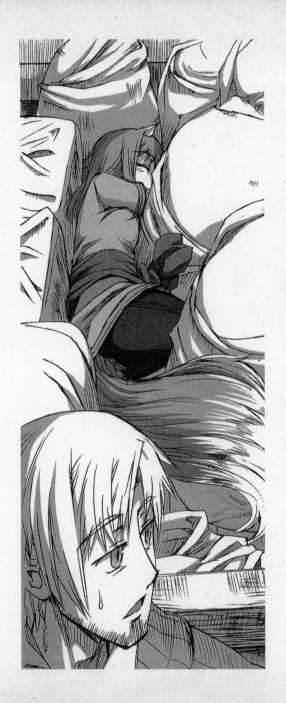

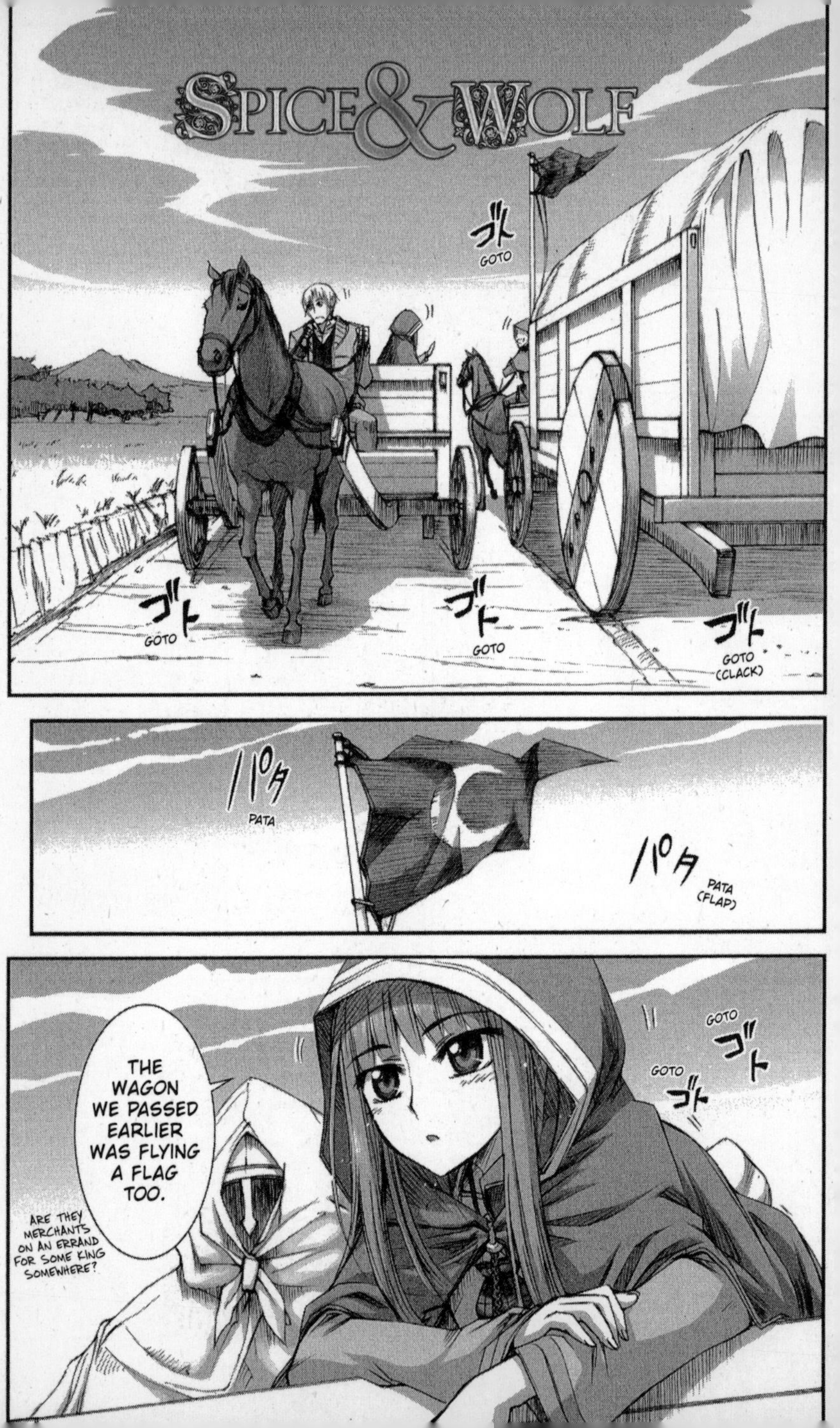
SPICE & WOLF
ゴト
GOTO
ゴト
GOTO
(CLACK)
ゴト
GOTO
ゴト
GOTO
パタ
PATA
(FLAP)
パタ
PATA
GOTO
ゴト
GOTO
ゴト
THE WAGON WE PASSED EARLIER WAS FLYING A FLAG TOO.
ARE THEY MERCHANTS ON AN ERRAND FOR SOME KING SOMEWHERE?

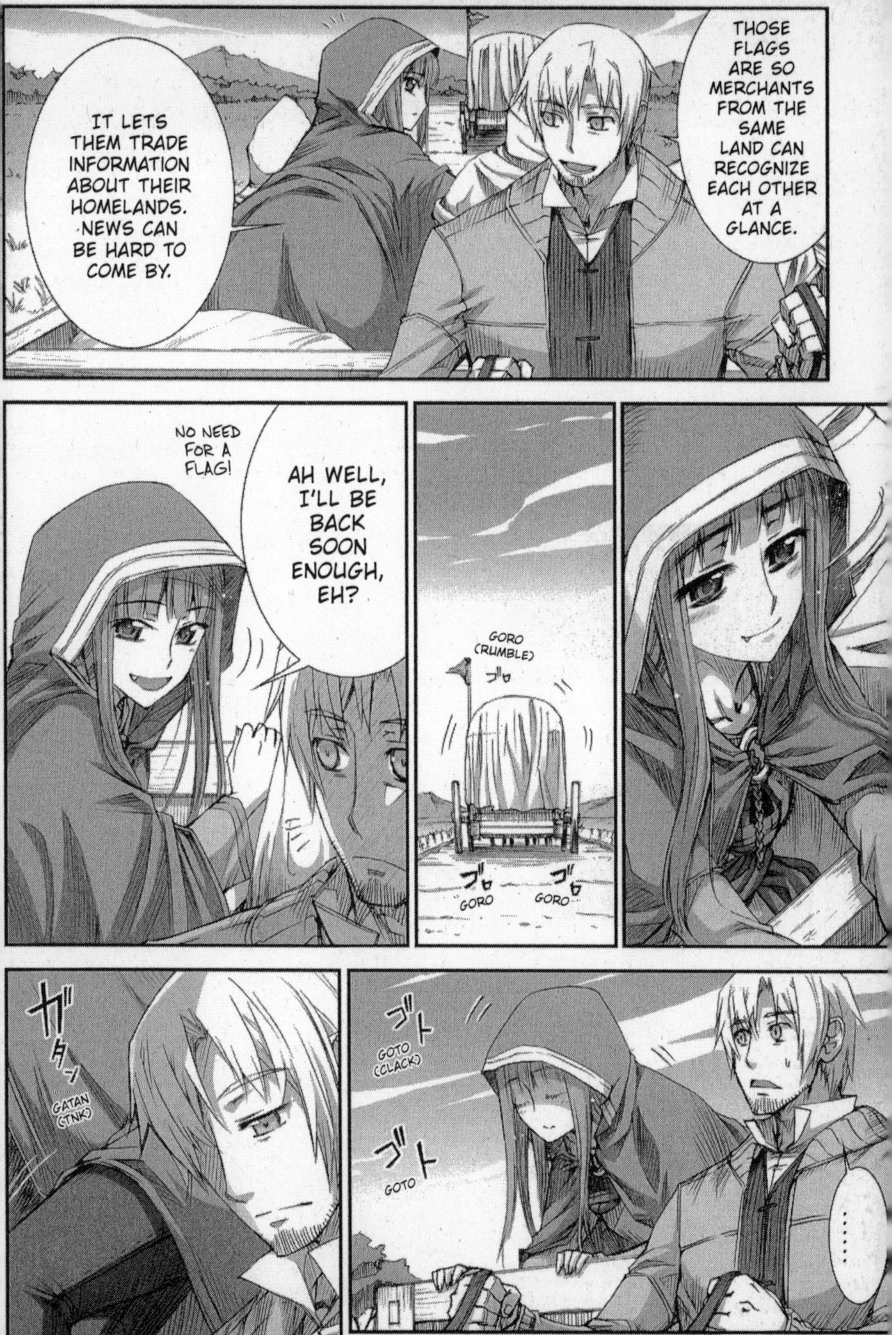
THOSE FLAGS ARE SO MERCHANTS FROM THE SAME LAND CAN RECOGNIZE EACH OTHER AT A GLANCE.
IT LETS THEM TRADE INFORMATION ABOUT THEIR HOMELANDS. NEWS CAN BE HARD TO COME BY.
GORO (RUMBLE)
GORO
GORO
AH WELL, I'LL BE BACK SOON ENOUGH, EH?
NO NEED FOR A FLAG!
GOTO (CLACK)
GOTO
......
GATAN (TNK)

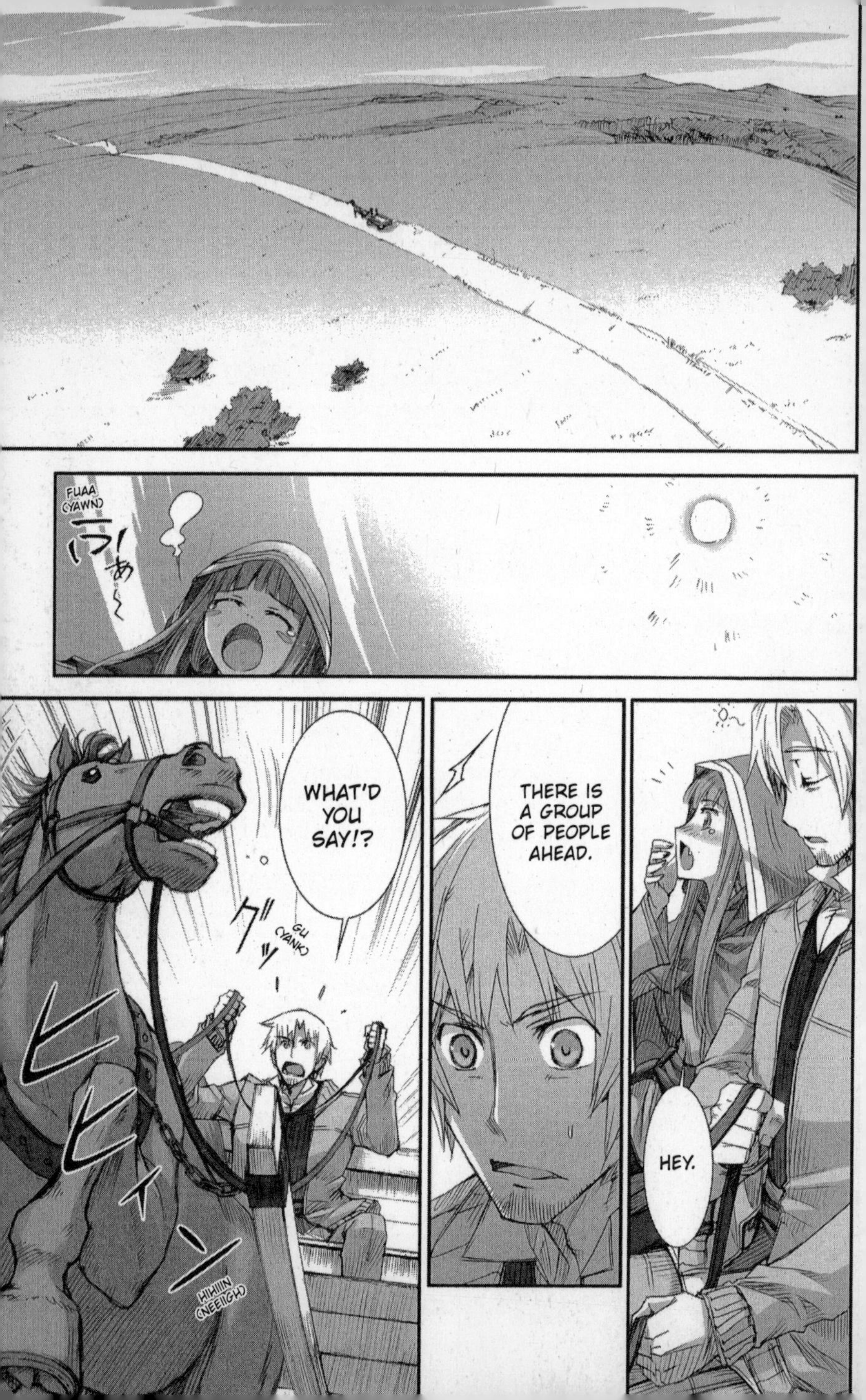
FUAA (YAWN)
HEY.
THERE IS A GROUP OF PEOPLE AHEAD.
WHAT'D YOU SAY!?
GU (YANK)
HIHIIIN (NEEIGH)

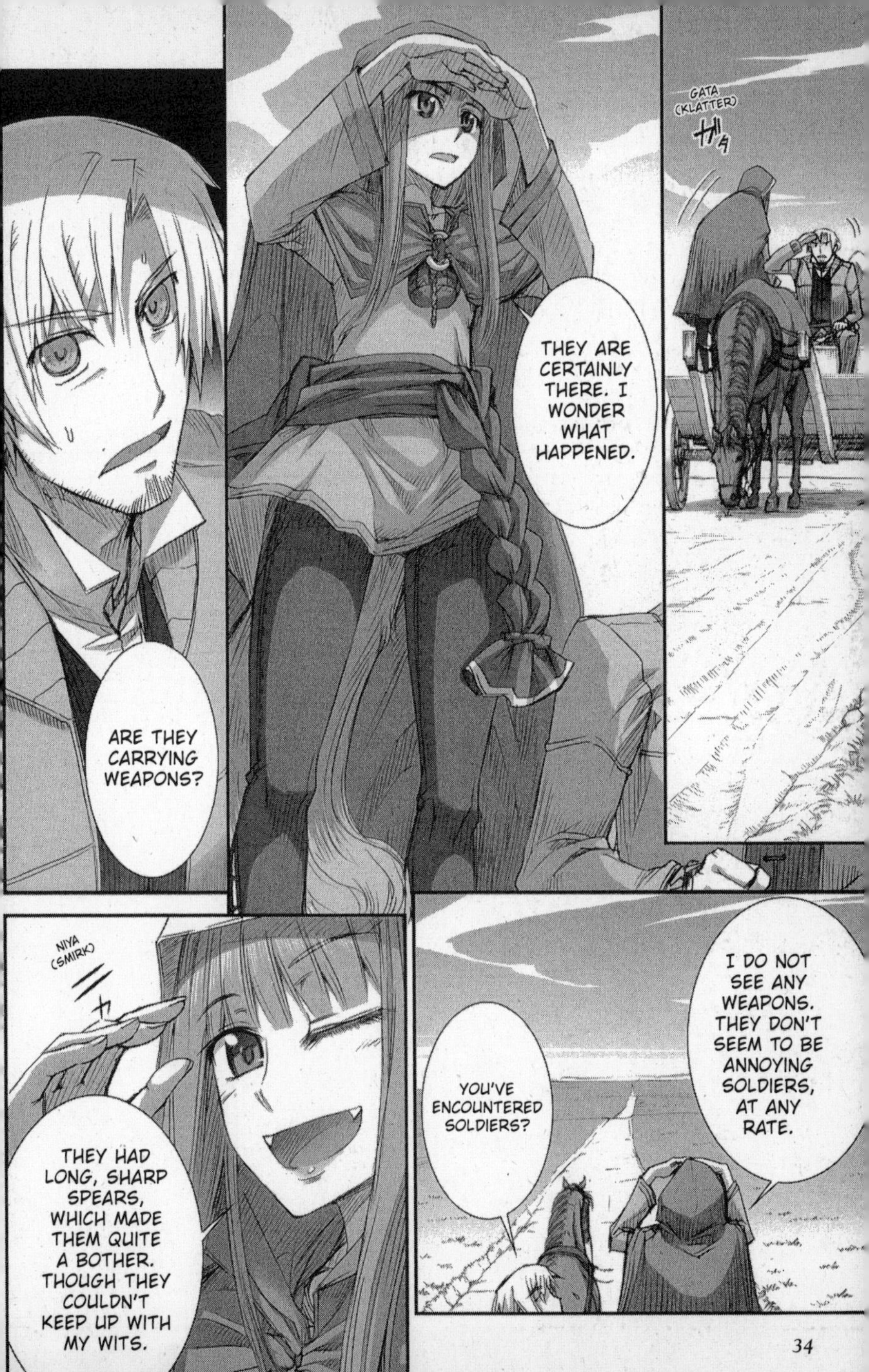
GATA (KLATTER)
THEY ARE CERTAINLY THERE. I WONDER WHAT HAPPENED.
ARE THEY CARRYING WEAPONS?
I DO NOT SEE ANY WEAPONS. THEY DON'T SEEM TO BE ANNOYING SOLDIERS, AT ANY RATE.
YOU'VE ENCOUNTERED SOLDIERS?
NIYA (SMIRK)
THEY HAD LONG, SHARP SPEARS, WHICH MADE THEM QUITE A BOTHER. THOUGH THEY COULDN'T KEEP UP WITH MY WITS.

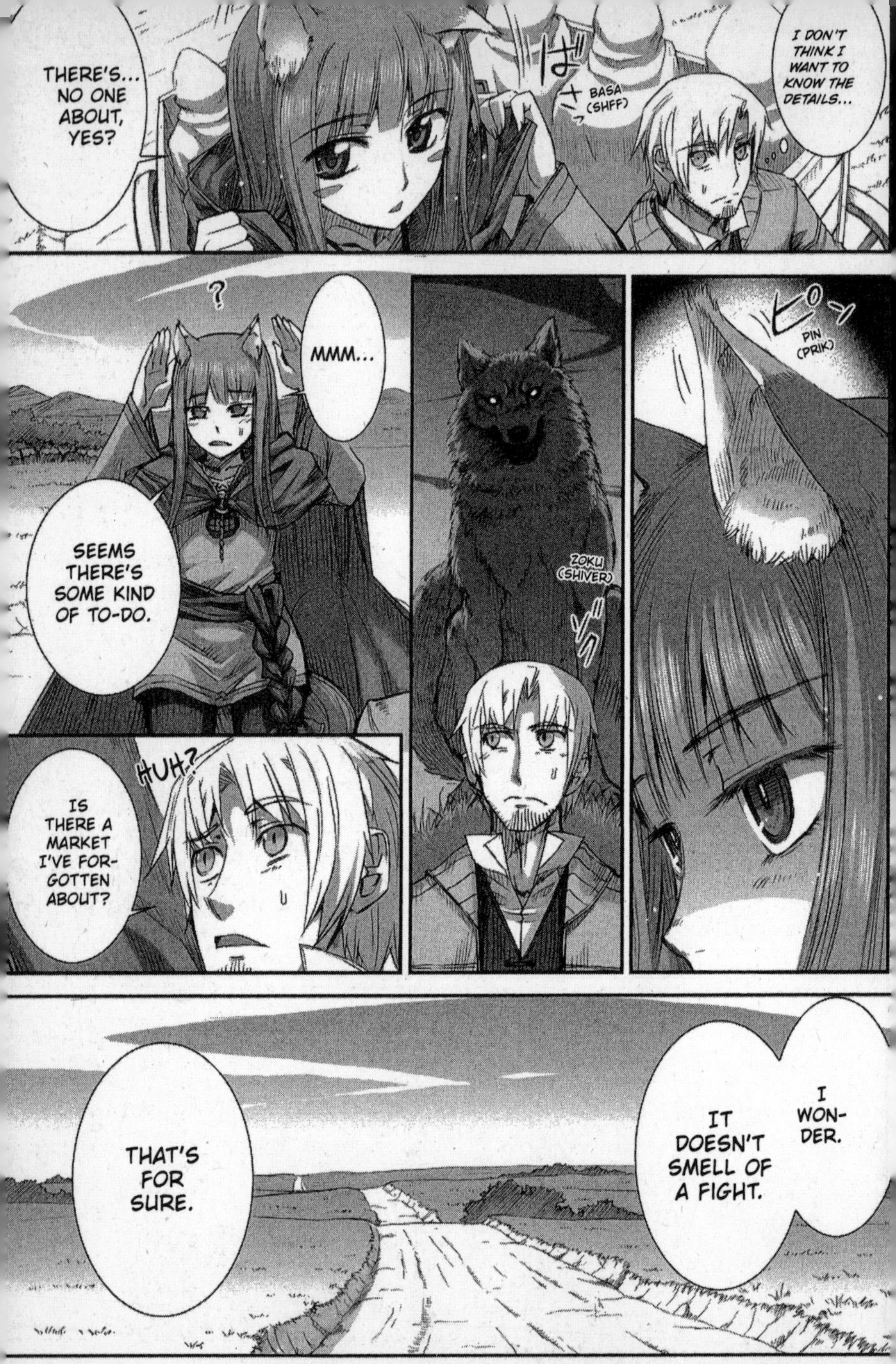
I DON'T THINK I WANT TO KNOW THE DETAILS...
BASA (SHFF)
THERE'S... NO ONE ABOUT, YES?
PIN (PRIK)
ZOKU (SHIVER)
?
MMM...
SEEMS THERE'S SOME KIND OF TO-DO.
HUH?
IS THERE A MARKET I'VE FOR-GOTTEN ABOUT?
I WON-DER.
IT DOESN'T SMELL OF A FIGHT.
THAT'S FOR SURE.

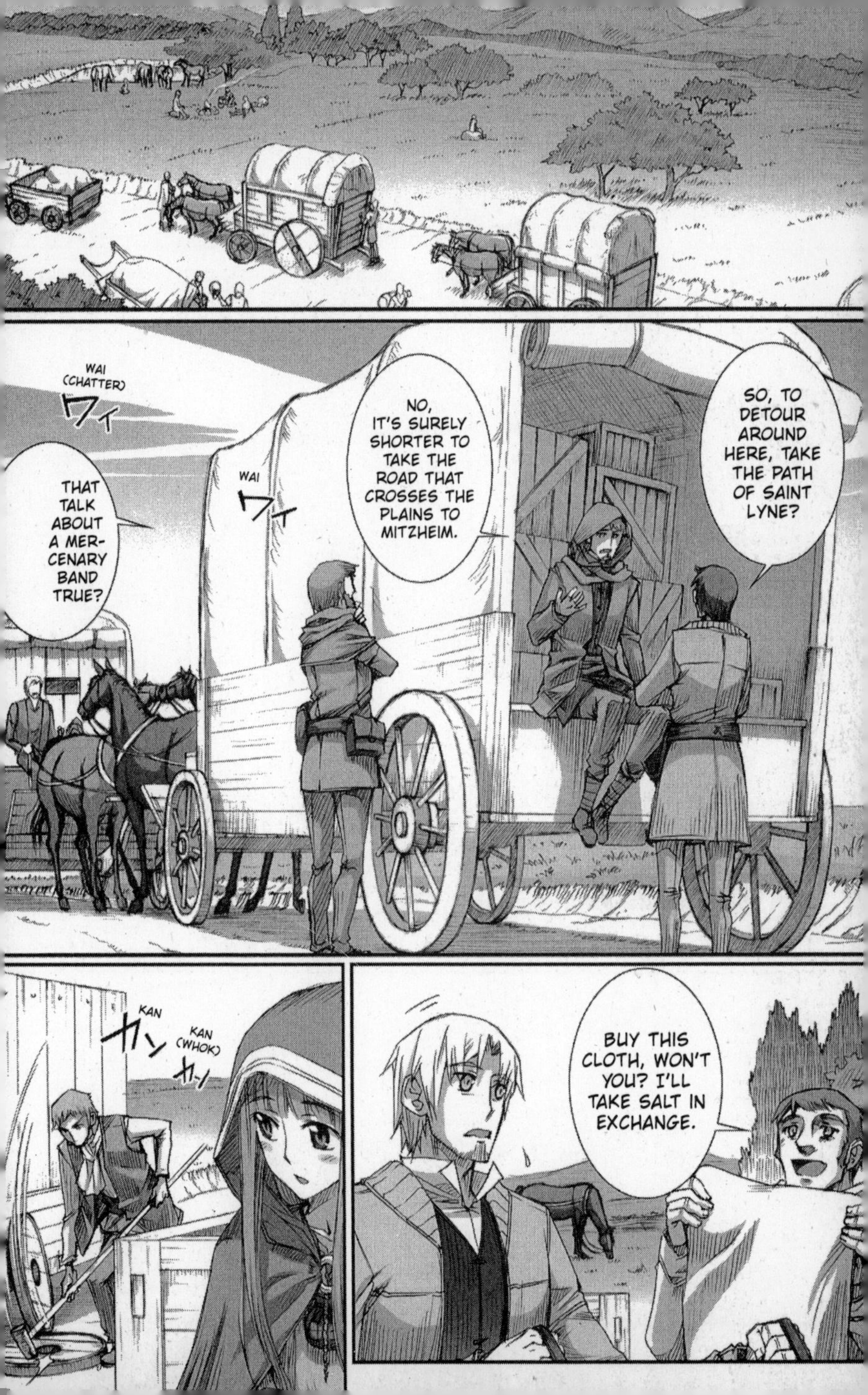
SO, TO DETOUR AROUND HERE, TAKE THE PATH OF SAINT LYNE?
NO, IT'S SURELY SHORTER TO TAKE THE ROAD THAT CROSSES THE PLAINS TO MITZHEIM.
WAI
ワイ
WAI (CHATTER)
ワイ
THAT TALK ABOUT A MER-CENARY BAND TRUE?
BUY THIS CLOTH, WON'T YOU? I'LL TAKE SALT IN EXCHANGE.
KAN
カン
KAN (WHOK)
カン

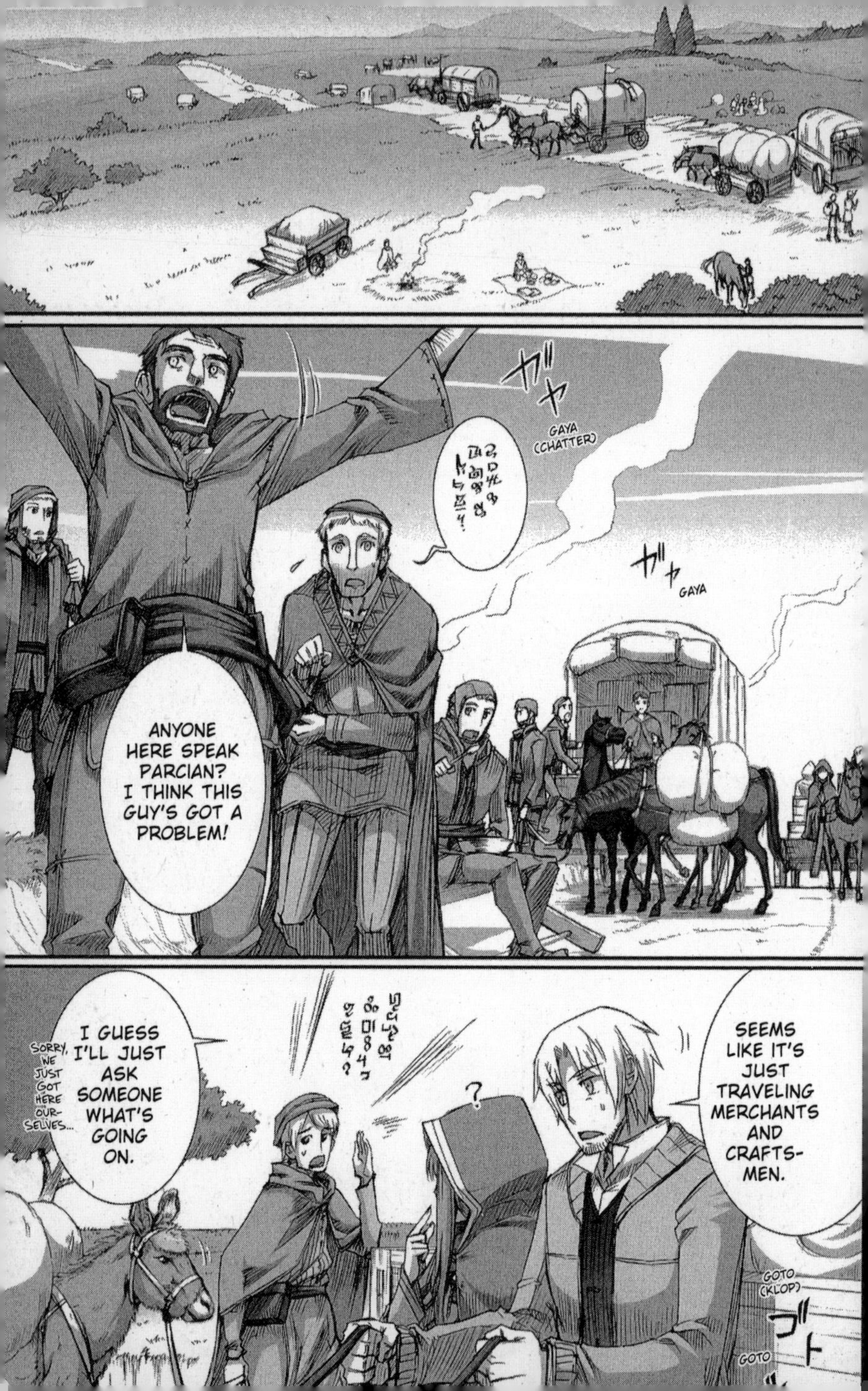
ガヤ
GAYA (CHATTER)
ガヤ
GAYA
ANYONE HERE SPEAK PARCIAN? I THINK THIS GUY'S GOT A PROBLEM!
SEEMS LIKE IT'S JUST TRAVELING MERCHANTS AND CRAFTS-MEN.
GOTO (KLOP)
ゴト
GOTO
I GUESS I'LL JUST ASK SOMEONE WHAT'S GOING ON.
SORRY, WE JUST GOT HERE OUR-SELVES...

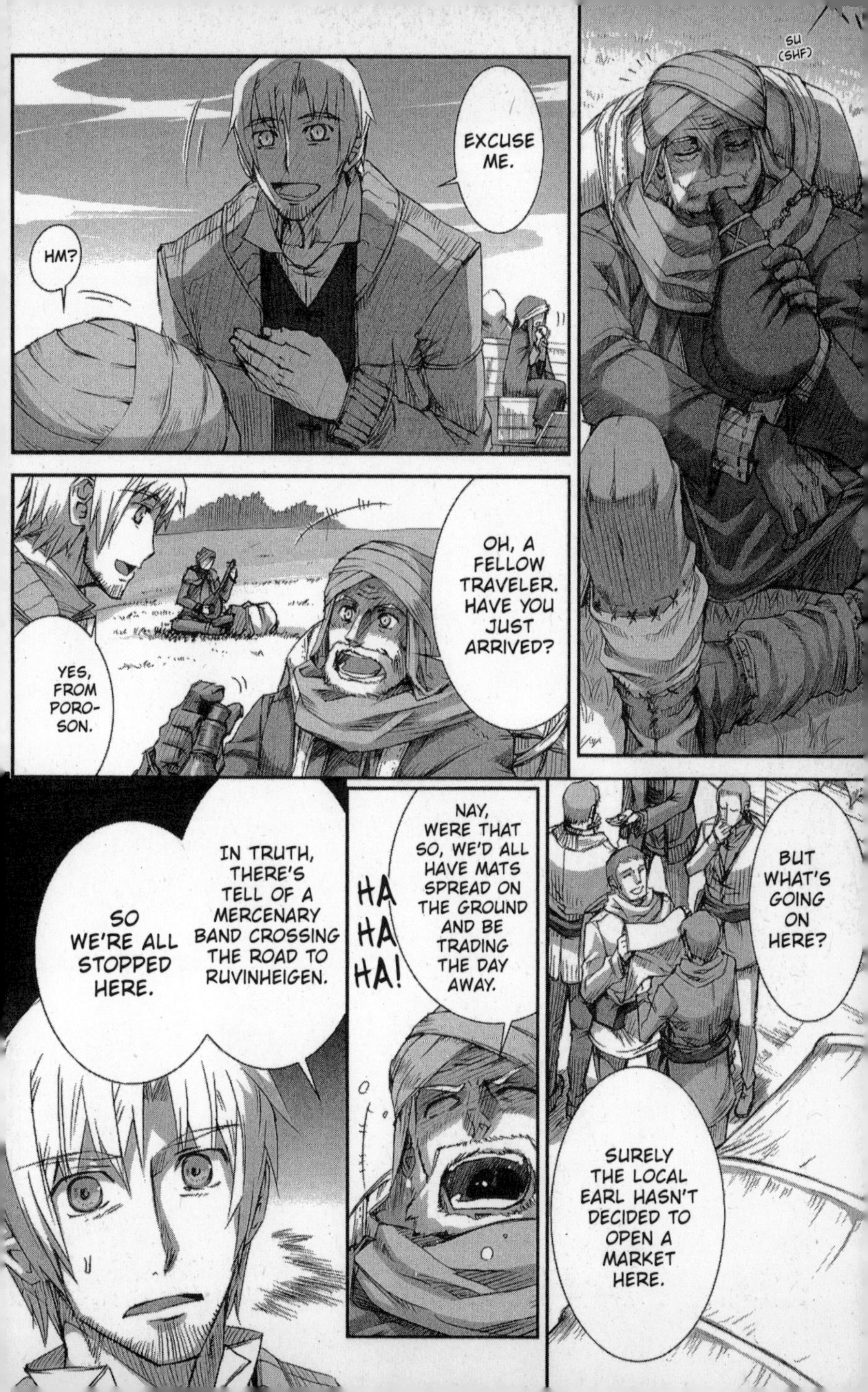
SU (SHF)
EXCUSE ME.
HM?
OH, A FELLOW TRAVELER. HAVE YOU JUST ARRIVED?
YES, FROM POROSON.
BUT WHAT'S GOING ON HERE?
SURELY THE LOCAL EARL HASN'T DECIDED TO OPEN A MARKET HERE.
NAY, WERE THAT SO, WE'D ALL HAVE MATS SPREAD ON THE GROUND AND BE TRADING THE DAY AWAY.
HA HA HA!
IN TRUTH, THERE'S TELL OF A MERCENARY BAND CROSSING THE ROAD TO RUVINHEIGEN.
SO WE'RE ALL STOPPED HERE.

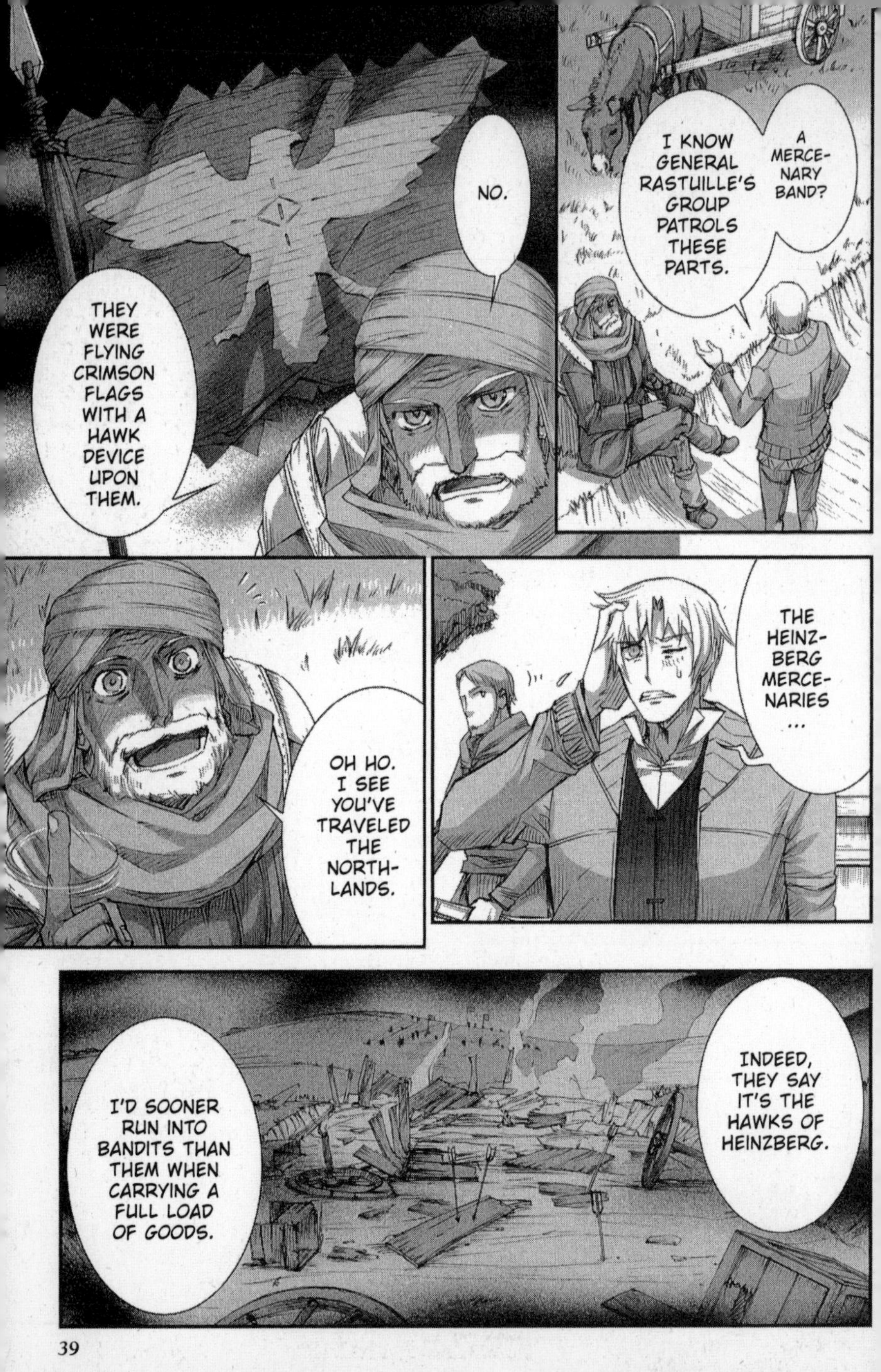
A MERCENARY BAND?
I KNOW GENERAL RASTUILLE'S GROUP PATROLS THESE PARTS.
NO.
THEY WERE FLYING CRIMSON FLAGS WITH A HAWK DEVICE UPON THEM.
THE HEINZBERG MERCENARIES...
OH HO. I SEE YOU'VE TRAVELED THE NORTHLANDS.
INDEED, THEY SAY IT'S THE HAWKS OF HEINZBERG.
I'D SOONER RUN INTO BANDITS THAN THEM WHEN CARRYING A FULL LOAD OF GOODS.

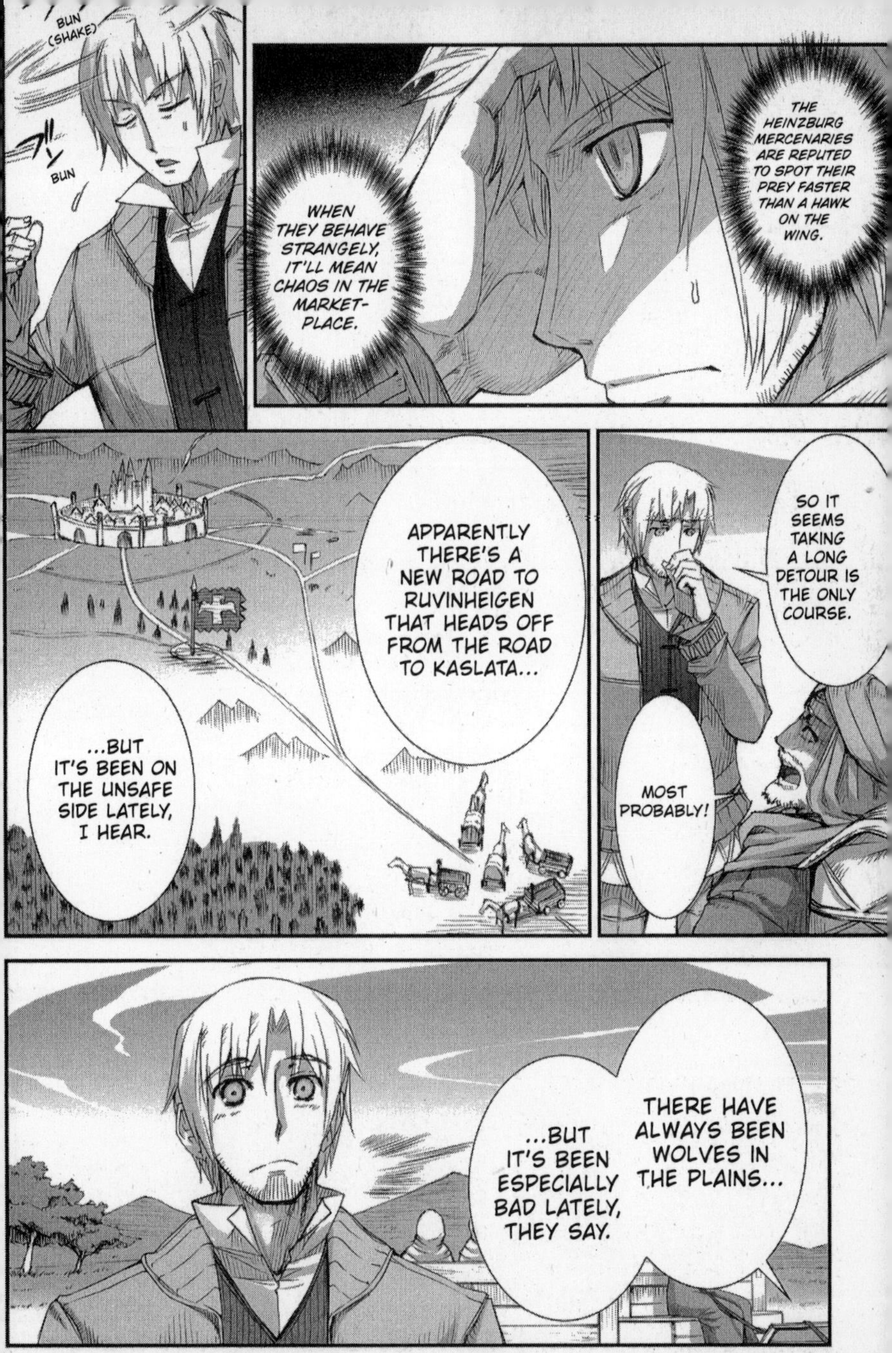
THE HEINZBURG MERCENARIES ARE REPUTED TO SPOT THEIR PREY FASTER THAN A HAWK ON THE WING.
WHEN THEY BEHAVE STRANGELY, IT'LL MEAN CHAOS IN THE MARKET-PLACE.
BUN (SHAKE)
BUN
SO IT SEEMS TAKING A LONG DETOUR IS THE ONLY COURSE.
MOST PROBABLY!
APPARENTLY THERE'S A NEW ROAD TO RUVINHEIGEN THAT HEADS OFF FROM THE ROAD TO KASLATA...
...BUT IT'S BEEN ON THE UNSAFE SIDE LATELY, I HEAR.
THERE HAVE ALWAYS BEEN WOLVES IN THE PLAINS...
...BUT IT'S BEEN ESPECIALLY BAD LATELY, THEY SAY.

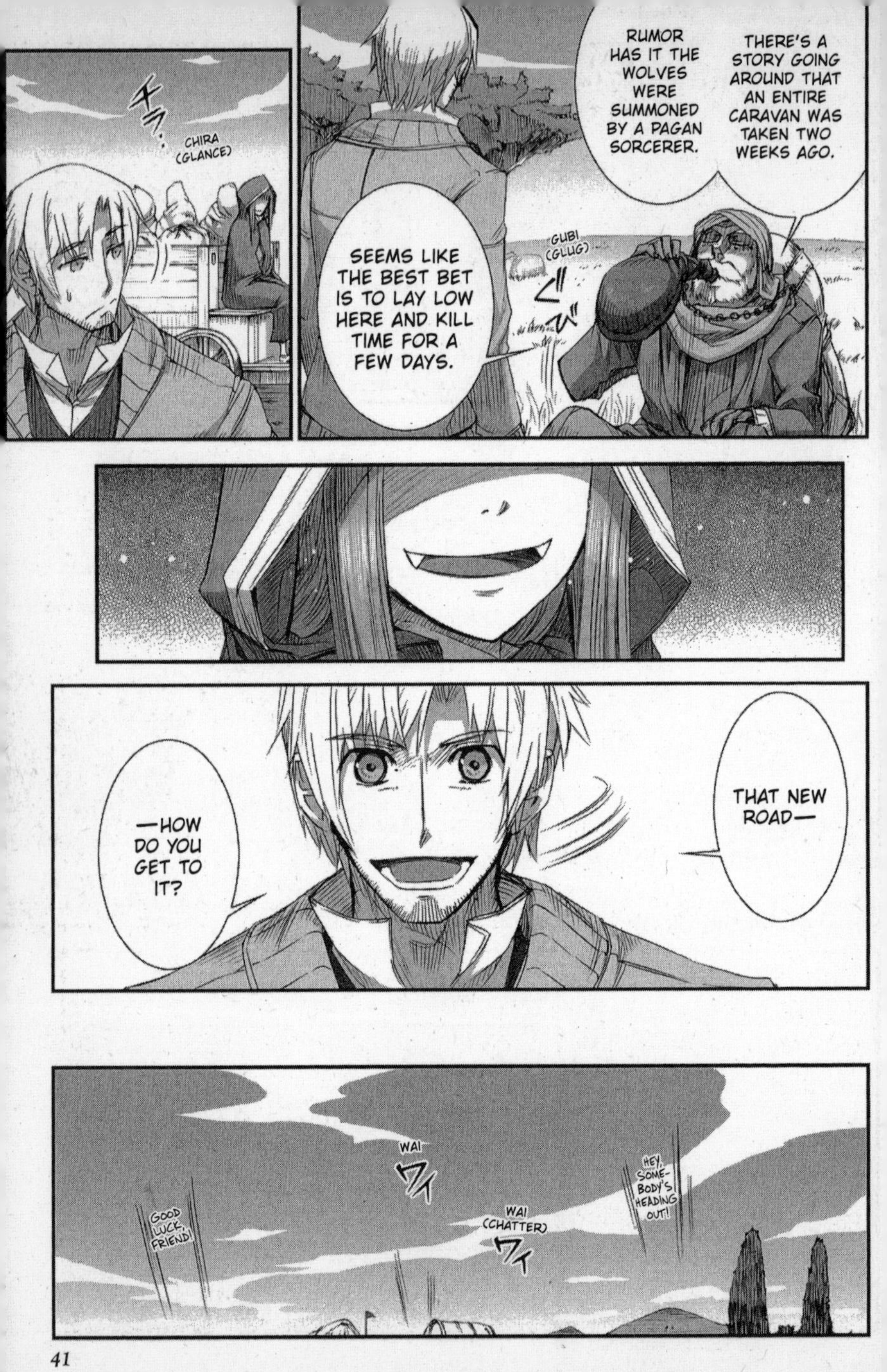
THERE'S A STORY GOING AROUND THAT AN ENTIRE CARAVAN WAS TAKEN TWO WEEKS AGO.
RUMOR HAS IT THE WOLVES WERE SUMMONED BY A PAGAN SORCERER.
GUBI (GLUG)
SEEMS LIKE THE BEST BET IS TO LAY LOW HERE AND KILL TIME FOR A FEW DAYS.
CHIRA (GLANCE)
THAT NEW ROAD—
—HOW DO YOU GET TO IT?
HEY, SOMEBODY'S HEADING OUT!
WAI
WAI (CHATTER)
GOOD LUCK, FRIEND!

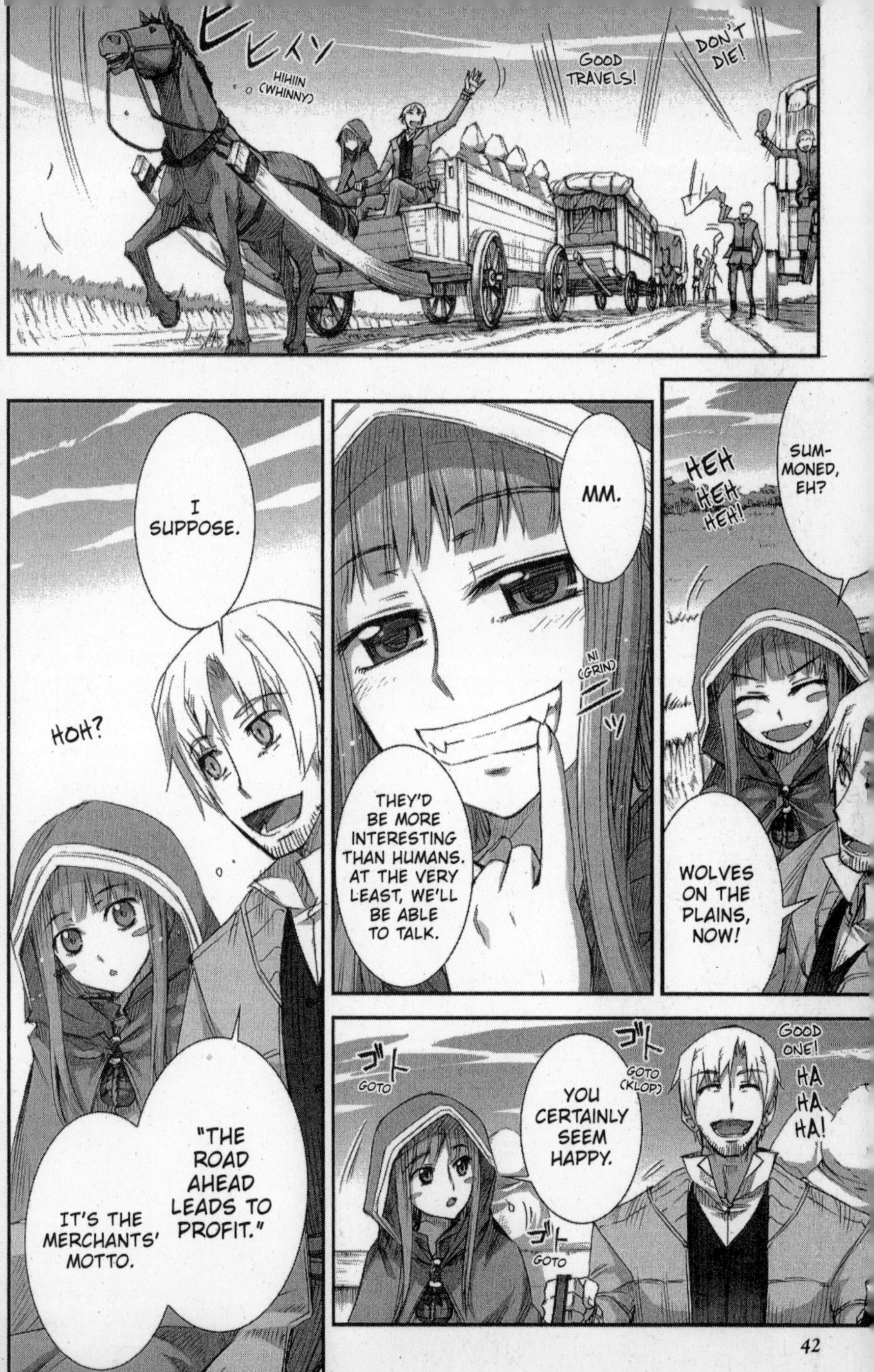
DON'T DIE!
GOOD TRAVELS!
HIHIIN (WHINNY)
SUM-MONED, EH?
HEH HEH HEH!
WOLVES ON THE PLAINS, NOW!
MM.
NI (GRIN)
THEY'D BE MORE INTERESTING THAN HUMANS. AT THE VERY LEAST, WE'LL BE ABLE TO TALK.
GOOD ONE!
HA HA HA!
GOTO (KLOP)
YOU CERTAINLY SEEM HAPPY.
GOTO
GOTO
I SUPPOSE.
HOH?
"THE ROAD AHEAD LEADS TO PROFIT."
IT'S THE MERCHANTS' MOTTO.

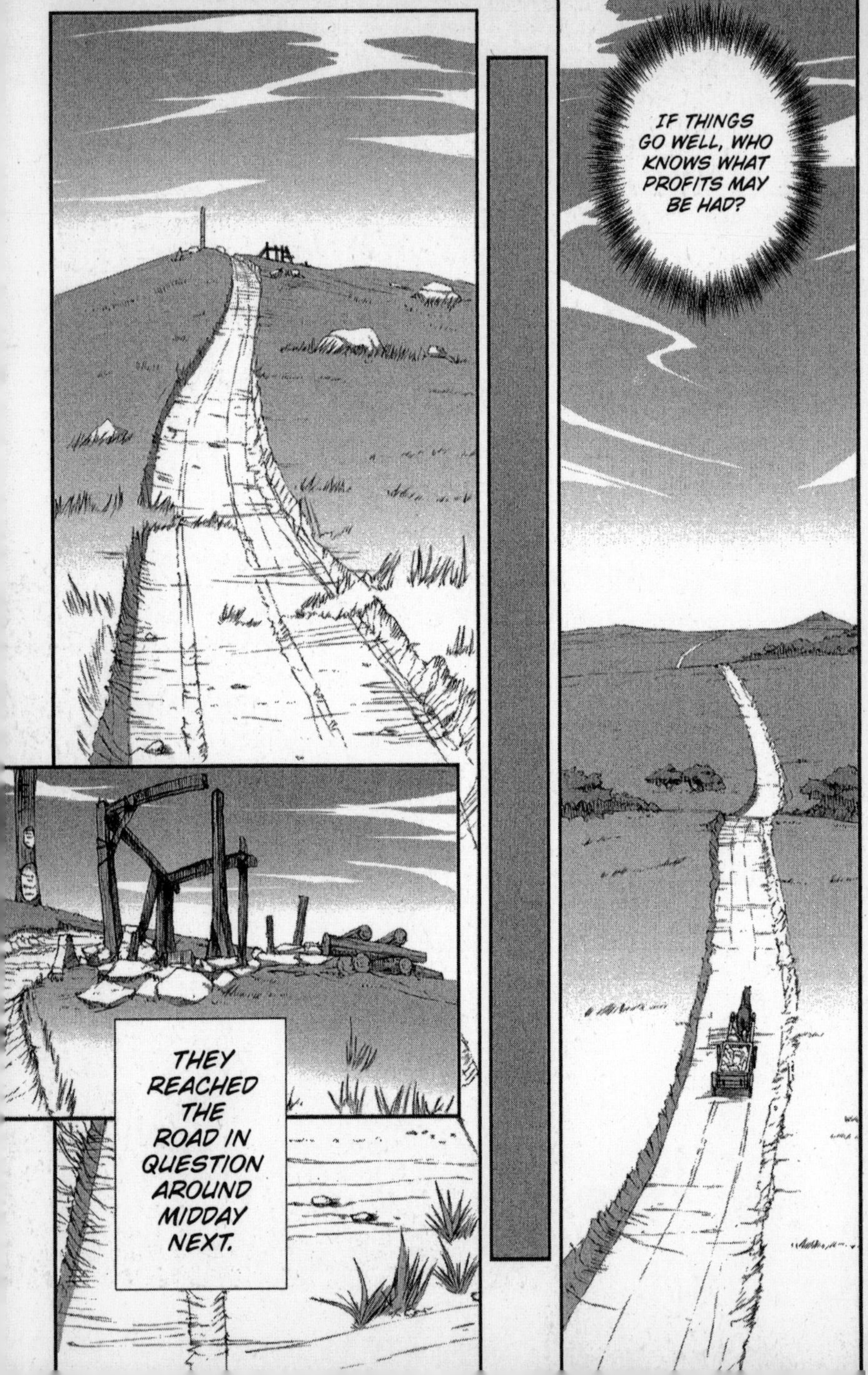
IF THINGS GO WELL, WHO KNOWS WHAT PROFITS MAY BE HAD?
THEY REACHED THE ROAD IN QUESTION AROUND MIDDAY NEXT.

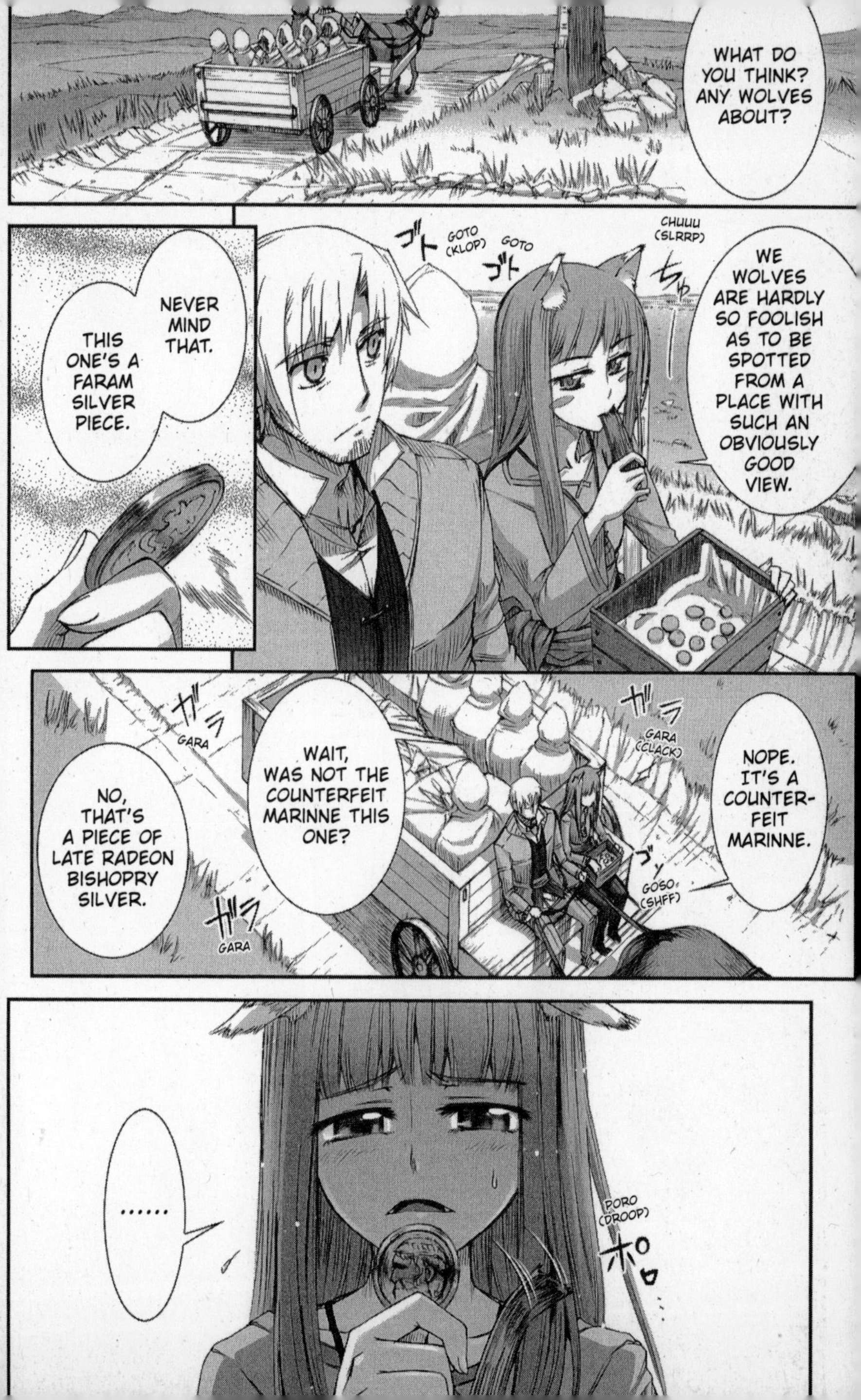
WHAT DO YOU THINK? ANY WOLVES ABOUT?
ちゅー
CHUUU (SLRRP)
ゴト
GOTO
ゴト
GOTO (KLOP)
WE WOLVES ARE HARDLY SO FOOLISH AS TO BE SPOTTED FROM A PLACE WITH SUCH AN OBVIOUSLY GOOD VIEW.
NEVER MIND THAT.
THIS ONE'S A FARAM SILVER PIECE.
ガラ
GARA (CLACK)
NOPE. IT'S A COUNTER-FEIT MARINNE.
ゴソ
GOSO (SHFF)
WAIT, WAS NOT THE COUNTERFEIT MARINNE THIS ONE?
ガラ
GARA
NO, THAT'S A PIECE OF LATE RADEON BISHOPRY SILVER.
ガラ
GARA
ポロ
PORO (DROOP)
......

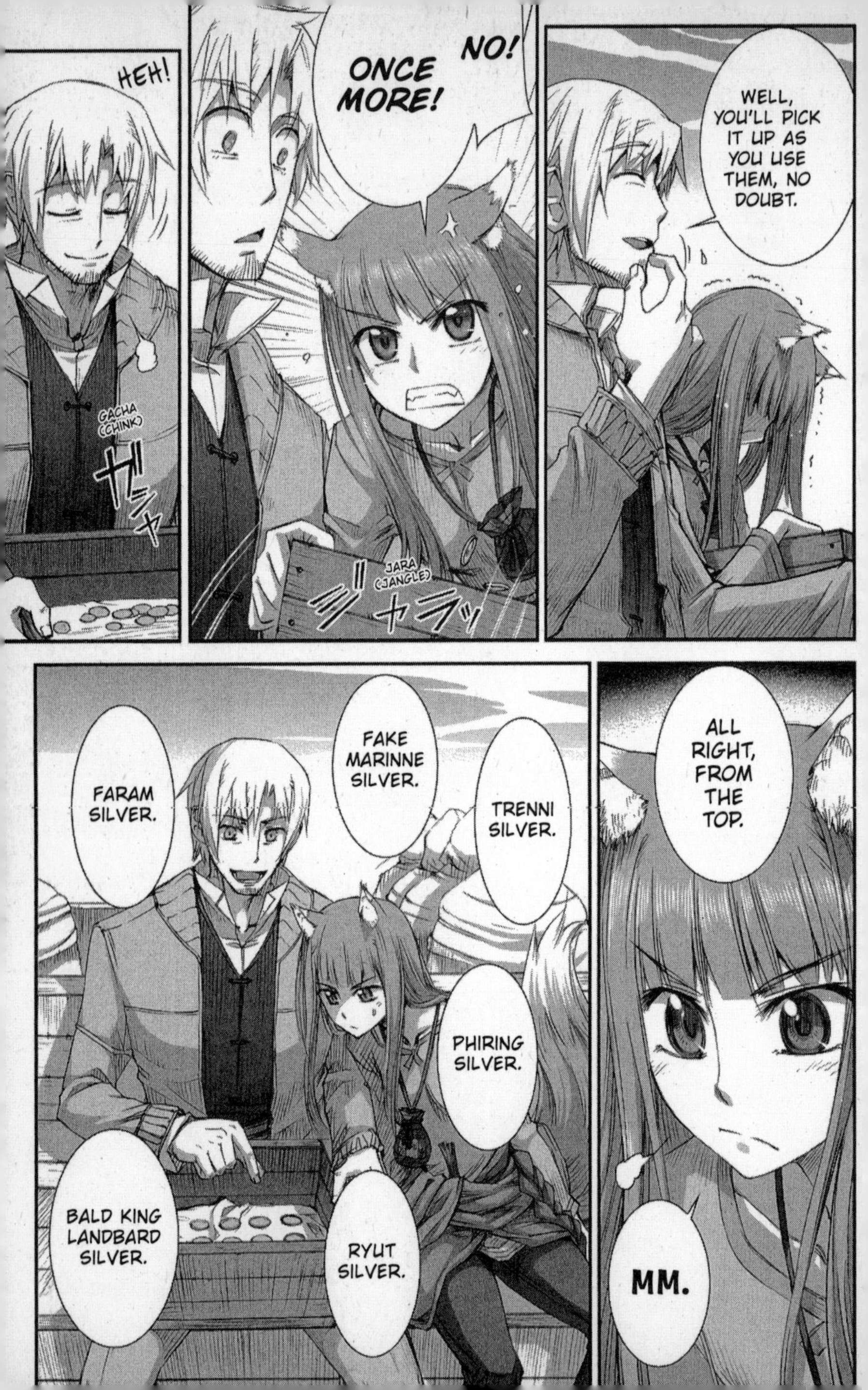
WELL, YOU'LL PICK IT UP AS YOU USE THEM, NO DOUBT.
NO!
ONCE MORE!
JARA (JANGLE)
ジャラッ
HEH!
GACHA (CHINK)
ガシャ
ALL RIGHT, FROM THE TOP.
MM.
TRENNI SILVER.
FAKE MARINNE SILVER.
FARAM SILVER.
PHIRING SILVER.
RYUT SILVER.
BALD KING LANDBARD SILVER.

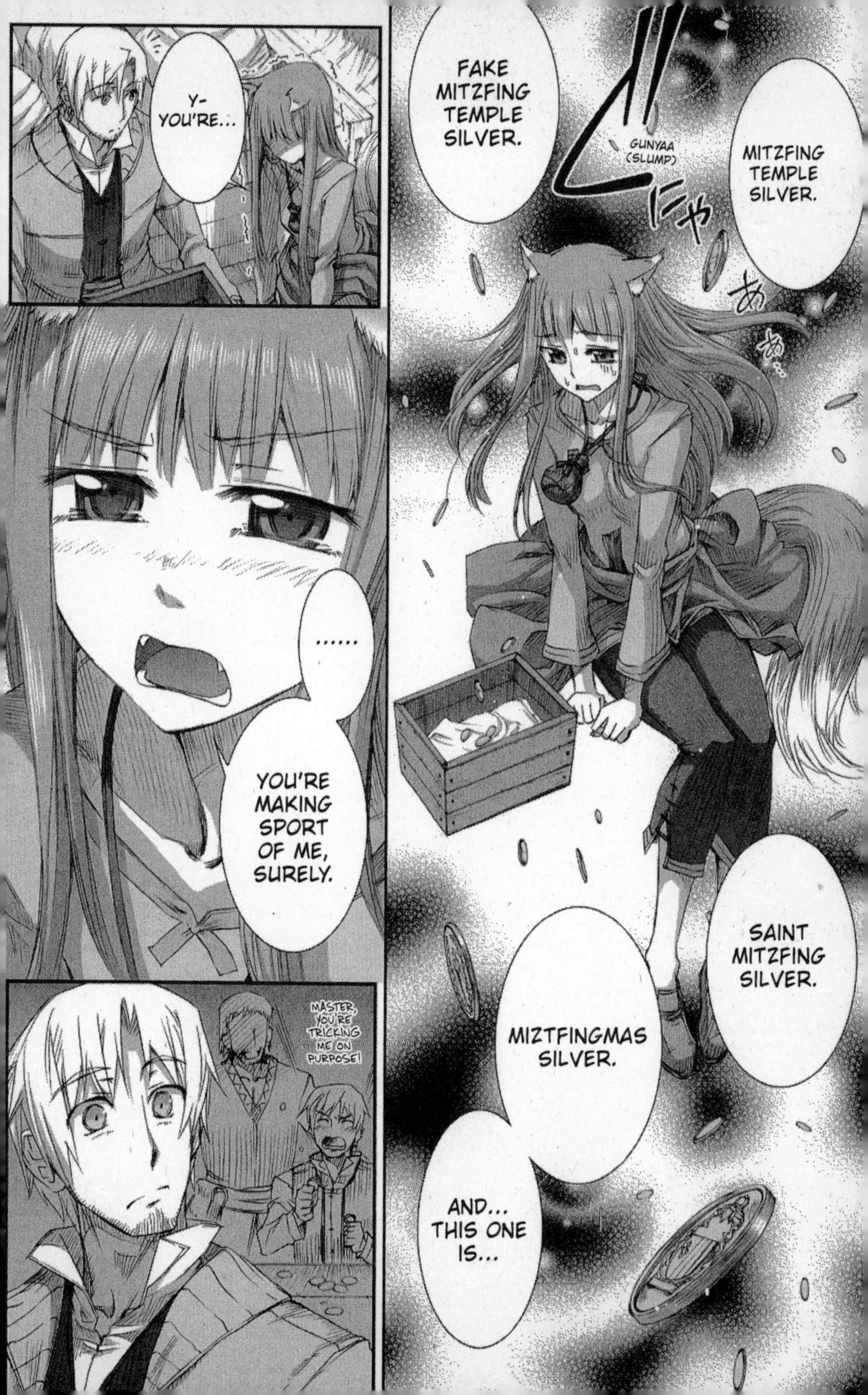
MITZFING TEMPLE SILVER.
FAKE MITZFING TEMPLE SILVER.
GUNYAA (SLUMP)
SAINT MITZFING SILVER.
MIZTFINGMAS SILVER.
AND... THIS ONE IS...
Y-YOU'RE...
......
YOU'RE MAKING SPORT OF ME, SURELY.
MASTER, YOU'RE TRICKING ME ON PURPOSE!

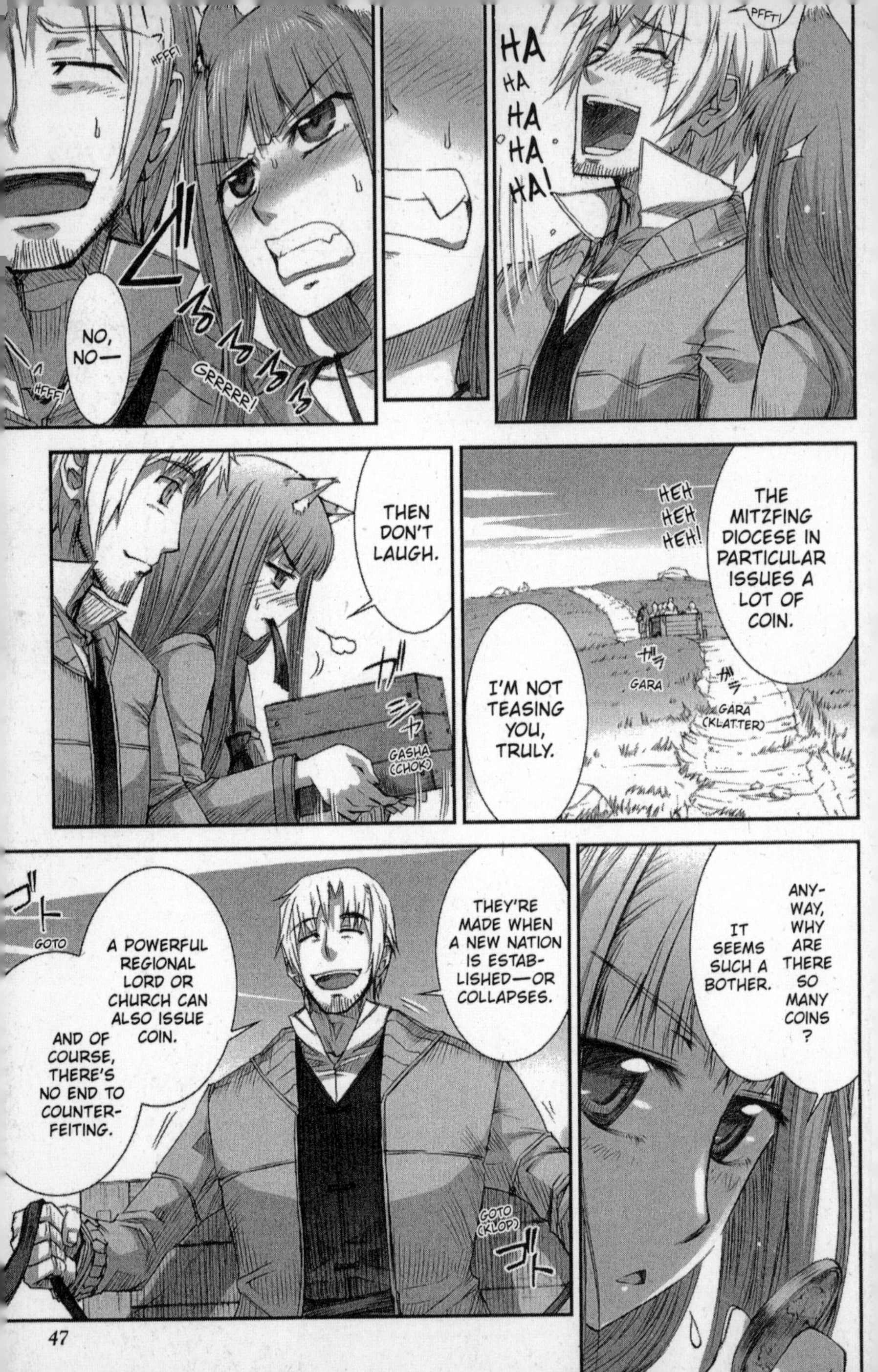
PFFT!
HA HA HA HA HA!
HFFF!
NO, NO—
HFFF!
GRRRRR!
HEH HEH HEH!
THE MITZFING DIOCESE IN PARTICULAR ISSUES A LOT OF COIN.
I'M NOT TEASING YOU, TRULY.
GARA
GARA (KLATTER)
THEN DON'T LAUGH.
GASHA (CHOK)
ANY-WAY, WHY ARE THERE SO MANY COINS?
IT SEEMS SUCH A BOTHER.
THEY'RE MADE WHEN A NEW NATION IS ESTAB-LISHED—OR COLLAPSES.
GOTO
A POWERFUL REGIONAL LORD OR CHURCH CAN ALSO ISSUE COIN.
AND OF COURSE, THERE'S NO END TO COUNTER-FEITING.
GOTO (KLOP)

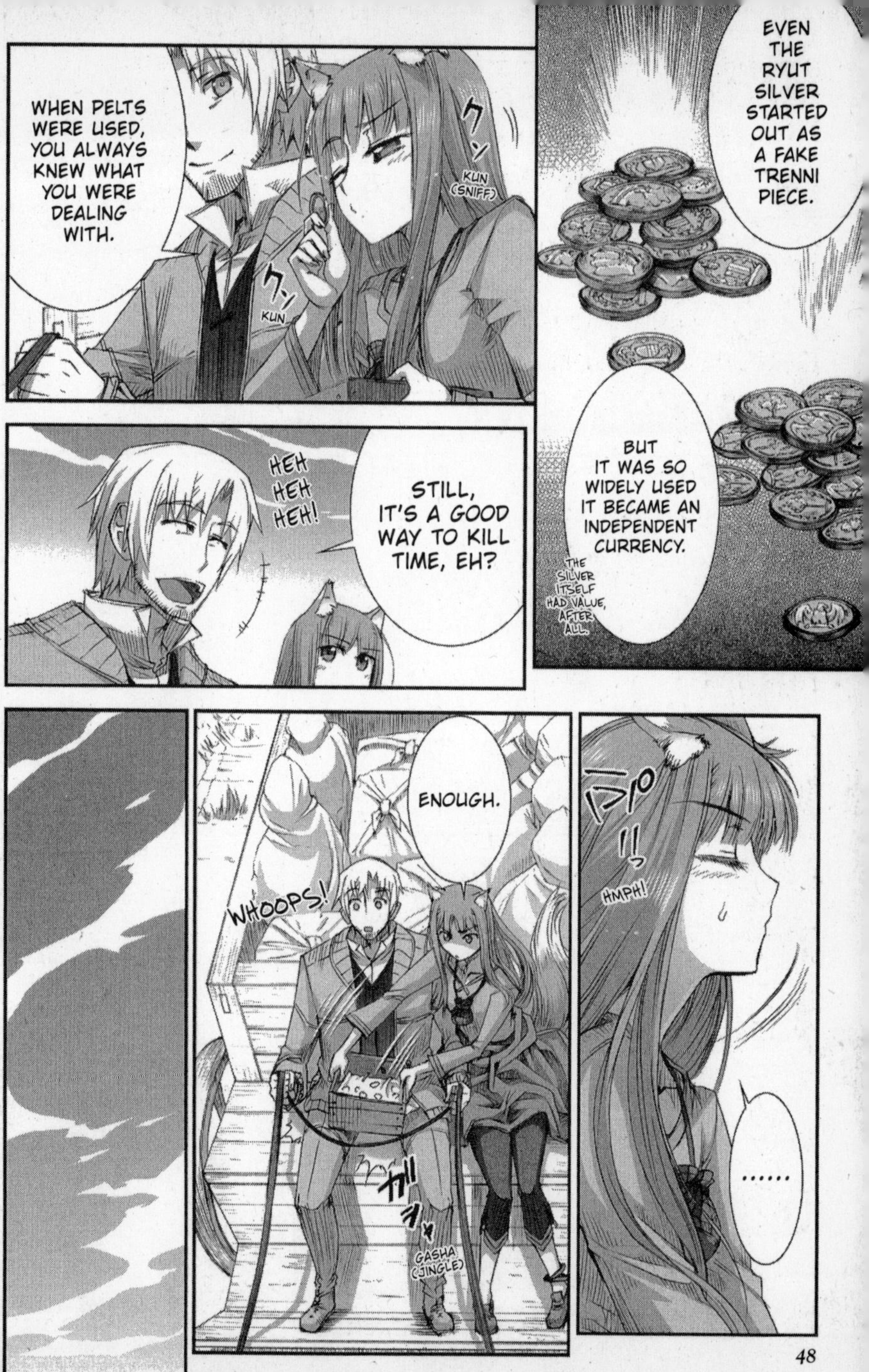

EVEN THE RYUT SILVER STARTED OUT AS A FAKE TRENNI PIECE.
BUT IT WAS SO WIDELY USED IT BECAME AN INDEPENDENT CURRENCY.
THE SILVER ITSELF HAD VALUE, AFTER ALL.
KUN (SNIFF)
WHEN PELTS WERE USED, YOU ALWAYS KNEW WHAT YOU WERE DEALING WITH.
KUN
STILL, IT'S A GOOD WAY TO KILL TIME, EH?
HEH HEH HEH!
HMPH!
......
ENOUGH.
WHOOPS!
GASHA (JINGLE)

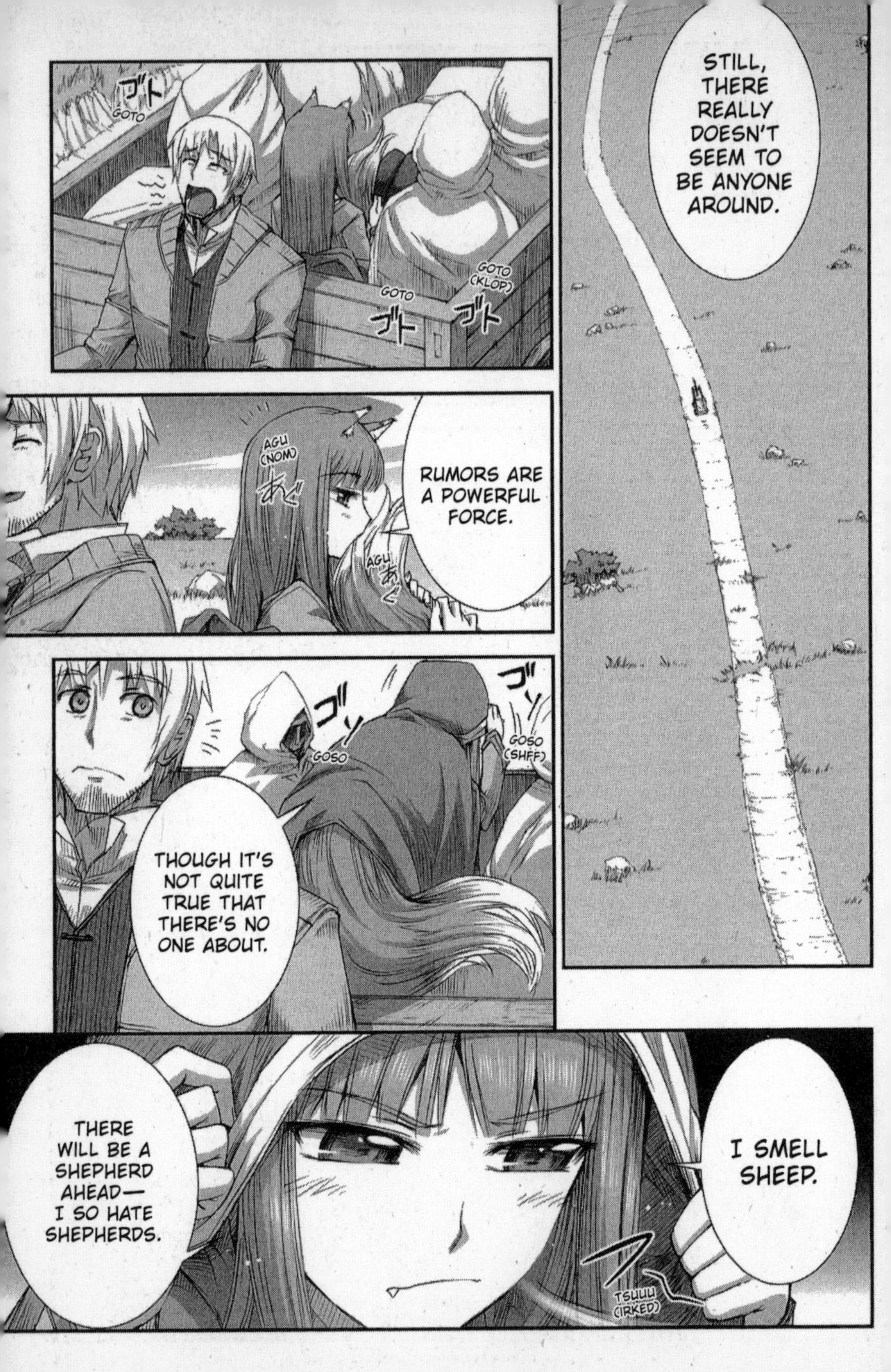
STILL, THERE REALLY DOESN'T SEEM TO BE ANYONE AROUND.
ゴト
GOTO (KLOP)
ゴト
GOTO
ゴト
GOTO
RUMORS ARE A POWERFUL FORCE.
AGU (NOM)
あぐ
AGU
あぐ
ゴソ
GOSO (SHFF)
ゴソ
GOSO
THOUGH IT'S NOT QUITE TRUE THAT THERE'S NO ONE ABOUT.
I SMELL SHEEP.
TSUUU (IRKED)
THERE WILL BE A SHEPHERD AHEAD— I SO HATE SHEPHERDS.

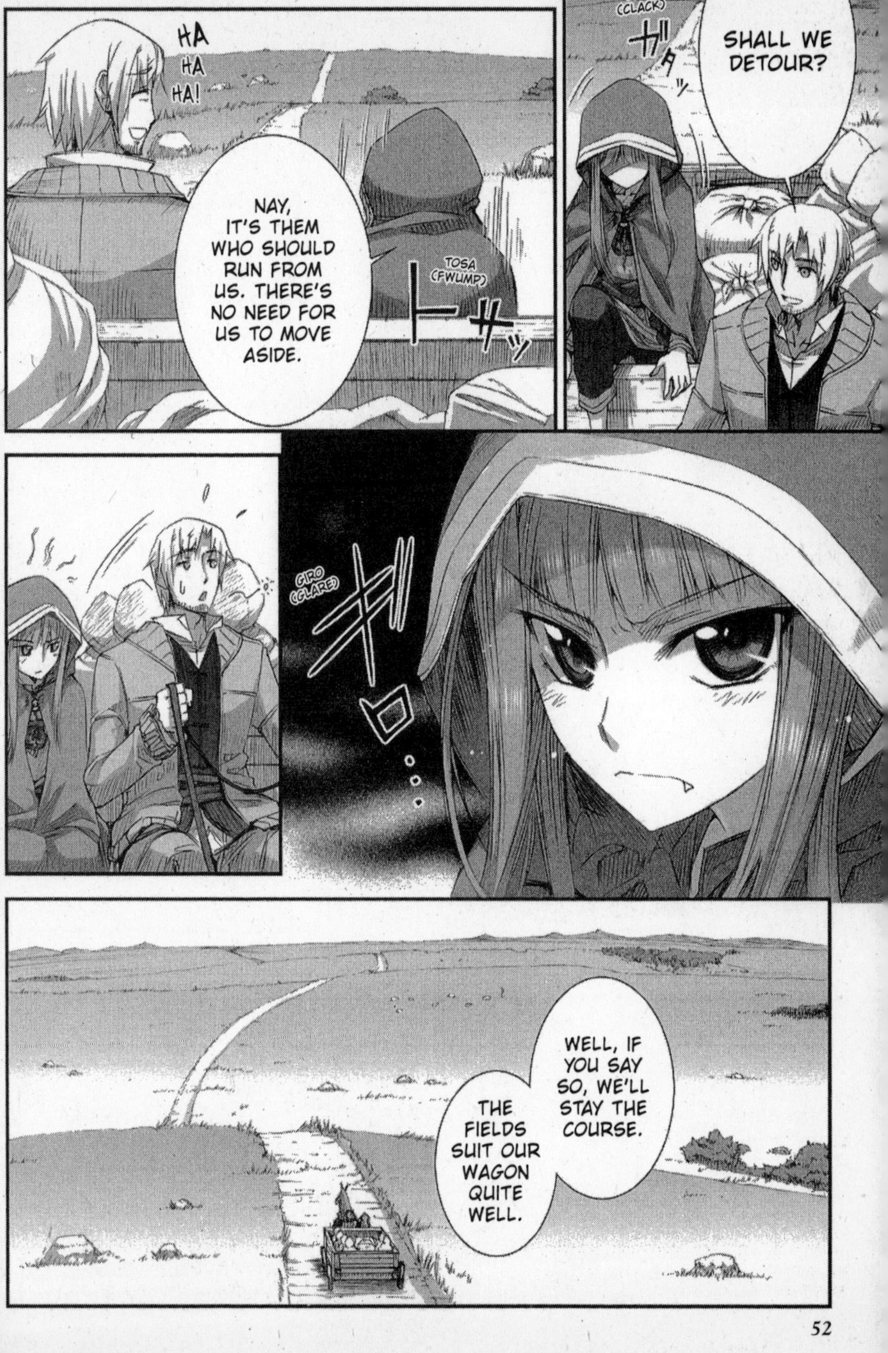
SHALL WE DETOUR?
GATA (CLACK)
HA HA HA!
NAY, IT'S THEM WHO SHOULD RUN FROM US. THERE'S NO NEED FOR US TO MOVE ASIDE.
TOSA (FWUMP)
GIRO (GLARE)
...
WELL, IF YOU SAY SO, WE'LL STAY THE COURSE.
THE FIELDS SUIT OUR WAGON QUITE WELL.

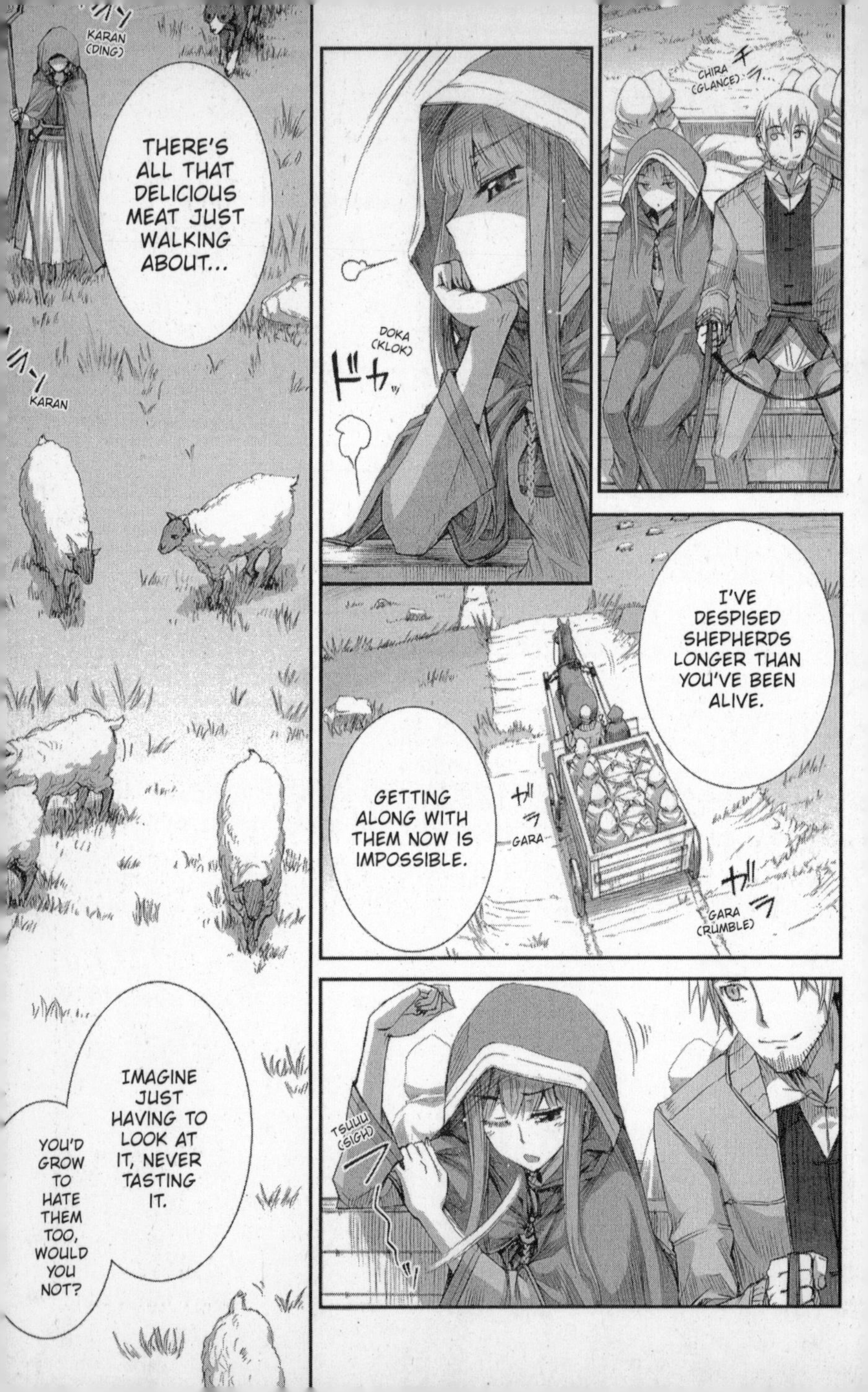
CHIRA (GLANCE)
DOKA (KLOK)
I'VE DESPISED SHEPHERDS LONGER THAN YOU'VE BEEN ALIVE.
GETTING ALONG WITH THEM NOW IS IMPOSSIBLE.
GARA
GARA (RUMBLE)
TSULUU (SIGH)
KARAN (DING)
THERE'S ALL THAT DELICIOUS MEAT JUST WALKING ABOUT...
KARAN
IMAGINE JUST HAVING TO LOOK AT IT, NEVER TASTING IT.
YOU'D GROW TO HATE THEM TOO, WOULD YOU NOT?

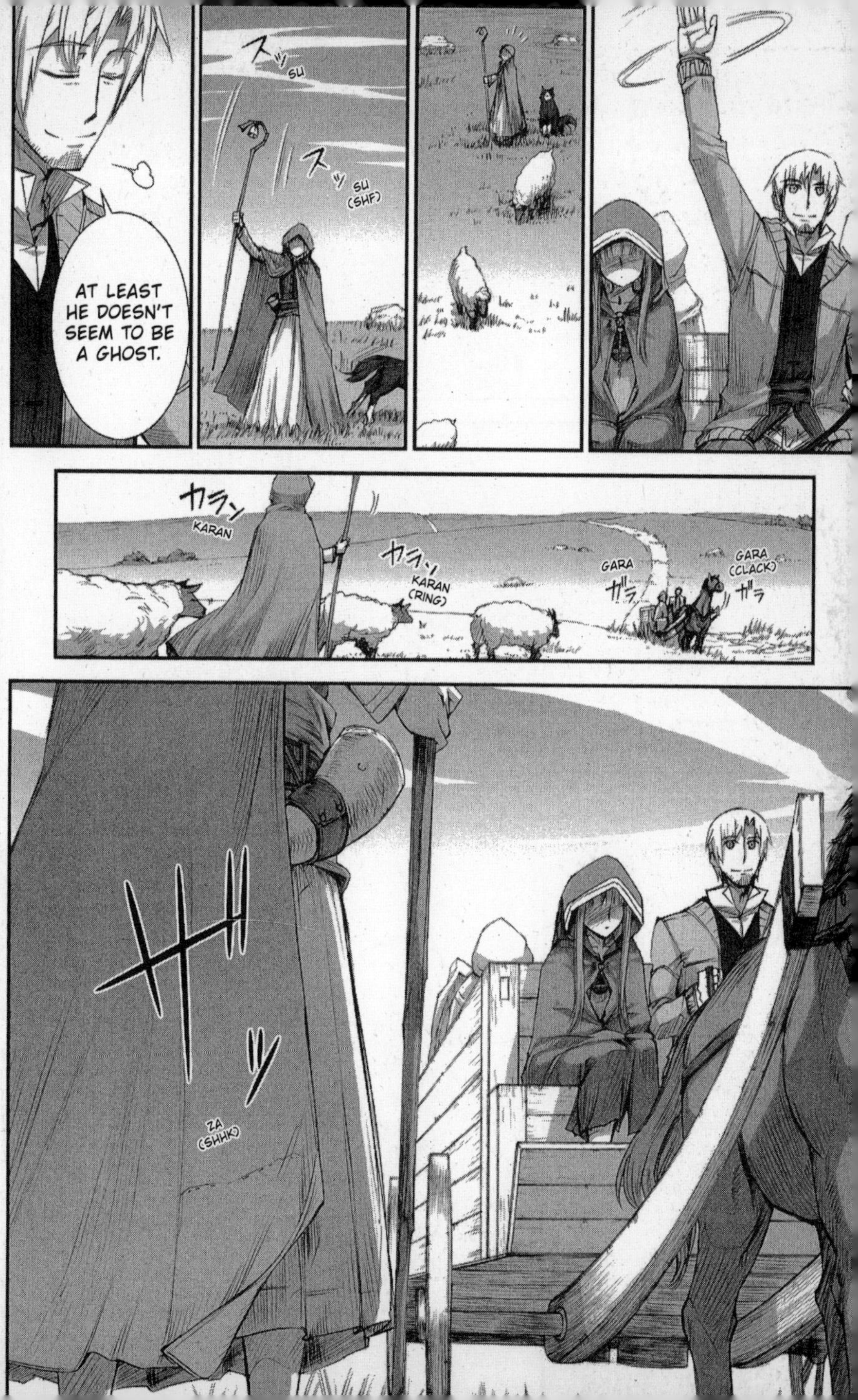
ズッ
SU
ズッ
SU (SHF)
AT LEAST HE DOESN'T SEEM TO BE A GHOST.
GARA (CLACK)
GARA
KARAN (RING)
KARAN
ZA (SHHK)

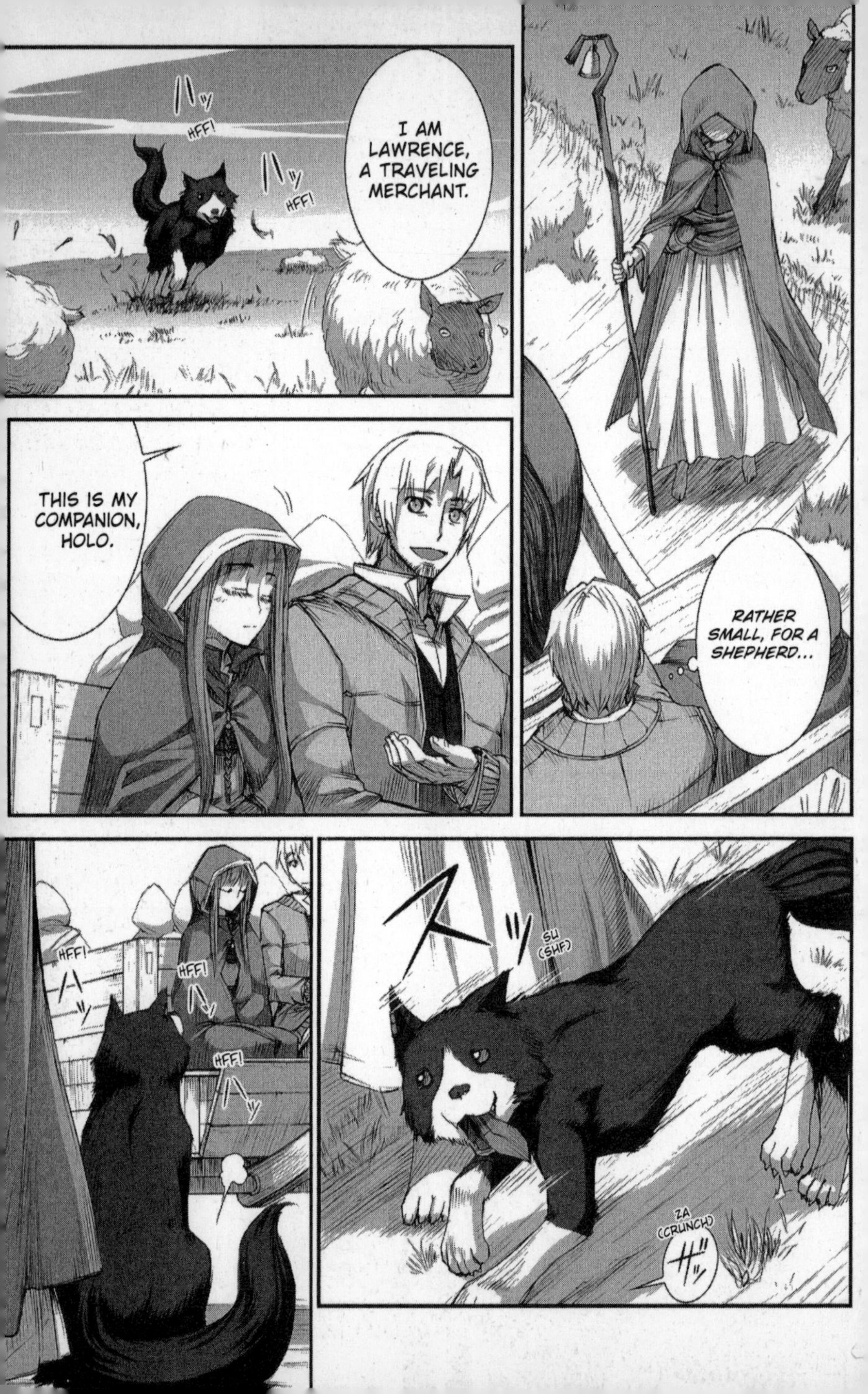
RATHER SMALL, FOR A SHEPHERD...
I AM LAWRENCE, A TRAVELING MERCHANT.
HFF!
HFF!
THIS IS MY COMPANION, HOLO.
SU (SHF)
ZA (CRUNCH)
HFF!
HFF!
HFF!

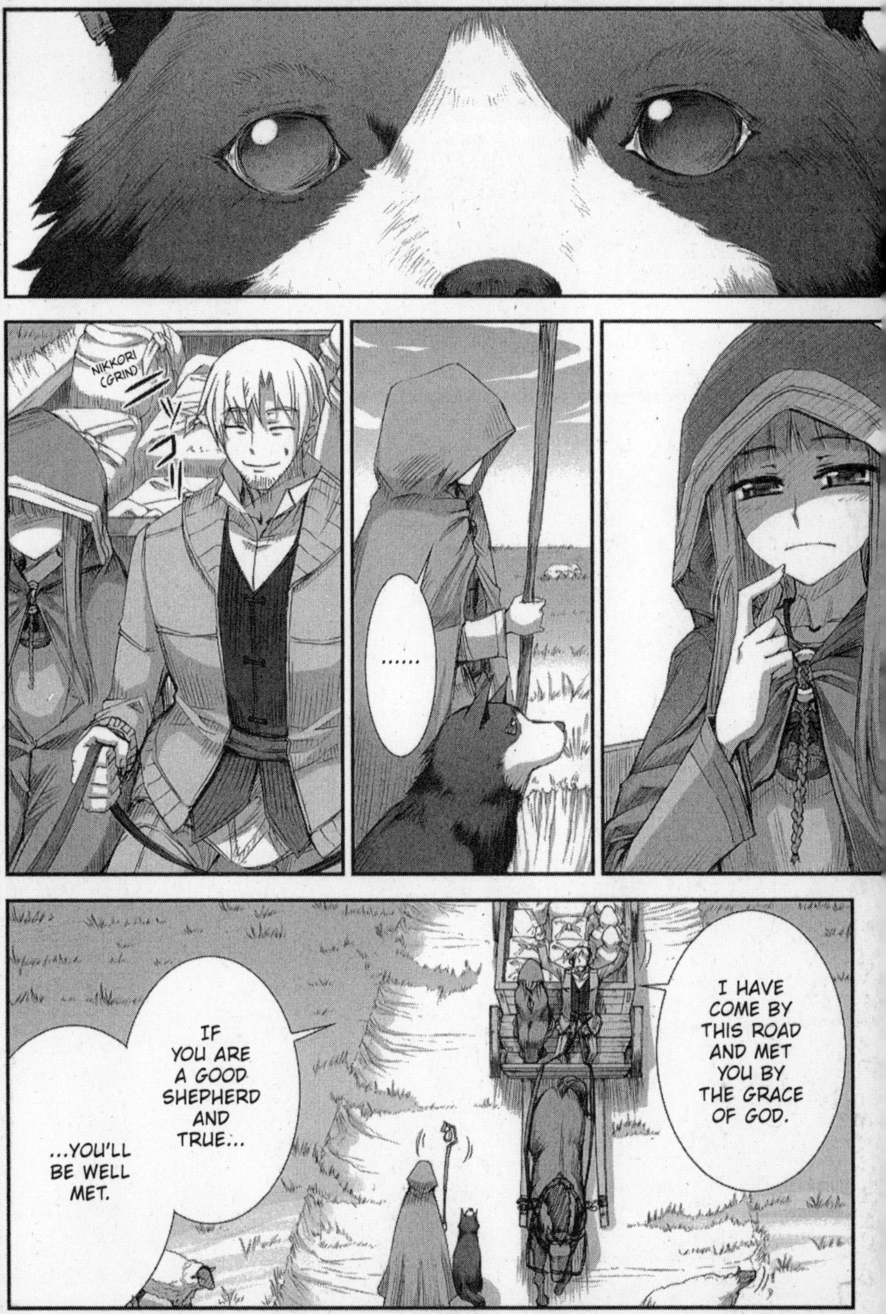
......
NIKKORI (GRIN)
I HAVE COME BY THIS ROAD AND MET YOU BY THE GRACE OF GOD.
IF YOU ARE A GOOD SHEPHERD AND TRUE...
...YOU'LL BE WELL MET.

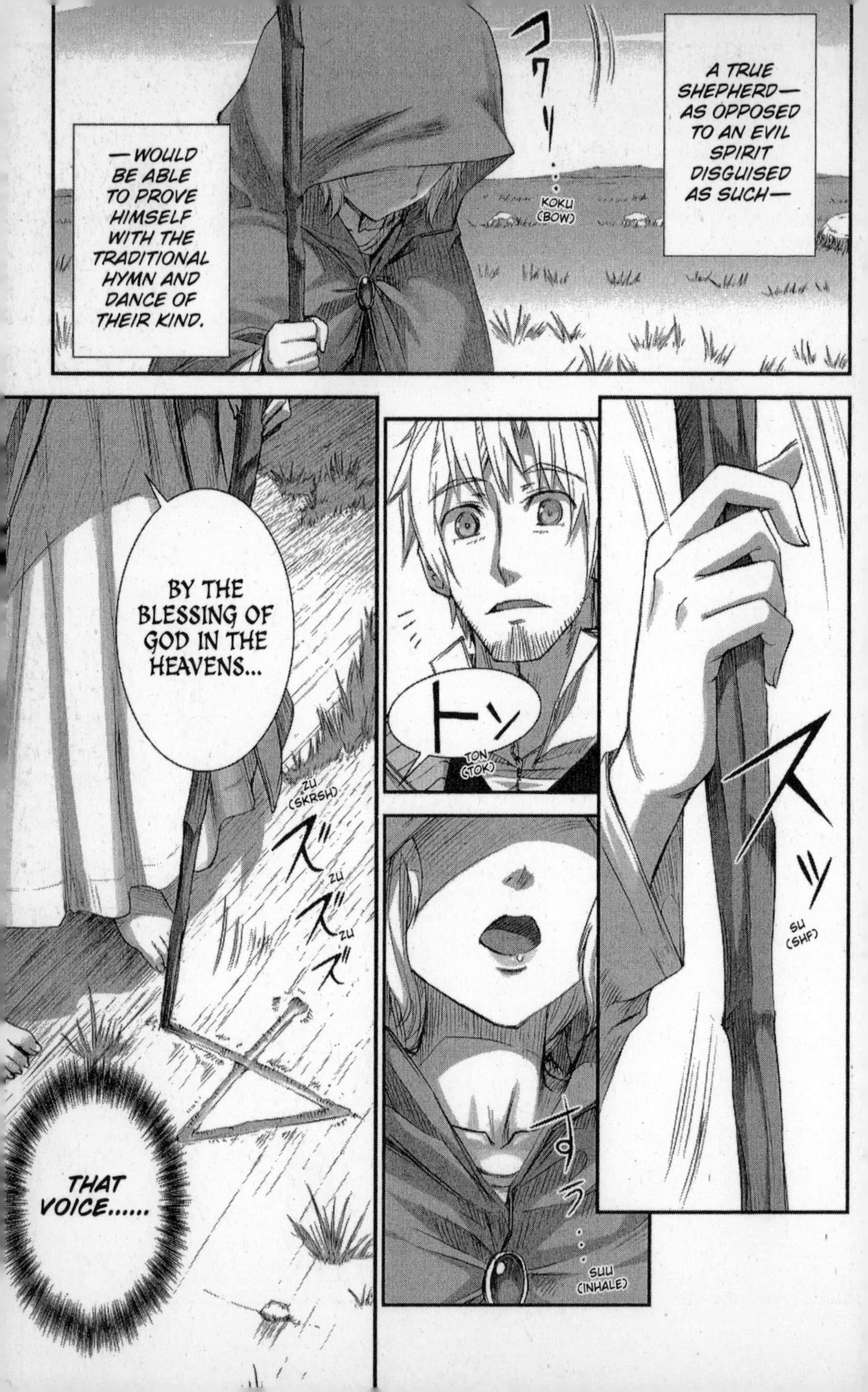
A TRUE SHEPHERD—AS OPPOSED TO AN EVIL SPIRIT DISGUISED AS SUCH—
コクリ…
KOKU (BOW)
—WOULD BE ABLE TO PROVE HIMSELF WITH THE TRADITIONAL HYMN AND DANCE OF THEIR KIND.
スッ
SU (SHF)
トッ
TON (TOK)
すぅ…
SUU (INHALE)
BY THE BLESSING OF GOD IN THE HEAVENS...
ZU (SKRSH)
ズ ZU ズ ZU ズ
THAT VOICE......

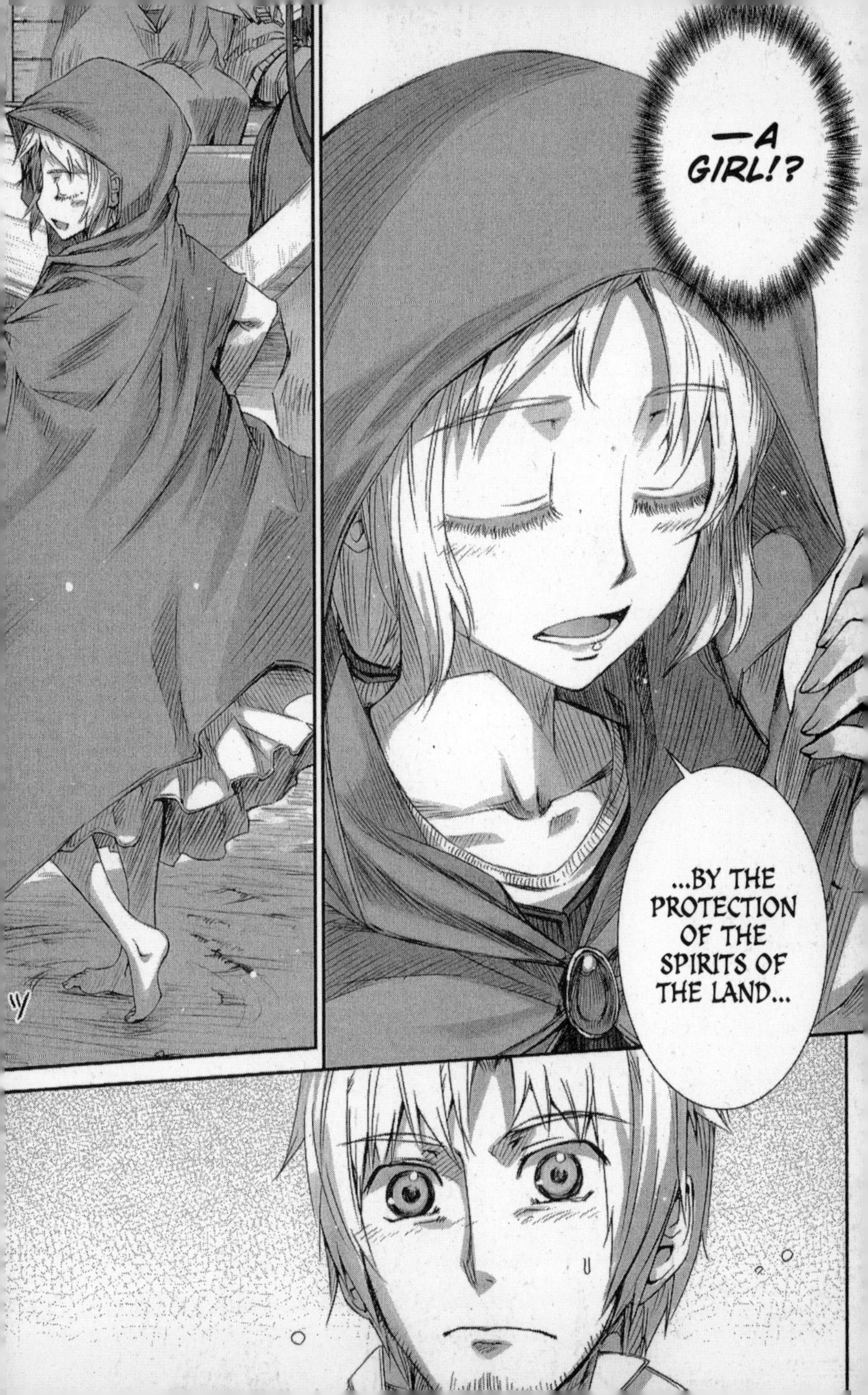
—A GIRL!?
...BY THE PROTECTION OF THE SPIRITS OF THE LAND...

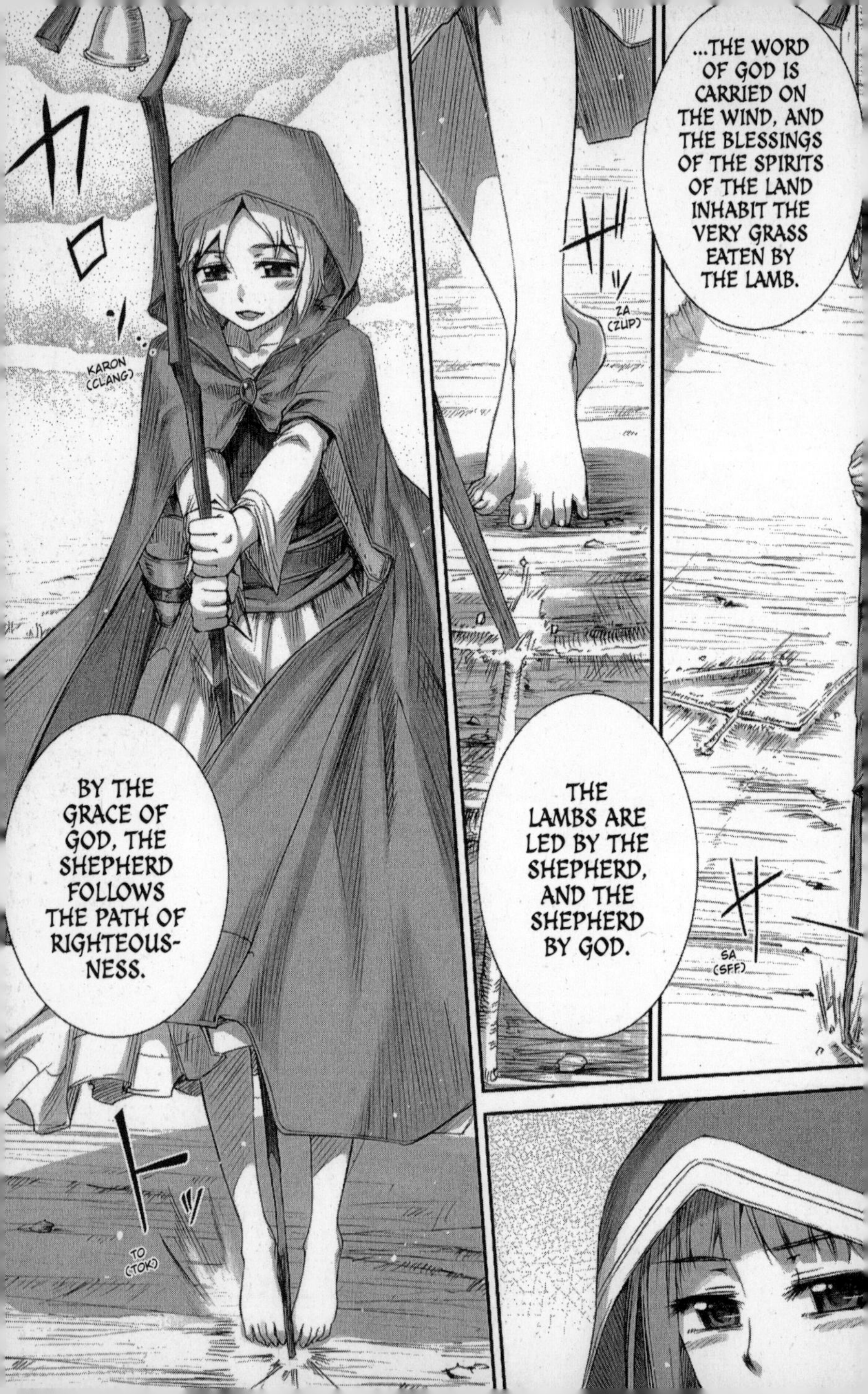
...THE WORD OF GOD IS CARRIED ON THE WIND, AND THE BLESSINGS OF THE SPIRITS OF THE LAND INHABIT THE VERY GRASS EATEN BY THE LAMB.
SA (SFF)
ZA (ZUP)
THE LAMBS ARE LED BY THE SHEPHERD, AND THE SHEPHERD BY GOD.
KARON (CLANG)
BY THE GRACE OF GOD, THE SHEPHERD FOLLOWS THE PATH OF RIGHTEOUS-NESS.
TO (TOK)

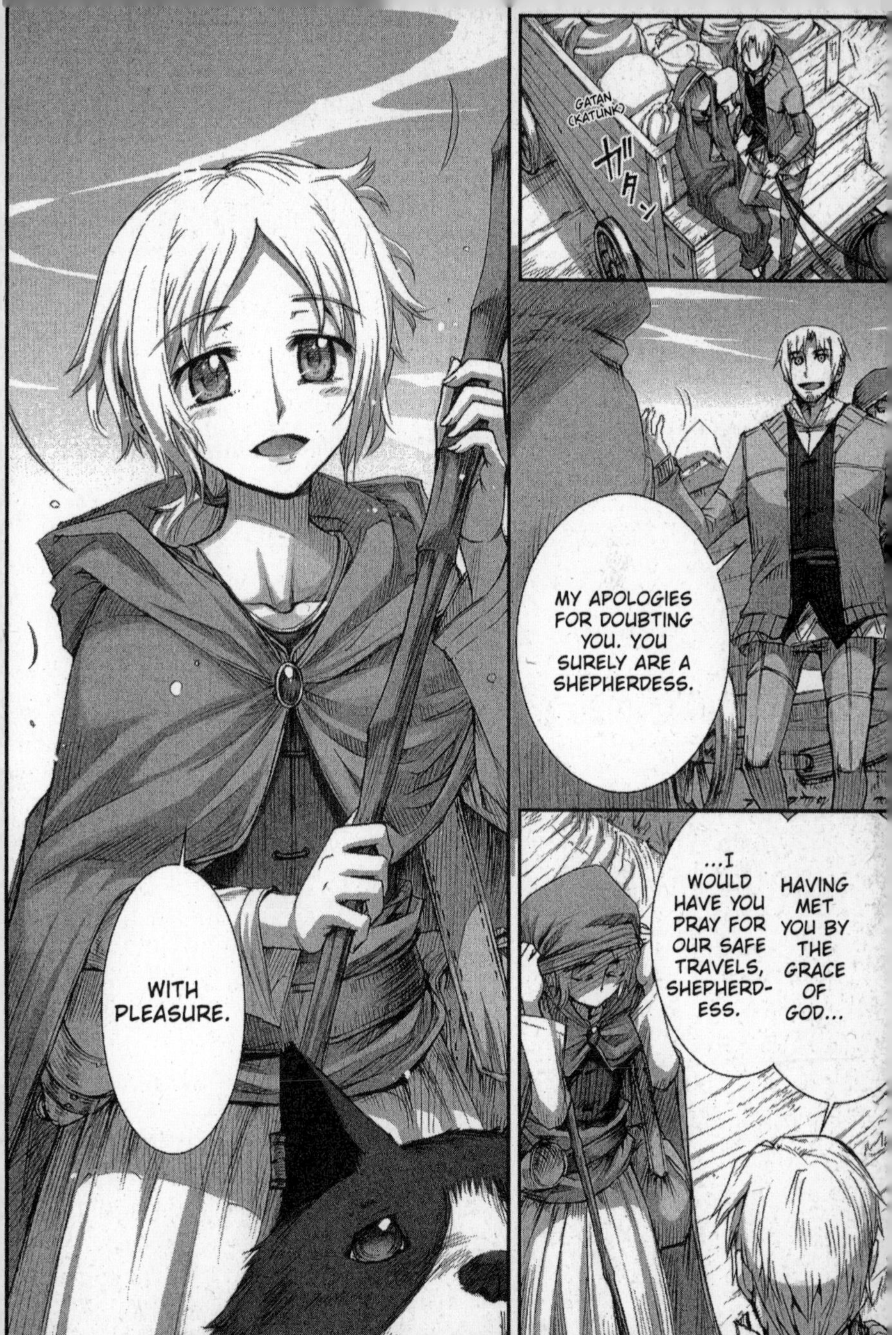
GATAN (KATUNK)
ガタン
MY APOLOGIES FOR DOUBTING YOU. YOU SURELY ARE A SHEPHERDESS.
HAVING MET YOU BY THE GRACE OF GOD...
...I WOULD HAVE YOU PRAY FOR OUR SAFE TRAVELS, SHEPHERD-ESS.
WITH PLEASURE.

SPICE&WOLF

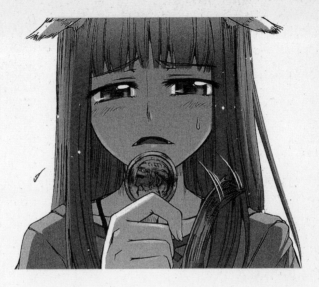

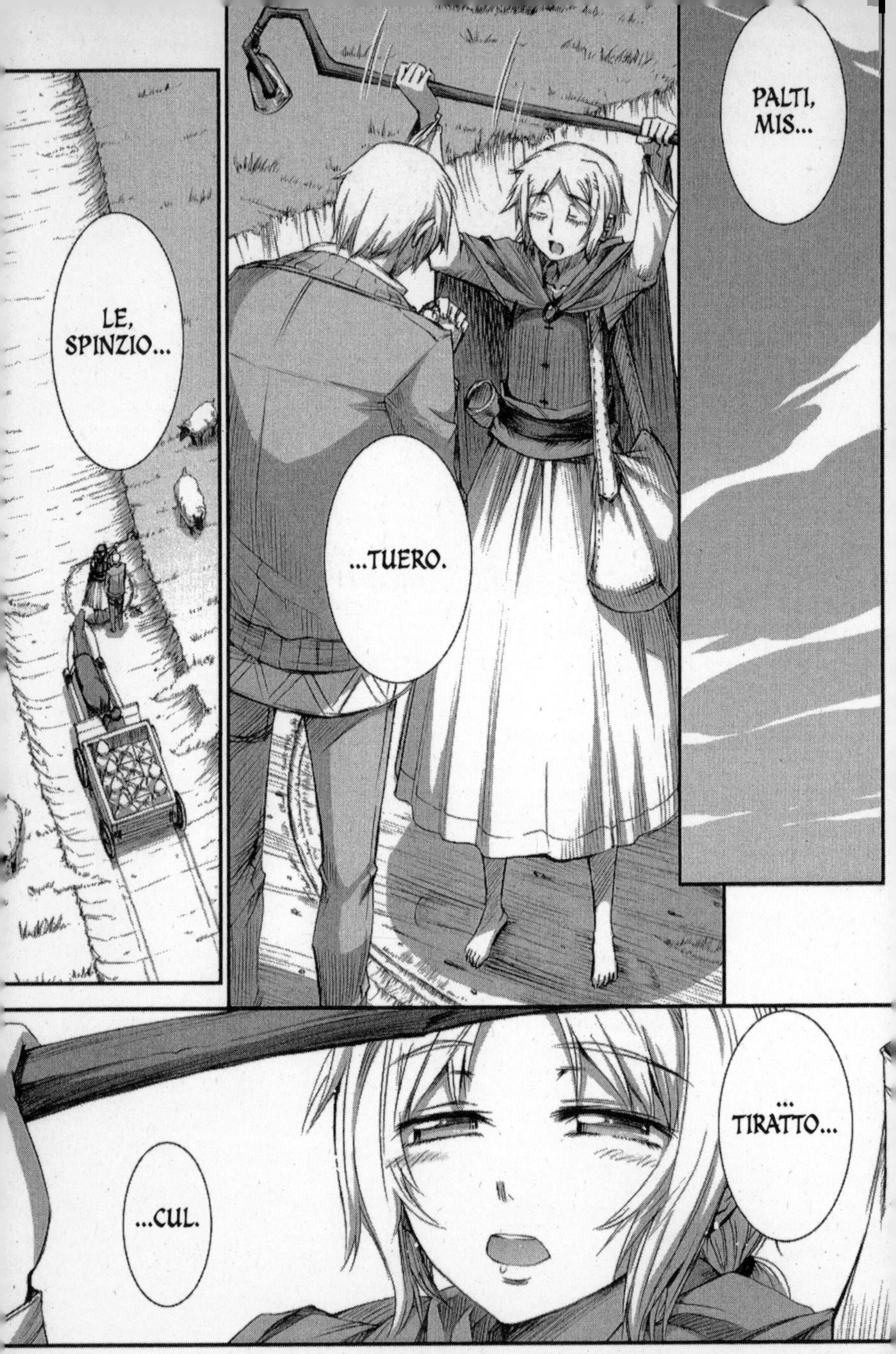
PALTI, MIS...
...TUERO.
LE, SPINZIO...
... TIRATTO...
...CUL.

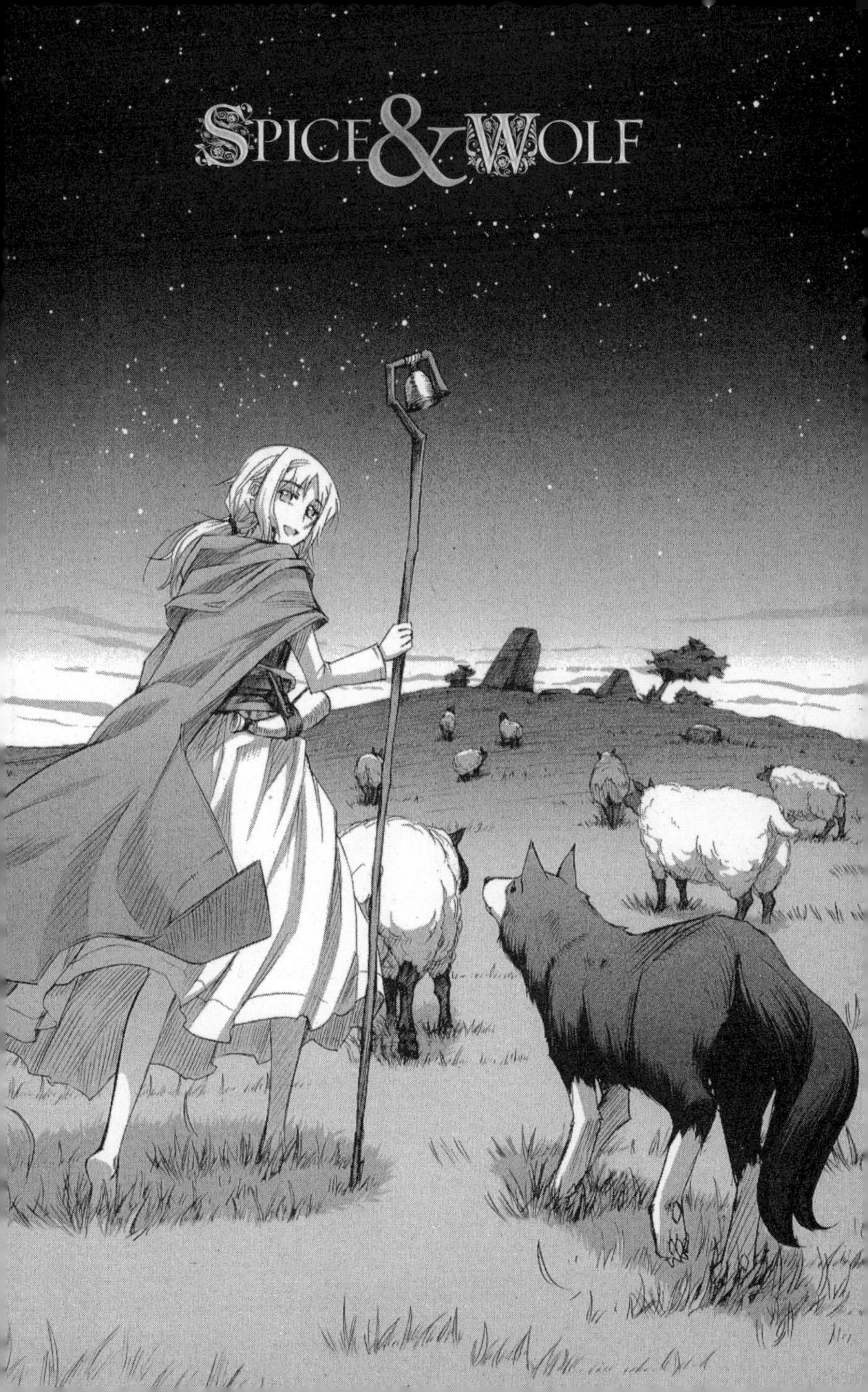
SPICE & WOLF

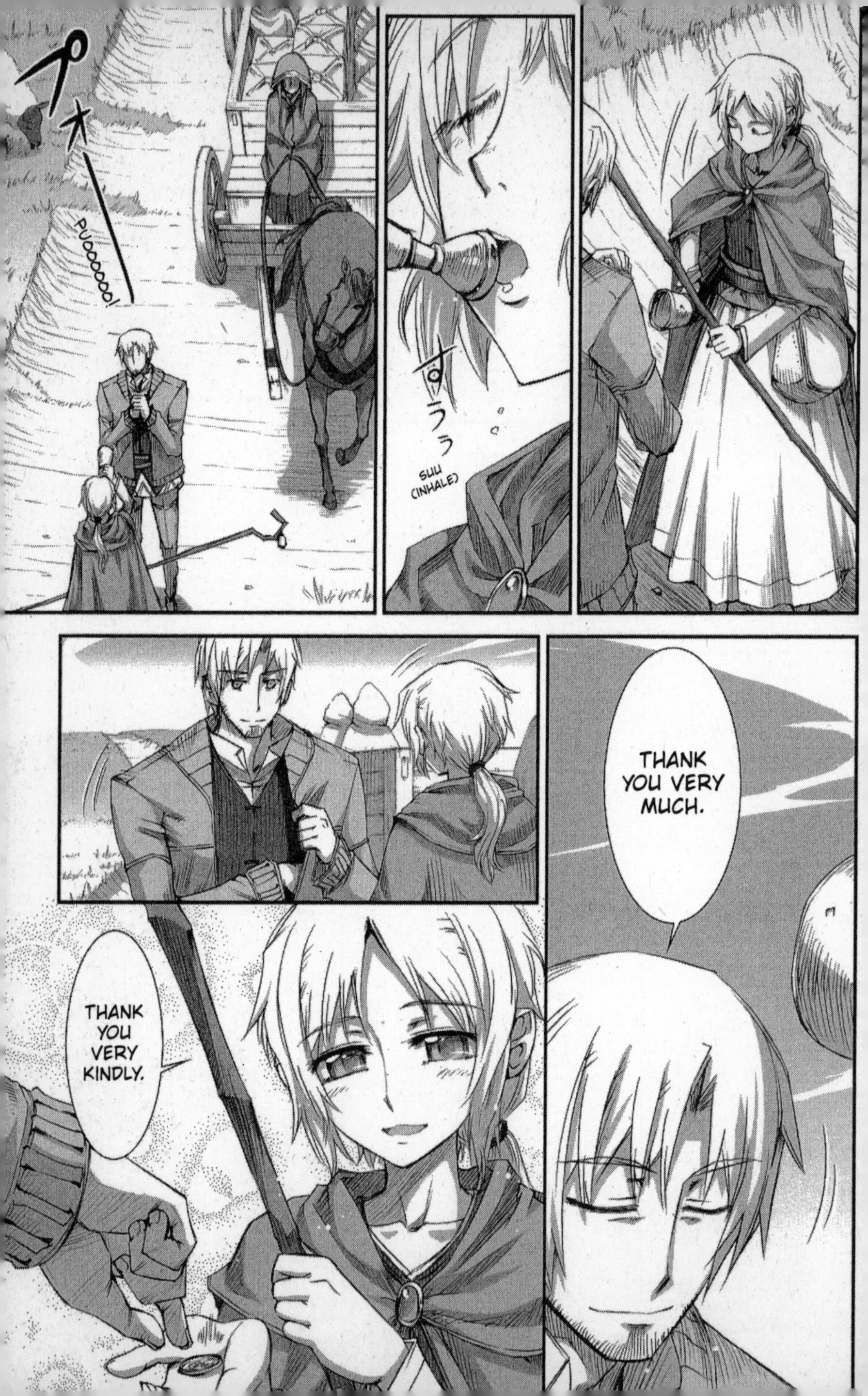
SUU (INHALE)
PUOOOOOO!
THANK YOU VERY MUCH.
THANK YOU VERY KINDLY.

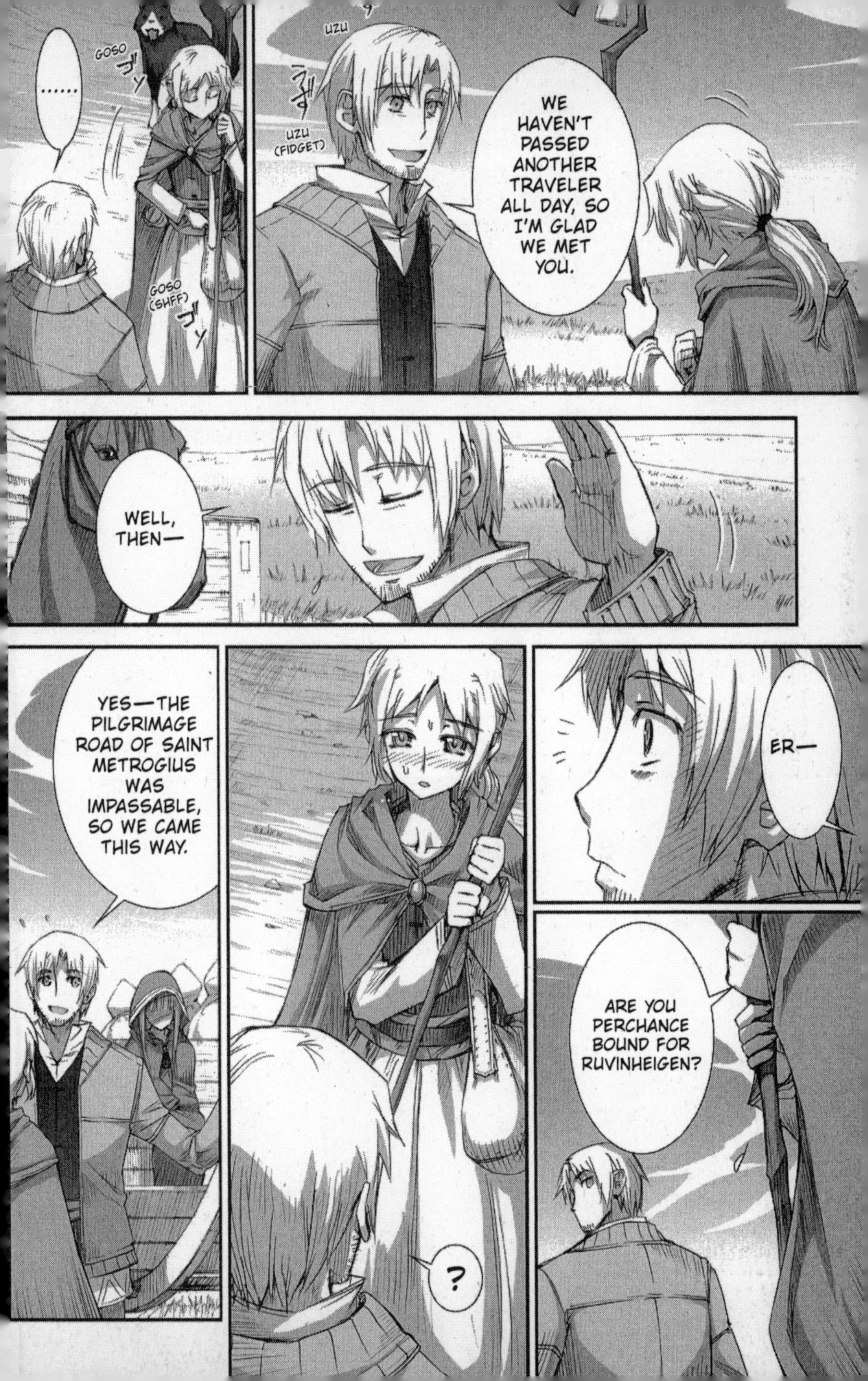
WE HAVEN'T PASSED ANOTHER TRAVELER ALL DAY, SO I'M GLAD WE MET YOU.
UZU
UZU (FIDGET)
......
GOSO
GOSO (SHFF)
WELL, THEN—
ER—
ARE YOU PERCHANCE BOUND FOR RUVINHEIGEN?
?
YES—THE PILGRIMAGE ROAD OF SAINT METROGIUS WAS IMPASSABLE, SO WE CAME THIS WAY.

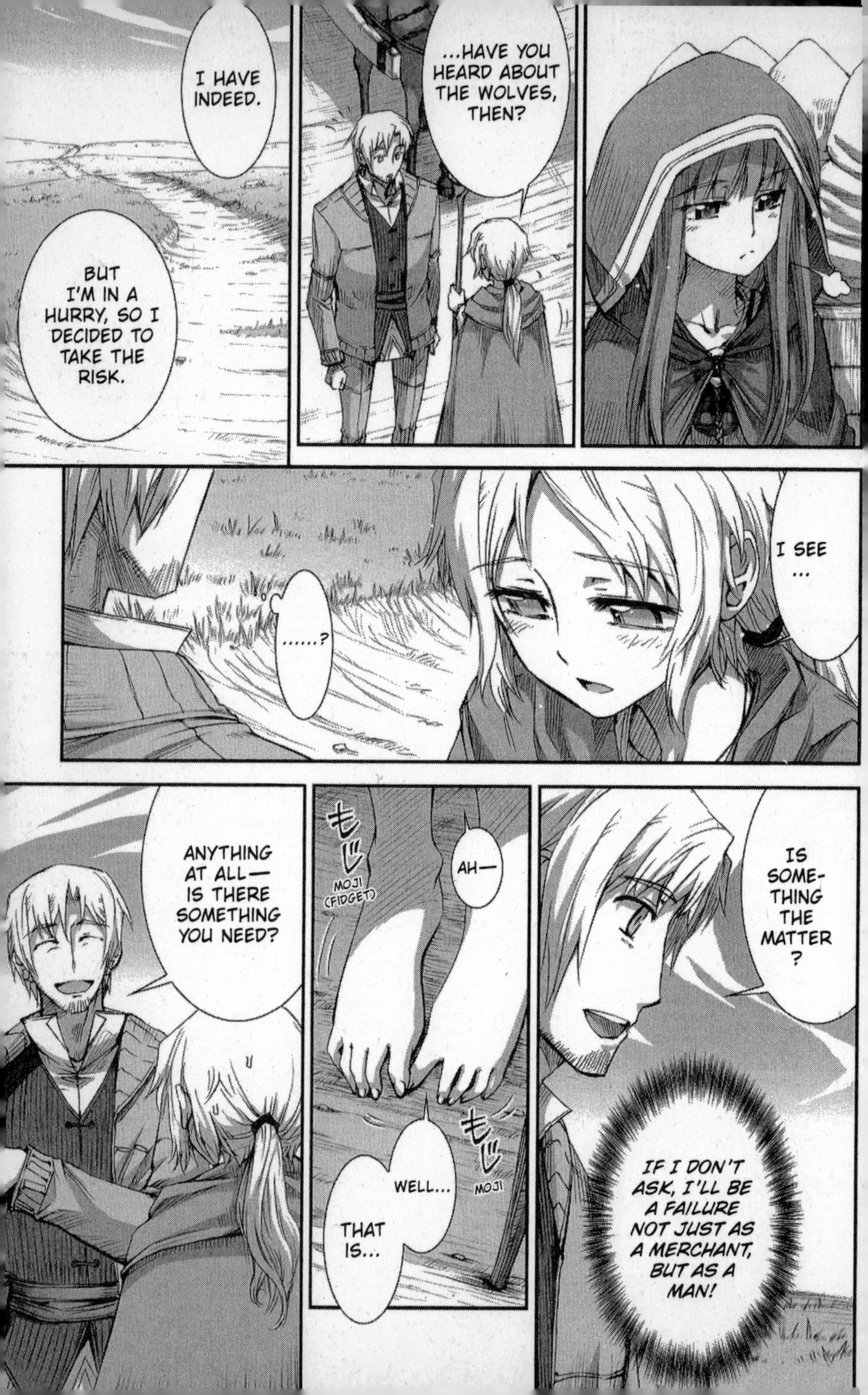
...HAVE YOU HEARD ABOUT THE WOLVES, THEN?
I HAVE INDEED.
BUT I'M IN A HURRY, SO I DECIDED TO TAKE THE RISK.
I SEE ...
......?
IS SOMETHING THE MATTER ?
IF I DON'T ASK, I'LL BE A FAILURE NOT JUST AS A MERCHANT, BUT AS A MAN!
AH—
もじ
MOJI (FIDGET)
もじ
MOJI
WELL...
THAT IS...
ANYTHING AT ALL— IS THERE SOMETHING YOU NEED?

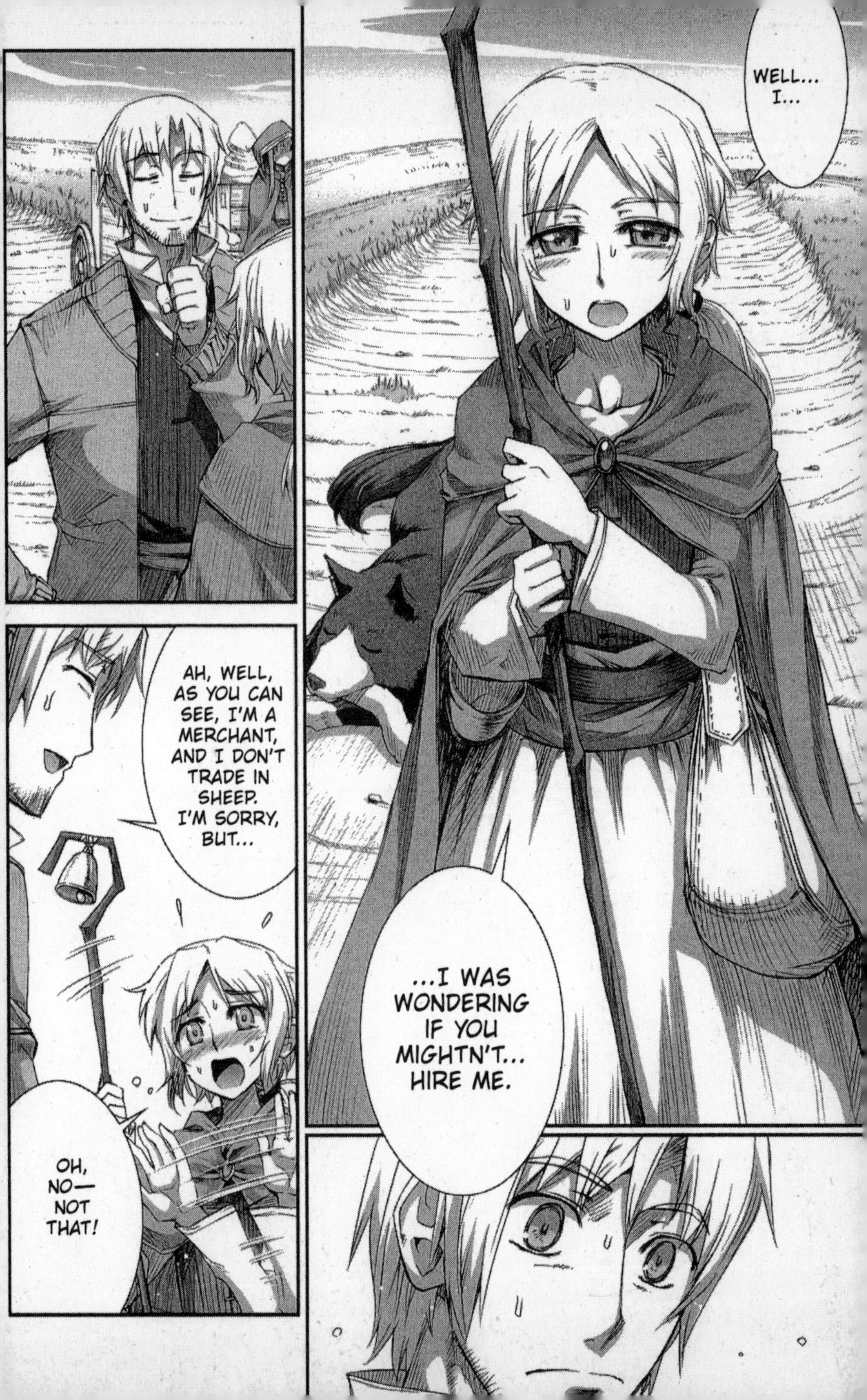
WELL... I...
...I WAS WONDERING IF YOU MIGHTN'T... HIRE ME.
AH, WELL, AS YOU CAN SEE, I'M A MERCHANT, AND I DON'T TRADE IN SHEEP. I'M SORRY, BUT...
OH, NO— NOT THAT!

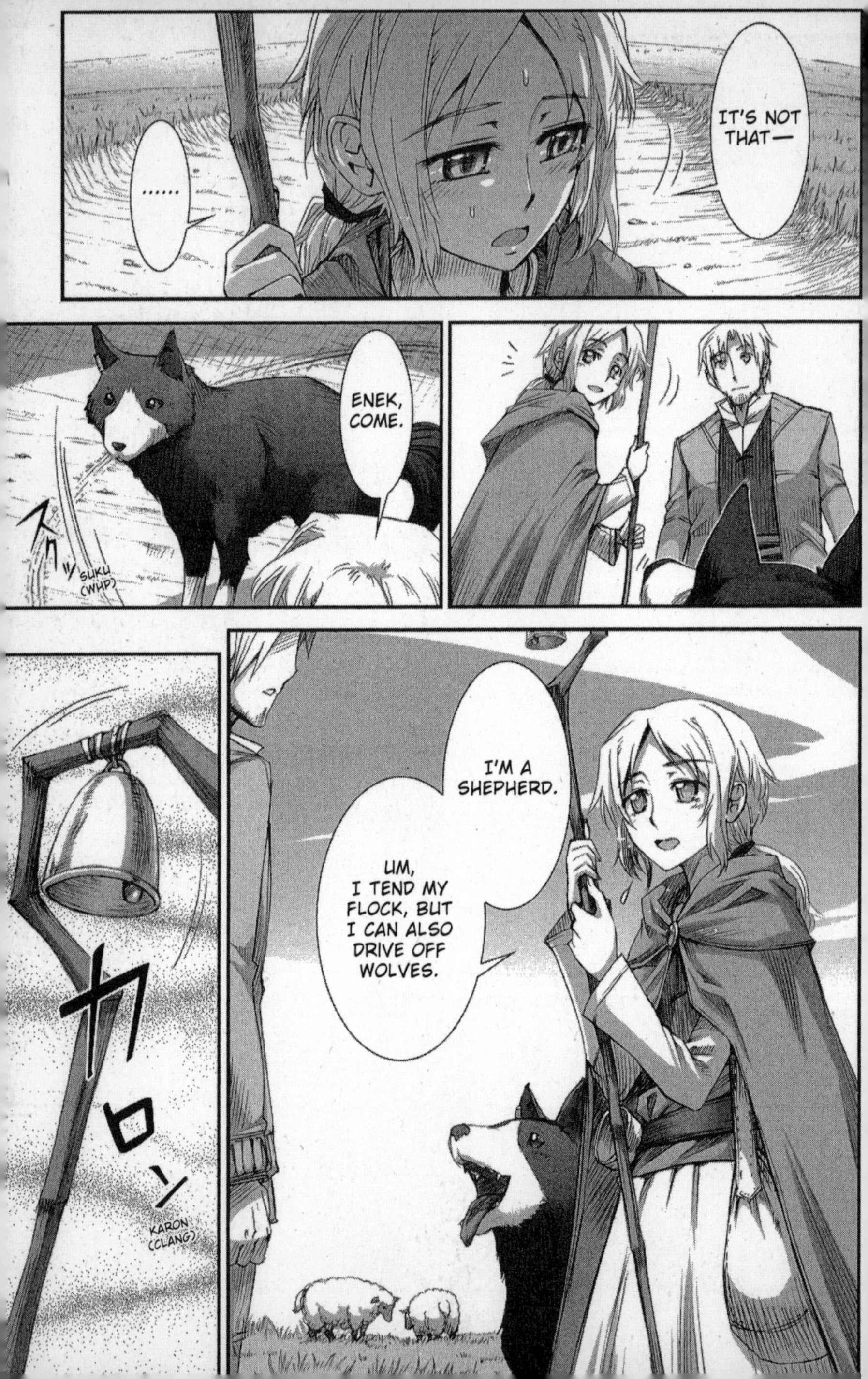
IT'S NOT THAT—
......
ENEK, COME.
SUKU (WHP)
I'M A SHEPHERD.
UM, I TEND MY FLOCK, BUT I CAN ALSO DRIVE OFF WOLVES.
KARON (CLANG)

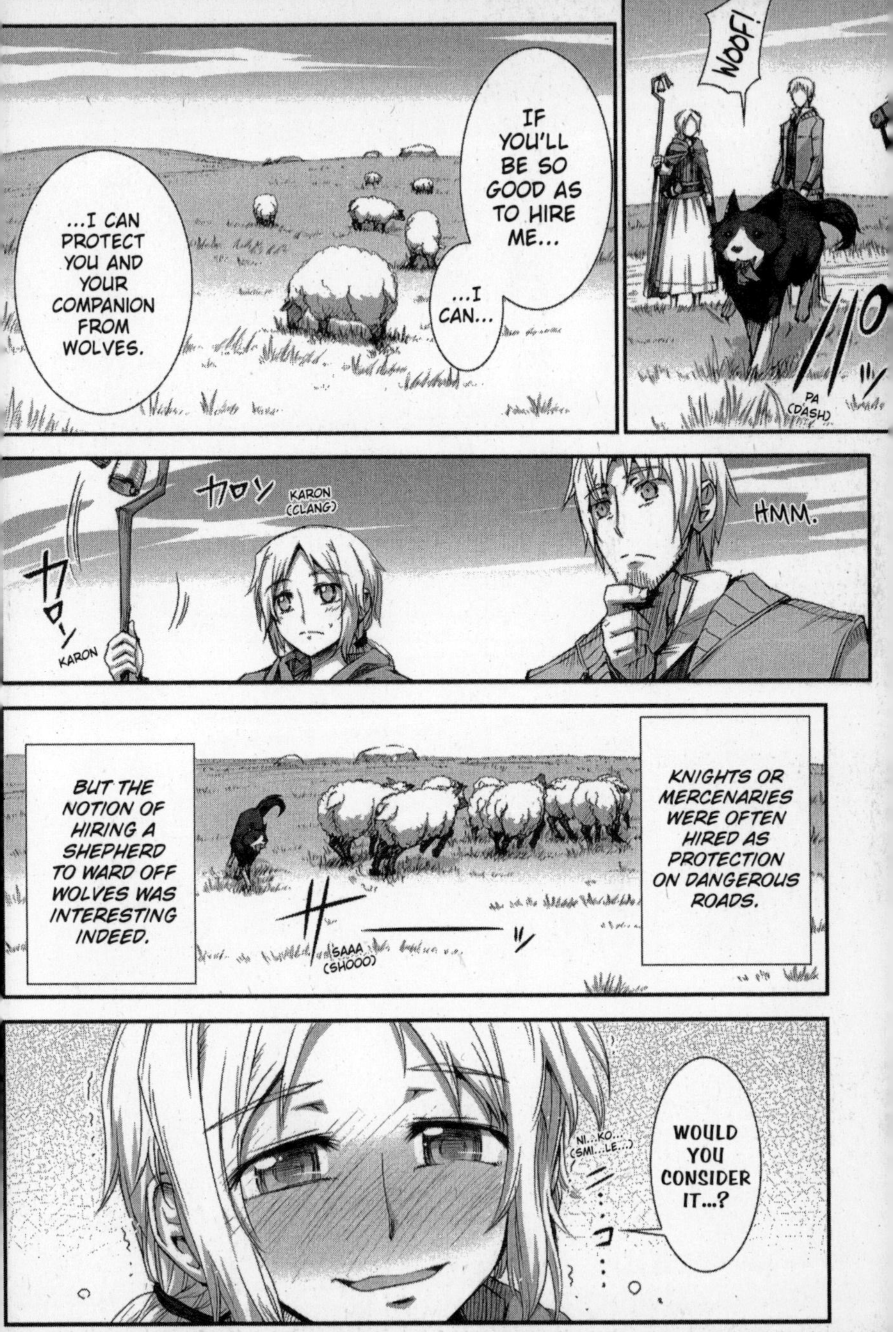
WOOF!
PA (DASH)
IF YOU'LL BE SO GOOD AS TO HIRE ME...
...I CAN...
...I CAN PROTECT YOU AND YOUR COMPANION FROM WOLVES.
HMM.
カロン
KARON (CLANG)
カローン
KARON
KNIGHTS OR MERCENARIES WERE OFTEN HIRED AS PROTECTION ON DANGEROUS ROADS.
SAAA (SHOOO)
BUT THE NOTION OF HIRING A SHEPHERD TO WARD OFF WOLVES WAS INTERESTING INDEED.
NI...KO... (SMI...LE...)
WOULD YOU CONSIDER IT...?

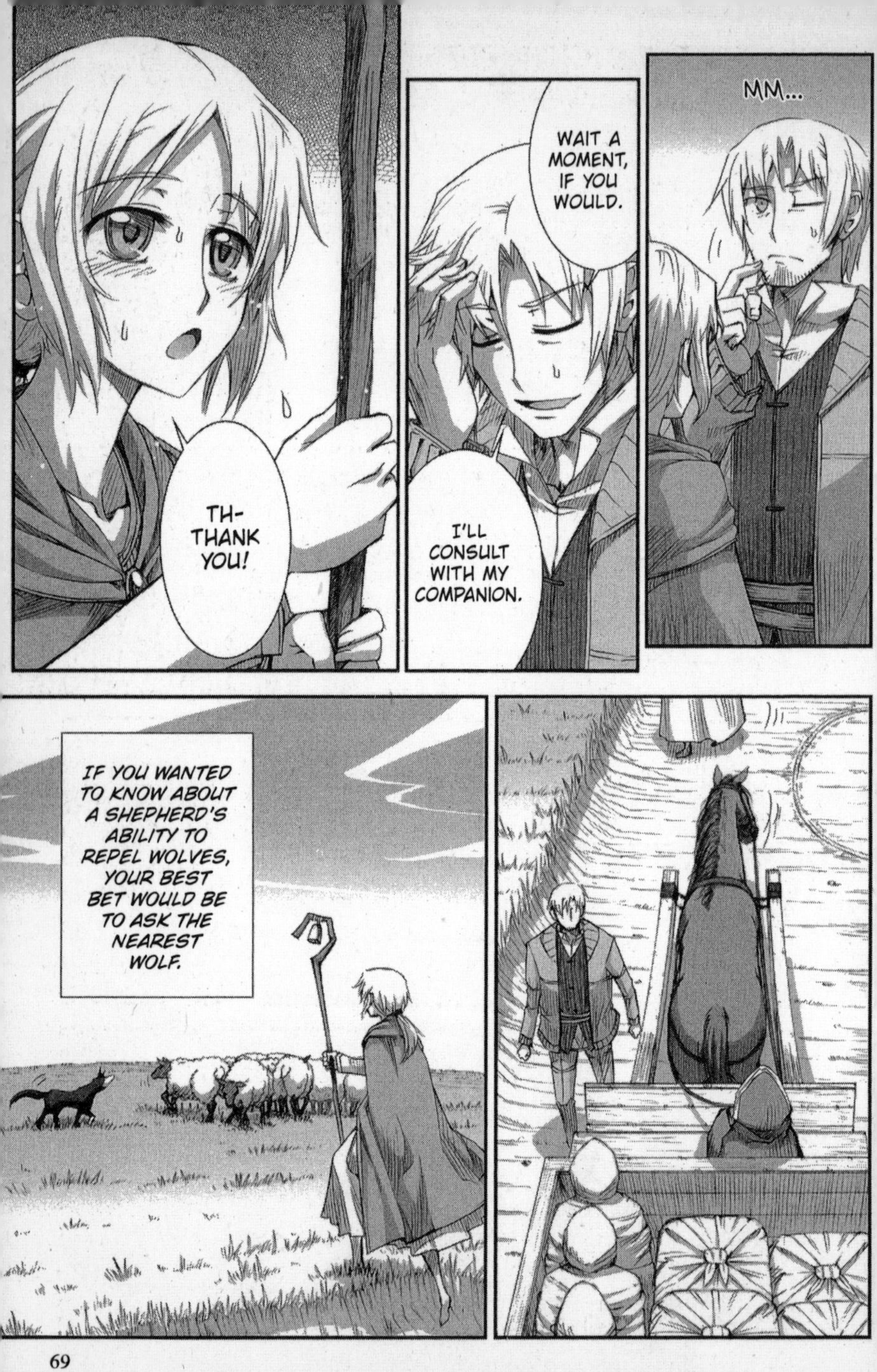
MM...
WAIT A MOMENT, IF YOU WOULD.
I'LL CONSULT WITH MY COMPANION.
TH- THANK YOU!
IF YOU WANTED TO KNOW ABOUT A SHEPHERD'S ABILITY TO REPEL WOLVES, YOUR BEST BET WOULD BE TO ASK THE NEAREST WOLF.

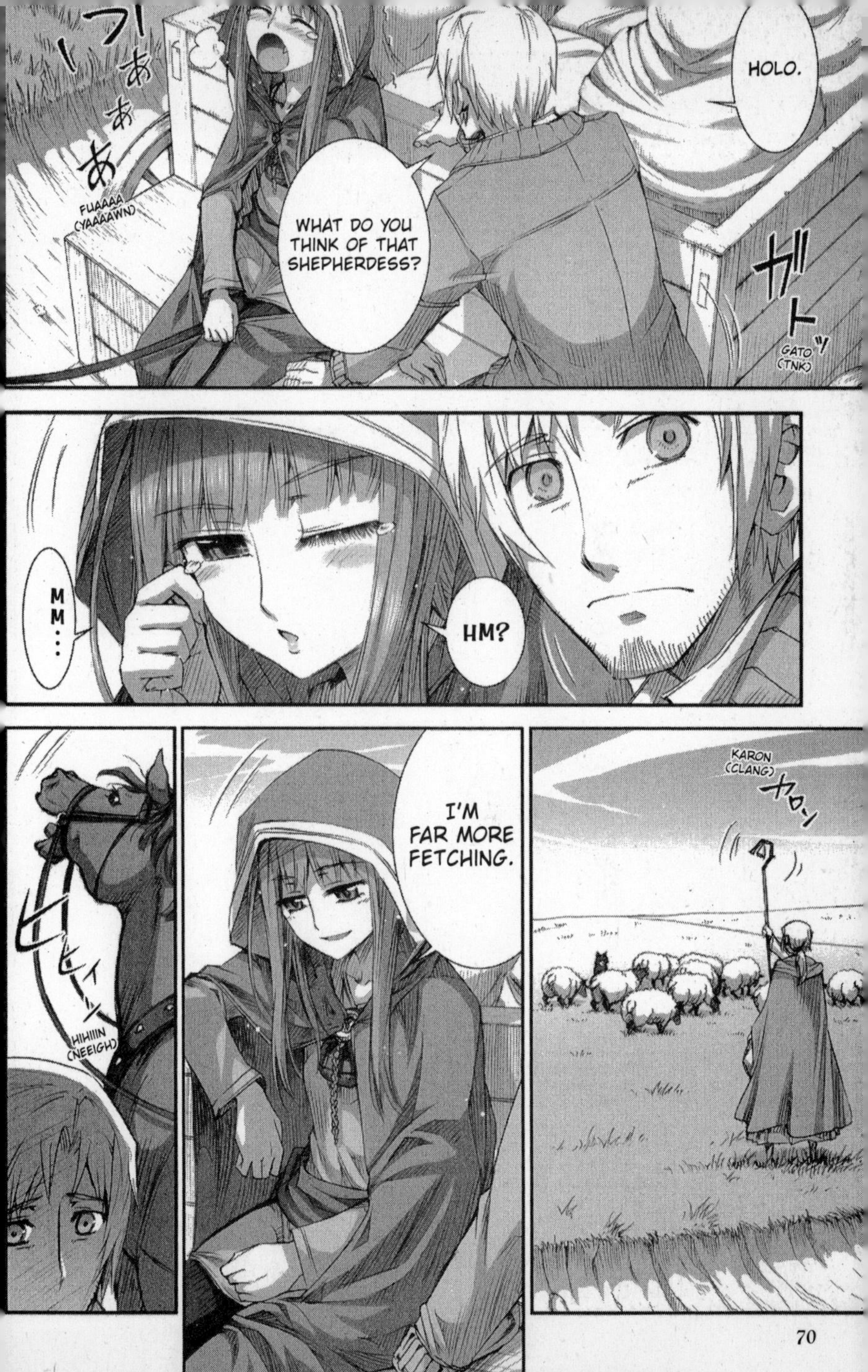
HOLO.
WHAT DO YOU THINK OF THAT SHEPHERDESS?
GATO (TNK)
FUAAAA (YAAAAWN)
HM?
MM...
KARON (CLANG)
I'M FAR MORE FETCHING.
HIHIIIN (NEEIGH)

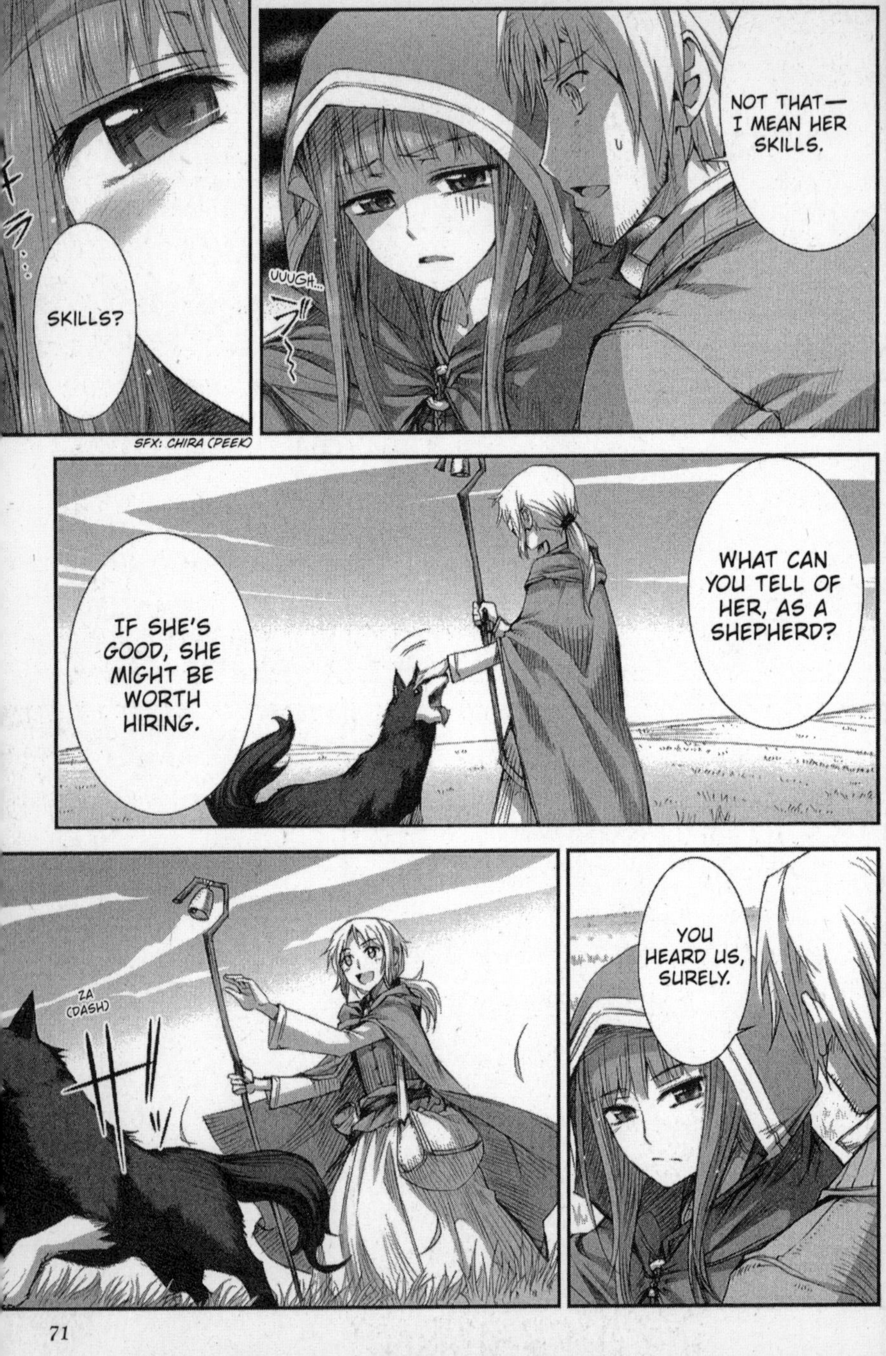
NOT THAT— I MEAN HER SKILLS.
UUUGH...
SKILLS?
SFX: CHIRA (PEEK)
WHAT CAN YOU TELL OF HER, AS A SHEPHERD?
IF SHE'S GOOD, SHE MIGHT BE WORTH HIRING.
YOU HEARD US, SURELY.
ZA (DASH)

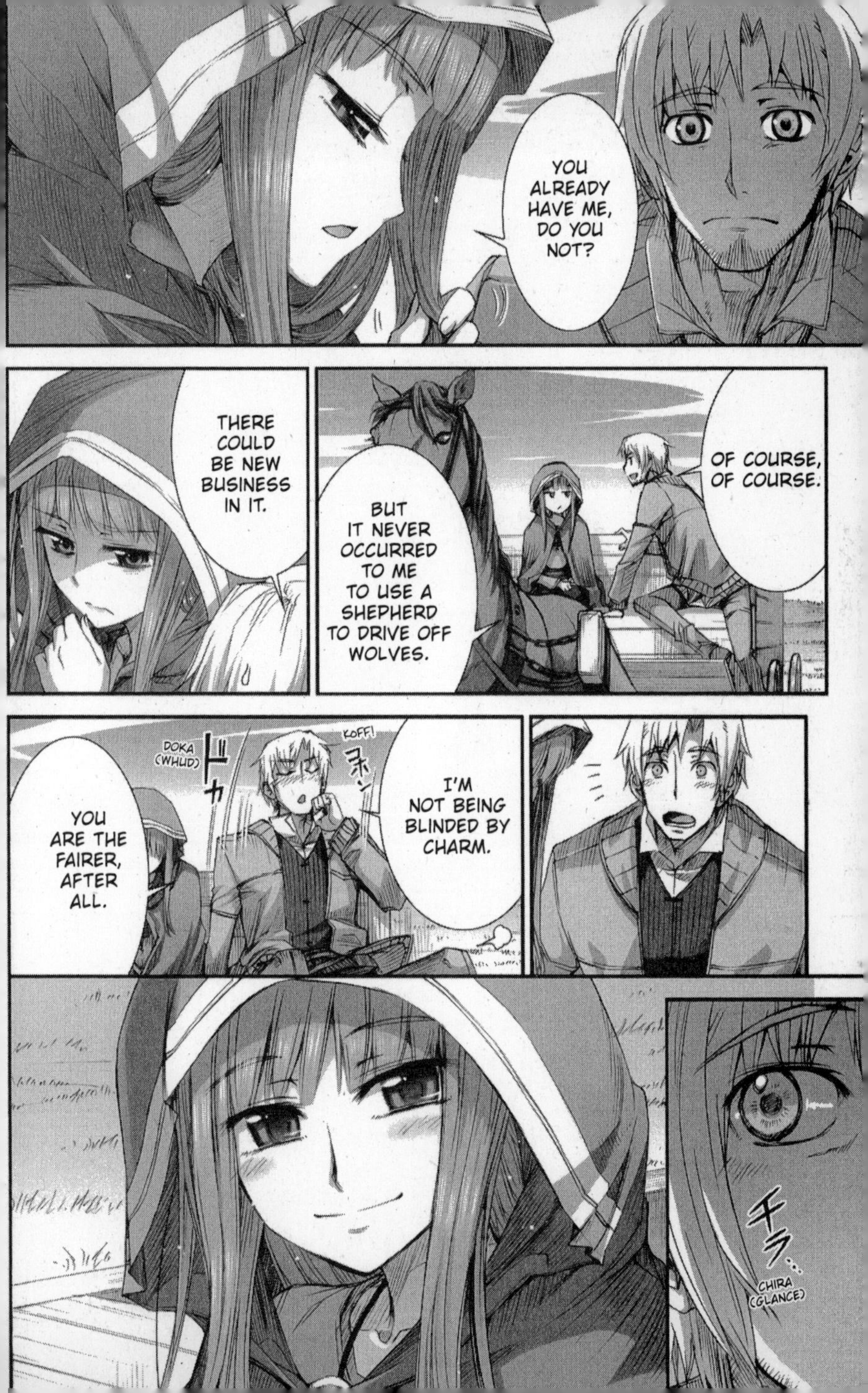
YOU ALREADY HAVE ME, DO YOU NOT?
OF COURSE, OF COURSE.
BUT IT NEVER OCCURRED TO ME TO USE A SHEPHERD TO DRIVE OFF WOLVES.
THERE COULD BE NEW BUSINESS IN IT.
KOFF!
I'M NOT BEING BLINDED BY CHARM.
ドカ
DOKA (WHUD)
YOU ARE THE FAIRER, AFTER ALL.
チラ…
CHIRA (GLANCE)

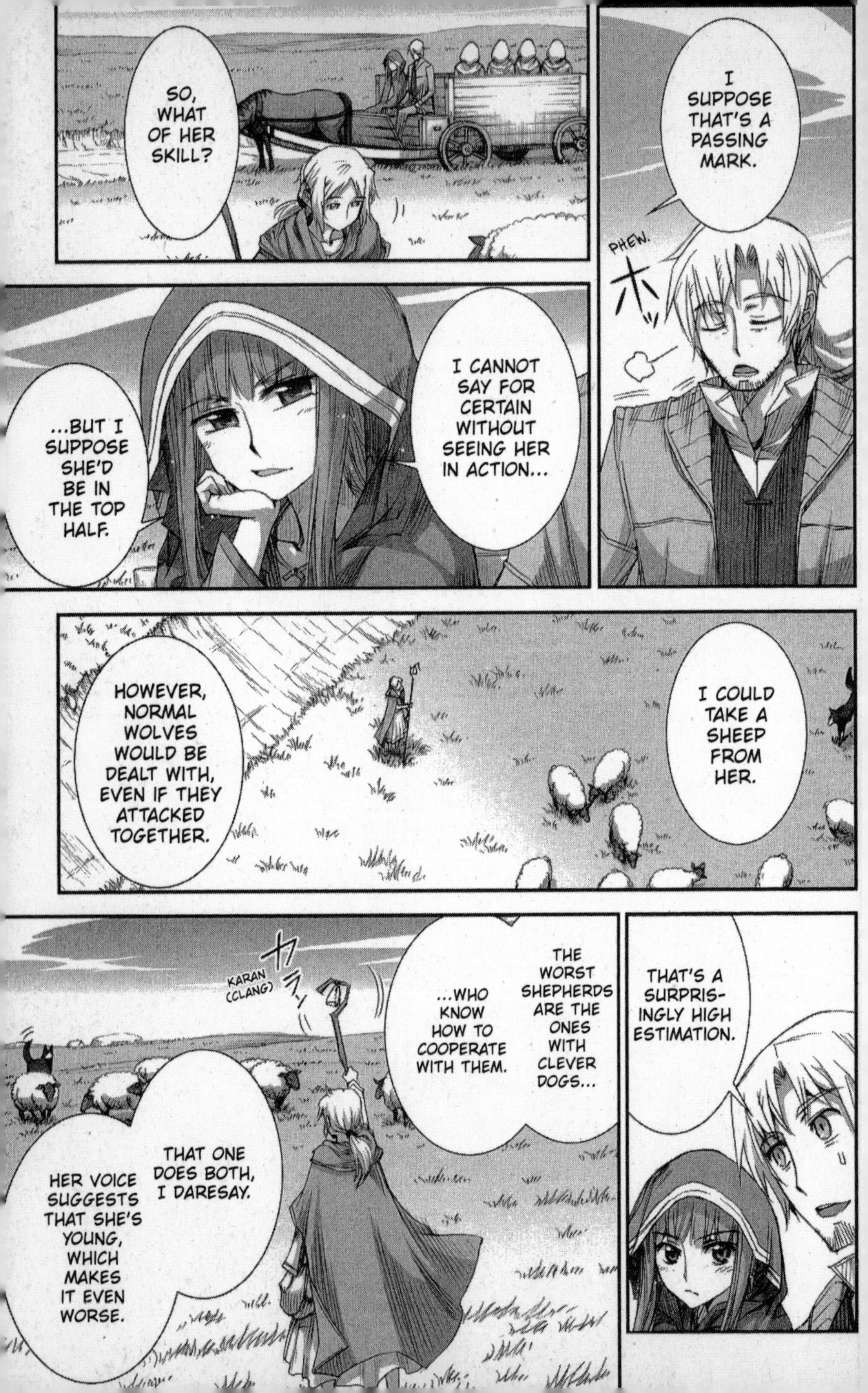
SO, WHAT OF HER SKILL?
I CANNOT SAY FOR CERTAIN WITHOUT SEEING HER IN ACTION...
...BUT I SUPPOSE SHE'D BE IN THE TOP HALF.
I SUPPOSE THAT'S A PASSING MARK.
PHEW.
I COULD TAKE A SHEEP FROM HER.
HOWEVER, NORMAL WOLVES WOULD BE DEALT WITH, EVEN IF THEY ATTACKED TOGETHER.
THAT'S A SURPRISINGLY HIGH ESTIMATION.
THE WORST SHEPHERDS ARE THE ONES WITH CLEVER DOGS...
...WHO KNOW HOW TO COOPERATE WITH THEM.
KARAN (CLANG)
THAT ONE DOES BOTH, I DARESAY.
HER VOICE SUGGESTS THAT SHE'S YOUNG, WHICH MAKES IT EVEN WORSE.

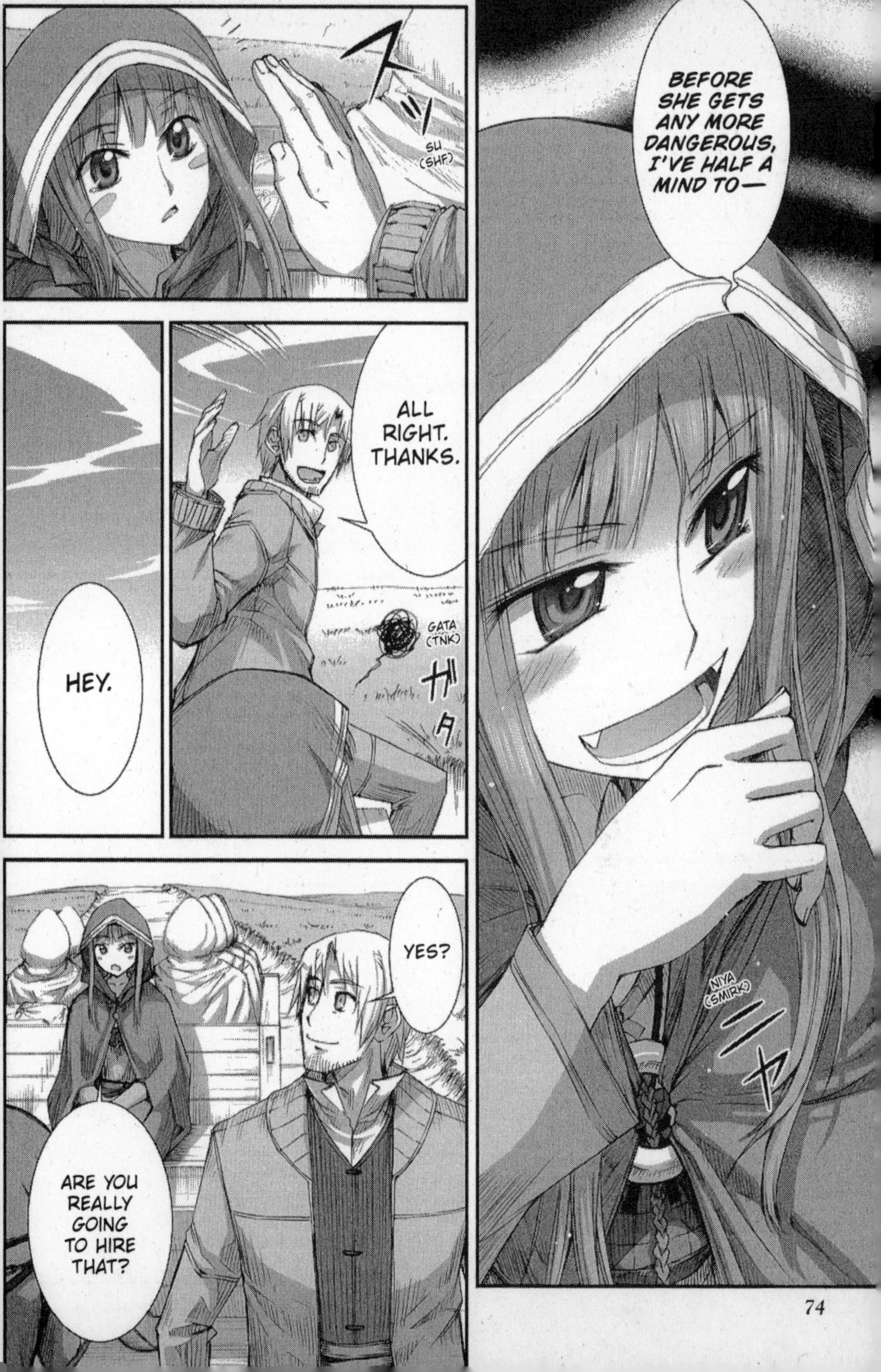
BEFORE SHE GETS ANY MORE DANGEROUS, I'VE HALF A MIND TO—
NIYA (SMIRK)
SU (SHF.)
ALL RIGHT. THANKS.
GATA (TNK)
HEY.
YES?
ARE YOU REALLY GOING TO HIRE THAT?

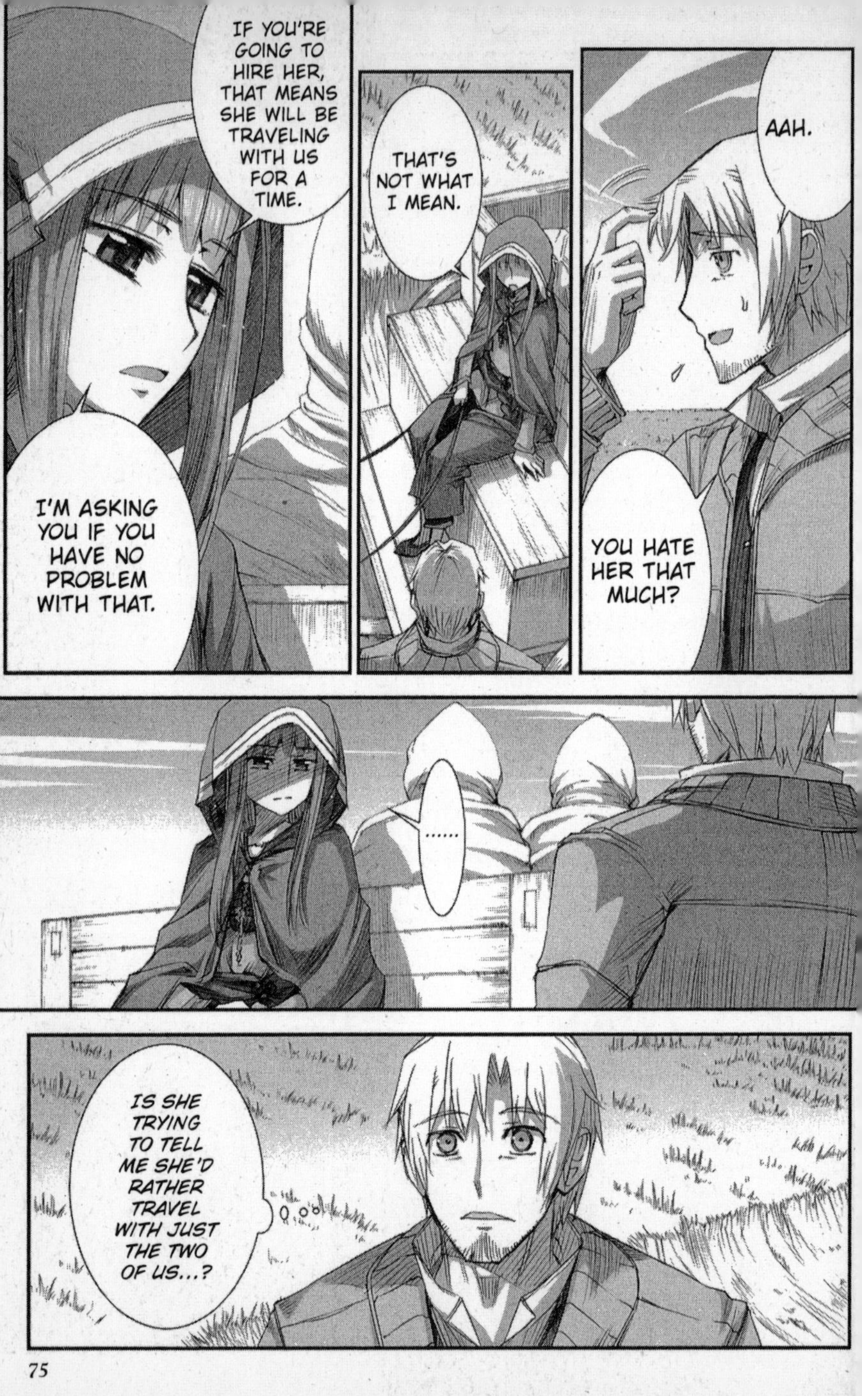
AAH.
YOU HATE HER THAT MUCH?
THAT'S NOT WHAT I MEAN.
IF YOU'RE GOING TO HIRE HER, THAT MEANS SHE WILL BE TRAVELING WITH US FOR A TIME.
I'M ASKING YOU IF YOU HAVE NO PROBLEM WITH THAT.
......
IS SHE TRYING TO TELL ME SHE'D RATHER TRAVEL WITH JUST THE TWO OF US...?

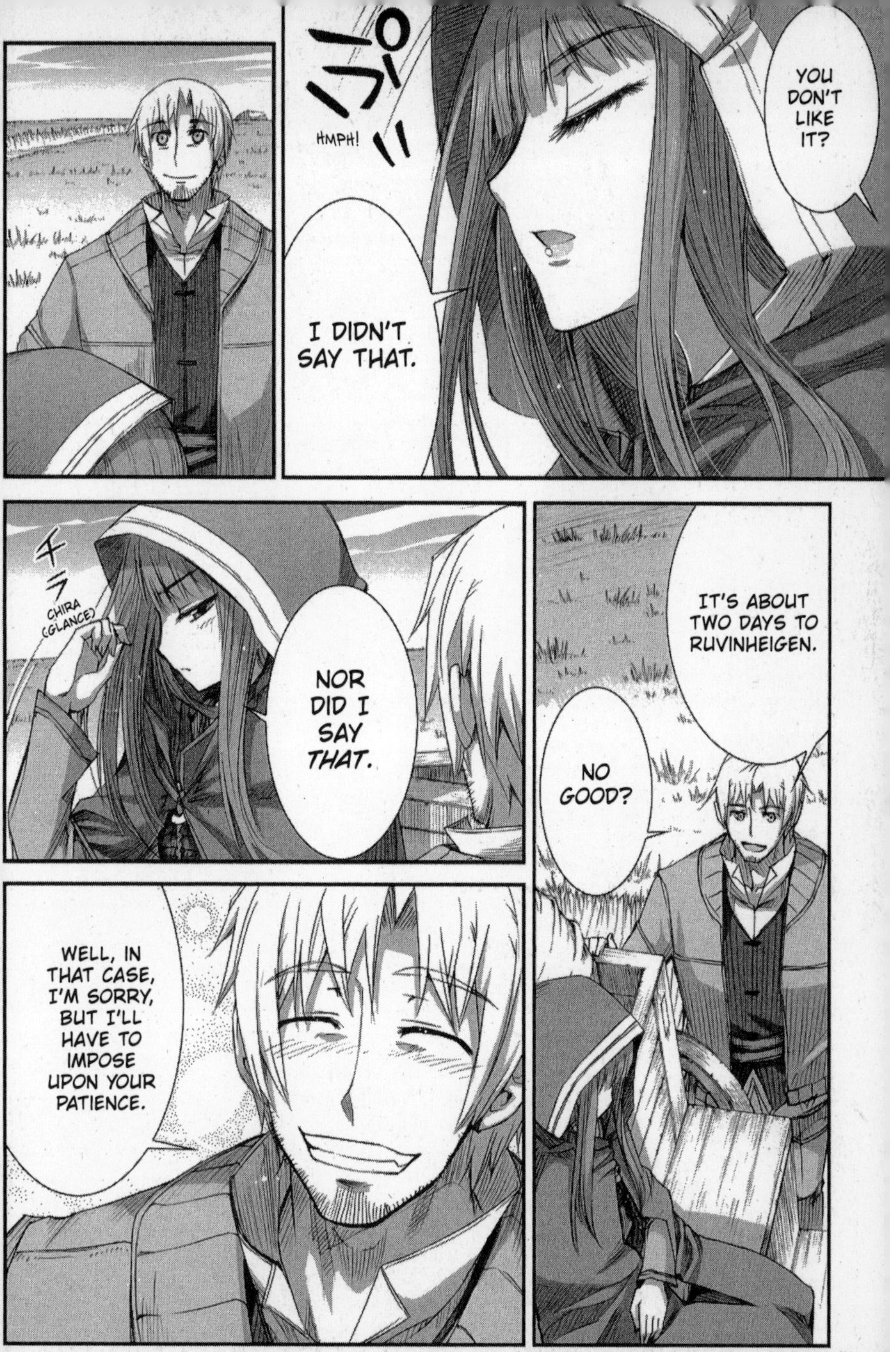
YOU DON'T LIKE IT?
ぷい
HMPH!
I DIDN'T SAY THAT.
IT'S ABOUT TWO DAYS TO RUVINHEIGEN.
NO GOOD?
NOR DID I SAY *THAT.*
チラ
CHIRA (GLANCE)
WELL, IN THAT CASE, I'M SORRY, BUT I'LL HAVE TO IMPOSE UPON YOUR PATIENCE.

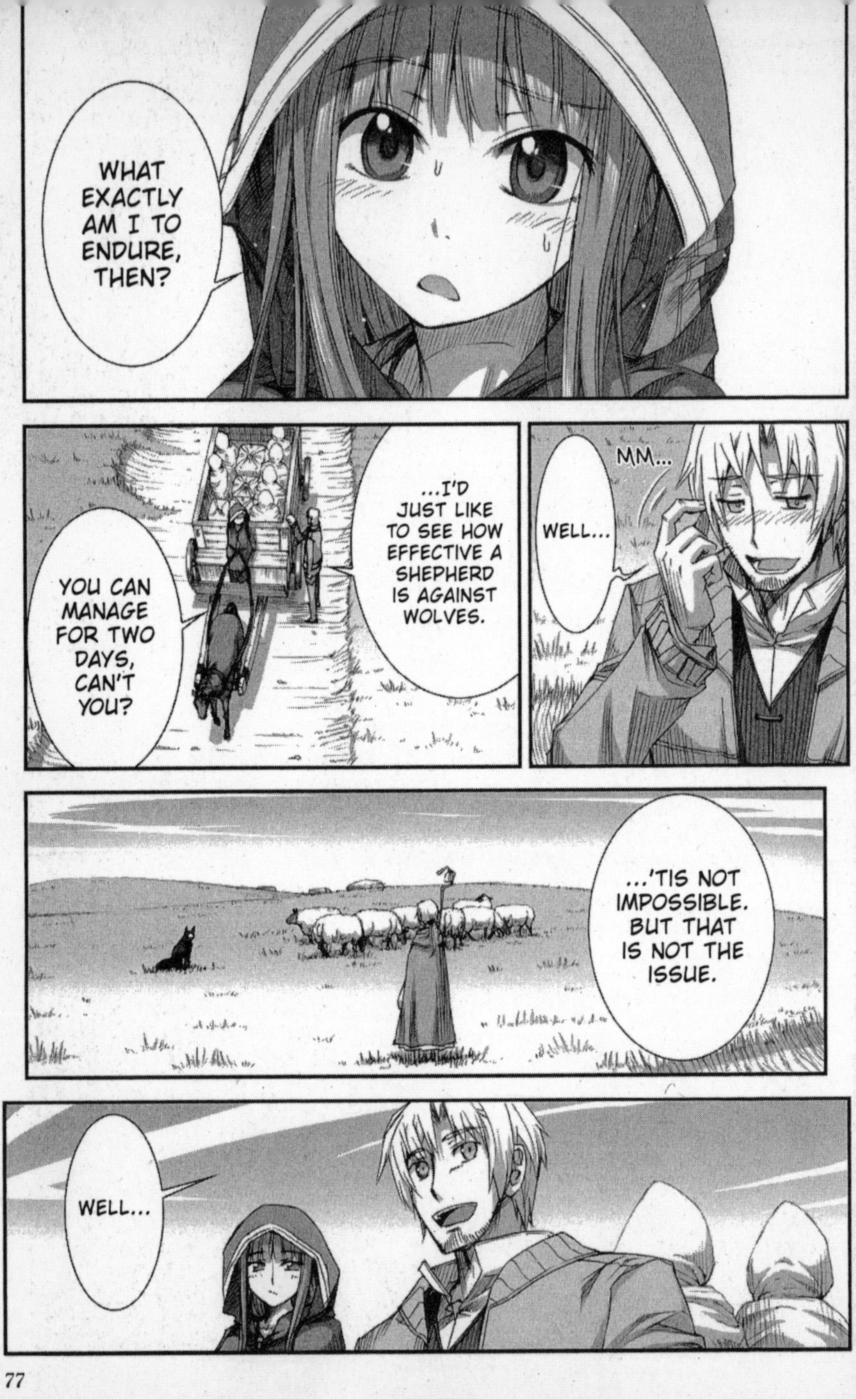
WHAT EXACTLY AM I TO ENDURE, THEN?
MM...
WELL...
...I'D JUST LIKE TO SEE HOW EFFECTIVE A SHEPHERD IS AGAINST WOLVES.
YOU CAN MANAGE FOR TWO DAYS, CAN'T YOU?
...'TIS NOT IMPOSSIBLE. BUT THAT IS NOT THE ISSUE.
WELL...

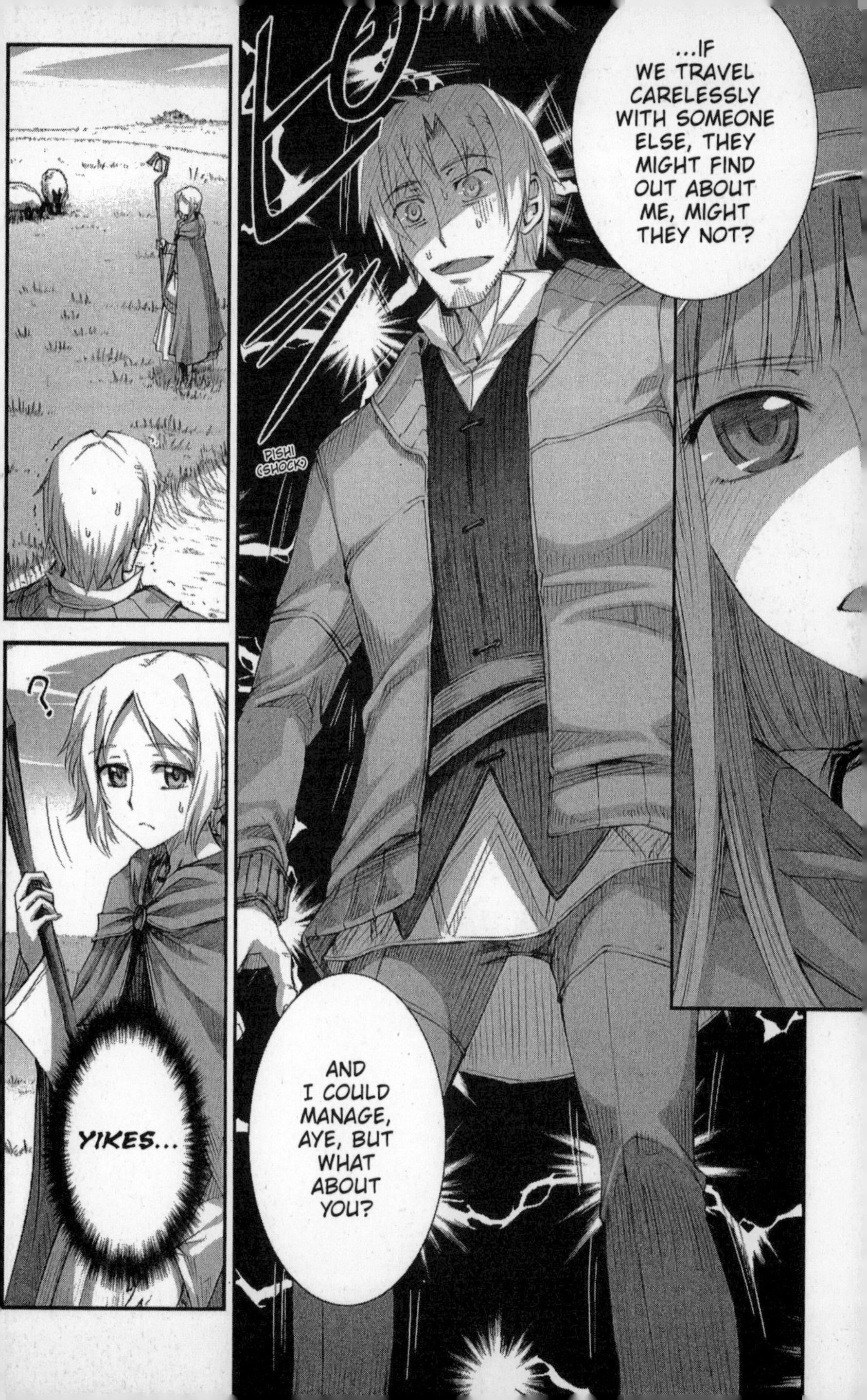
...IF WE TRAVEL CARELESSLY WITH SOMEONE ELSE, THEY MIGHT FIND OUT ABOUT ME, MIGHT THEY NOT?
AND I COULD MANAGE, AYE, BUT WHAT ABOUT YOU?
PISHI (SHOCK)
?
YIKES...

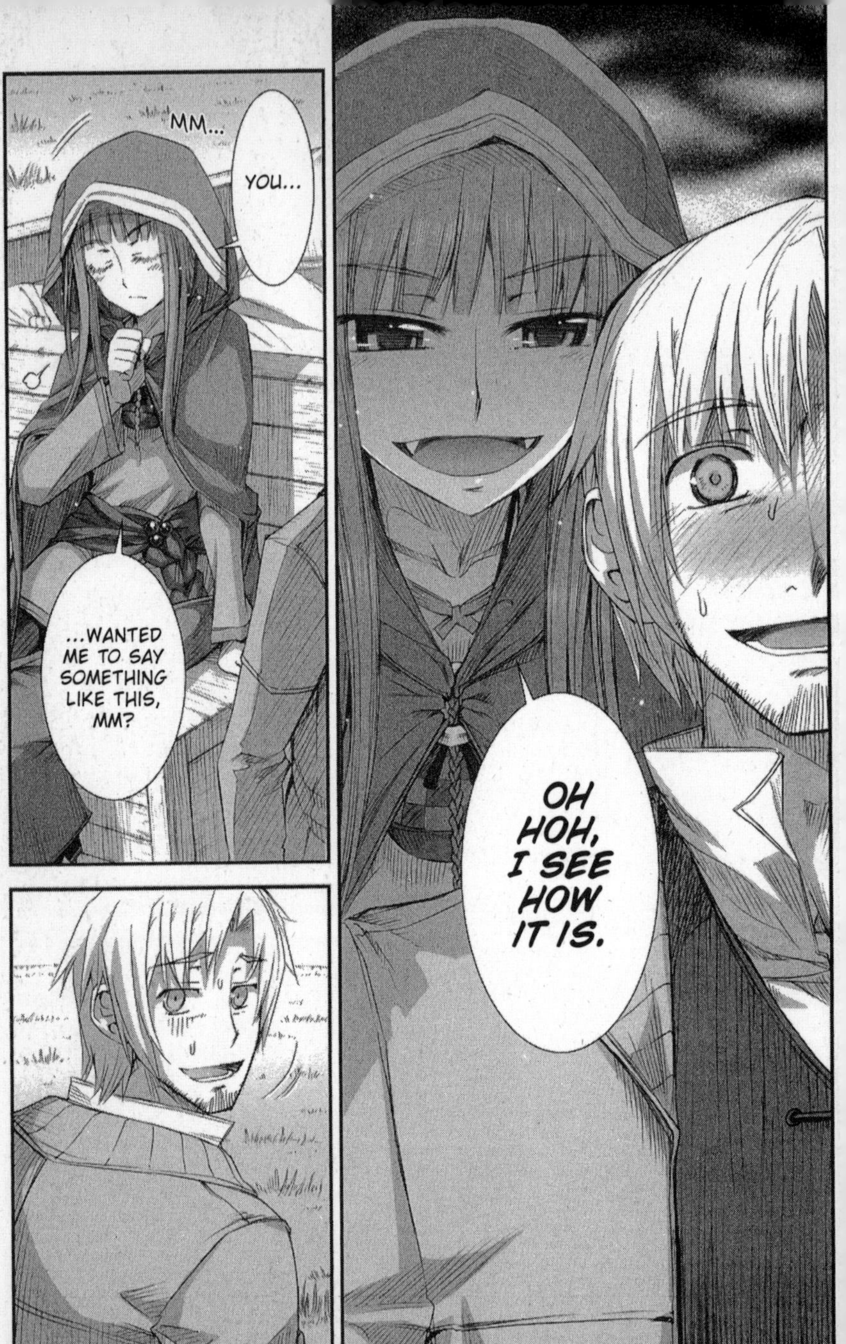
OH HOH, I SEE HOW IT IS.
MM...
YOU...
...WANTED ME TO SAY SOMETHING LIKE THIS, MM?

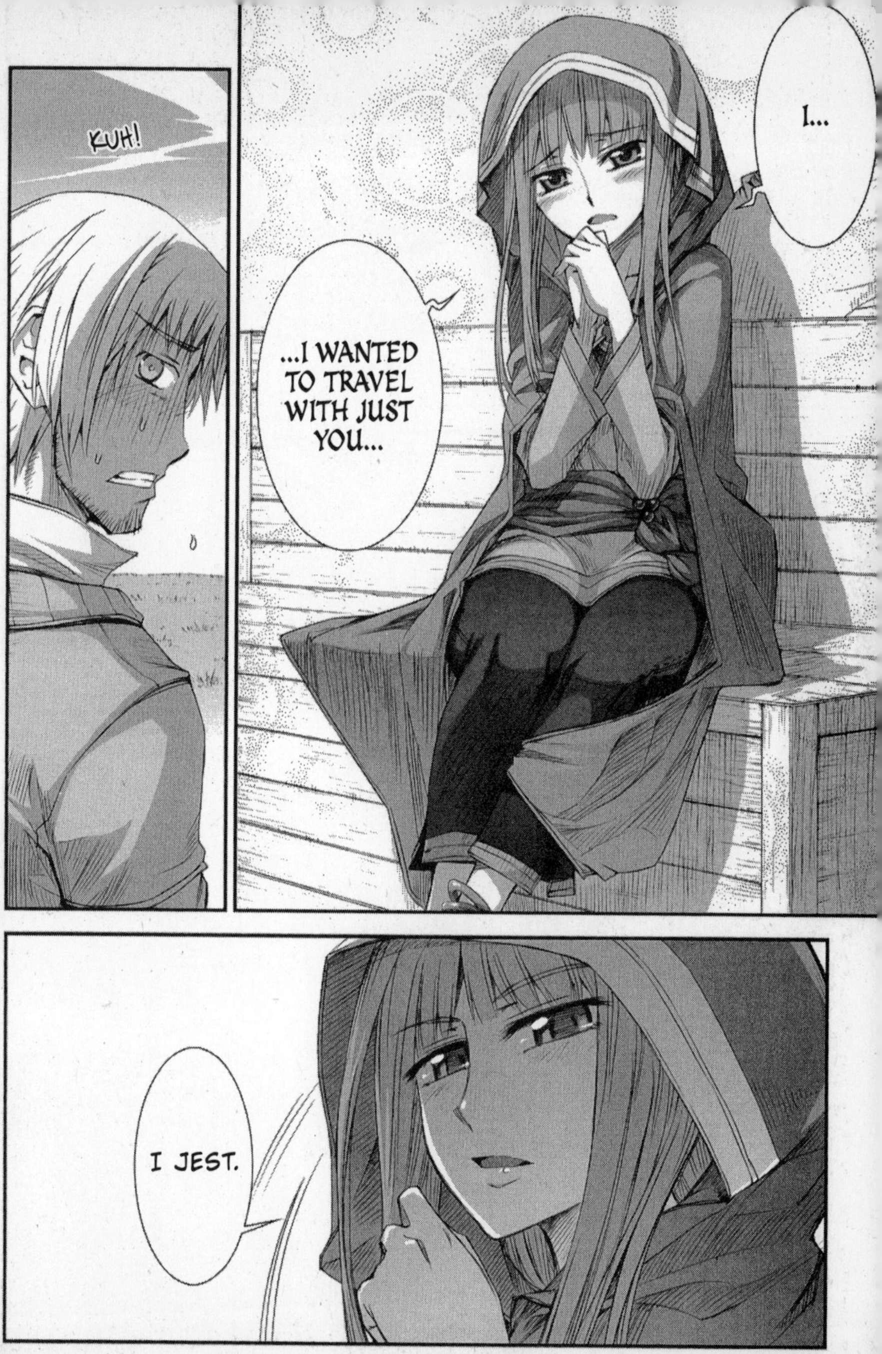
I...
...I WANTED TO TRAVEL WITH JUST YOU...
KUH!
I JEST.

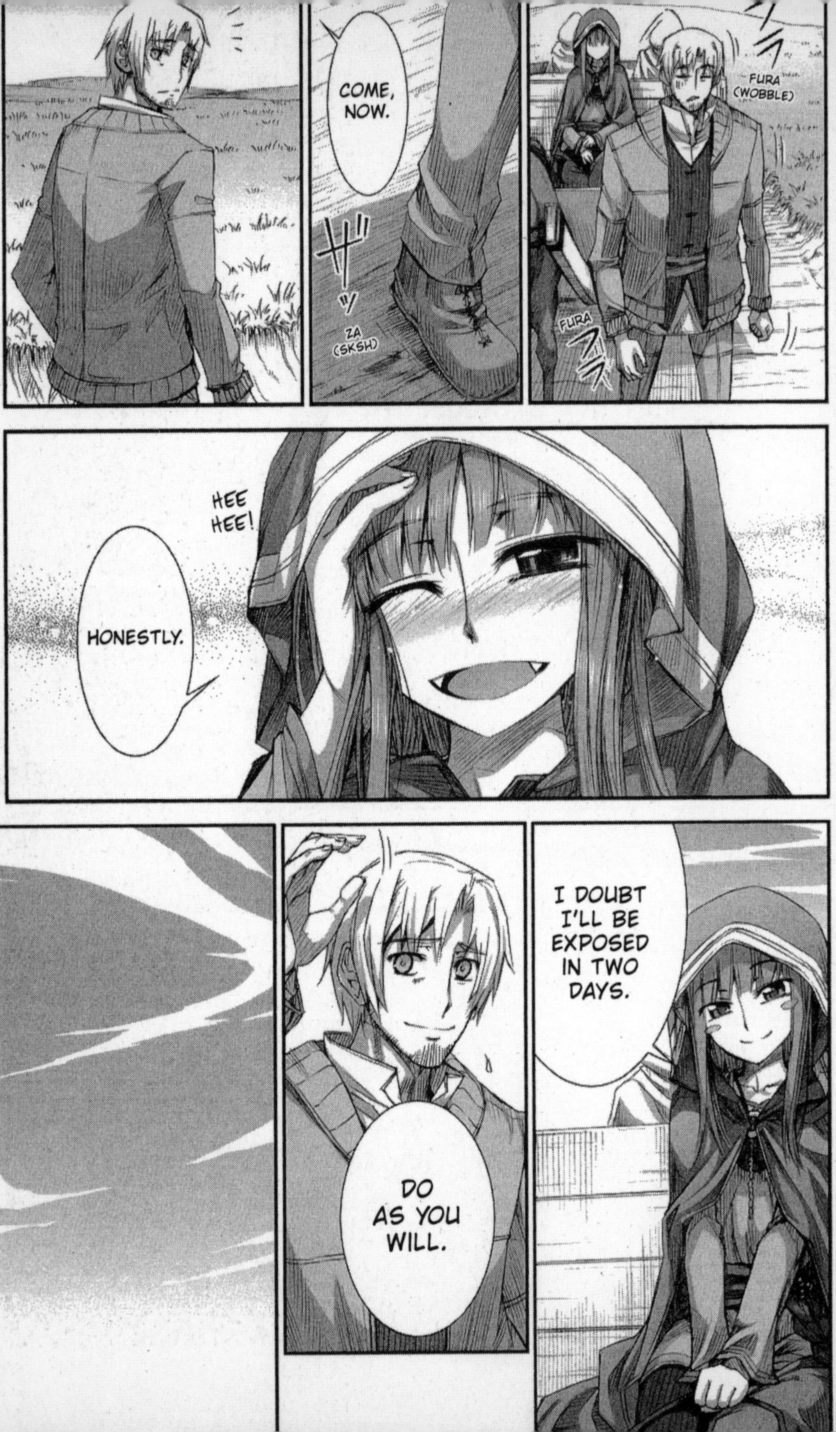
FURA (WOBBLE)
FURA
COME, NOW.
ZA (SKSH)
HEE HEE!
HONESTLY.
I DOUBT I'LL BE EXPOSED IN TWO DAYS.
DO AS YOU WILL.

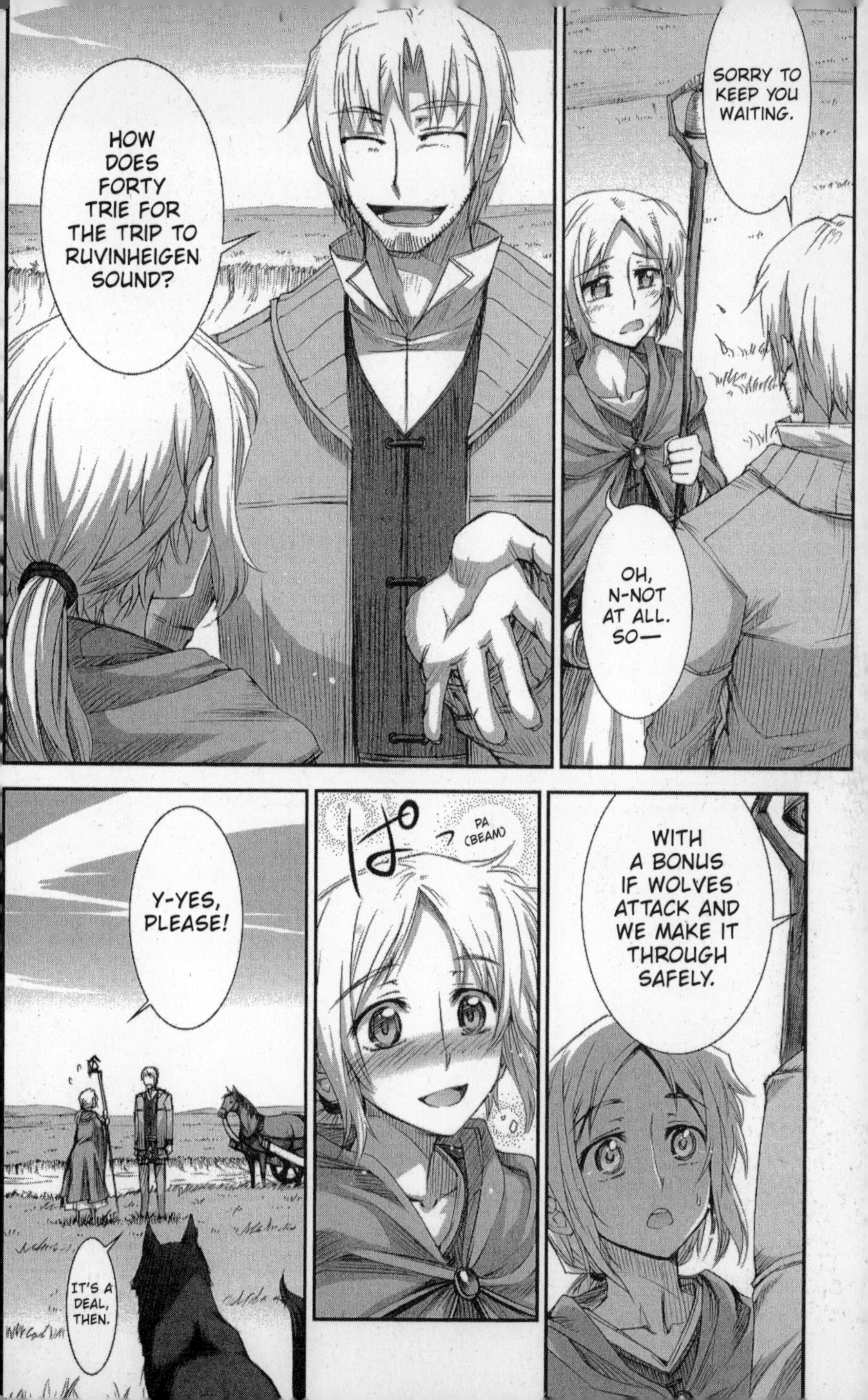
SORRY TO KEEP YOU WAITING.
OH, N-NOT AT ALL. SO—
HOW DOES FORTY TRIE FOR THE TRIP TO RUVINHEIGEN SOUND?
WITH A BONUS IF WOLVES ATTACK AND WE MAKE IT THROUGH SAFELY.
ぱ
PA (BEAM)
Y-YES, PLEASE!
IT'S A DEAL, THEN.

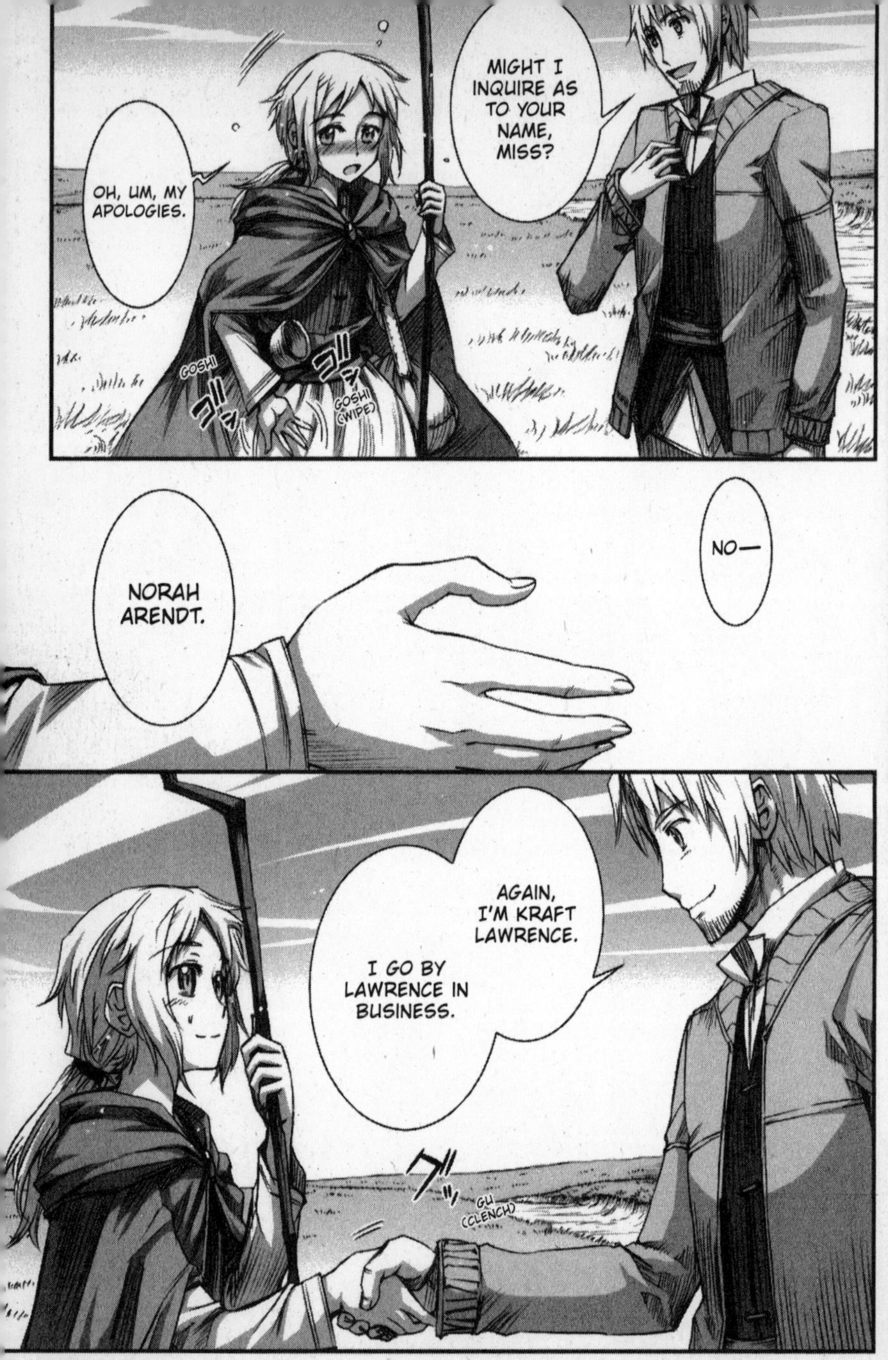
MIGHT I INQUIRE AS TO YOUR NAME, MISS?
OH, UM, MY APOLOGIES.
GOSHI
GOSHI (WIPE)
NO—
NORAH ARENDT.
AGAIN, I'M KRAFT LAWRENCE.
I GO BY LAWRENCE IN BUSINESS.
GU (CLENCH)

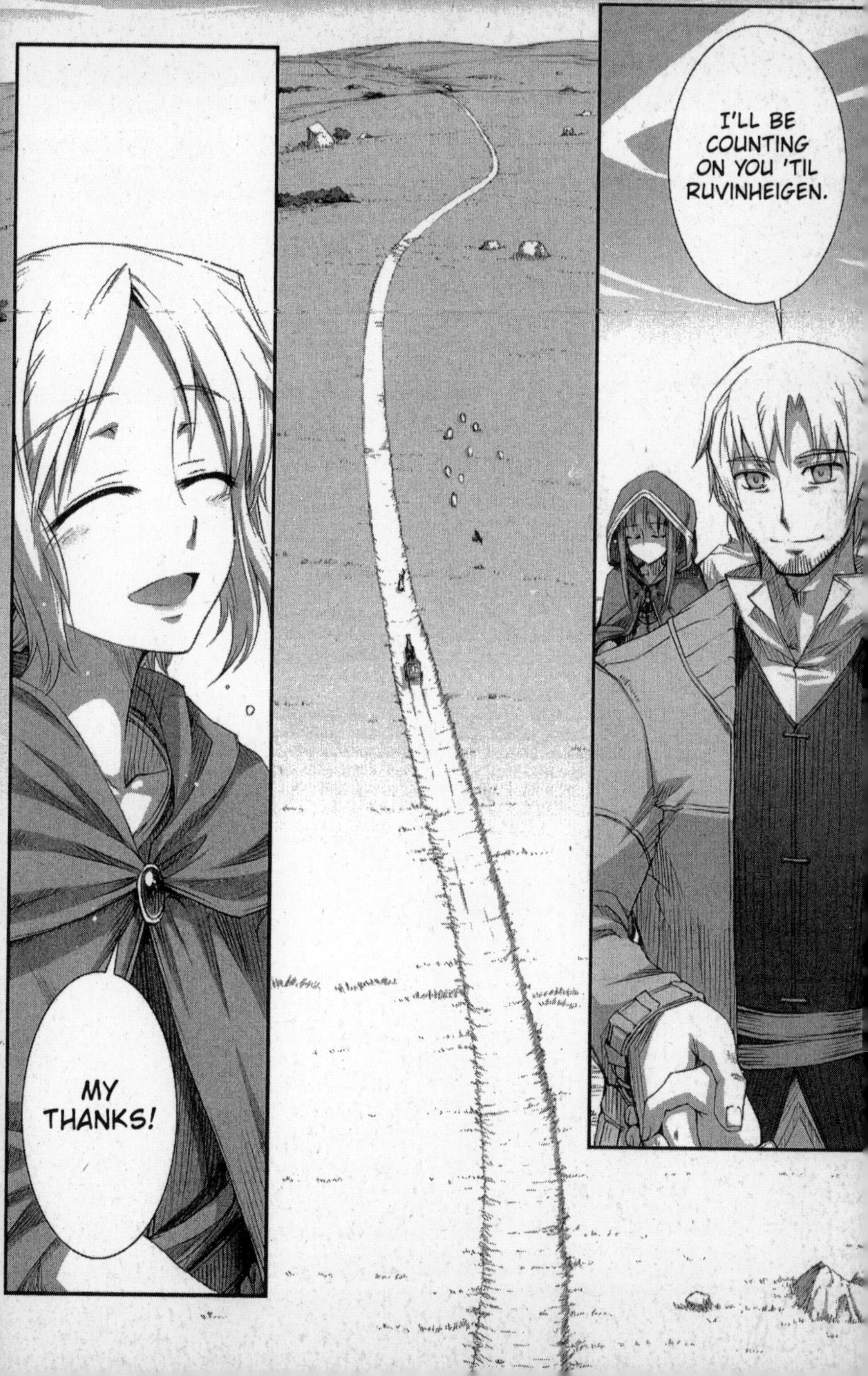
I'LL BE COUNTING ON YOU 'TIL RUVINHEIGEN.
MY THANKS!

SPICE & WOLF

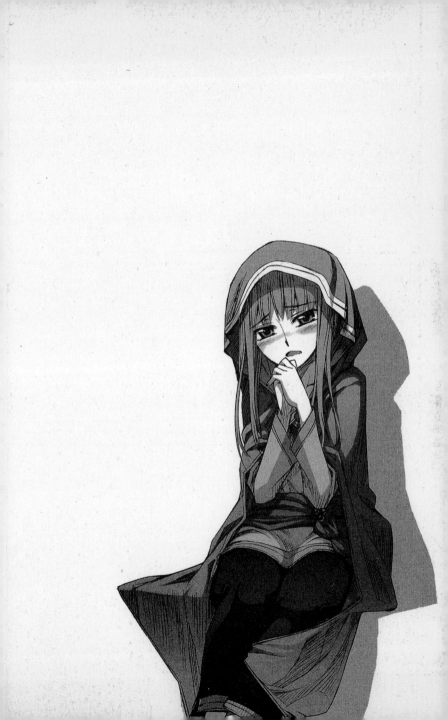

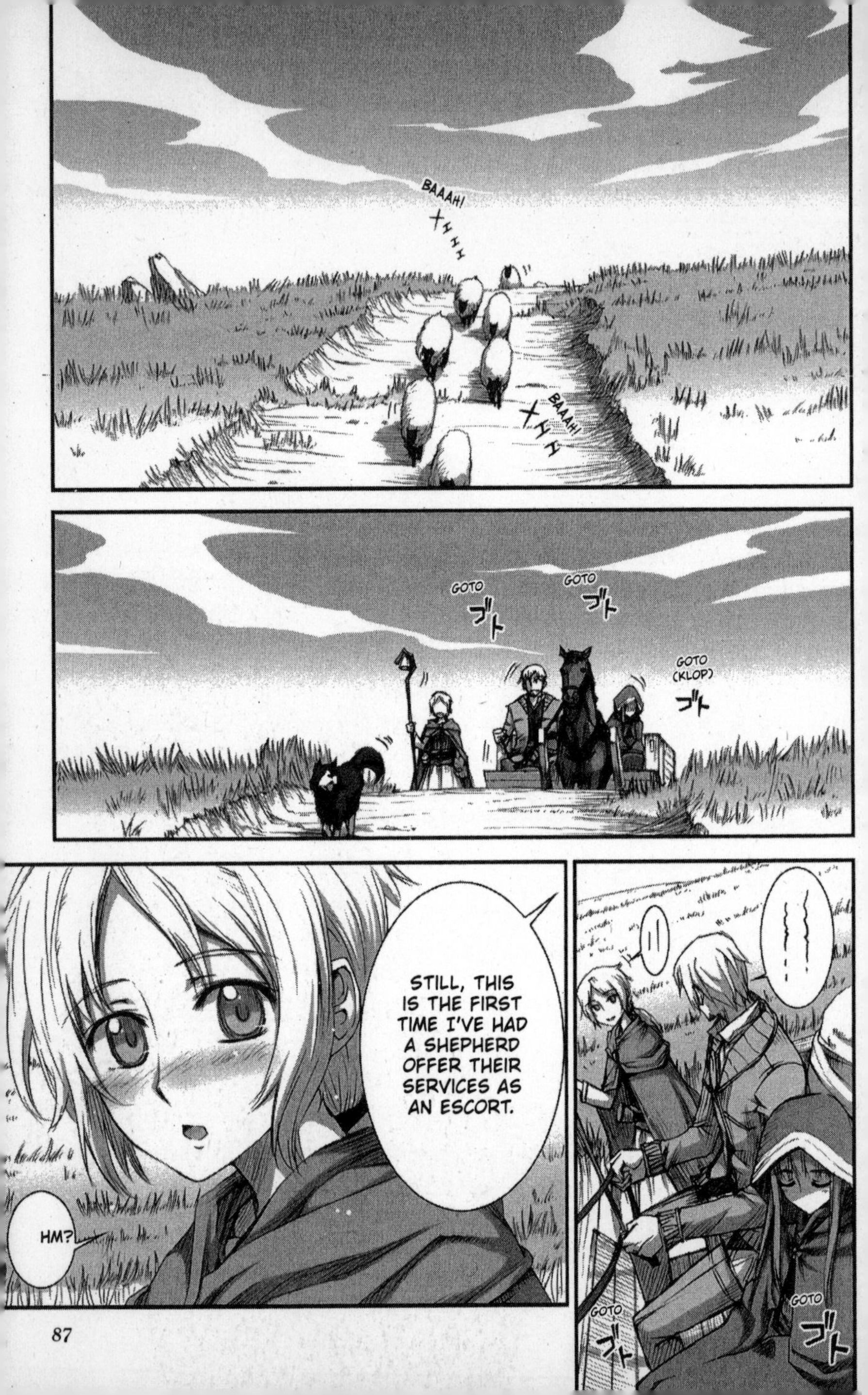
BAAAH!
BAAAH!
GOTO
GOTO
GOTO (KLOP)
GOTO
GOTO
STILL, THIS IS THE FIRST TIME I'VE HAD A SHEPHERD OFFER THEIR SERVICES AS AN ESCORT.
HM?

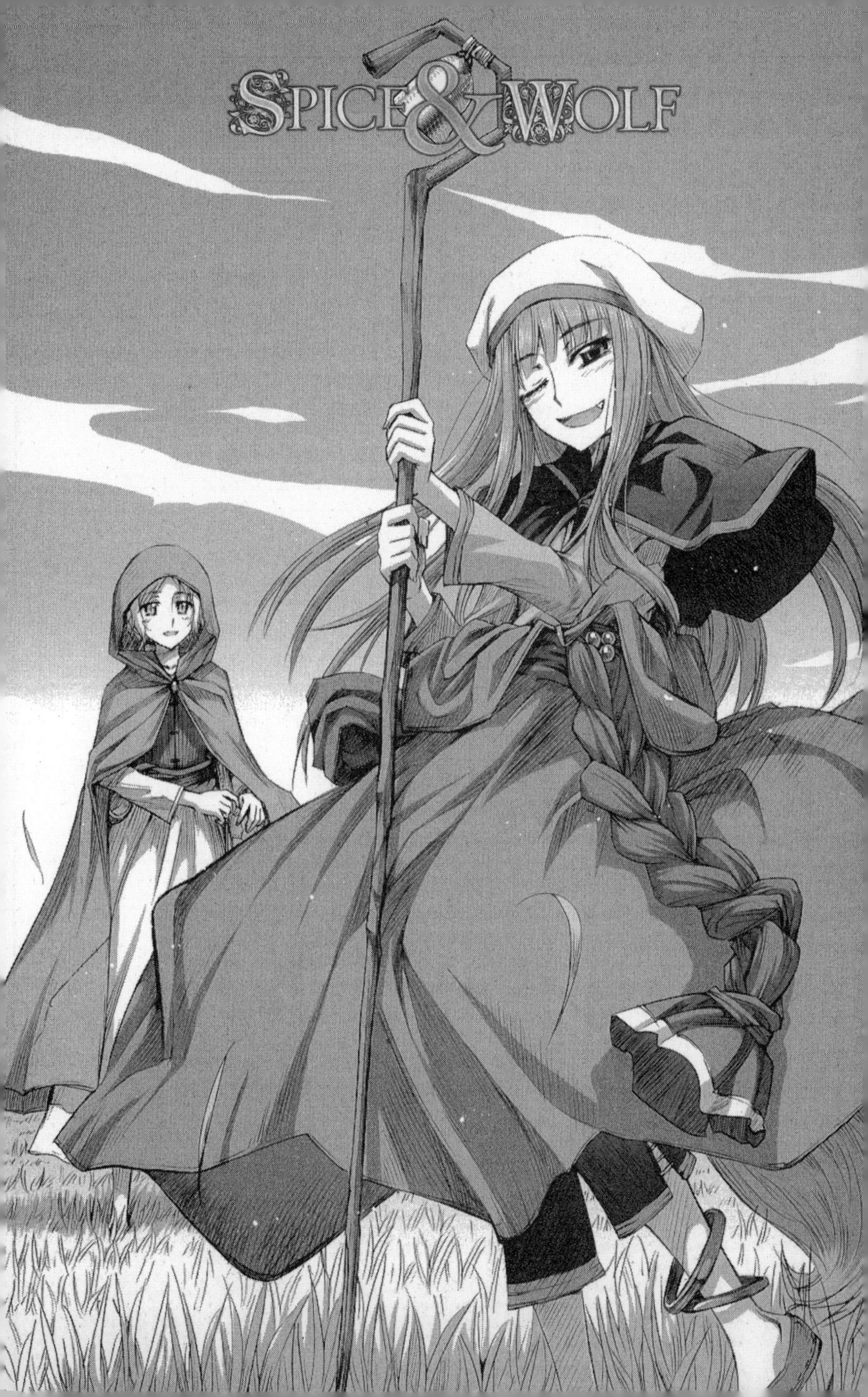
SPICE & WOLF

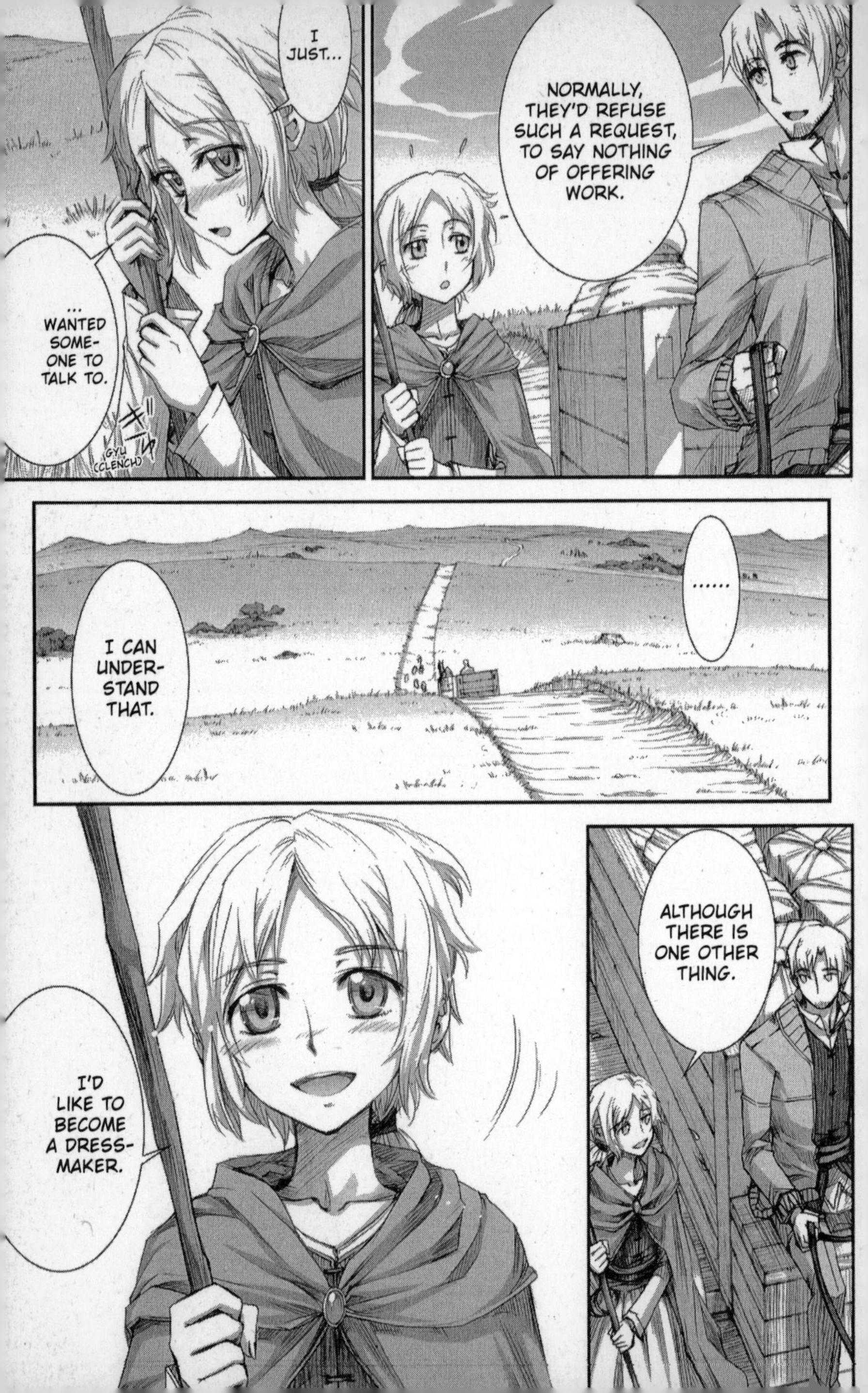
NORMALLY, THEY'D REFUSE SUCH A REQUEST, TO SAY NOTHING OF OFFERING WORK.
I JUST...
...WANTED SOME-ONE TO TALK TO.
GYU (CLENCH)
......
I CAN UNDER-STAND THAT.
ALTHOUGH THERE IS ONE OTHER THING.
I'D LIKE TO BECOME A DRESS-MAKER.

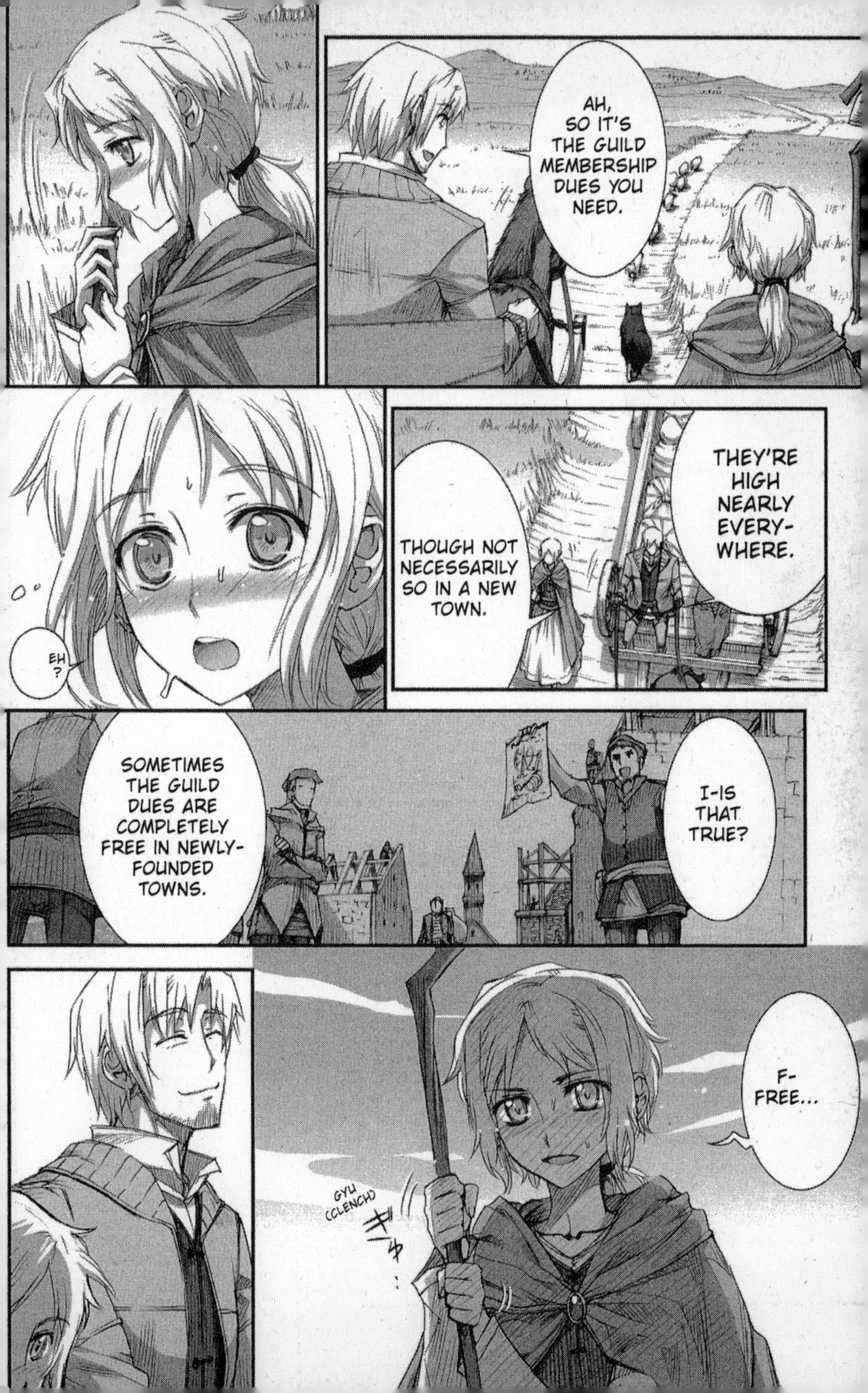
AH, SO IT'S THE GUILD MEMBERSHIP DUES YOU NEED.
THEY'RE HIGH NEARLY EVERY-WHERE.
THOUGH NOT NECESSARILY SO IN A NEW TOWN.
EH?
I-IS THAT TRUE?
SOMETIMES THE GUILD DUES ARE COMPLETELY FREE IN NEWLY-FOUNDED TOWNS.
F- FREE...
GYU (CLENCH)

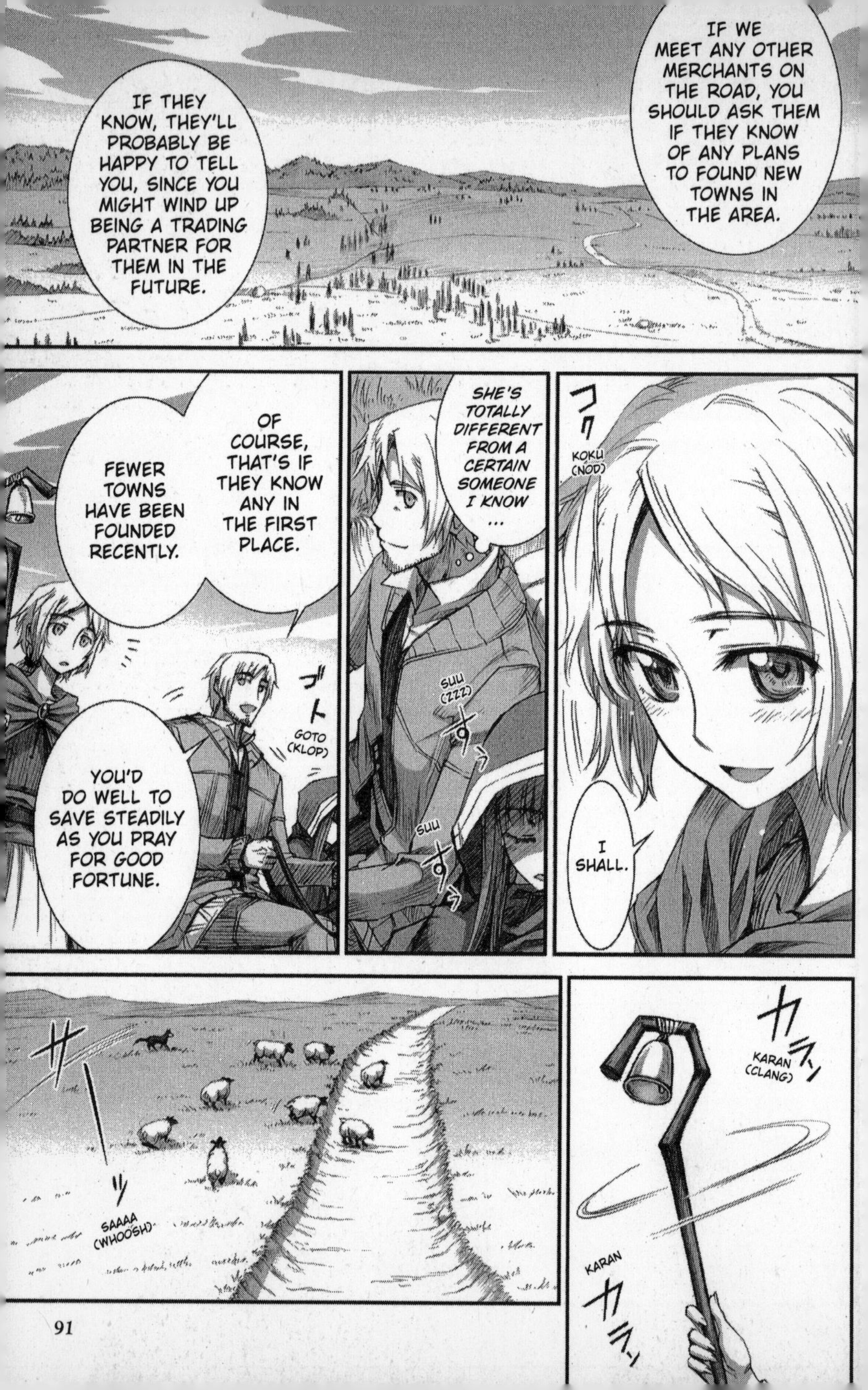
IF WE MEET ANY OTHER MERCHANTS ON THE ROAD, YOU SHOULD ASK THEM IF THEY KNOW OF ANY PLANS TO FOUND NEW TOWNS IN THE AREA.
IF THEY KNOW, THEY'LL PROBABLY BE HAPPY TO TELL YOU, SINCE YOU MIGHT WIND UP BEING A TRADING PARTNER FOR THEM IN THE FUTURE.
KOKU (NOD)
I SHALL.
SHE'S TOTALLY DIFFERENT FROM A CERTAIN SOMEONE I KNOW ...
SUU (ZZZ)
SUU
OF COURSE, THAT'S IF THEY KNOW ANY IN THE FIRST PLACE.
FEWER TOWNS HAVE BEEN FOUNDED RECENTLY.
GOTO (KLOP)
YOU'D DO WELL TO SAVE STEADILY AS YOU PRAY FOR GOOD FORTUNE.
KARAN (CLANG)
KARAN
SAAAA (WHOOSH)

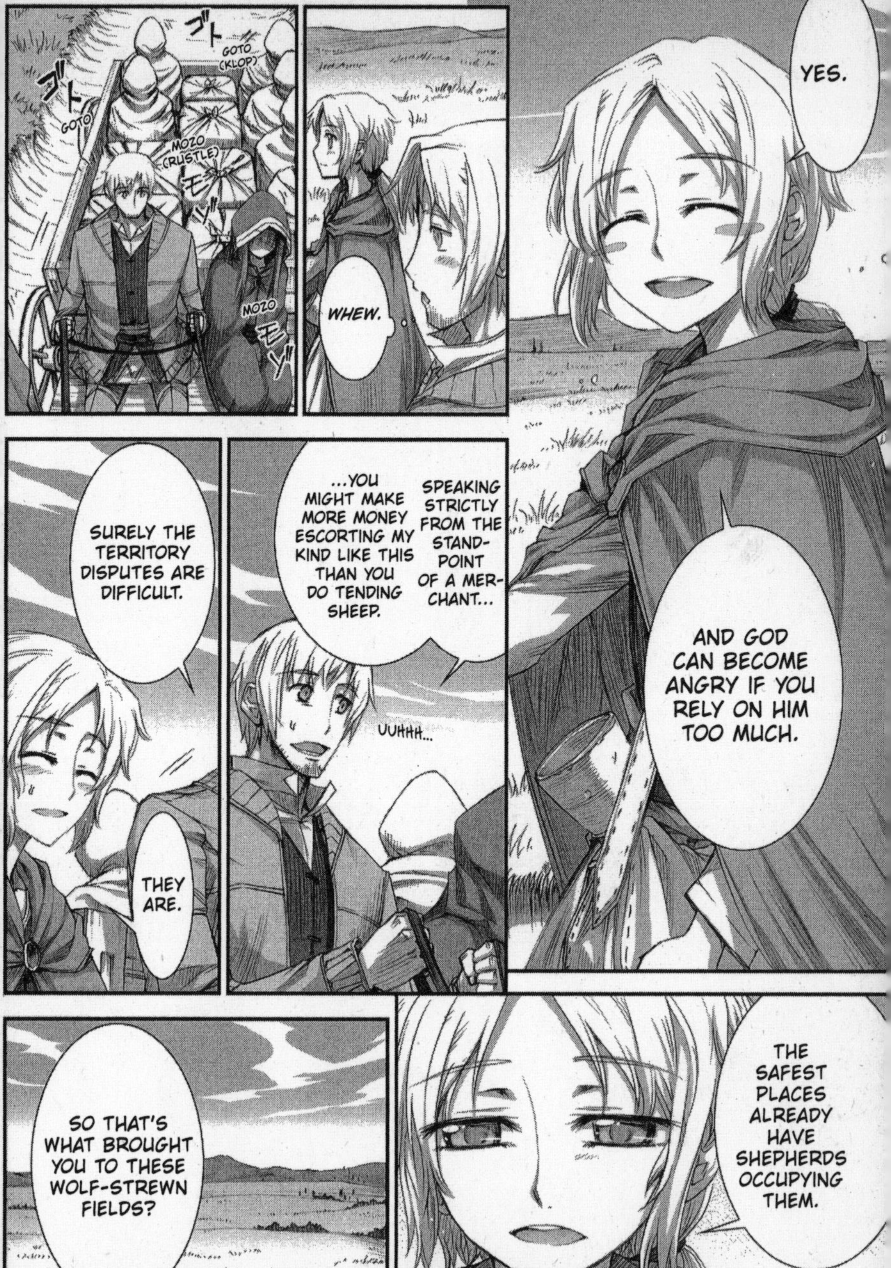
YES.
AND GOD CAN BECOME ANGRY IF YOU RELY ON HIM TOO MUCH.
WHEW.
ゴト
GOTO (KLOP)
ゴト
GOTO
モゾ
MOZO (RUSTLE)
モゾ
MOZO
SPEAKING STRICTLY FROM THE STANDPOINT OF A MERCHANT...
...YOU MIGHT MAKE MORE MONEY ESCORTING MY KIND LIKE THIS THAN YOU DO TENDING SHEEP.
UUHHH...
SURELY THE TERRITORY DISPUTES ARE DIFFICULT.
THEY ARE.
THE SAFEST PLACES ALREADY HAVE SHEPHERDS OCCUPYING THEM.
SO THAT'S WHAT BROUGHT YOU TO THESE WOLF-STREWN FIELDS?

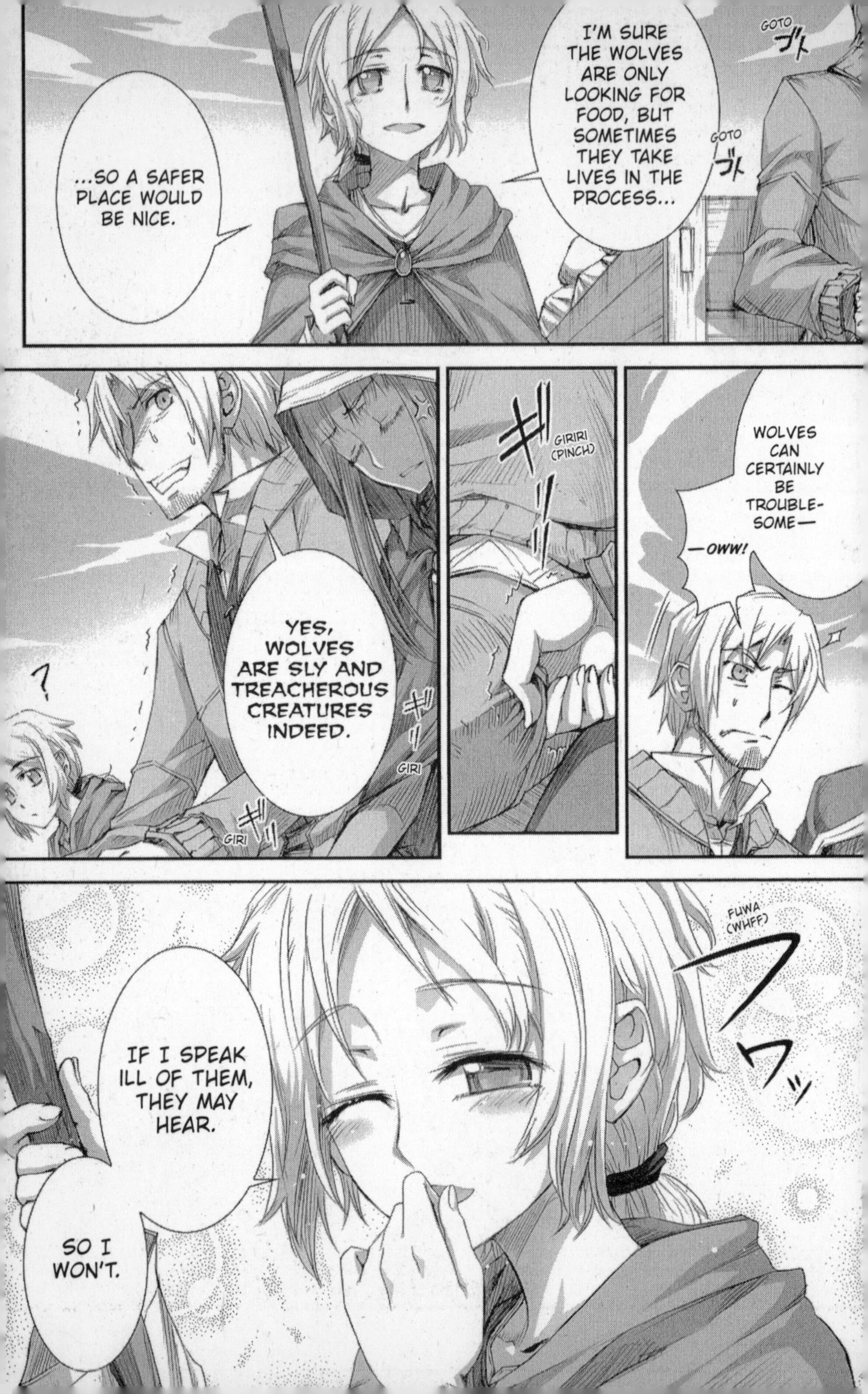
GOTO
GOTO
I'M SURE THE WOLVES ARE ONLY LOOKING FOR FOOD, BUT SOMETIMES THEY TAKE LIVES IN THE PROCESS...
...SO A SAFER PLACE WOULD BE NICE.
WOLVES CAN CERTAINLY BE TROUBLE-SOME—
—OWW!
GIRIRI (PINCH)
YES, WOLVES ARE SLY AND TREACHEROUS CREATURES INDEED.
GIRI
GIRI
?
FUWA (WHFF)
IF I SPEAK ILL OF THEM, THEY MAY HEAR.
SO I WON'T.

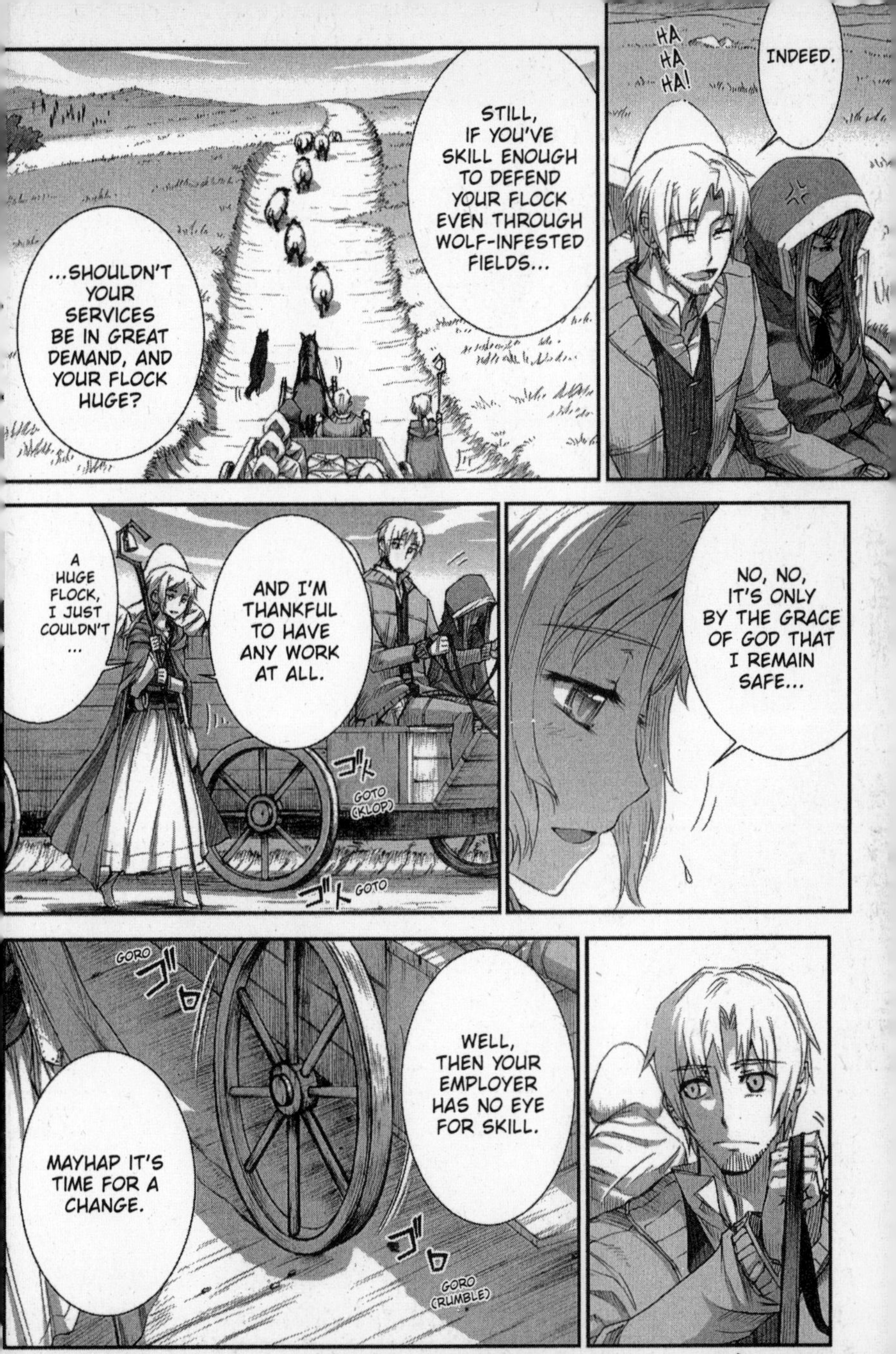
INDEED.
HA HA HA!
STILL, IF YOU'VE SKILL ENOUGH TO DEFEND YOUR FLOCK EVEN THROUGH WOLF-INFESTED FIELDS...
...SHOULDN'T YOUR SERVICES BE IN GREAT DEMAND, AND YOUR FLOCK HUGE?
NO, NO, IT'S ONLY BY THE GRACE OF GOD THAT I REMAIN SAFE...
AND I'M THANKFUL TO HAVE ANY WORK AT ALL.
A HUGE FLOCK, I JUST COULDN'T ...
GOTO (KLOP)
GOTO
WELL, THEN YOUR EMPLOYER HAS NO EYE FOR SKILL.
GORO
GORO (RUMBLE)
MAYHAP IT'S TIME FOR A CHANGE.

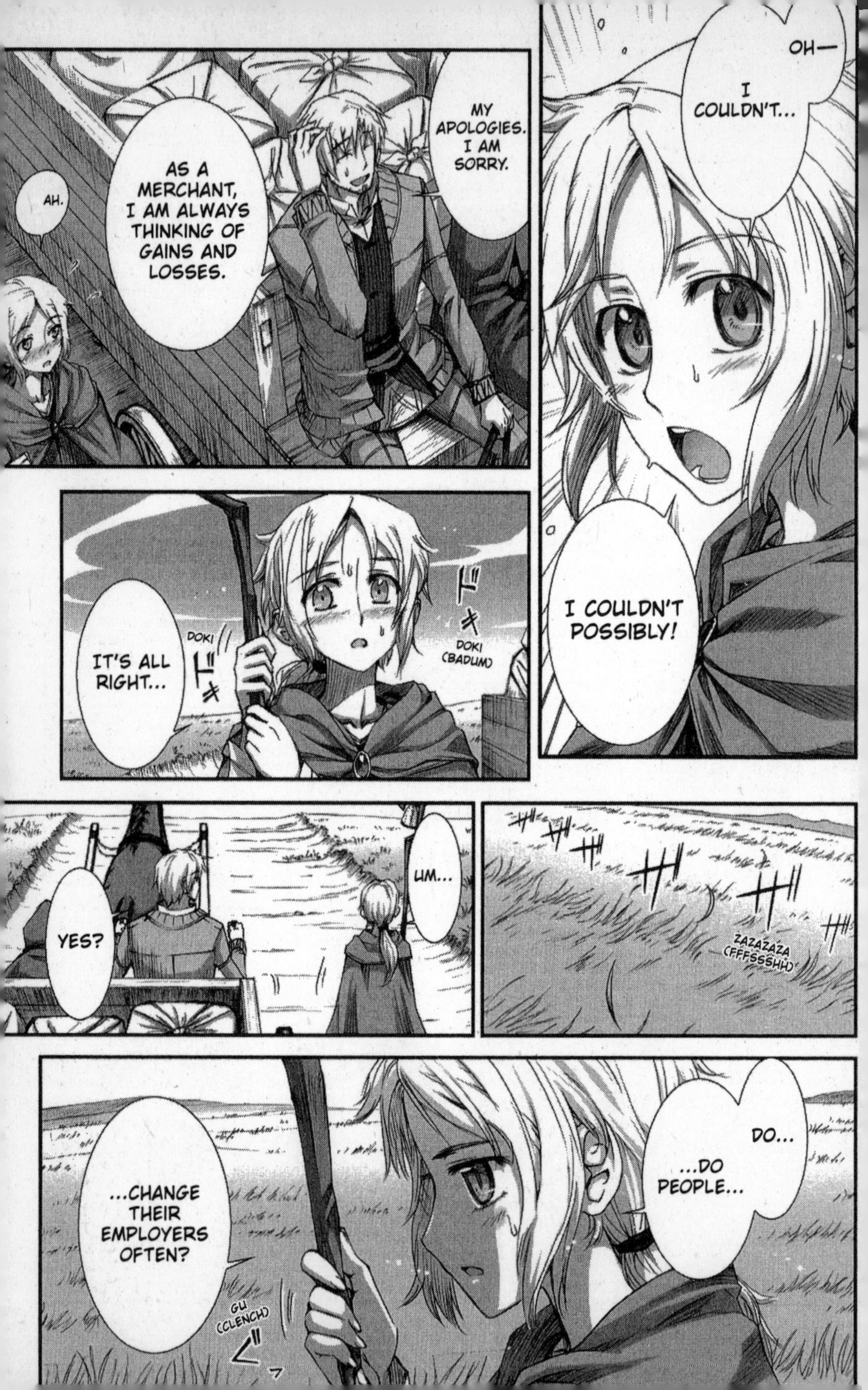
OH—
I COULDN'T...
I COULDN'T POSSIBLY!
MY APOLOGIES. I AM SORRY.
AS A MERCHANT, I AM ALWAYS THINKING OF GAINS AND LOSSES.
AH.
ドキ
DOKI (BADUM)
IT'S ALL RIGHT...
ドキ
DOKI
ZAZAZAZA (FFFSSSHH)
UM...
YES?
DO...
...DO PEOPLE...
...CHANGE THEIR EMPLOYERS OFTEN?
GU (CLENCH)

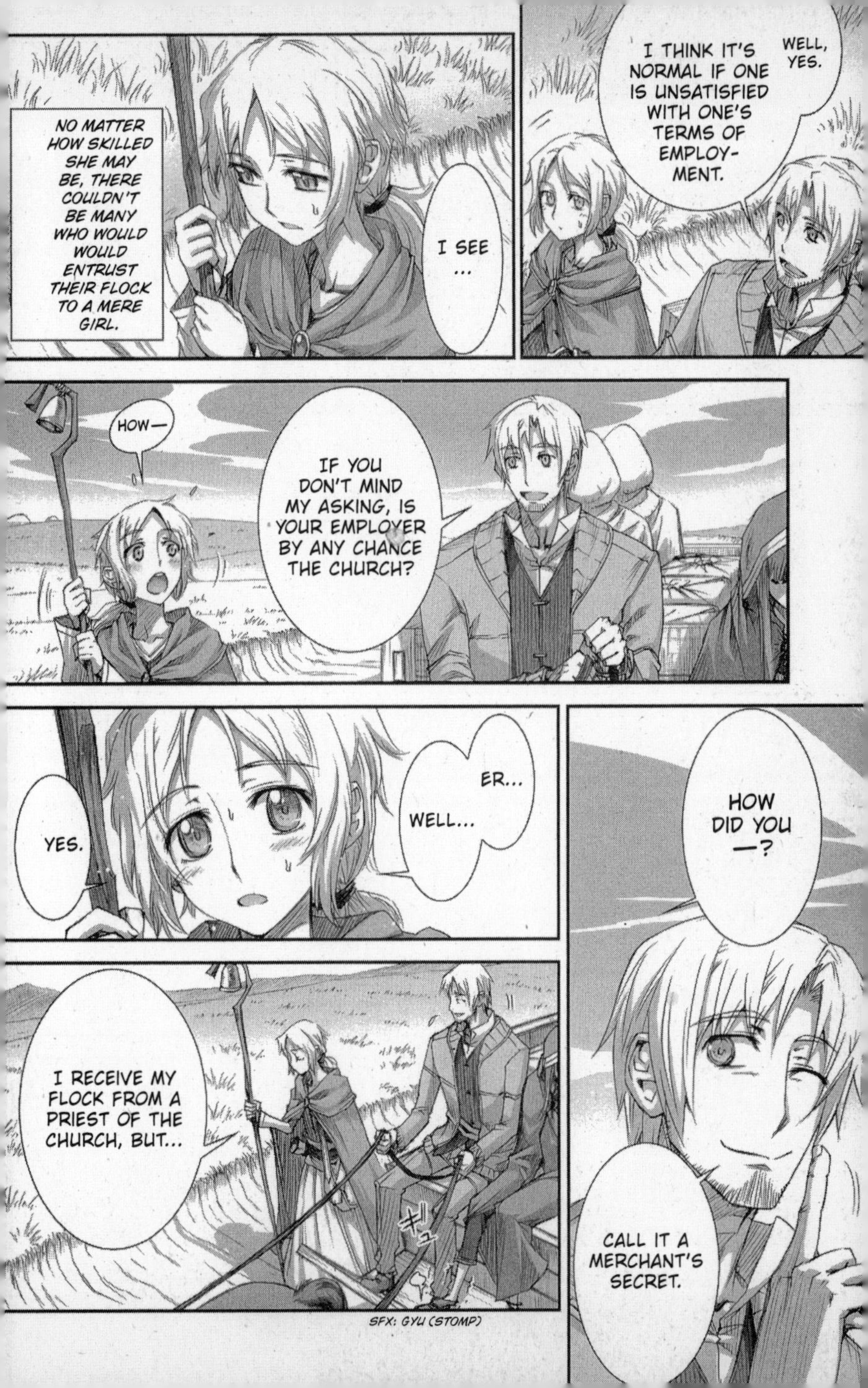
WELL, YES.
I THINK IT'S NORMAL IF ONE IS UNSATISFIED WITH ONE'S TERMS OF EMPLOYMENT.
I SEE ...
NO MATTER HOW SKILLED SHE MAY BE, THERE COULDN'T BE MANY WHO WOULD WOULD ENTRUST THEIR FLOCK TO A MERE GIRL.
IF YOU DON'T MIND MY ASKING, IS YOUR EMPLOYER BY ANY CHANCE THE CHURCH?
HOW—
HOW DID YOU —?
CALL IT A MERCHANT'S SECRET.
ER...
WELL...
YES.
I RECEIVE MY FLOCK FROM A PRIEST OF THE CHURCH, BUT...
SFX: GYU (STOMP)

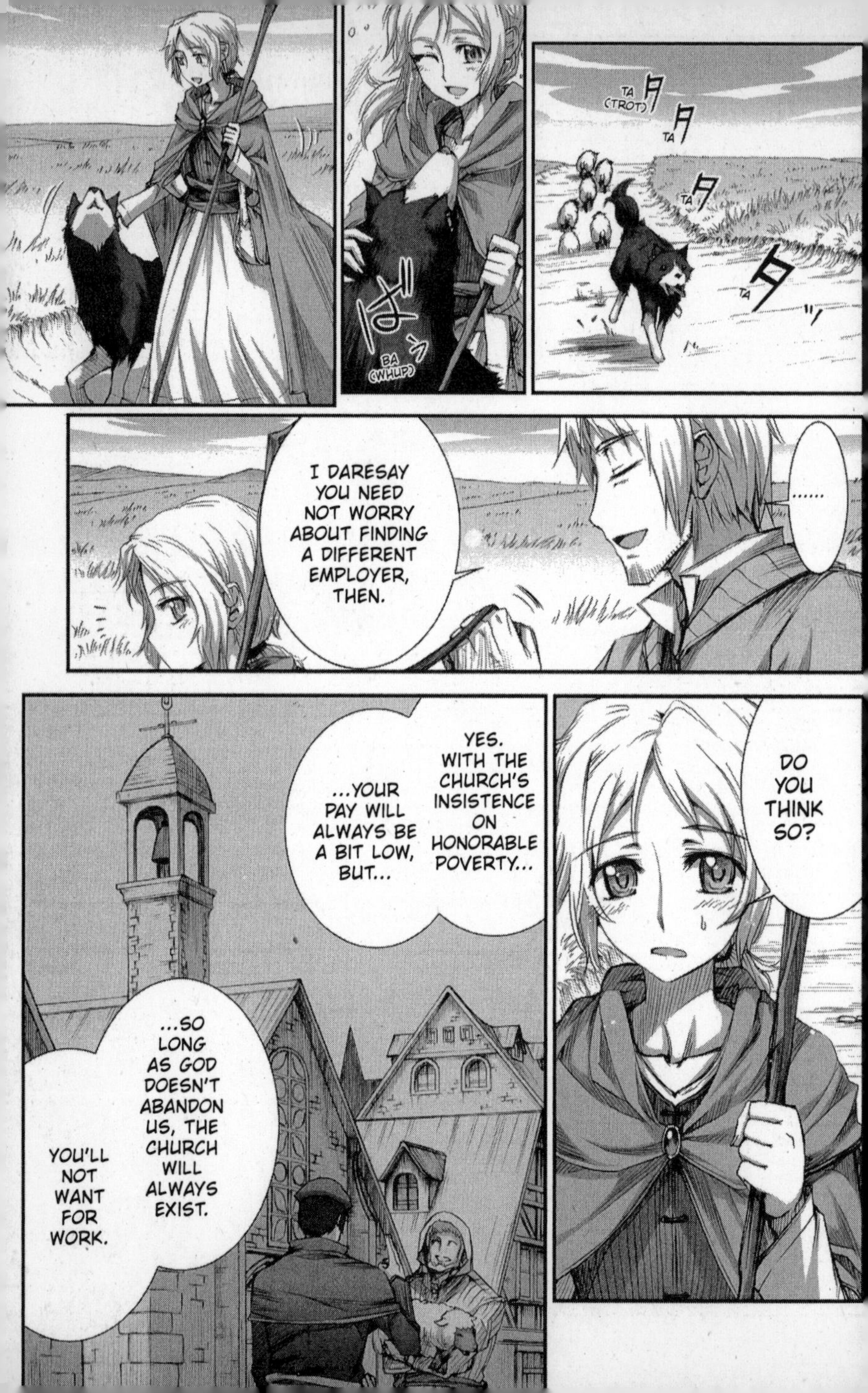
TA (TROT)
TA
TA
TA
BA (WHUP)
......
I DARESAY YOU NEED NOT WORRY ABOUT FINDING A DIFFERENT EMPLOYER, THEN.
DO YOU THINK SO?
YES. WITH THE CHURCH'S INSISTENCE ON HONORABLE POVERTY...
...YOUR PAY WILL ALWAYS BE A BIT LOW, BUT...
...SO LONG AS GOD DOESN'T ABANDON US, THE CHURCH WILL ALWAYS EXIST.
YOU'LL NOT WANT FOR WORK.

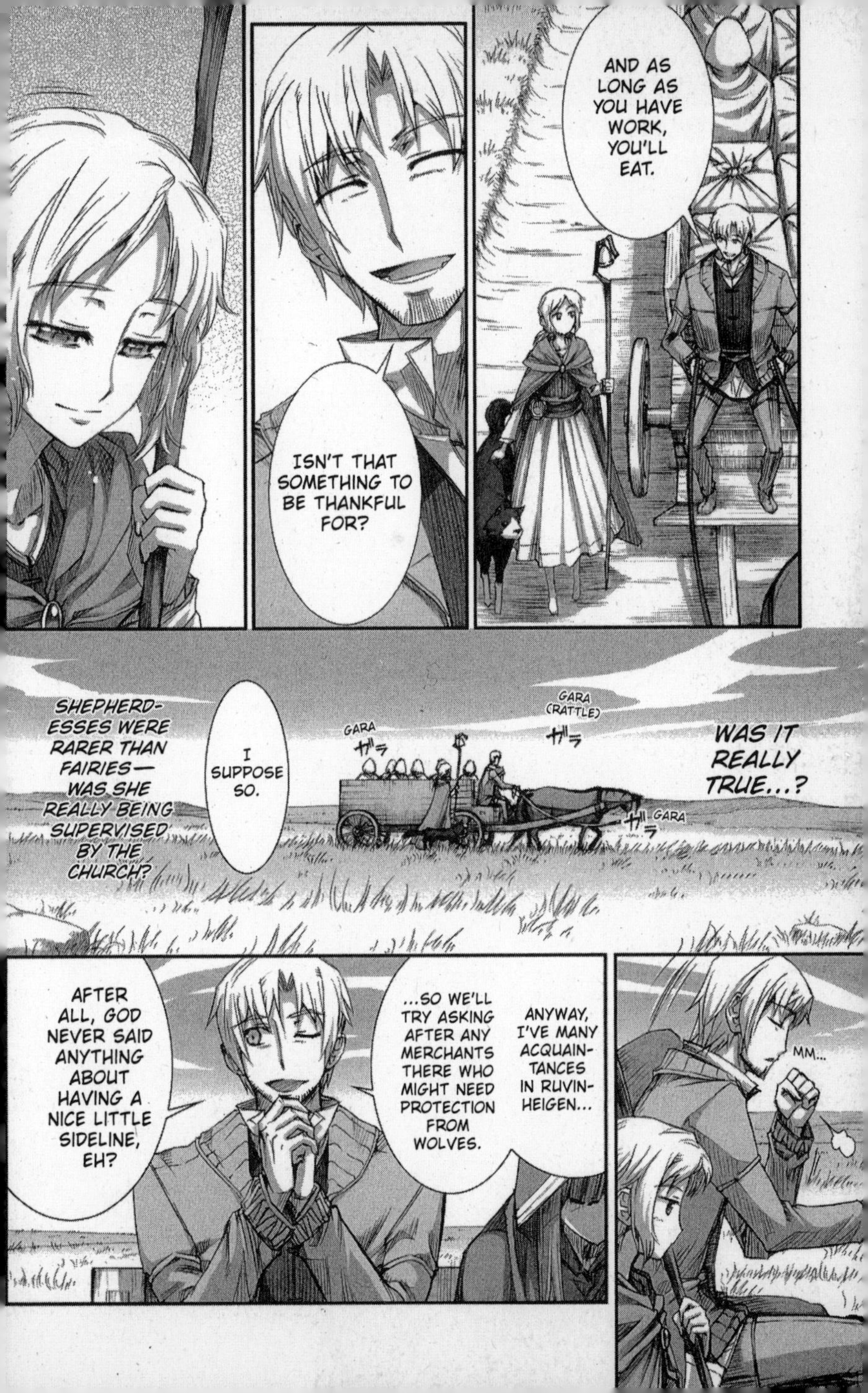
AND AS LONG AS YOU HAVE WORK, YOU'LL EAT.
ISN'T THAT SOMETHING TO BE THANKFUL FOR?
WAS IT REALLY TRUE...?
GARA (RATTLE)
GARA
GARA
I SUPPOSE SO.
SHEPHERD-ESSES WERE RARER THAN FAIRIES—WAS SHE REALLY BEING SUPERVISED BY THE CHURCH?
MM...
ANYWAY, I'VE MANY ACQUAIN-TANCES IN RUVIN-HEIGEN...
...SO WE'LL TRY ASKING AFTER ANY MERCHANTS THERE WHO MIGHT NEED PROTECTION FROM WOLVES.
AFTER ALL, GOD NEVER SAID ANYTHING ABOUT HAVING A NICE LITTLE SIDELINE, EH?

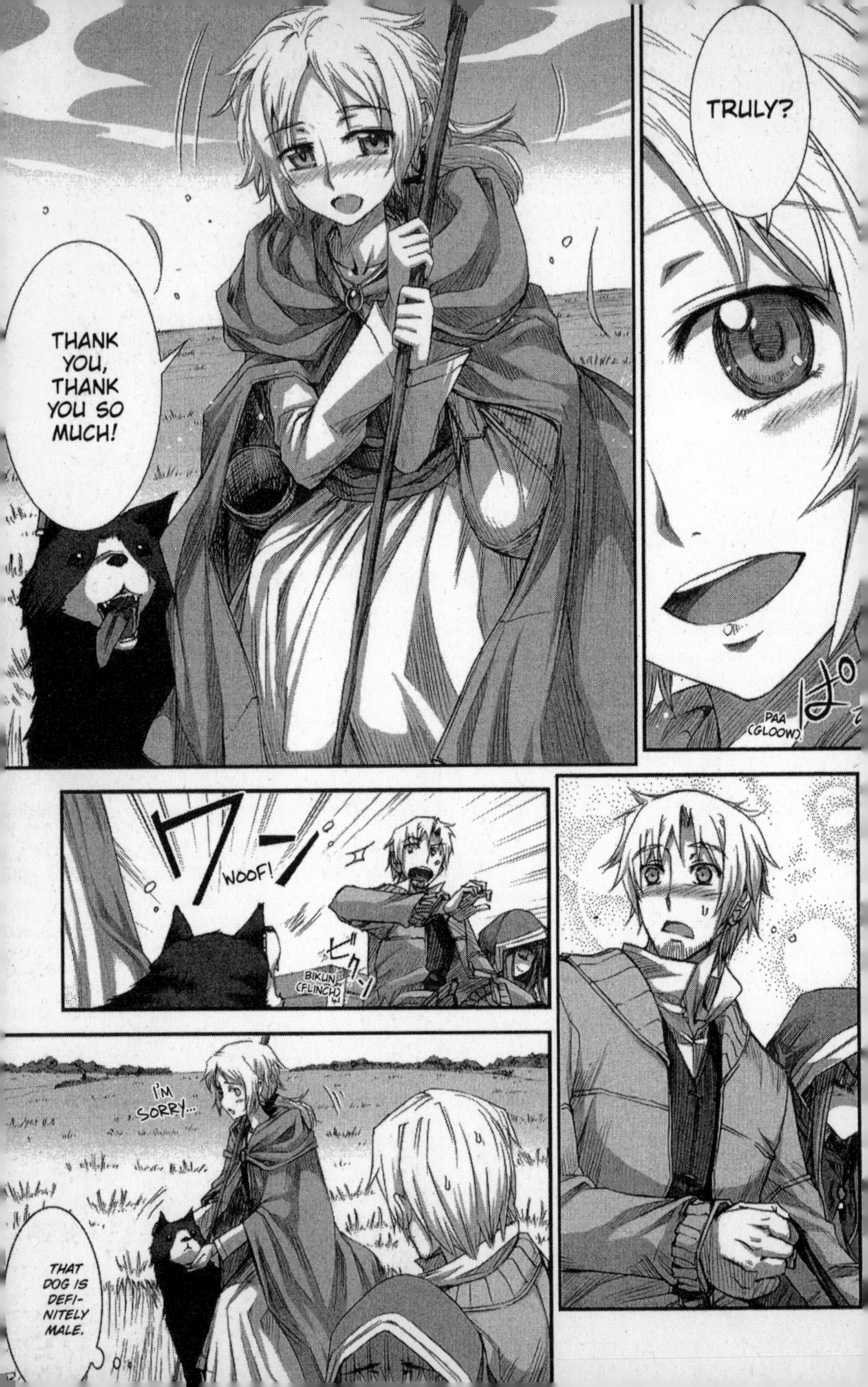
TRULY?
PAA (GLOOW)
THANK YOU, THANK YOU SO MUCH!
WOOF!
BIKUN (FLINCH)
I'M SORRY...
THAT DOG IS DEFI-NITELY MALE.

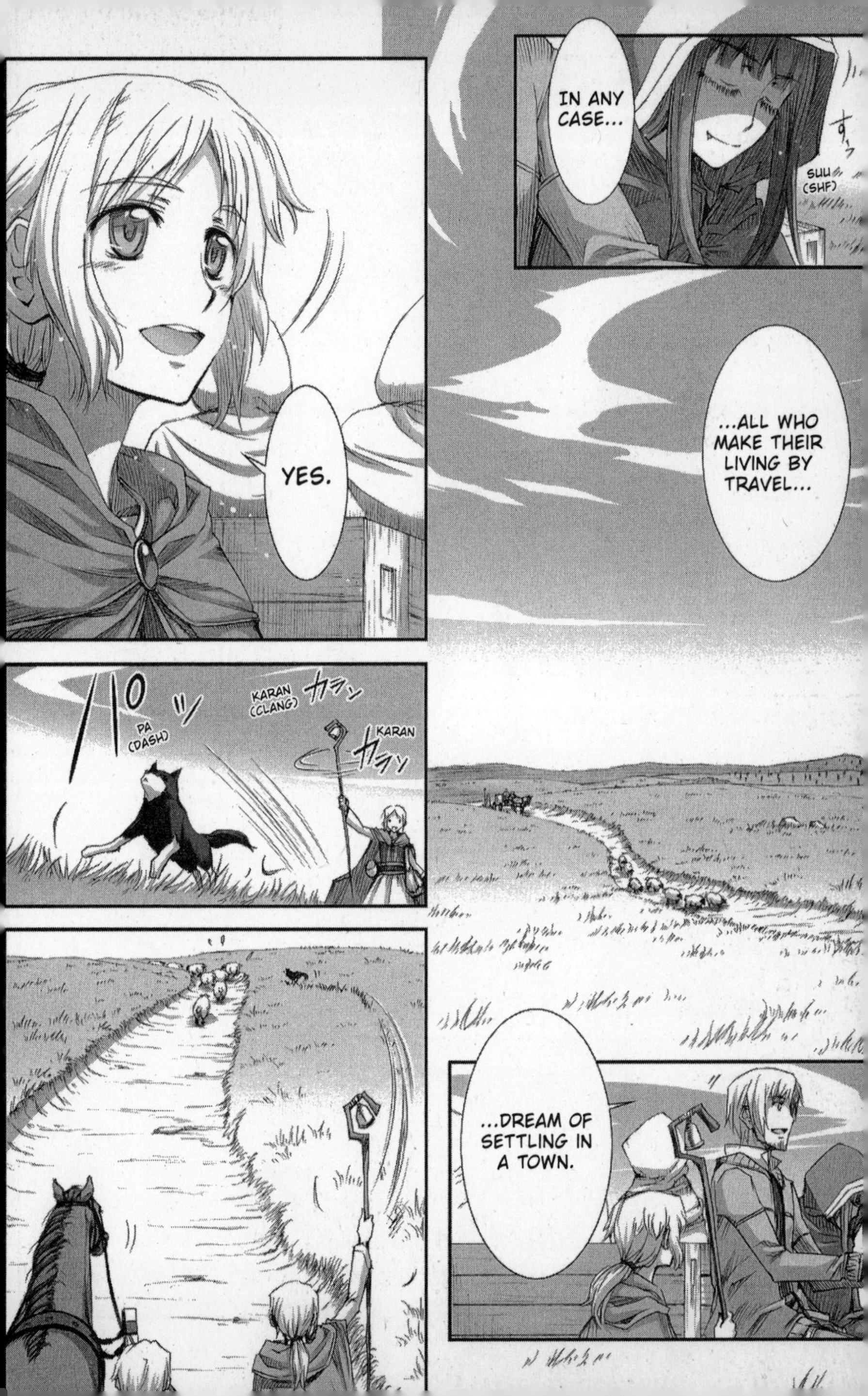
IN ANY CASE...
SUU (SHF)
YES.
...ALL WHO MAKE THEIR LIVING BY TRAVEL...
KARAN (CLANG)
PA (DASH)
KARAN
...DREAM OF SETTLING IN A TOWN.

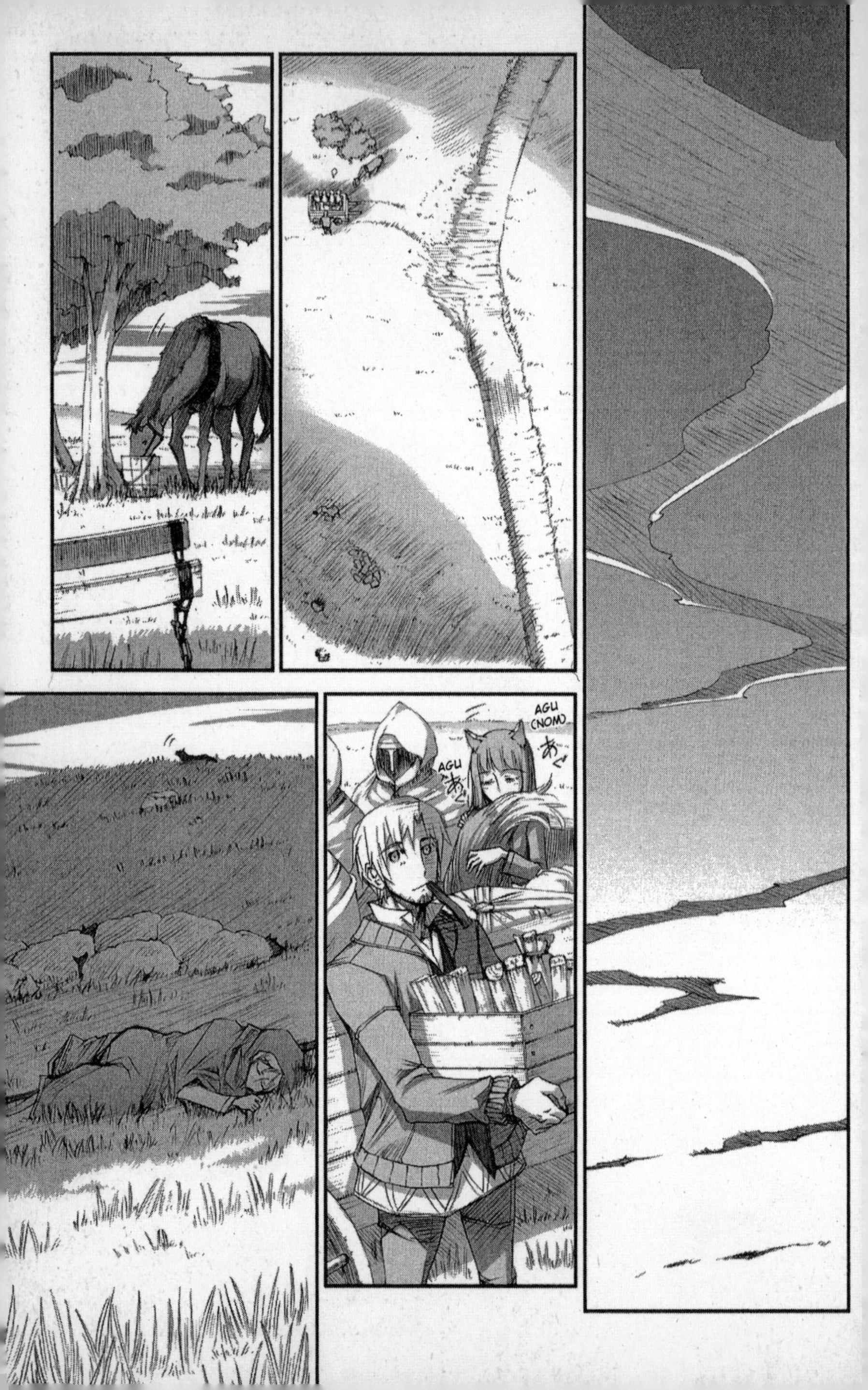
AGU (NOM)
あぐ
AGU
あぐ

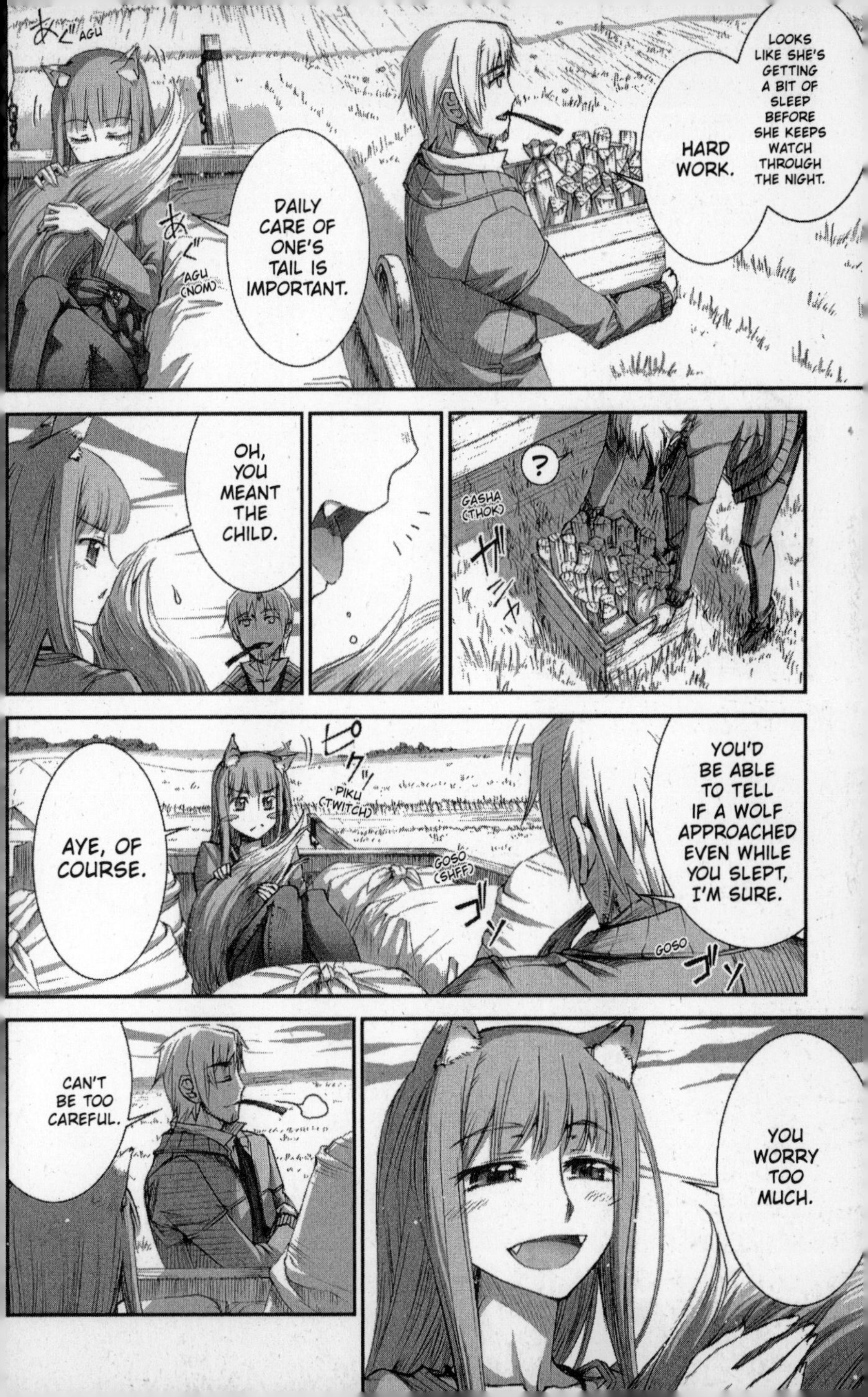

あぐ AGU
LOOKS LIKE SHE'S GETTING A BIT OF SLEEP BEFORE SHE KEEPS WATCH THROUGH THE NIGHT.
HARD WORK.
DAILY CARE OF ONE'S TAIL IS IMPORTANT.
あぐ AGU (NOM)
?
GASHA (THOK)
OH, YOU MEANT THE CHILD.
YOU'D BE ABLE TO TELL IF A WOLF APPROACHED EVEN WHILE YOU SLEPT, I'M SURE.
GOSO (SHFF)
GOSO
PIKU (TWITCH)
AYE, OF COURSE.
YOU WORRY TOO MUCH.
CAN'T BE TOO CAREFUL.

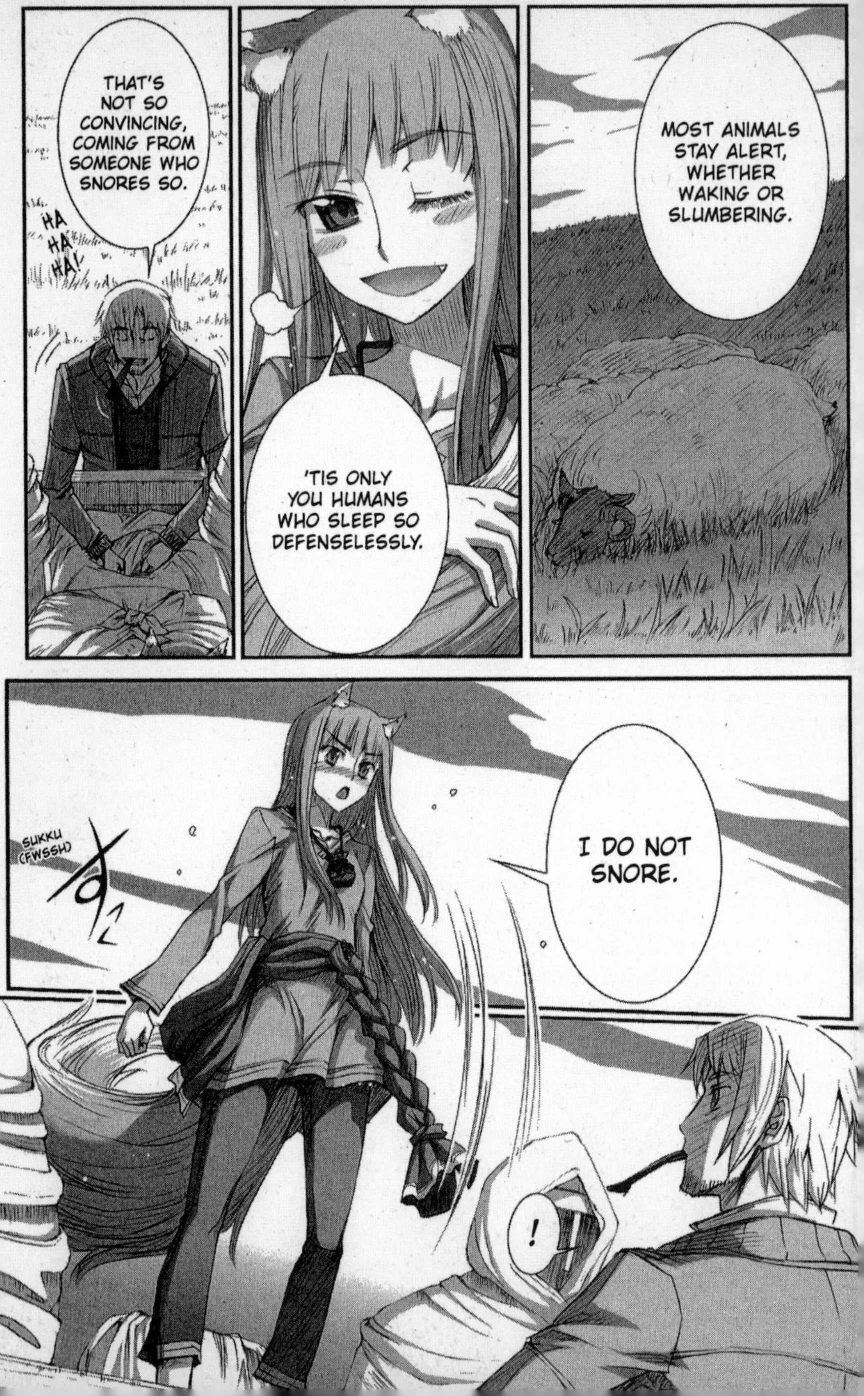
MOST ANIMALS STAY ALERT, WHETHER WAKING OR SLUMBERING.
'TIS ONLY YOU HUMANS WHO SLEEP SO DEFENSELESSLY.
THAT'S NOT SO CONVINCING, COMING FROM SOMEONE WHO SNORES SO.
HA HA HA!
I DO NOT SNORE.
SUKKU (FWSSH)
!

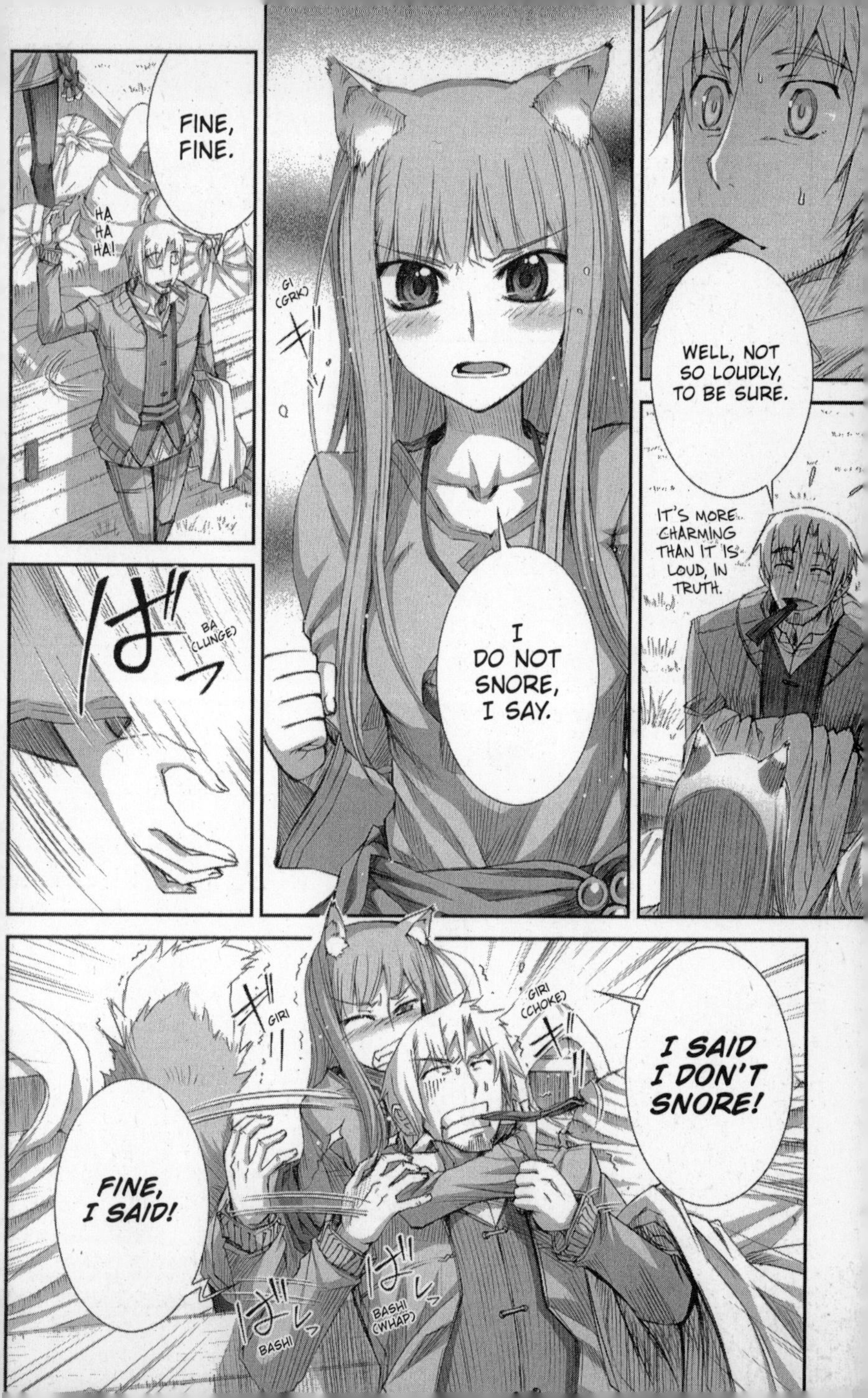
WELL, NOT SO LOUDLY, TO BE SURE.
IT'S MORE CHARMING THAN IT IS LOUD, IN TRUTH.
GI (GRK)
I DO NOT SNORE, I SAY.
FINE, FINE.
HA HA HA!
BA (LUNGE)
I SAID I DON'T SNORE!
GIRI (CHOKE)
GIRI
FINE, I SAID!
BASHI (WHAP)
BASHI

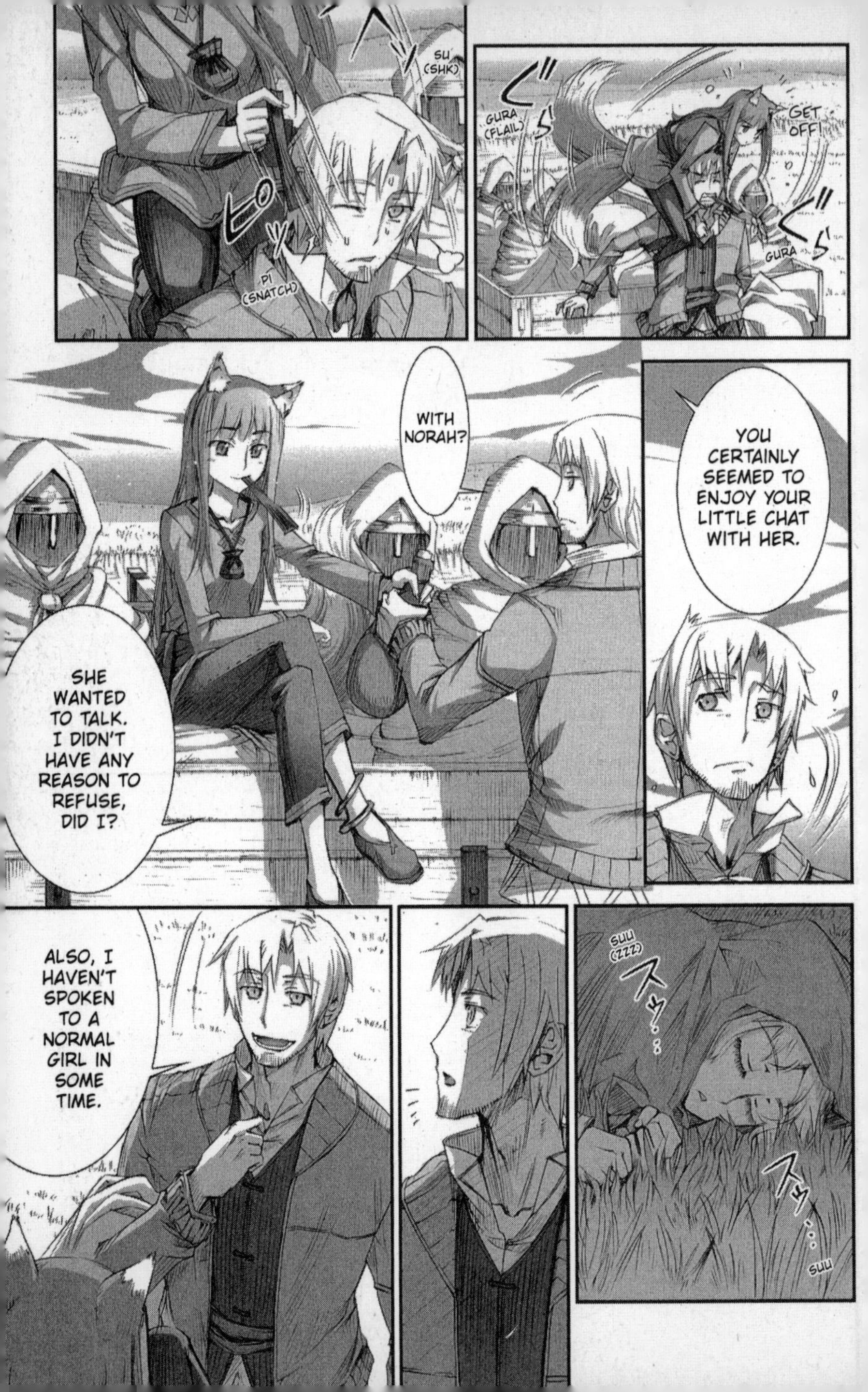
GURA (FLAIL)
GET OFF!
GURA
SU (SHK)
PI (SNATCH)
YOU CERTAINLY SEEMED TO ENJOY YOUR LITTLE CHAT WITH HER.
WITH NORAH?
SHE WANTED TO TALK. I DIDN'T HAVE ANY REASON TO REFUSE, DID I?
SUU (ZZZ)
SUU
ALSO, I HAVEN'T SPOKEN TO A NORMAL GIRL IN SOME TIME.

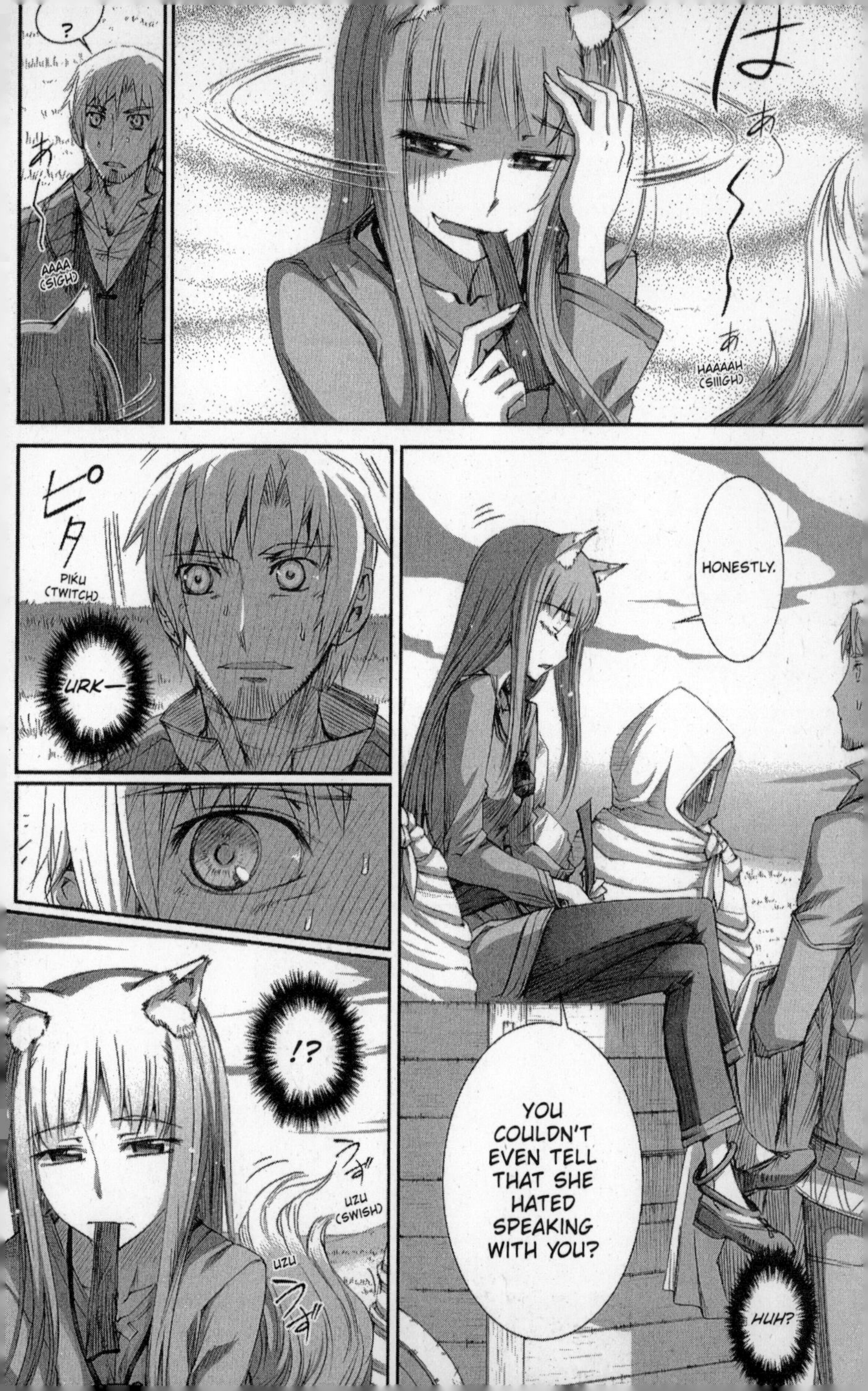

はあ〜〜あ
HAAAAH (SIIIGH)
?
あ〜
AAAA (SIGH)
HONESTLY.
YOU COULDN'T EVEN TELL THAT SHE HATED SPEAKING WITH YOU?
HUH?
ピク
PIKU (TWITCH)
URK—
!?
うず
UZU (SWISH)
うず
UZU

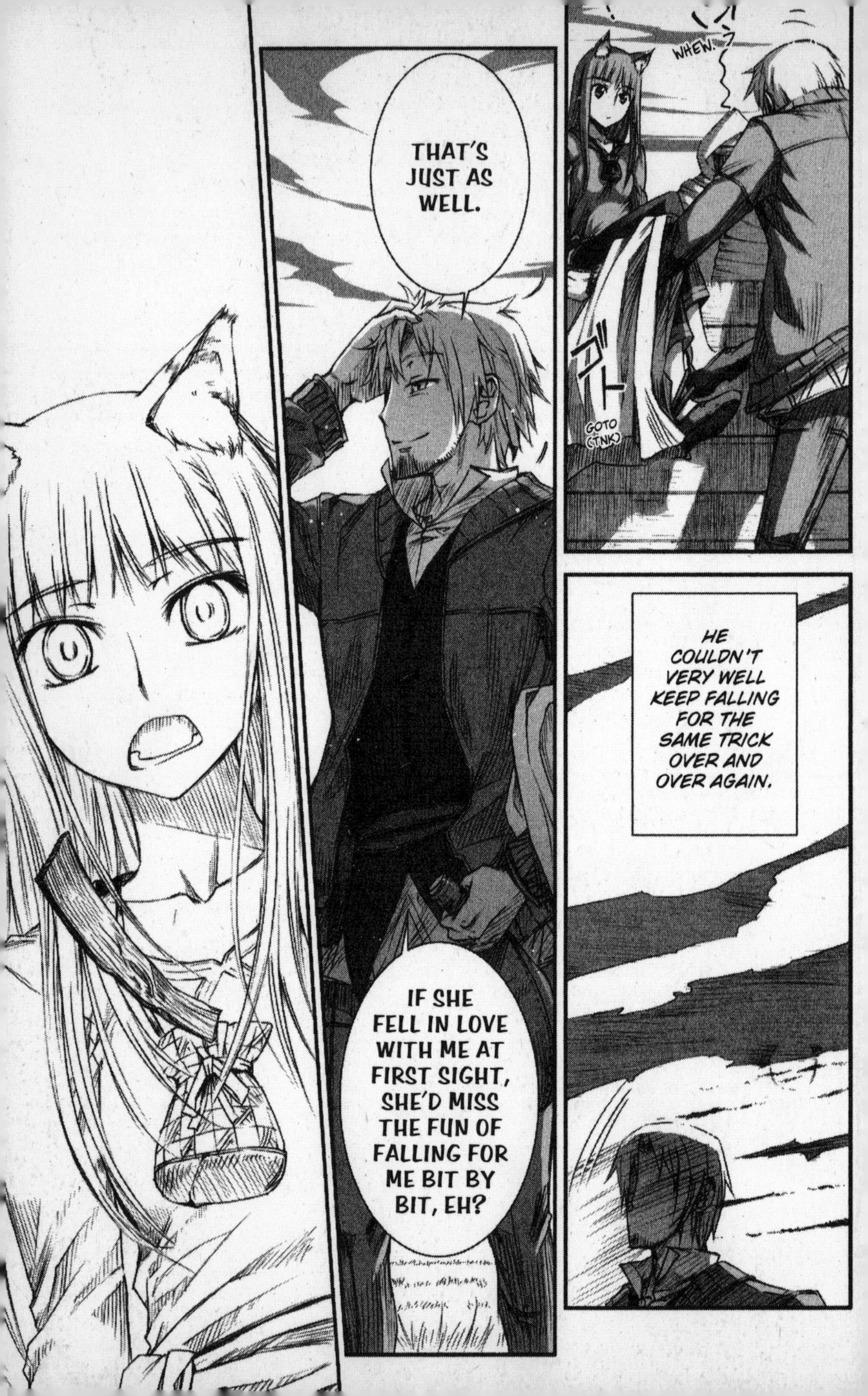
WHEW.
ゴト
GOTO (TNK)
HE COULDN'T VERY WELL KEEP FALLING FOR THE SAME TRICK OVER AND OVER AGAIN.
THAT'S JUST AS WELL.
IF SHE FELL IN LOVE WITH ME AT FIRST SIGHT, SHE'D MISS THE FUN OF FALLING FOR ME BIT BY BIT, EH?

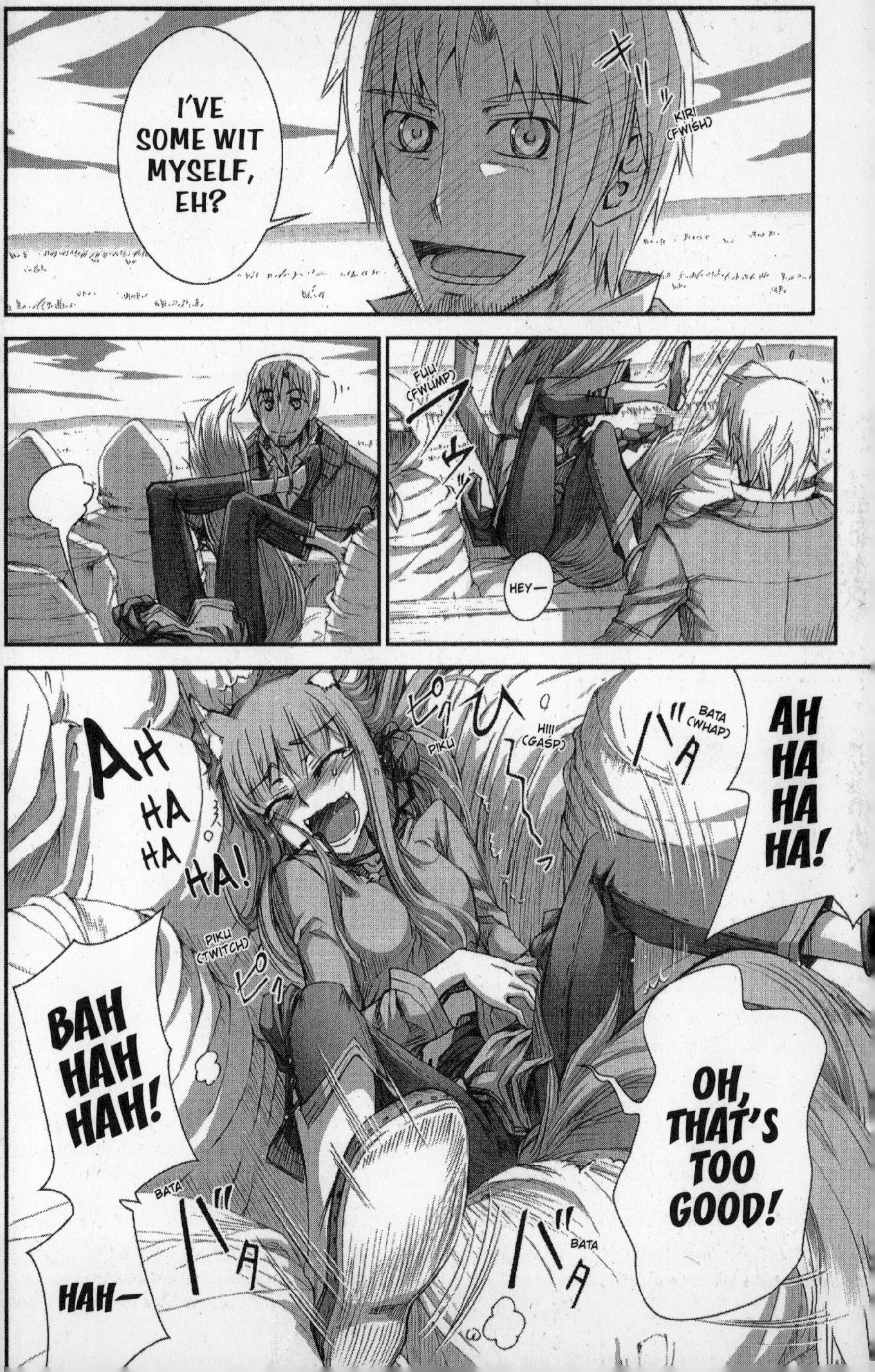
KIRI (FWISH)
I'VE SOME WIT MYSELF, EH?
FUU (FWUMP)
HEY—
AH HA HA HA HA!
BATA (WHAP)
HIII (GASP)
PIKU
AH HA HA HA!
PIKU (TWITCH)
OH, THAT'S TOO GOOD!
BATA
BAH HAH HAH!
BATA
HAH—

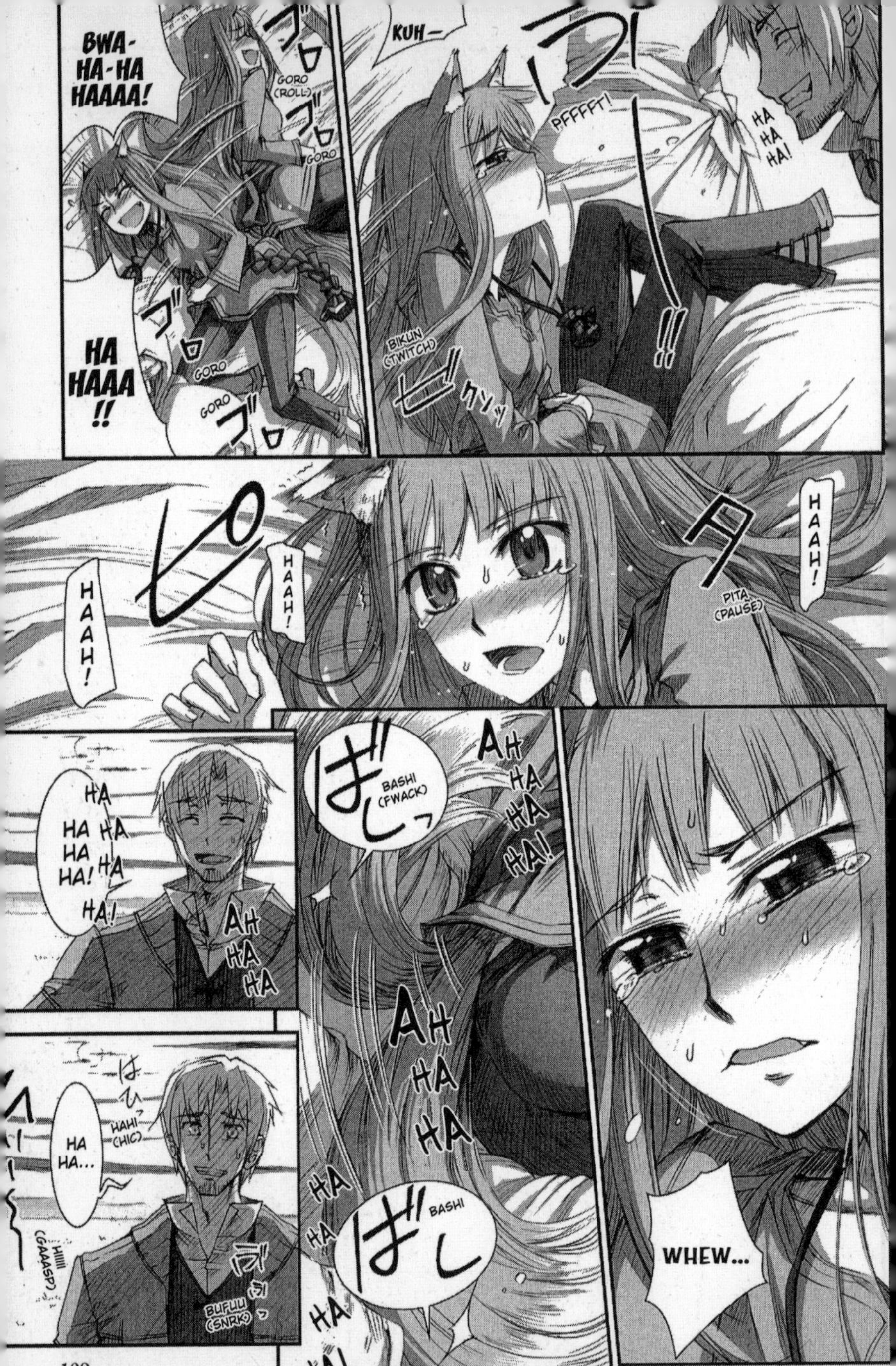
KUH—
PFFFFT!
HA HA HA!
!!
BIKUN (TWITCH)
BWA-HA-HA HAAAA!
GORO (ROLL)
GORO
HA HAAAA!!
GORO
GORO
HAAAH!
PITA (PAUSE)
HAAAH!
HAAAH!
WHEW...
BASHI (FWACK)
AH HA HA HA HA!
AH HA HA HA
HA HA HA HA!
BASHI
HA HA HA HA HA HA! HA HA!
AH HA HA HA
HAHI (HIC)
HA HA...
HIIIII (GAAASP)
BUFUU (SNRK)

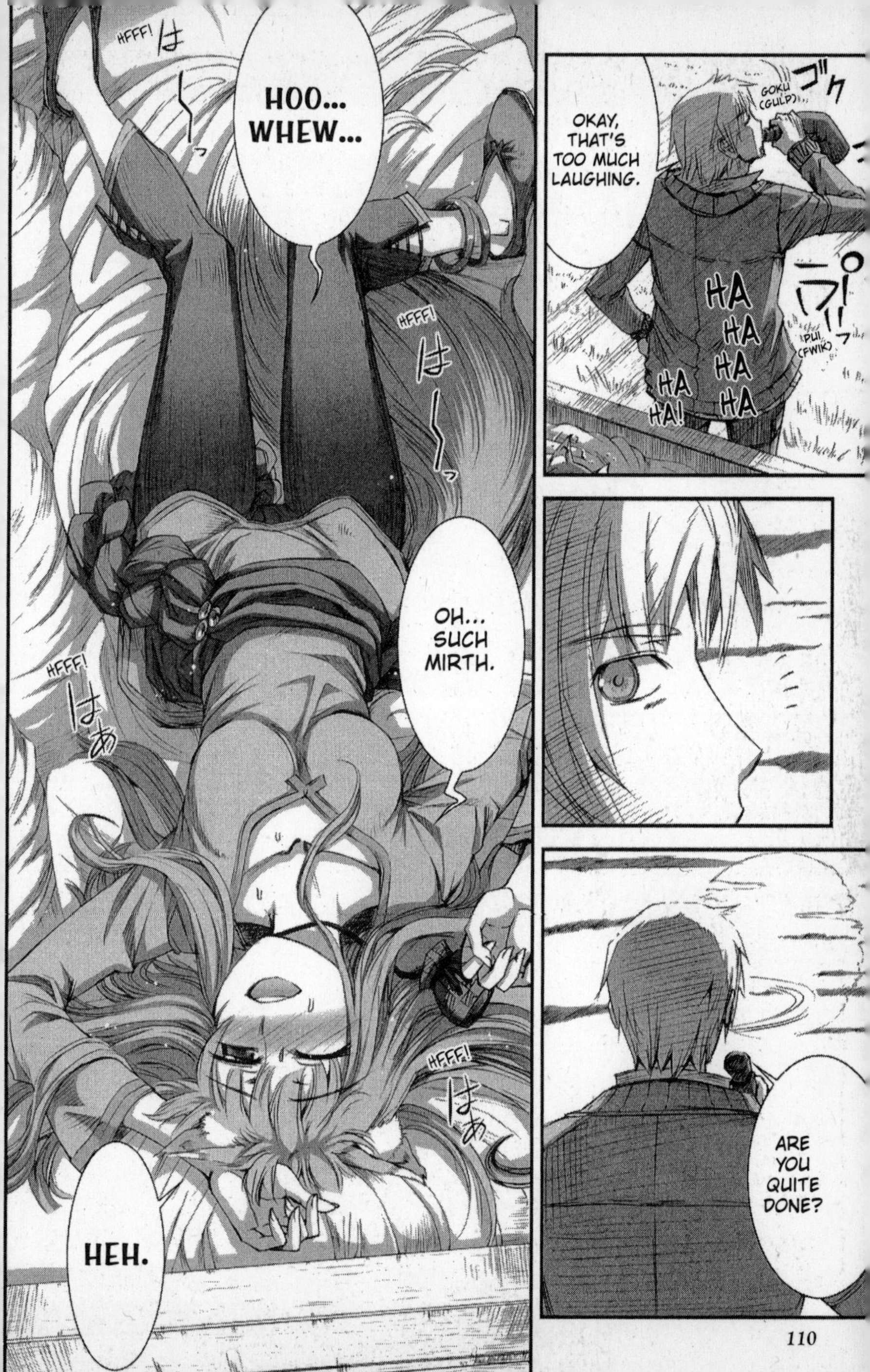
ゴク
GOKU (GULP)
OKAY, THAT'S TOO MUCH LAUGHING.
プイッ
PUI (FWIK)
HA HA HA HA HA
HA HA!
ARE YOU QUITE DONE?
HFFF! は〜っ
HOO... WHEW...
HFFF! は〜っ
OH... SUCH MIRTH.
HFFF! はあ
HFFF! はあ
HEH.

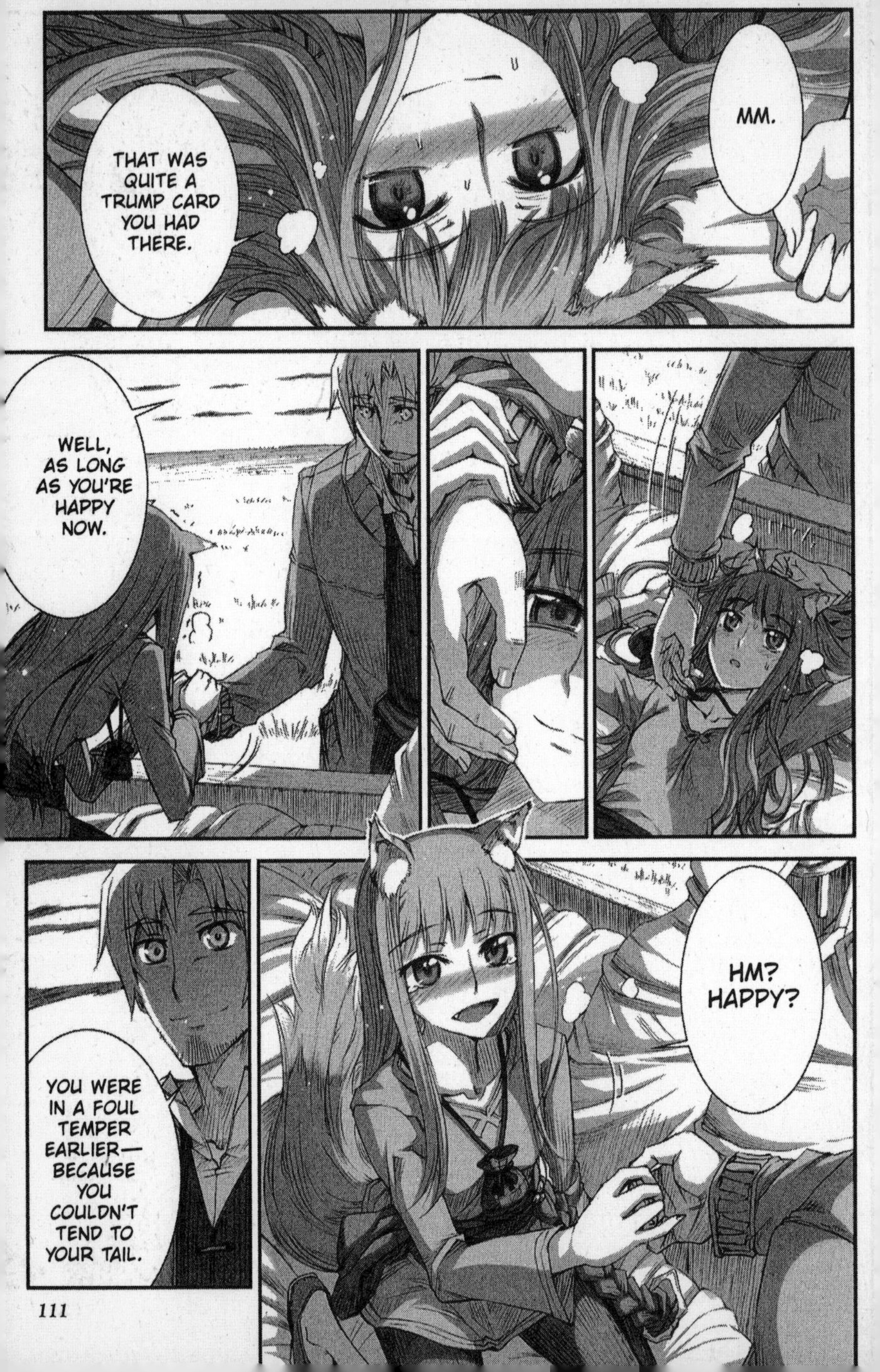
MM.
THAT WAS QUITE A TRUMP CARD YOU HAD THERE.
WELL, AS LONG AS YOU'RE HAPPY NOW.
HM? HAPPY?
YOU WERE IN A FOUL TEMPER EARLIER—BECAUSE YOU COULDN'T TEND TO YOUR TAIL.

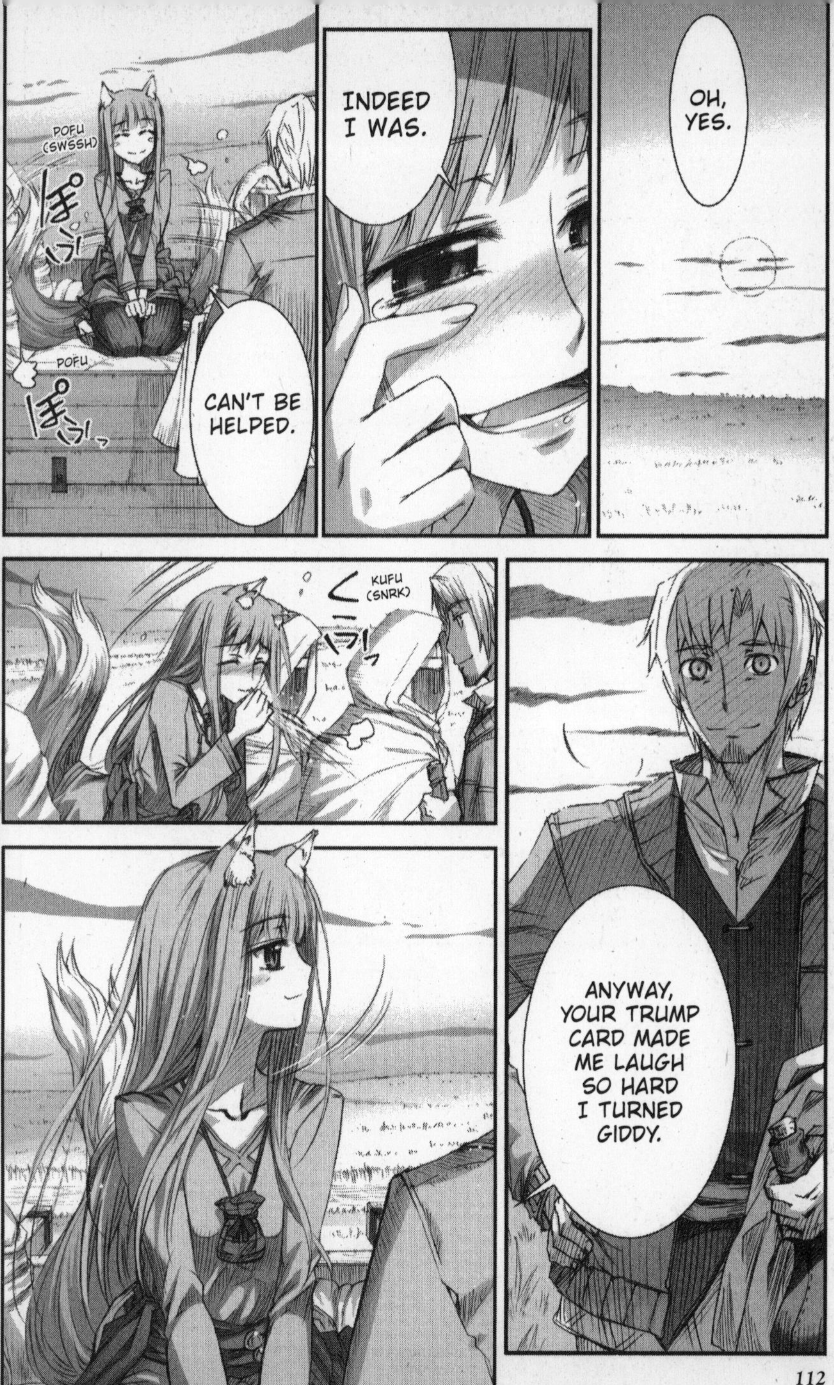

OH, YES.
INDEED I WAS.
POFU (SWSSH)
CAN'T BE HELPED.
POFU
ANYWAY, YOUR TRUMP CARD MADE ME LAUGH SO HARD I TURNED GIDDY.
KUFU (SNRK)

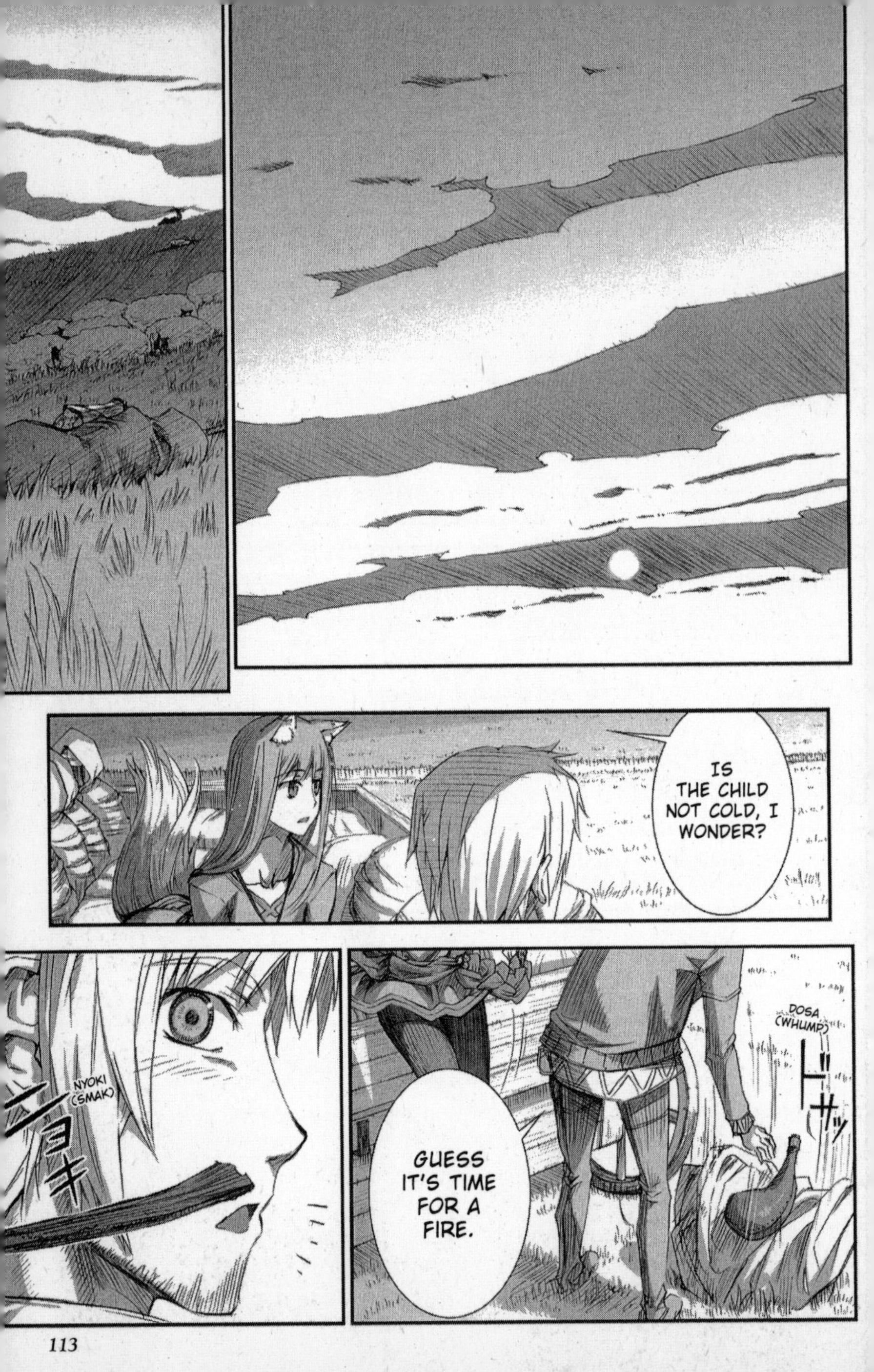
IS THE CHILD NOT COLD, I WONDER?
DOSA (WHUMP)
ドサッ
GUESS IT'S TIME FOR A FIRE.
NYOKI (SMAK)
ニョキ

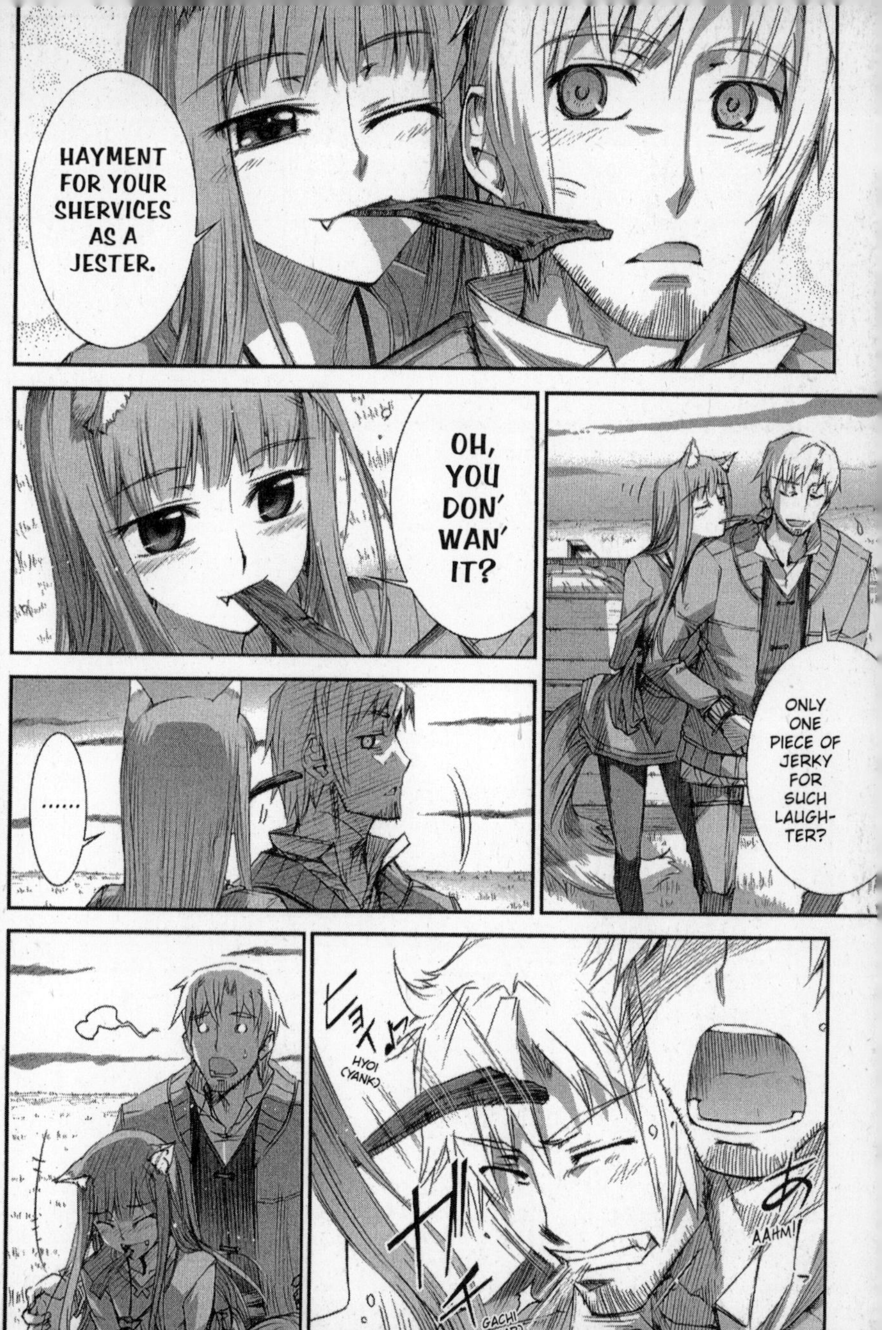
HAYMENT FOR YOUR SHERVICES AS A JESTER.
ONLY ONE PIECE OF JERKY FOR SUCH LAUGHTER?
OH, YOU DON' WAN' IT?
......
HYOI (YANK)
AAHM!
GACHI (SNAP)

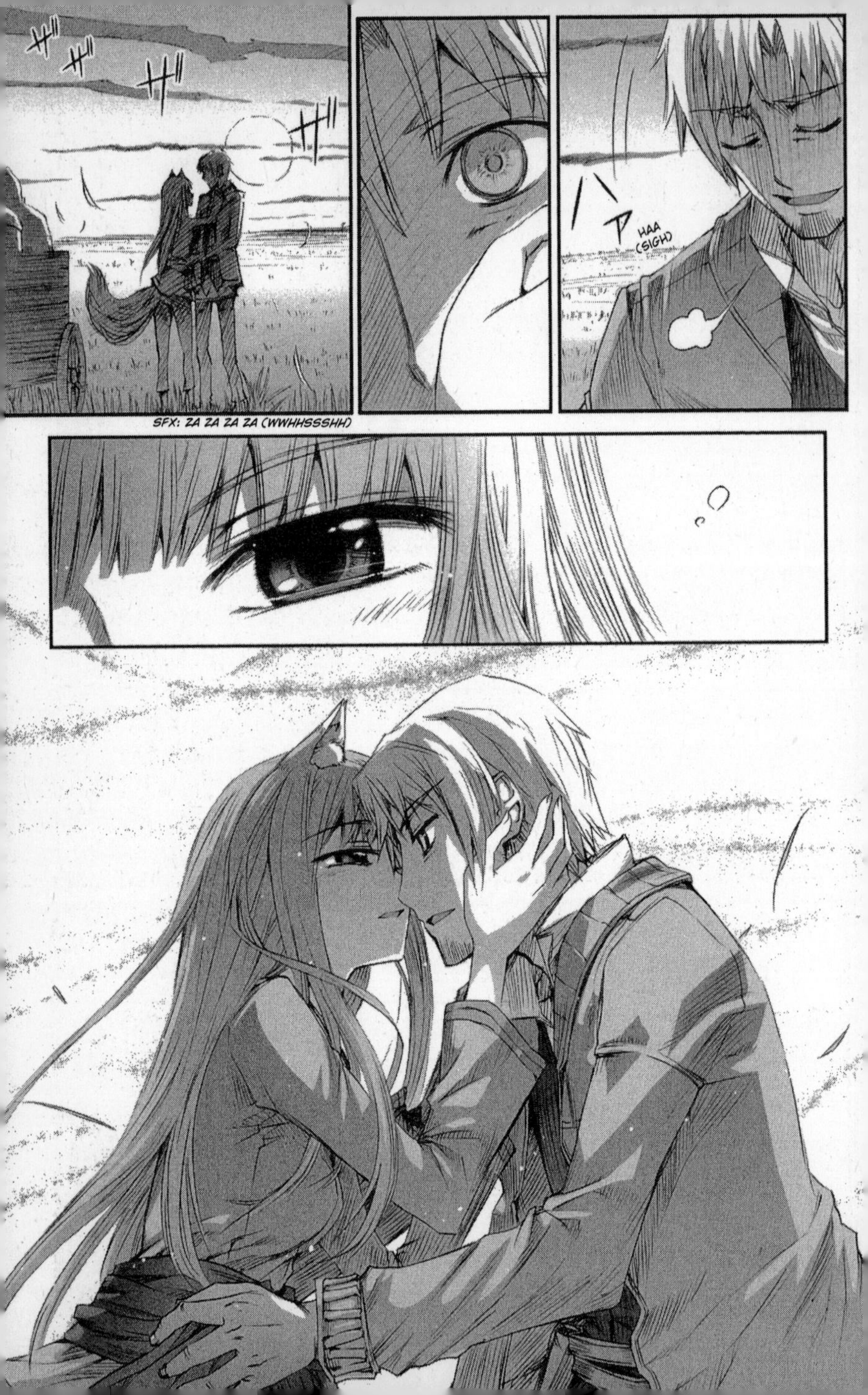
HAA
(SIGH)
SFX: ZA ZA ZA ZA (WWHHSSSHH)

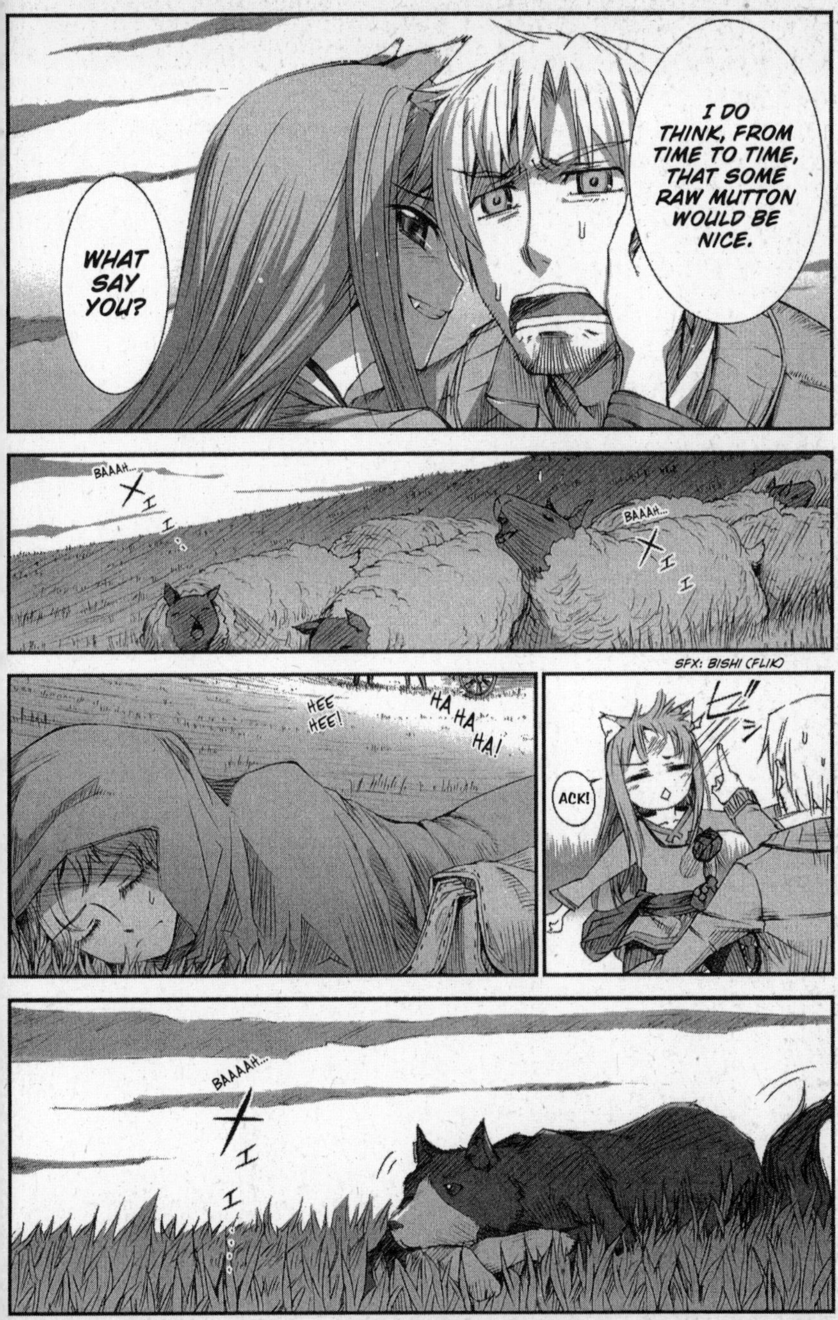
I DO THINK, FROM TIME TO TIME, THAT SOME RAW MUTTON WOULD BE NICE.
WHAT SAY YOU?
BAAAH...
BAAAH...
SFX: BISHI (FLIK)
ACK!
HA HA HA!
HEE HEE!
BAAAAH...

SPICE & WOLF

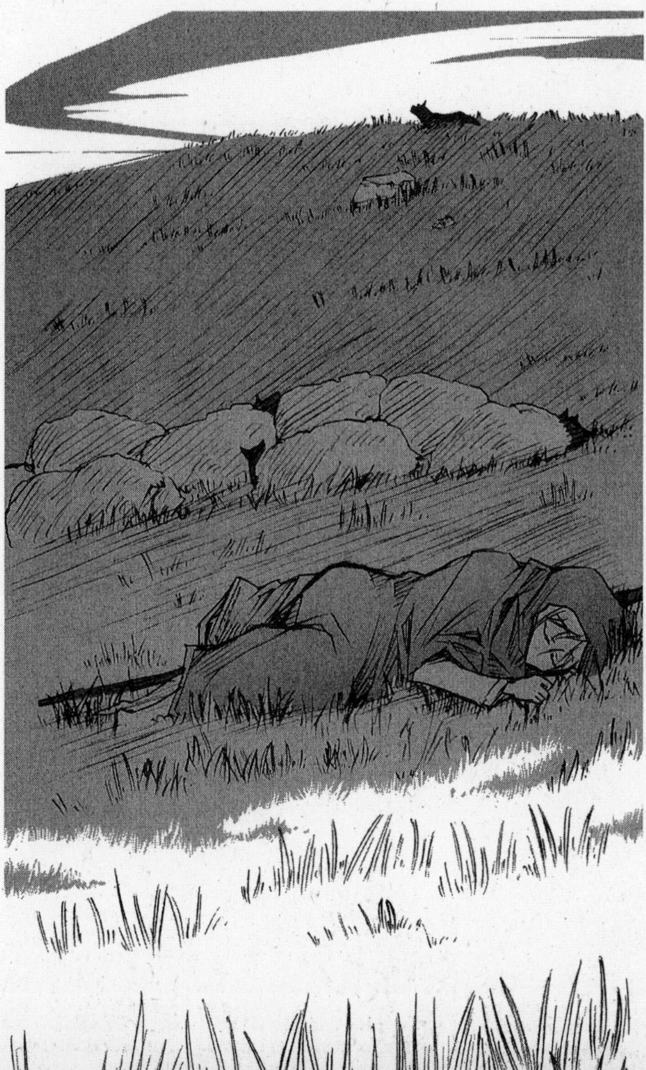

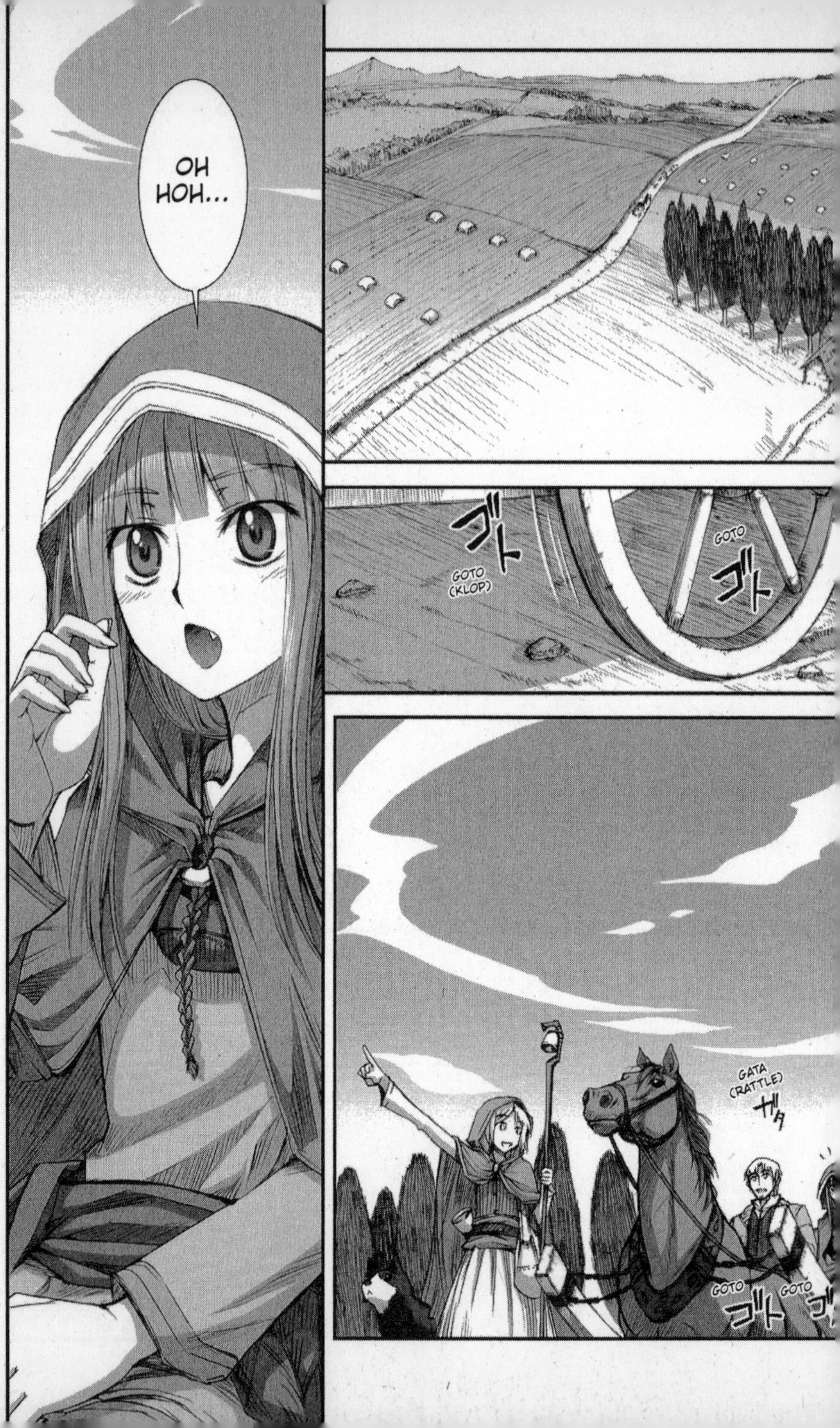
GOTO
ゴト
GOTO
(KLOP)
ゴト
GATA
(RATTLE)
ガタ
GOTO
ゴト
GOTO
ゴト
OH HOH...

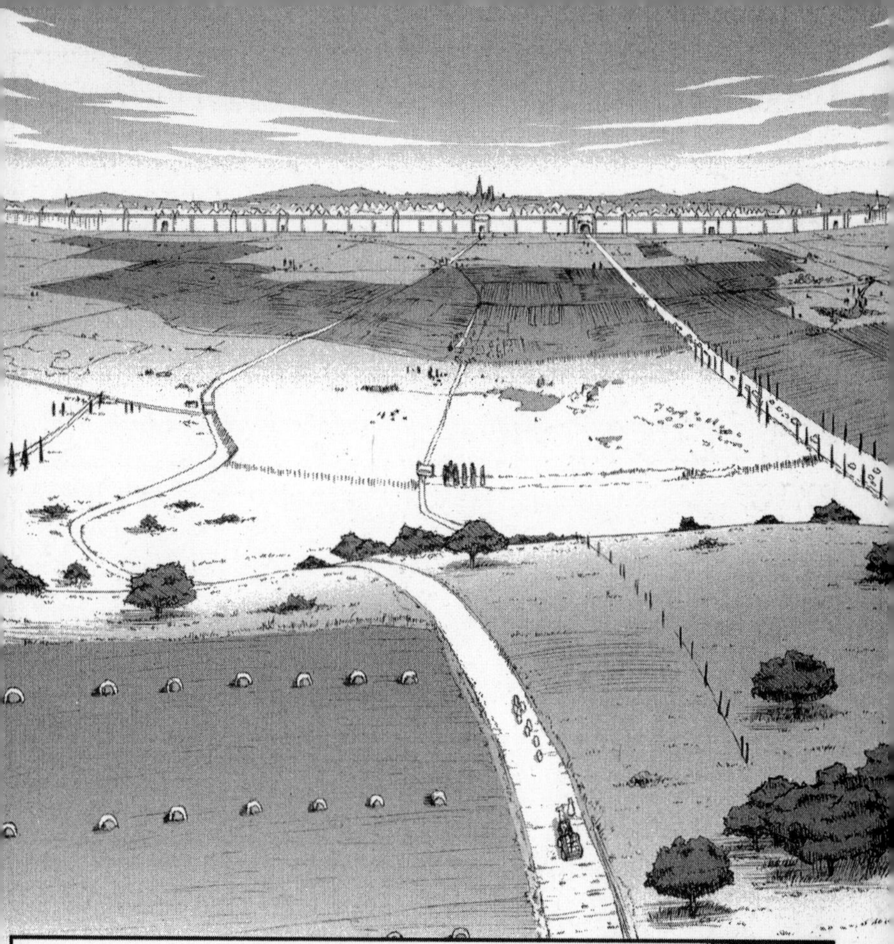

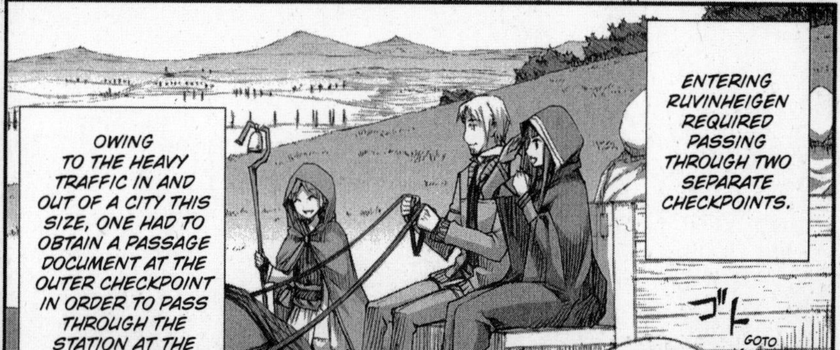
ENTERING RUVINHEIGEN REQUIRED PASSING THROUGH TWO SEPARATE CHECKPOINTS.
OWING TO THE HEAVY TRAFFIC IN AND OUT OF A CITY THIS SIZE, ONE HAD TO OBTAIN A PASSAGE DOCUMENT AT THE OUTER CHECKPOINT IN ORDER TO PASS THROUGH THE STATION AT THE CITY WALLS.
ゴト
GOTO (KLOP)
ゴト
GOTO

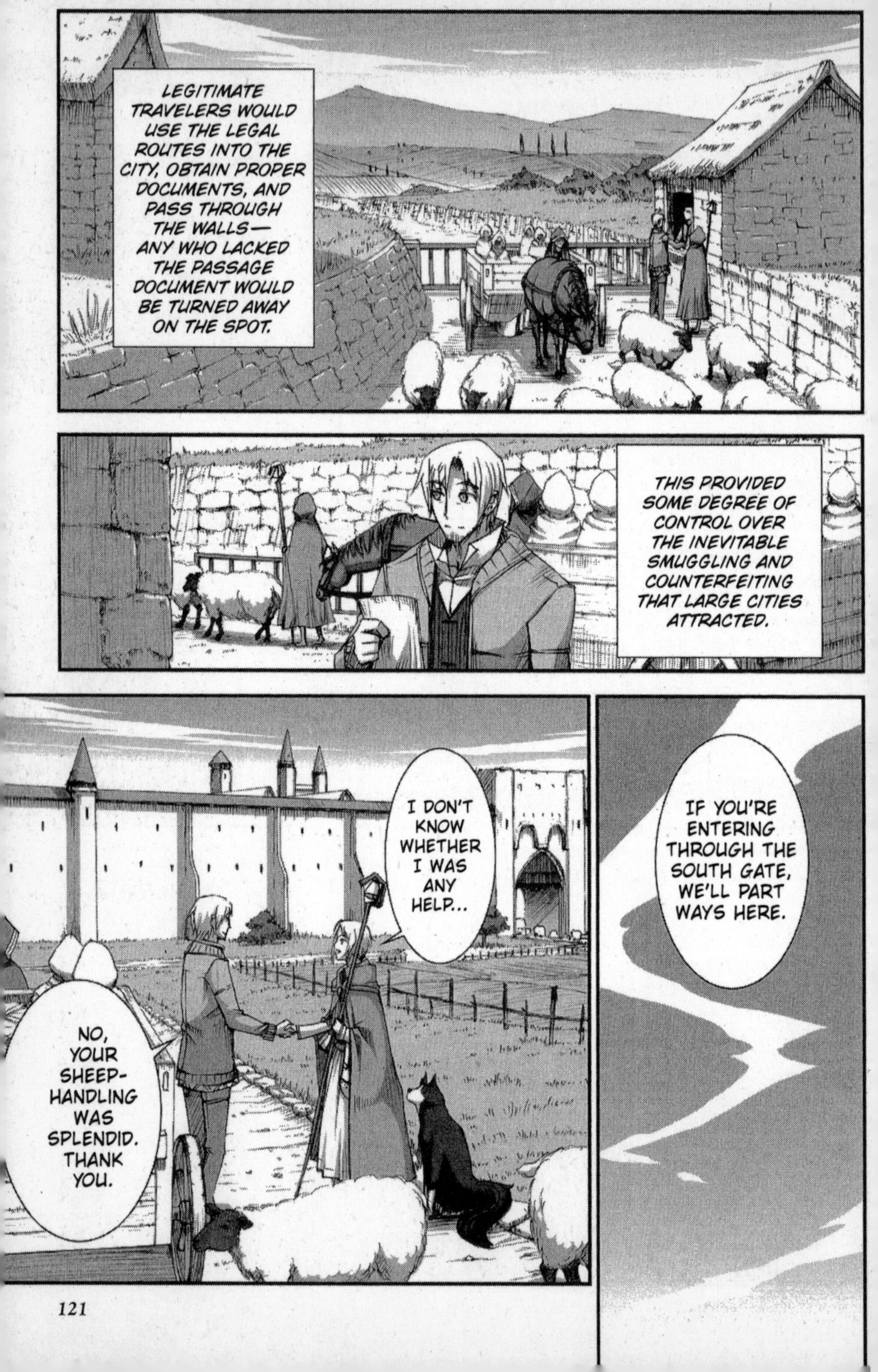
LEGITIMATE TRAVELERS WOULD USE THE LEGAL ROUTES INTO THE CITY, OBTAIN PROPER DOCUMENTS, AND PASS THROUGH THE WALLS—ANY WHO LACKED THE PASSAGE DOCUMENT WOULD BE TURNED AWAY ON THE SPOT.
THIS PROVIDED SOME DEGREE OF CONTROL OVER THE INEVITABLE SMUGGLING AND COUNTERFEITING THAT LARGE CITIES ATTRACTED.
IF YOU'RE ENTERING THROUGH THE SOUTH GATE, WE'LL PART WAYS HERE.
I DON'T KNOW WHETHER I WAS ANY HELP...
NO, YOUR SHEEP-HANDLING WAS SPLENDID. THANK YOU.

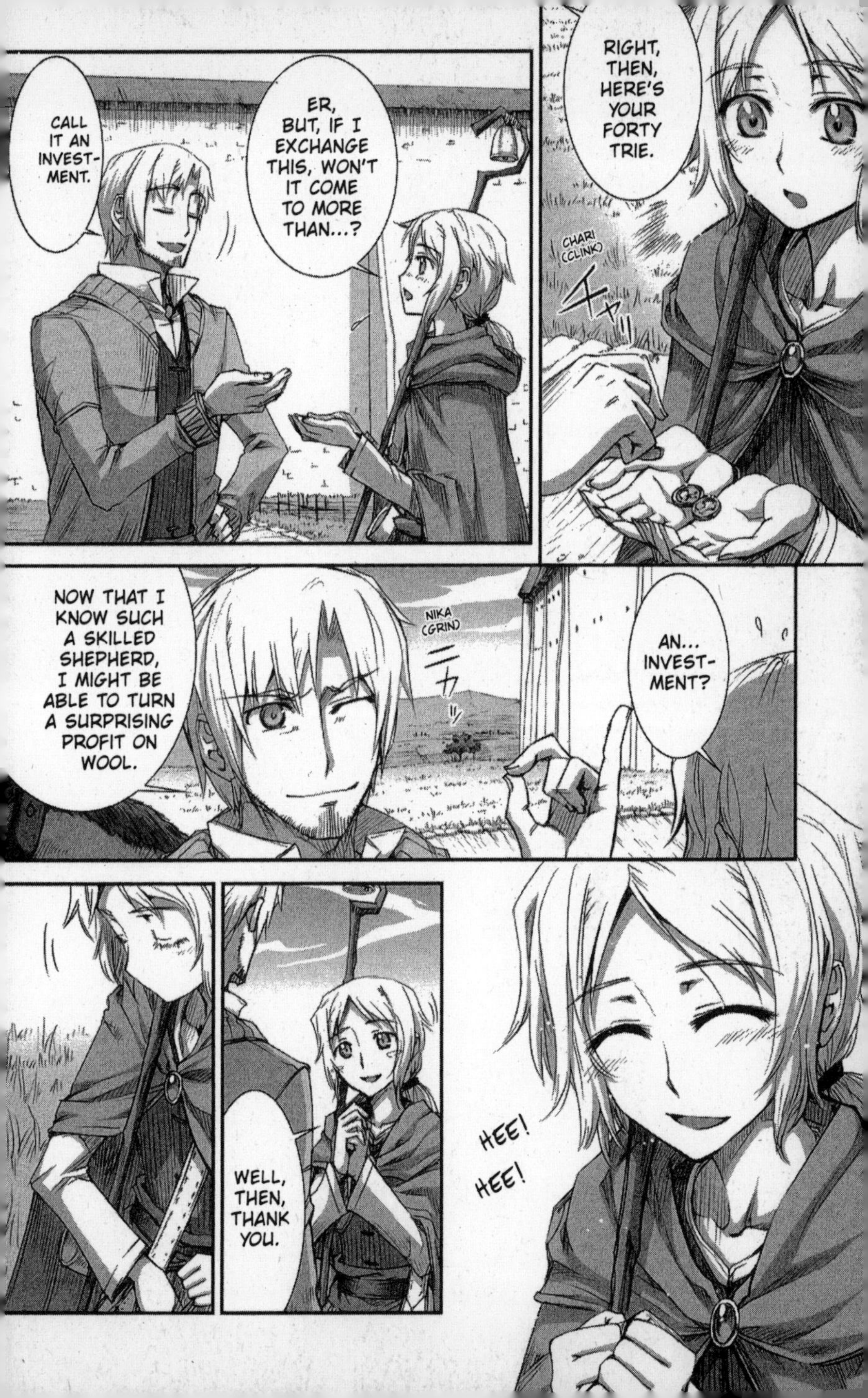

RIGHT, THEN, HERE'S YOUR FORTY TRIE.
CHARI (CLINK)
ER, BUT, IF I EXCHANGE THIS, WON'T IT COME TO MORE THAN...?
CALL IT AN INVESTMENT.
AN... INVESTMENT?
NIKA (GRIN)
NOW THAT I KNOW SUCH A SKILLED SHEPHERD, I MIGHT BE ABLE TO TURN A SURPRISING PROFIT ON WOOL.
HEE! HEE!
WELL, THEN, THANK YOU.

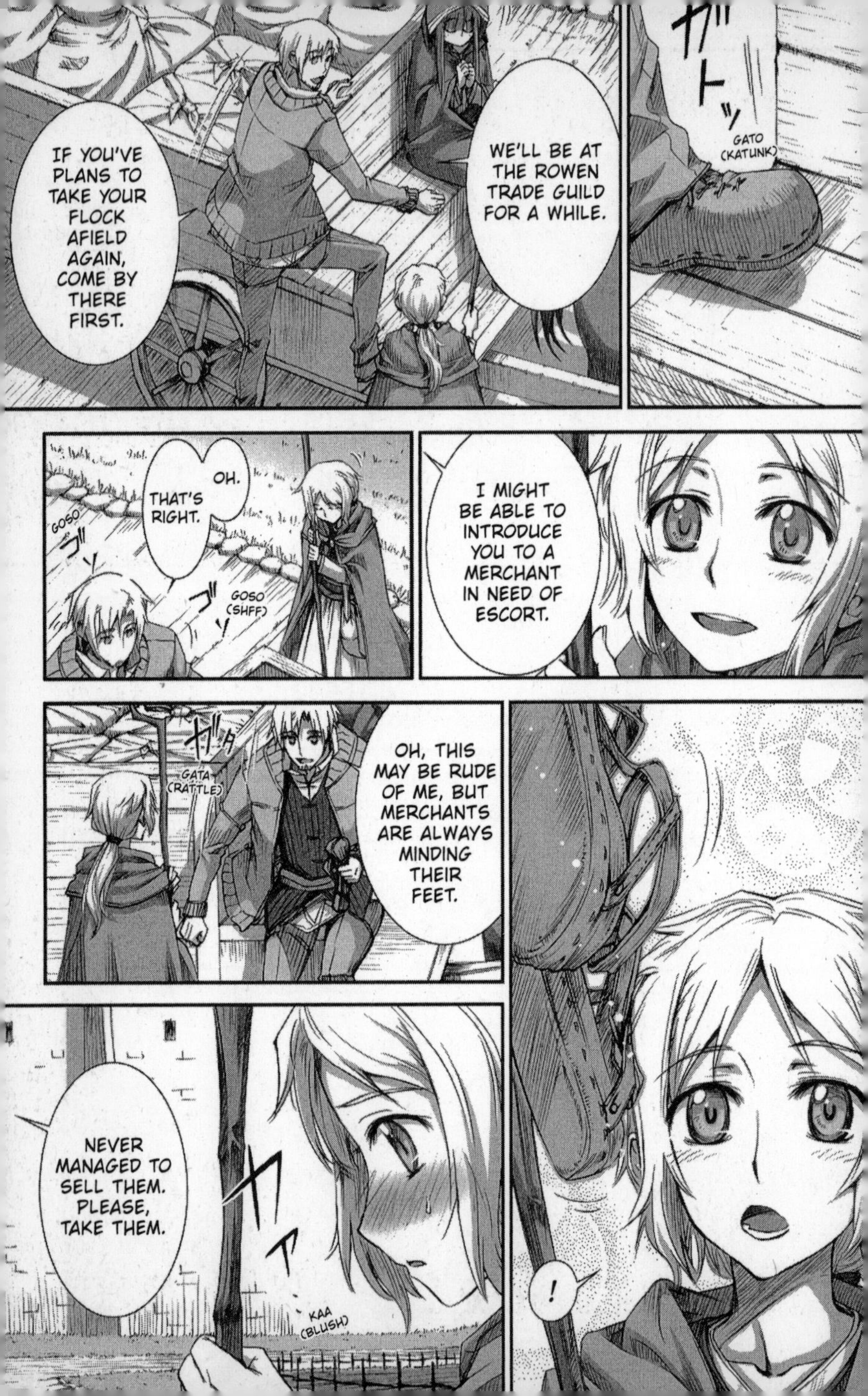
GATO
(KATUNK)
WE'LL BE AT THE ROWEN TRADE GUILD FOR A WHILE.
IF YOU'VE PLANS TO TAKE YOUR FLOCK AFIELD AGAIN, COME BY THERE FIRST.
I MIGHT BE ABLE TO INTRODUCE YOU TO A MERCHANT IN NEED OF ESCORT.
OH. THAT'S RIGHT.
GOSO
GOSO
(SHFF)
!
OH, THIS MAY BE RUDE OF ME, BUT MERCHANTS ARE ALWAYS MINDING THEIR FEET.
GATA
(RATTLE)
NEVER MANAGED TO SELL THEM. PLEASE, TAKE THEM.
KAA
(BLUSH)

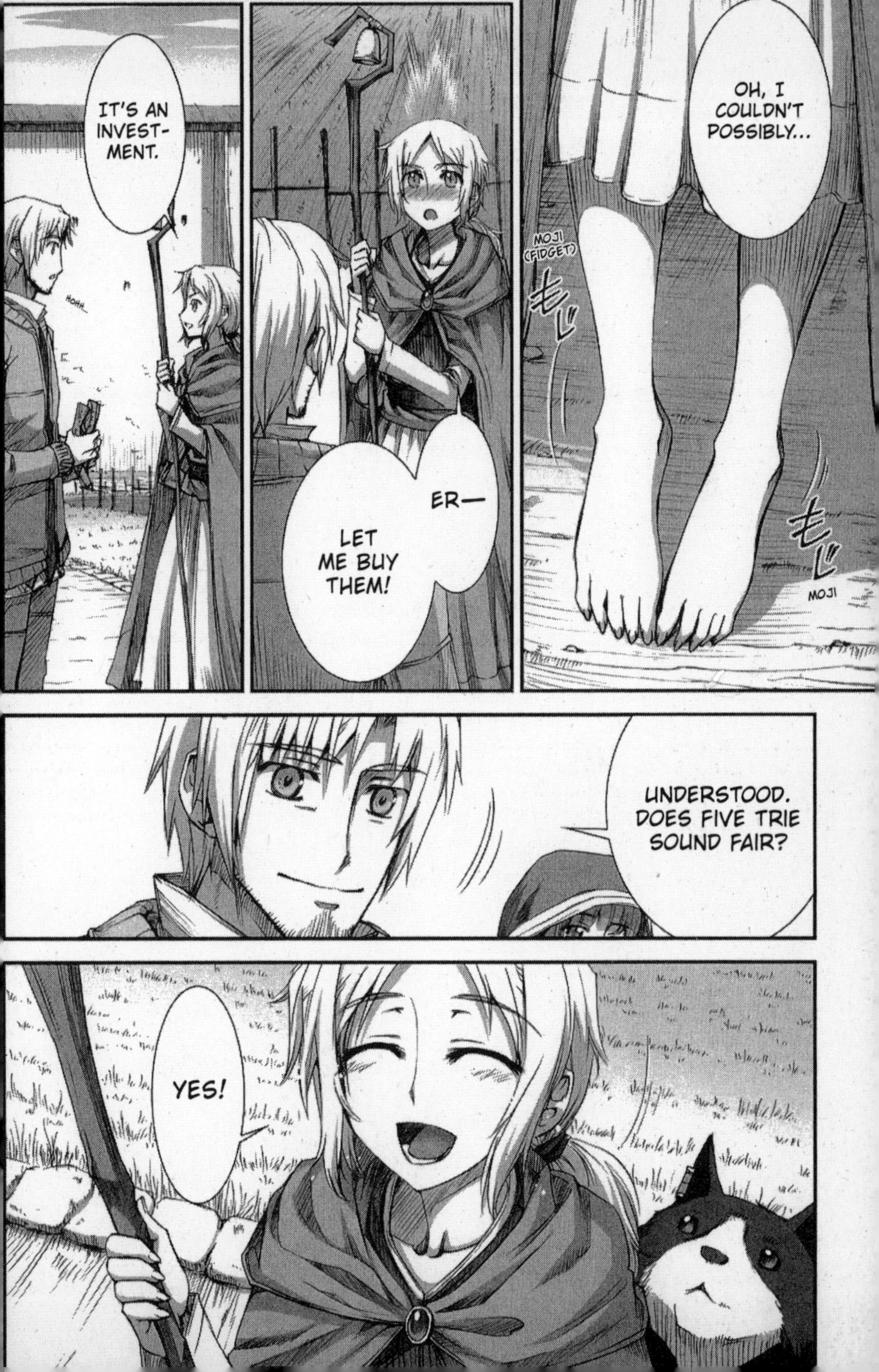
OH, I COULDN'T POSSIBLY...
MOJI (FIDGET)
モジ
モジ
MOJI
ER—
LET ME BUY THEM!
IT'S AN INVEST-MENT.
UNDERSTOOD. DOES FIVE TRIE SOUND FAIR?
YES!

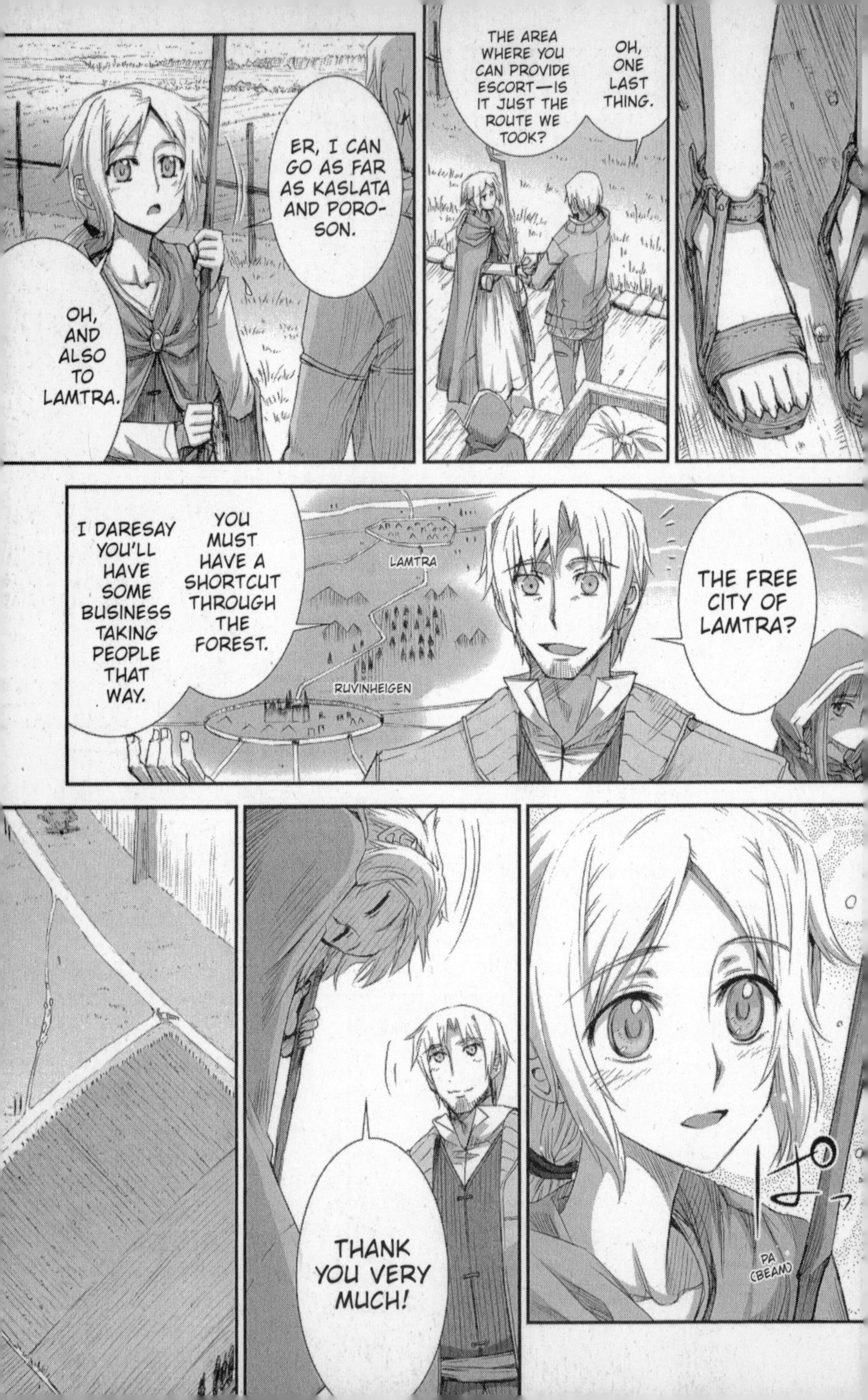

OH, ONE LAST THING.
THE AREA WHERE YOU CAN PROVIDE ESCORT—IS IT JUST THE ROUTE WE TOOK?
ER, I CAN GO AS FAR AS KASLATA AND POROSON.
OH, AND ALSO TO LAMTRA.
THE FREE CITY OF LAMTRA?
LAMTRA
RUVINHEIGEN
YOU MUST HAVE A SHORTCUT THROUGH THE FOREST.
I DARESAY YOU'LL HAVE SOME BUSINESS TAKING PEOPLE THAT WAY.
PA (BEAM)
THANK YOU VERY MUCH!

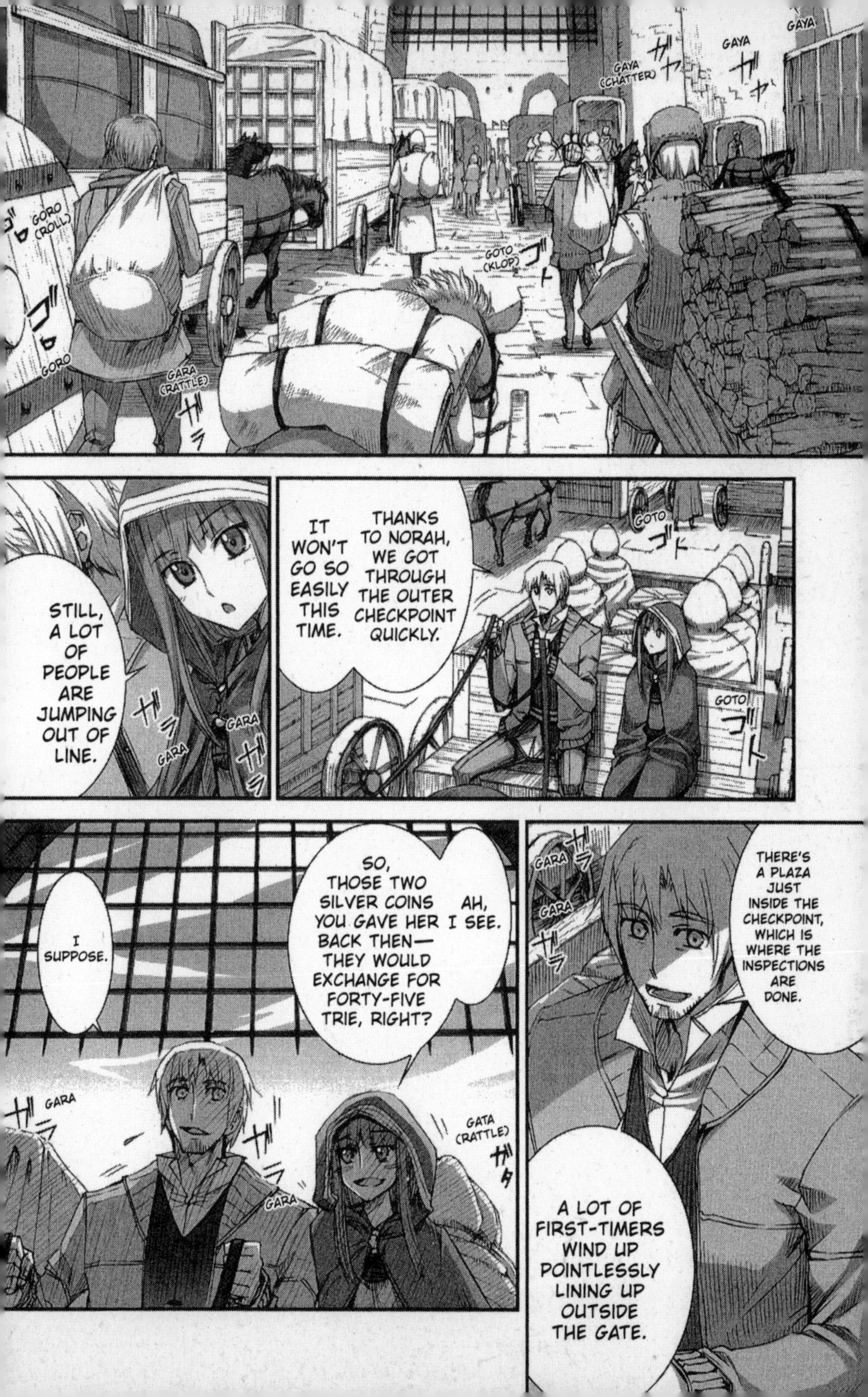
GAYA
GAYA
GAYA (CHATTER)
GOTO (KLOP)
GORO (ROLL)
GORO
GARA (RATTLE)
THANKS TO NORAH, WE GOT THROUGH THE OUTER CHECKPOINT QUICKLY.
IT WON'T GO SO EASILY THIS TIME.
GOTO
GOTO
STILL, A LOT OF PEOPLE ARE JUMPING OUT OF LINE.
GARA
GARA
THERE'S A PLAZA JUST INSIDE THE CHECKPOINT, WHICH IS WHERE THE INSPECTIONS ARE DONE.
GARA
GARA
A LOT OF FIRST-TIMERS WIND UP POINTLESSLY LINING UP OUTSIDE THE GATE.
AH, I SEE.
SO, THOSE TWO SILVER COINS YOU GAVE HER BACK THEN—THEY WOULD EXCHANGE FOR FORTY-FIVE TRIE, RIGHT?
I SUPPOSE.
GATA (RATTLE)
GARA
GARA

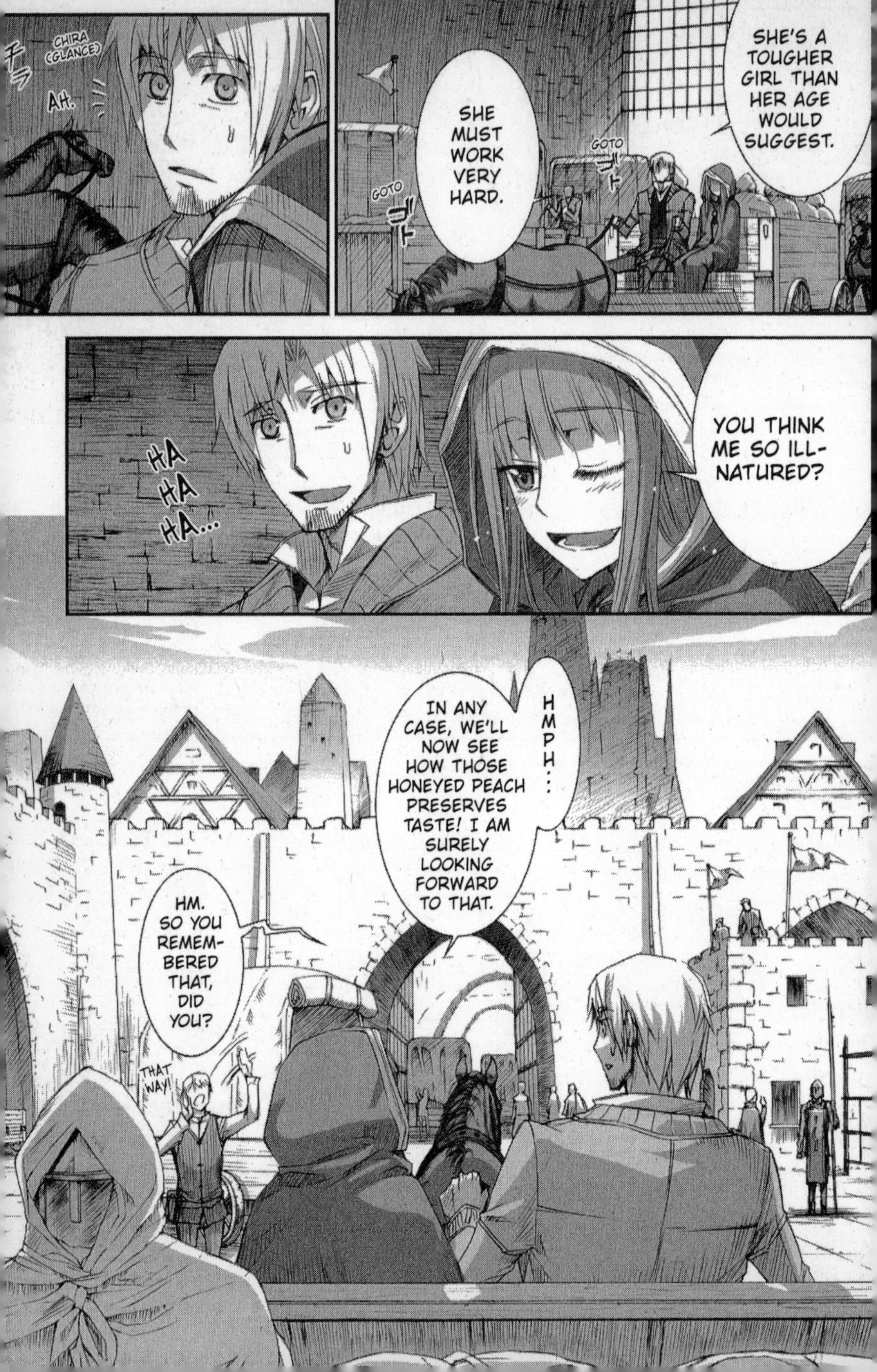

SHE'S A TOUGHER GIRL THAN HER AGE WOULD SUGGEST.
GOTO
SHE MUST WORK VERY HARD.
GOTO
CHIRA (GLANCE)
AH.
YOU THINK ME SO ILL-NATURED?
HA HA HA...
HMPH...
IN ANY CASE, WE'LL NOW SEE HOW THOSE HONEYED PEACH PRESERVES TASTE! I AM SURELY LOOKING FORWARD TO THAT.
HM. SO YOU REMEMBERED THAT, DID YOU?
THAT WAY!

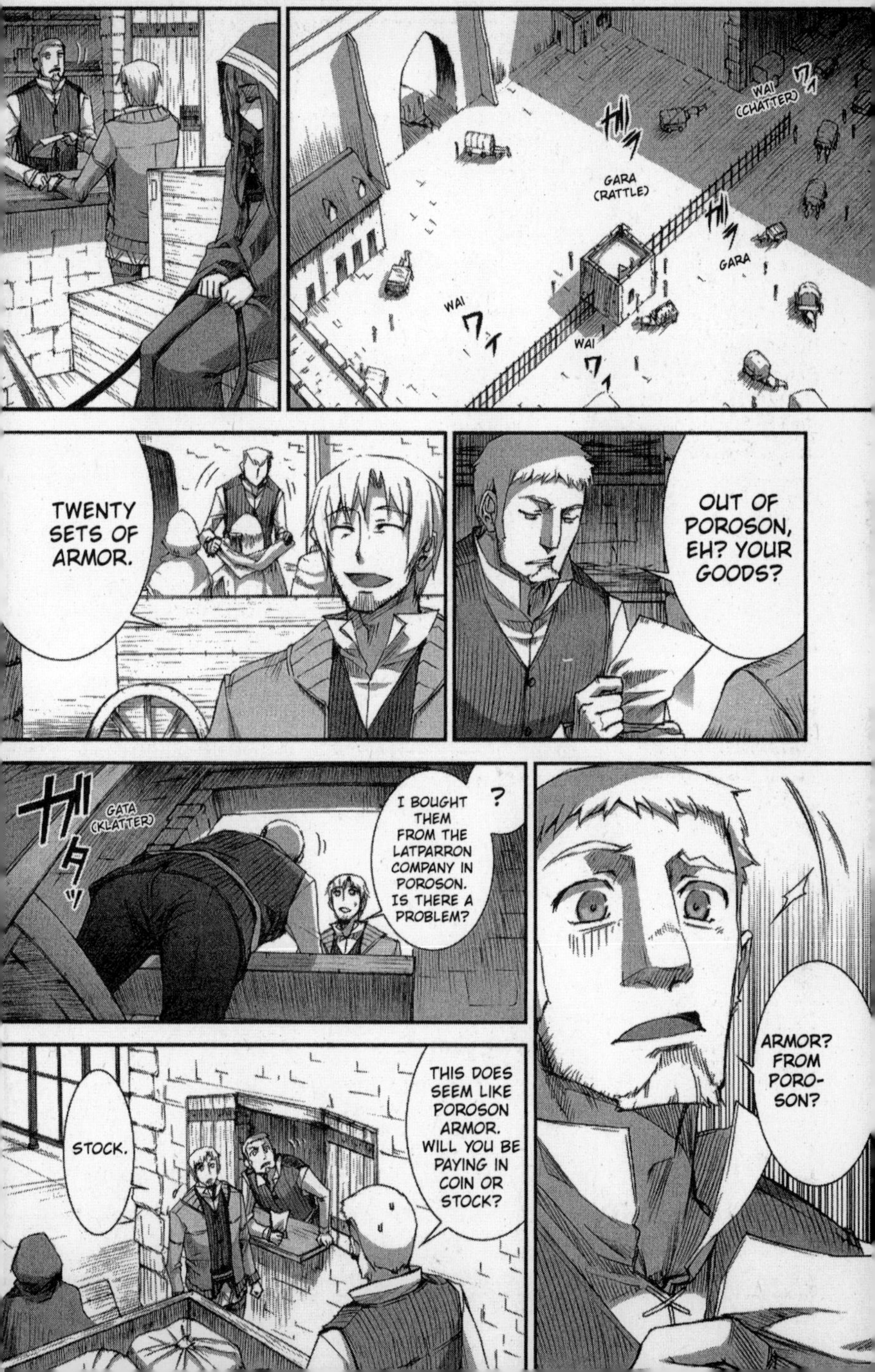

ワイ
WAI (CHATTER)
ガラ
GARA (RATTLE)
ガラ
GARA
WAI
ワイ
WAI
ワイ
OUT OF POROSON, EH? YOUR GOODS?
TWENTY SETS OF ARMOR.
ARMOR? FROM PORO-SON?
?
I BOUGHT THEM FROM THE LATPARRON COMPANY IN POROSON. IS THERE A PROBLEM?
ガタッ
GATA (KLATTER)
THIS DOES SEEM LIKE POROSON ARMOR. WILL YOU BE PAYING IN COIN OR STOCK?
STOCK.

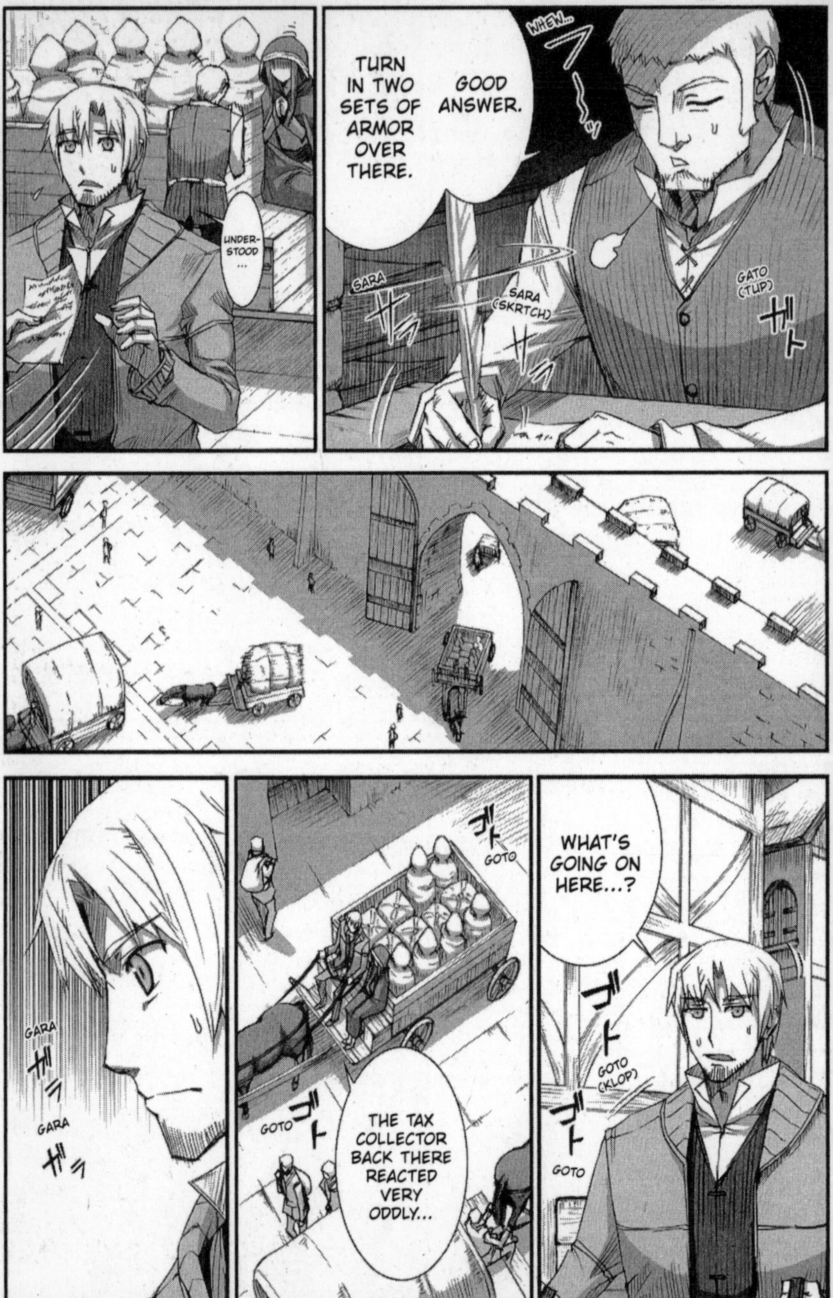
WHEW...
GOOD ANSWER.
TURN IN TWO SETS OF ARMOR OVER THERE.
SARA (SKRTCH)
SARA
GATO (TUP)
UNDER-STOOD...
WHAT'S GOING ON HERE...?
GOTO (KLOP)
GOTO
GOTO
THE TAX COLLECTOR BACK THERE REACTED VERY ODDLY...
GOTO
GARA
GARA

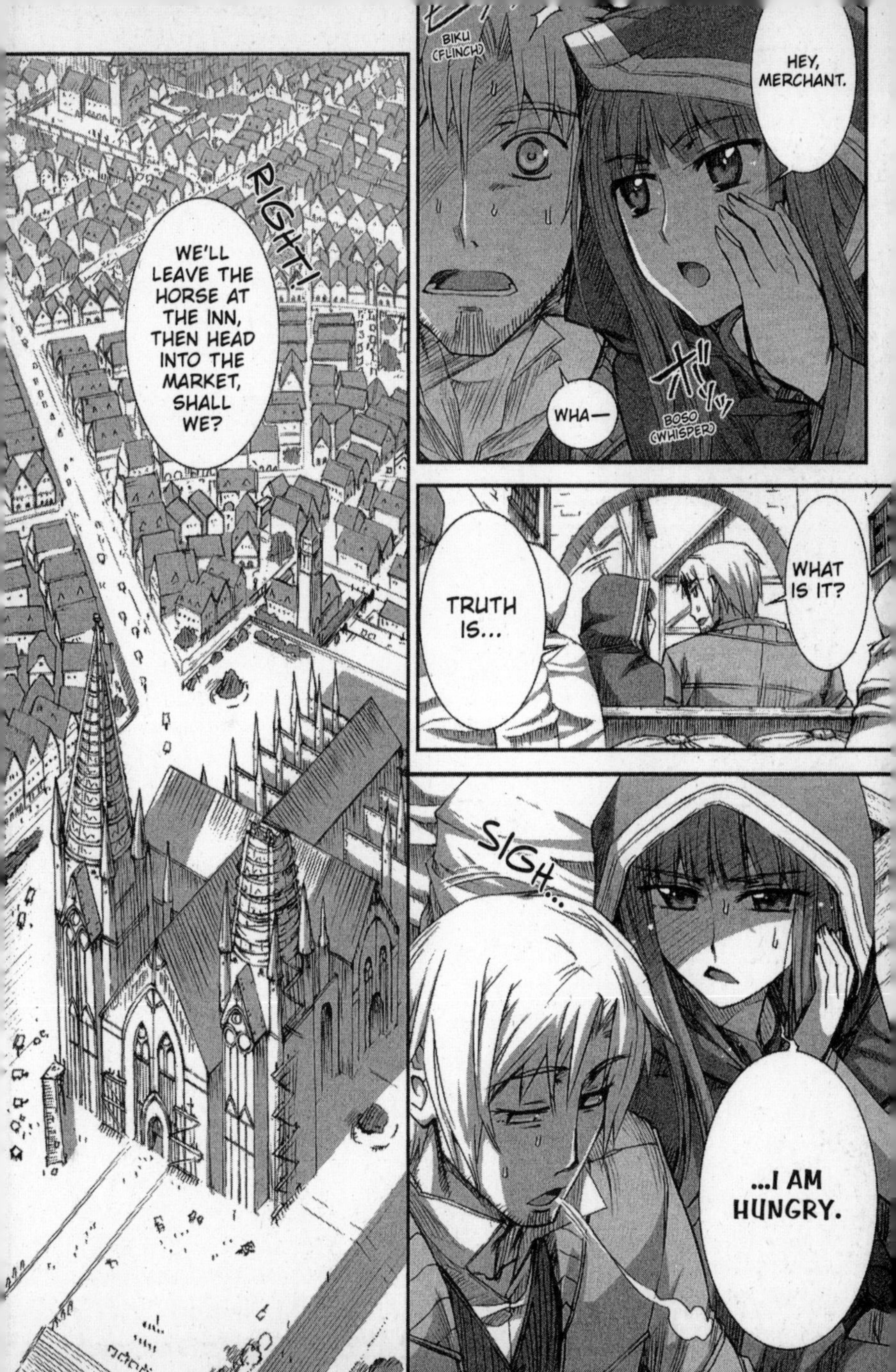
HEY, MERCHANT.
BOSO (WHISPER)
BIKU (FLINCH)
WHA—
WHAT IS IT?
TRUTH IS...
SIGH...
...I AM HUNGRY.
WE'LL LEAVE THE HORSE AT THE INN, THEN HEAD INTO THE MARKET, SHALL WE?
RIGHT!

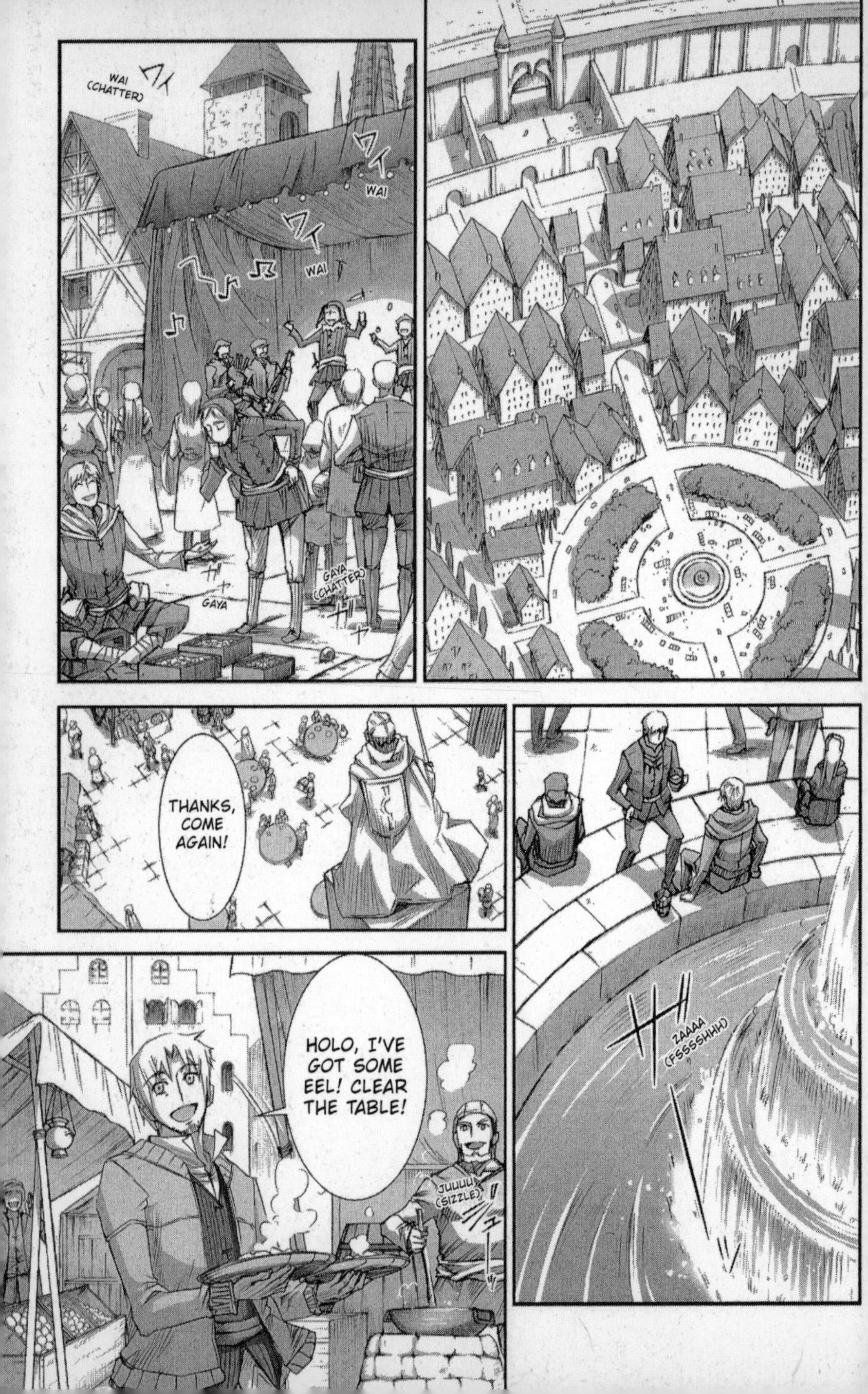
WAI (CHATTER)
WAI
WAI
GAYA (CHATTER)
GAYA
ZAAAA (FSSSSHHH)
THANKS, COME AGAIN!
HOLO, I'VE GOT SOME EEL! CLEAR THE TABLE!
JUUUU (SIZZLE)

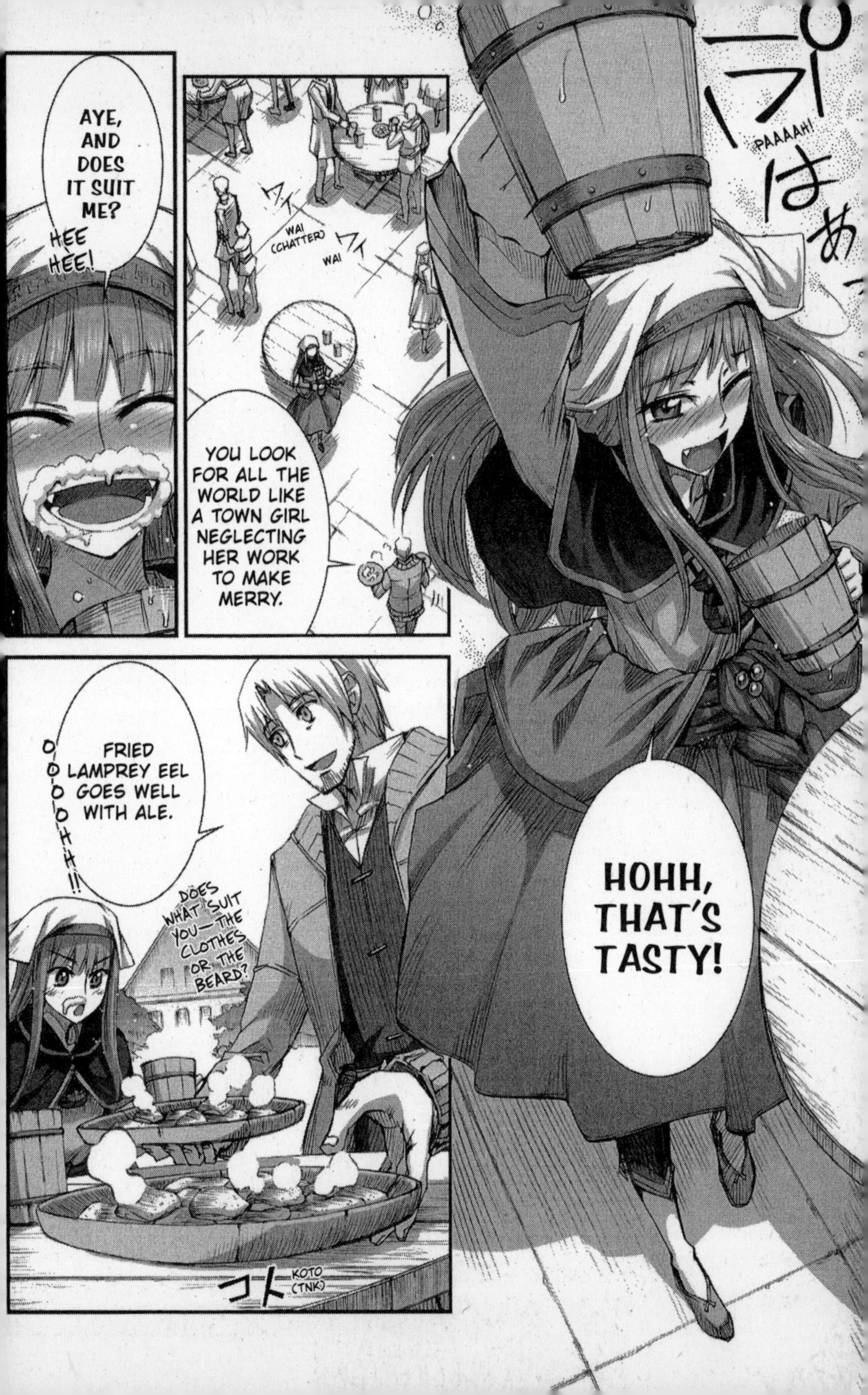

ぷはぁっ
PAAAAH!
HOHH, THAT'S TASTY!
ワイ WAI (CHATTER) ワイ WAI
YOU LOOK FOR ALL THE WORLD LIKE A TOWN GIRL NEGLECTING HER WORK TO MAKE MERRY.
AYE, AND DOES IT SUIT ME?
HEE HEE!
FRIED LAMPREY EEL GOES WELL WITH ALE.
OOOOOOHHH!!
DOES WHAT SUIT YOU—THE CLOTHES OR THE BEARD?
コト KOTO (TNK)

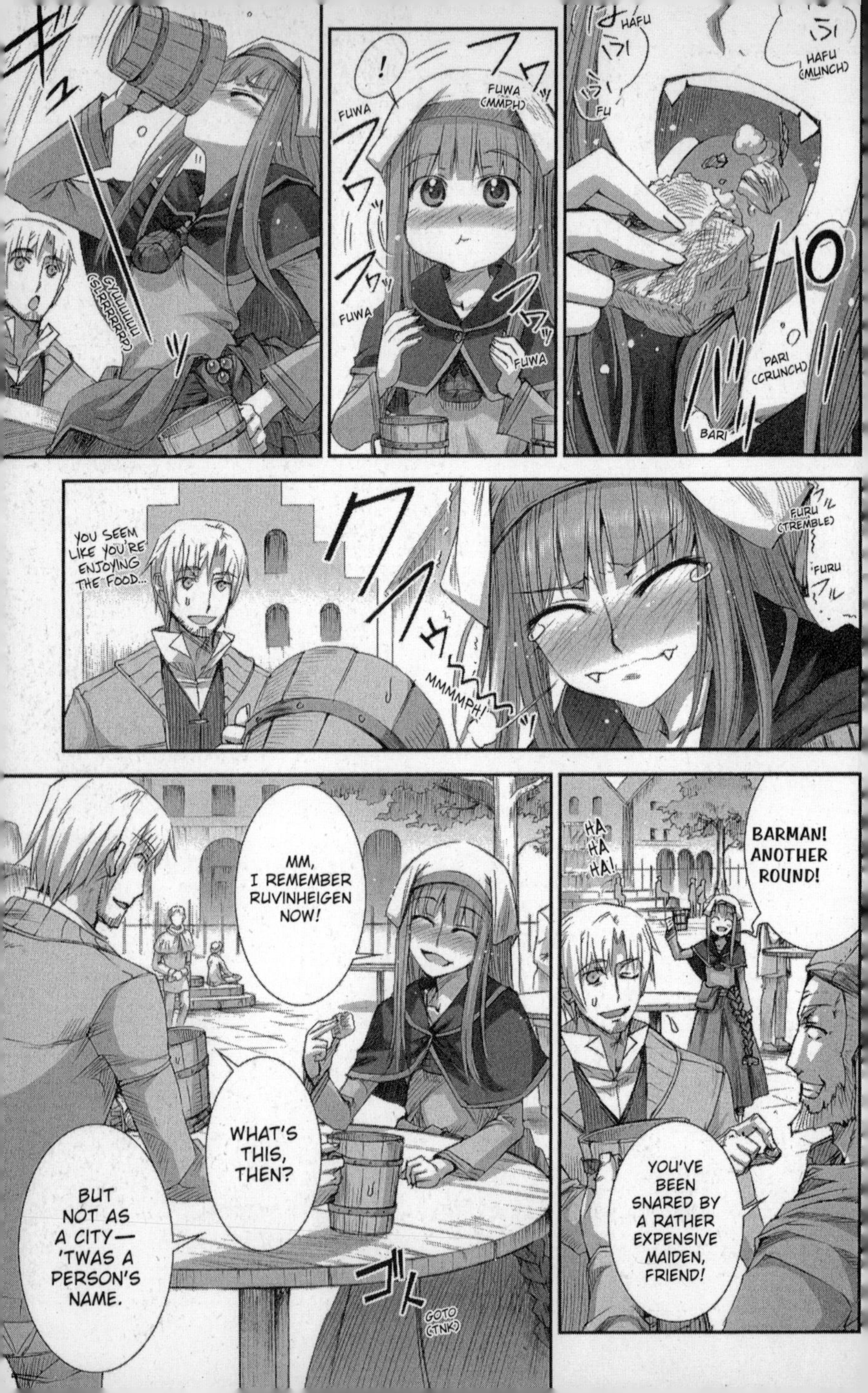
HAFU
HAFU (MUNCH)
FU
PARI (CRUNCH)
BARI
!
FUWA (MMPH)
FUWA
FUWA
FUWA
GYUUUUU (SLRRRRRP)
FURU (TREMBLE)
FURU
MMMMPH!
YOU SEEM LIKE YOU'RE ENJOYING THE FOOD...
BARMAN! ANOTHER ROUND!
HA HA HA!
YOU'VE BEEN SNARED BY A RATHER EXPENSIVE MAIDEN, FRIEND!
MM, I REMEMBER RUVINHEIGEN NOW!
WHAT'S THIS, THEN?
BUT NOT AS A CITY—'TWAS A PERSON'S NAME.
GOTO (TNK)

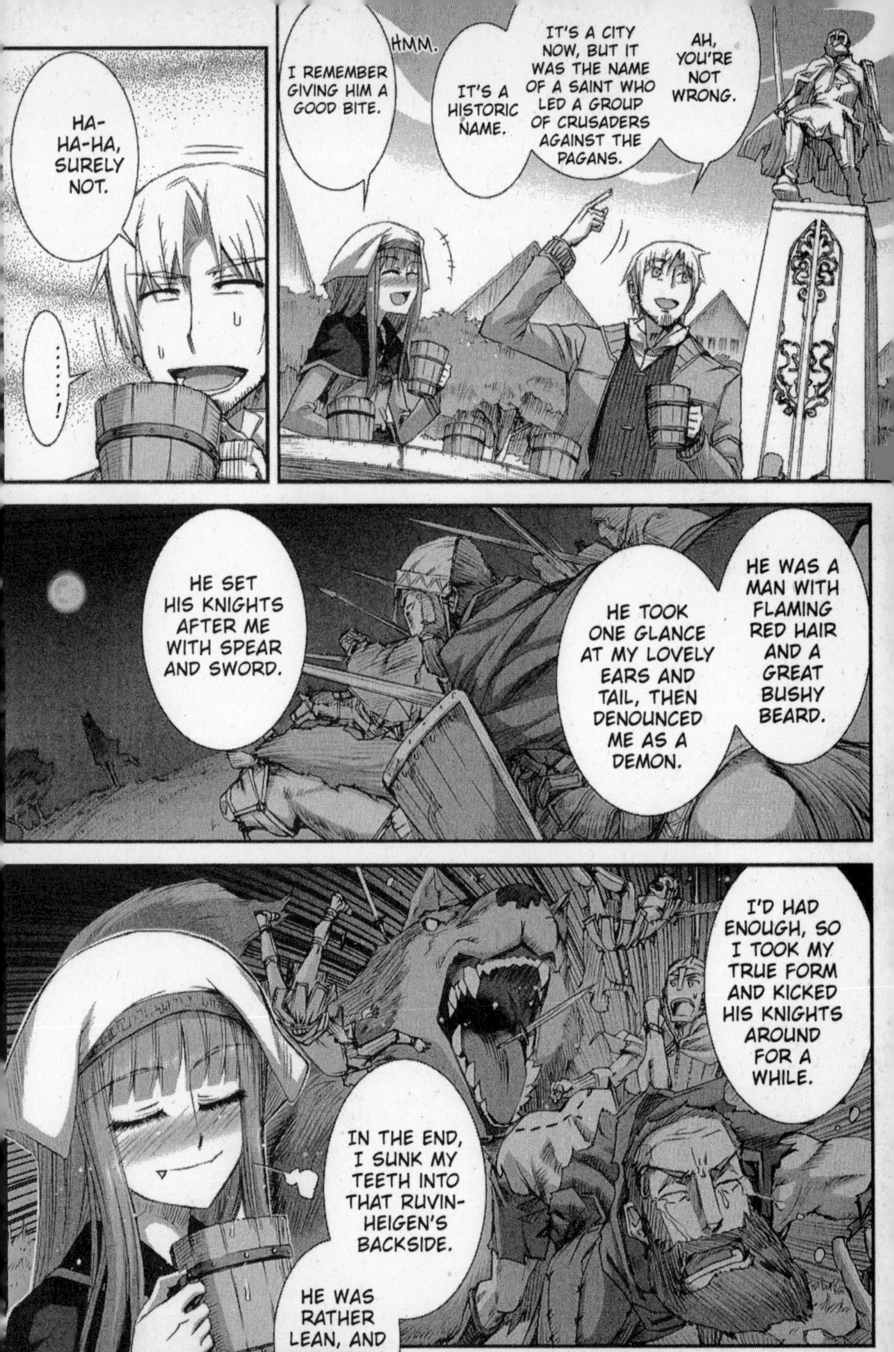
AH, YOU'RE NOT WRONG.
IT'S A CITY NOW, BUT IT WAS THE NAME OF A SAINT WHO LED A GROUP OF CRUSADERS AGAINST THE PAGANS.
IT'S A HISTORIC NAME.
HMM.
I REMEMBER GIVING HIM A GOOD BITE.
HA-HA-HA, SURELY NOT.
......!
HE WAS A MAN WITH FLAMING RED HAIR AND A GREAT BUSHY BEARD.
HE TOOK ONE GLANCE AT MY LOVELY EARS AND TAIL, THEN DENOUNCED ME AS A DEMON.
HE SET HIS KNIGHTS AFTER ME WITH SPEAR AND SWORD.
I'D HAD ENOUGH, SO I TOOK MY TRUE FORM AND KICKED HIS KNIGHTS AROUND FOR A WHILE.
IN THE END, I SUNK MY TEETH INTO THAT RUVIN-HEIGEN'S BACKSIDE.
HE WAS RATHER LEAN, AND FAR FROM TASTY.

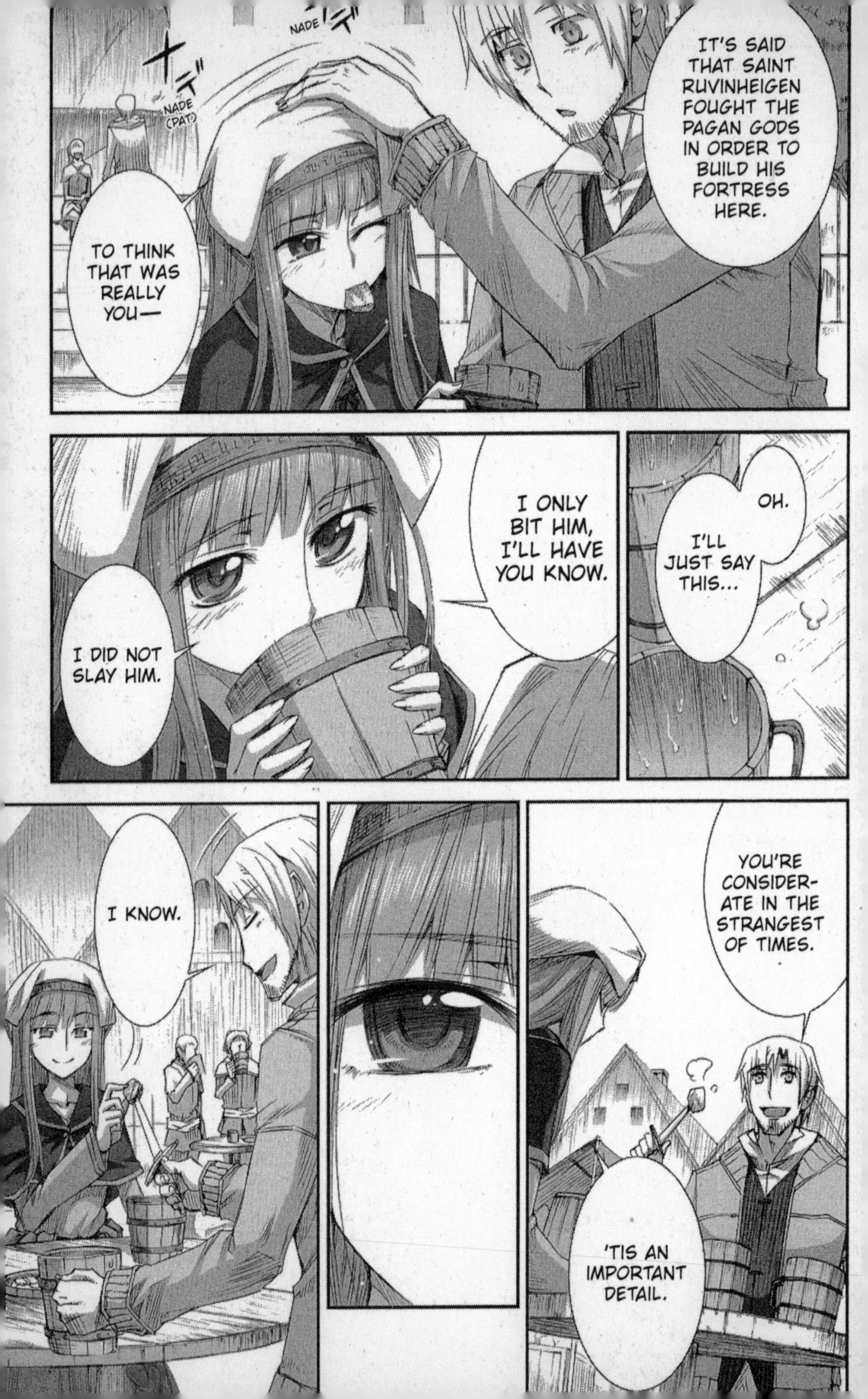
NADE
IT'S SAID THAT SAINT RUVINHEIGEN FOUGHT THE PAGAN GODS IN ORDER TO BUILD HIS FORTRESS HERE.
NADE (PAT)
TO THINK THAT WAS REALLY YOU—
OH.
I'LL JUST SAY THIS...
I ONLY BIT HIM, I'LL HAVE YOU KNOW.
I DID NOT SLAY HIM.
YOU'RE CONSIDER-ATE IN THE STRANGEST OF TIMES.
'TIS AN IMPORTANT DETAIL.
I KNOW.

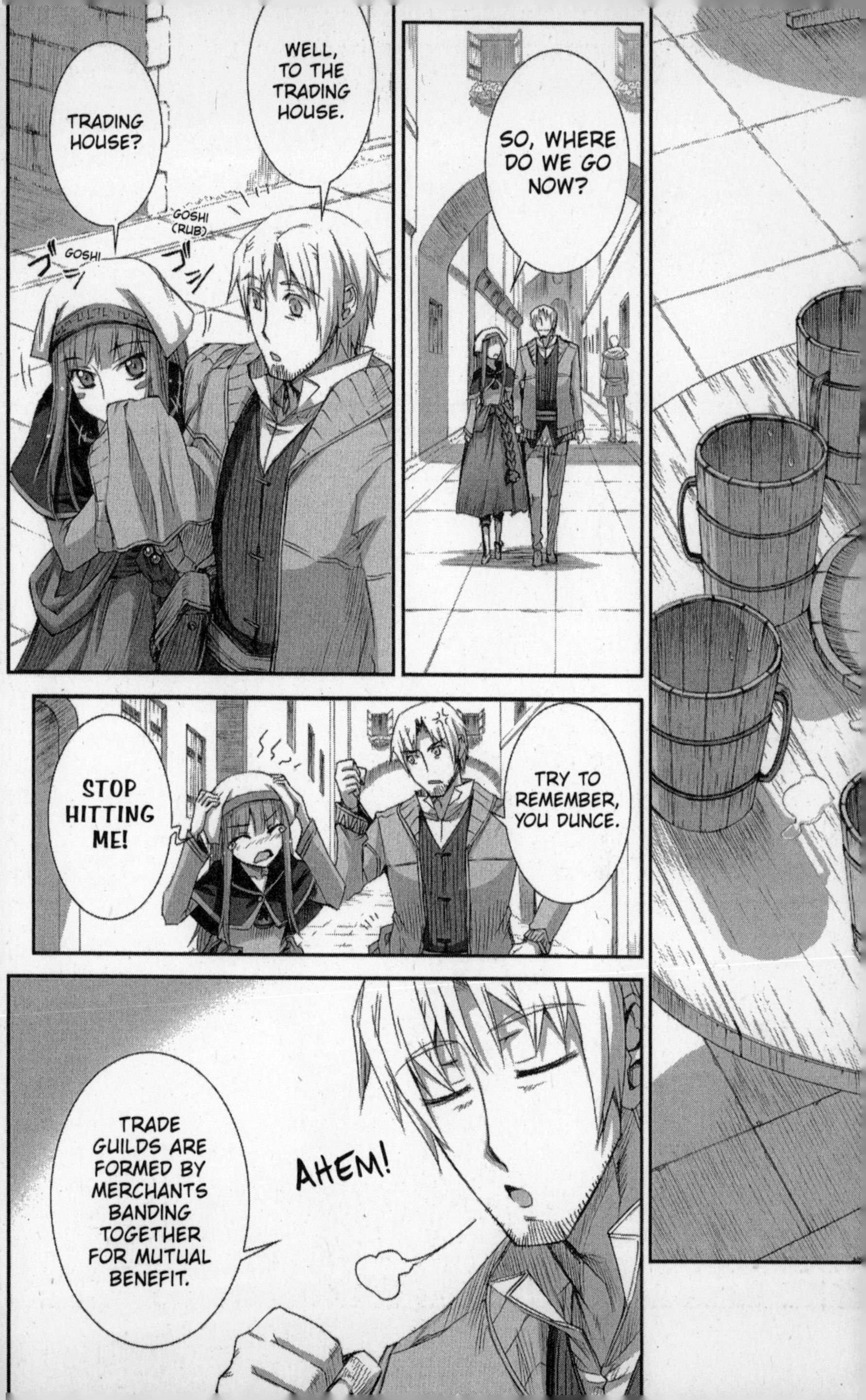
SO, WHERE DO WE GO NOW?
WELL, TO THE TRADING HOUSE.
TRADING HOUSE?
GOSHI (RUB)
GOSHI
TRY TO REMEMBER, YOU DUNCE.
STOP HITTING ME!
AHEM!
TRADE GUILDS ARE FORMED BY MERCHANTS BANDING TOGETHER FOR MUTUAL BENEFIT.

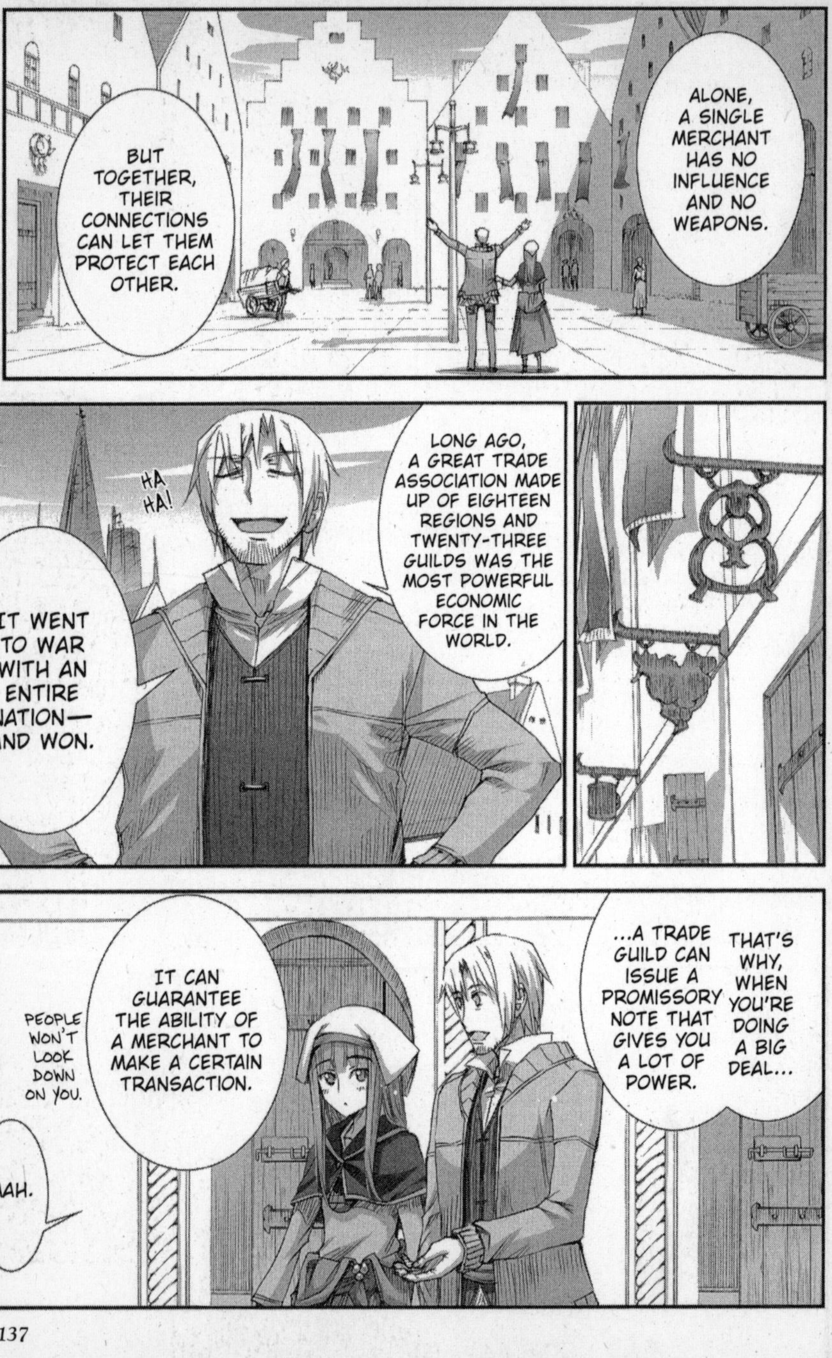
ALONE, A SINGLE MERCHANT HAS NO INFLUENCE AND NO WEAPONS.
BUT TOGETHER, THEIR CONNECTIONS CAN LET THEM PROTECT EACH OTHER.
LONG AGO, A GREAT TRADE ASSOCIATION MADE UP OF EIGHTEEN REGIONS AND TWENTY-THREE GUILDS WAS THE MOST POWERFUL ECONOMIC FORCE IN THE WORLD.
HA HA!
IT WENT TO WAR WITH AN ENTIRE NATION—AND WON.
THAT'S WHY, WHEN YOU'RE DOING A BIG DEAL...
...A TRADE GUILD CAN ISSUE A PROMISSORY NOTE THAT GIVES YOU A LOT OF POWER.
IT CAN GUARANTEE THE ABILITY OF A MERCHANT TO MAKE A CERTAIN TRANSACTION.
PEOPLE WON'T LOOK DOWN ON YOU.
AAH.

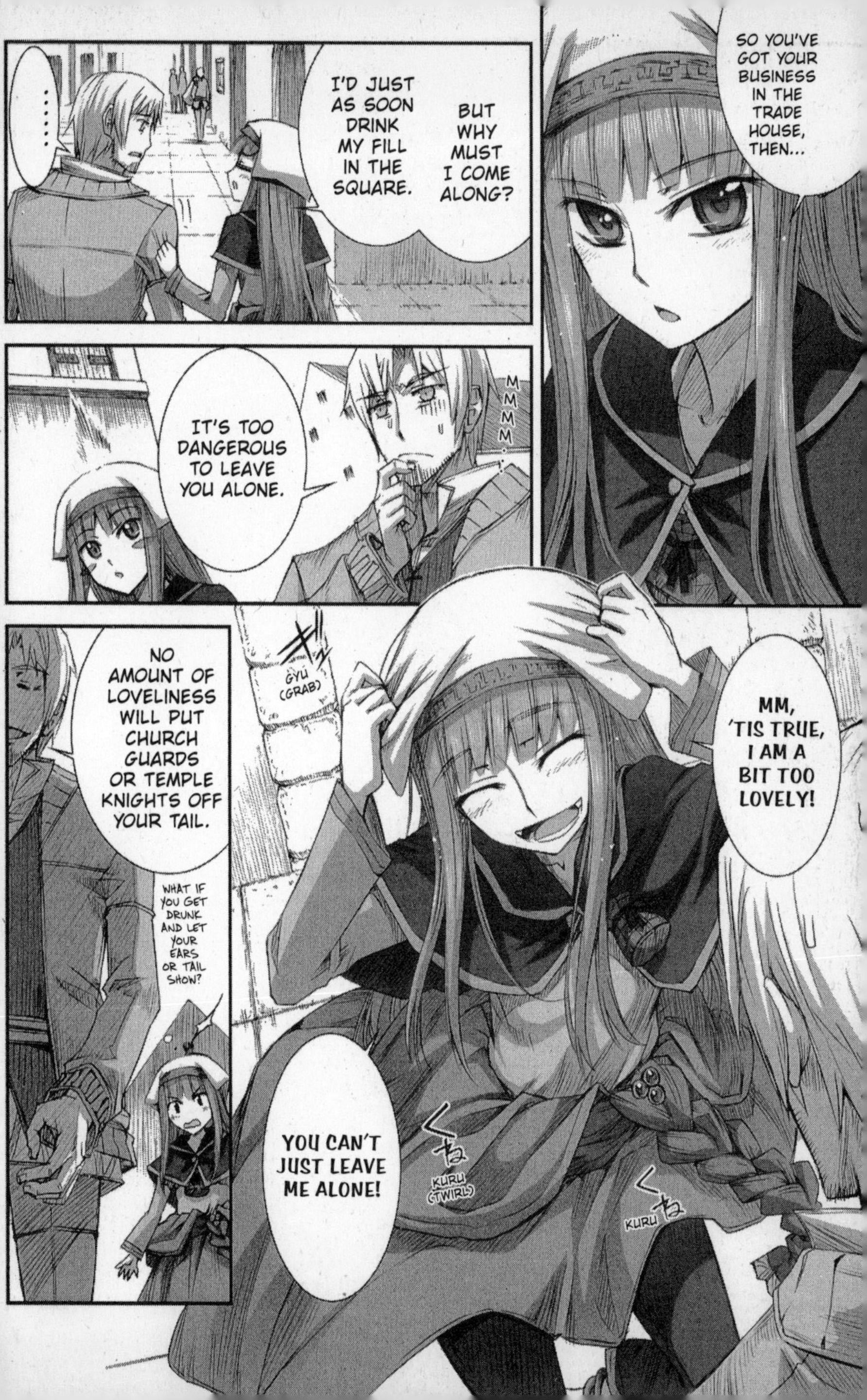

SO YOU'VE GOT YOUR BUSINESS IN THE TRADE HOUSE, THEN...
BUT WHY MUST I COME ALONG?
I'D JUST AS SOON DRINK MY FILL IN THE SQUARE.
......
MMMM...
IT'S TOO DANGEROUS TO LEAVE YOU ALONE.
GYU (GRAB)
MM, 'TIS TRUE, I AM A BIT TOO LOVELY!
KURU (TWIRL)
KURU
YOU CAN'T JUST LEAVE ME ALONE!
NO AMOUNT OF LOVELINESS WILL PUT CHURCH GUARDS OR TEMPLE KNIGHTS OFF YOUR TAIL.
WHAT IF YOU GET DRUNK AND LET YOUR EARS OR TAIL SHOW?

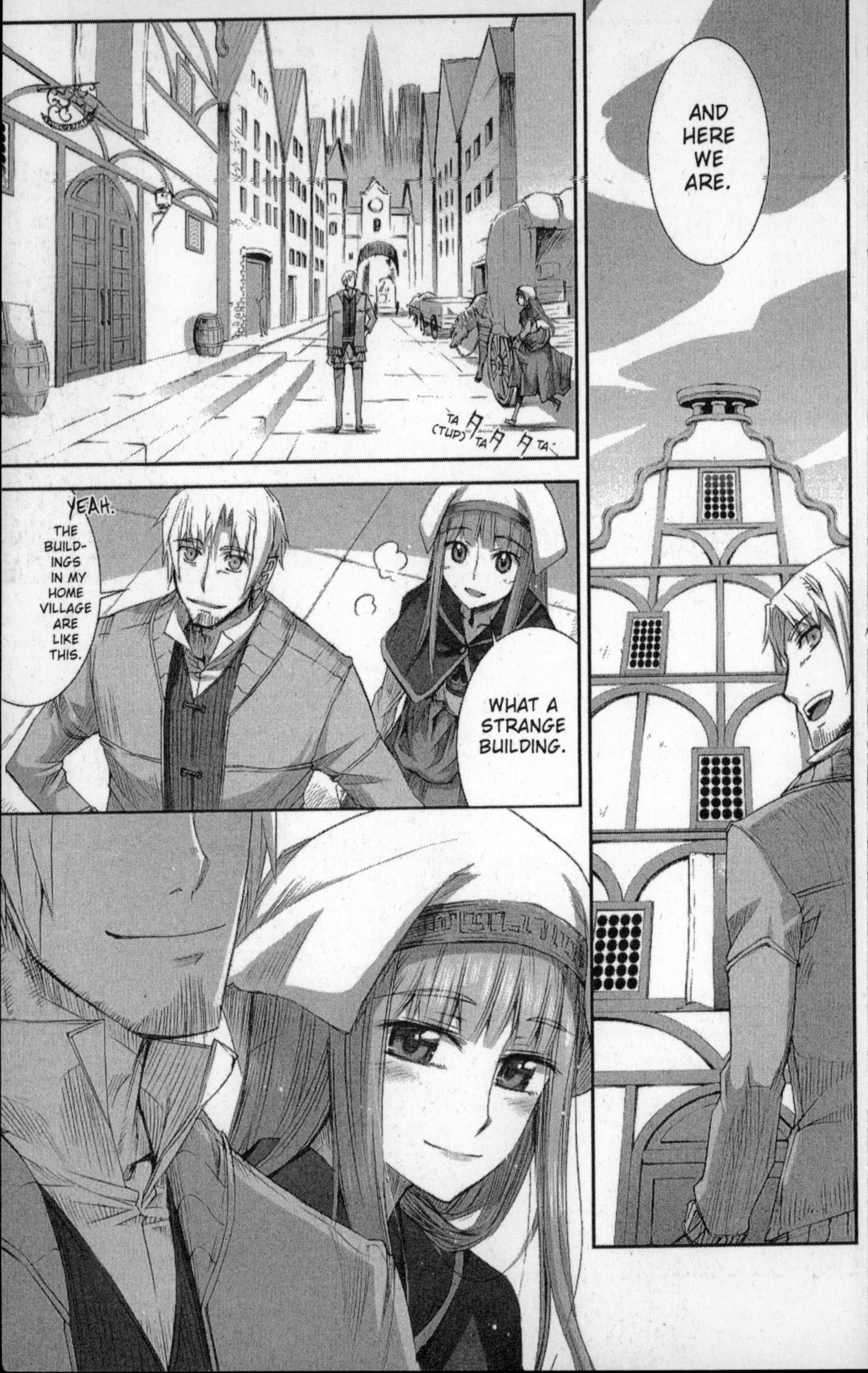
AND HERE WE ARE.
TA (TUP) TA TA TA
WHAT A STRANGE BUILDING.
YEAH.
THE BUILDINGS IN MY HOME VILLAGE ARE LIKE THIS.

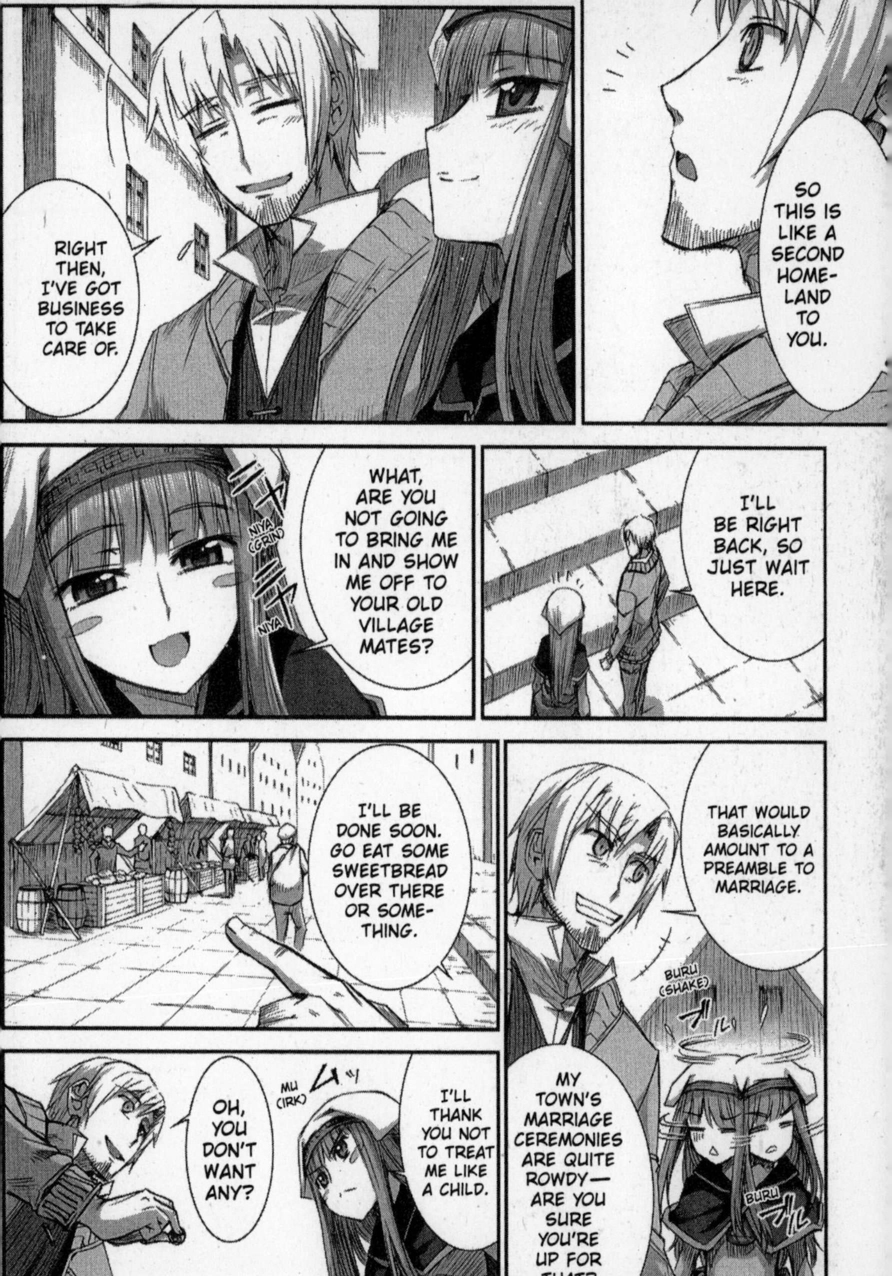
SO THIS IS LIKE A SECOND HOME-LAND TO YOU.
RIGHT THEN, I'VE GOT BUSINESS TO TAKE CARE OF.
I'LL BE RIGHT BACK, SO JUST WAIT HERE.
WHAT, ARE YOU NOT GOING TO BRING ME IN AND SHOW ME OFF TO YOUR OLD VILLAGE MATES?
NIYA (GRIN)
NIYA
THAT WOULD BASICALLY AMOUNT TO A PREAMBLE TO MARRIAGE.
BURU (SHAKE)
MY TOWN'S MARRIAGE CEREMONIES ARE QUITE ROWDY—ARE YOU SURE YOU'RE UP FOR THAT?
BURU
I'LL BE DONE SOON. GO EAT SOME SWEETBREAD OVER THERE OR SOME-THING.
I'LL THANK YOU NOT TO TREAT ME LIKE A CHILD.
MU (IRK)
OH, YOU DON'T WANT ANY?

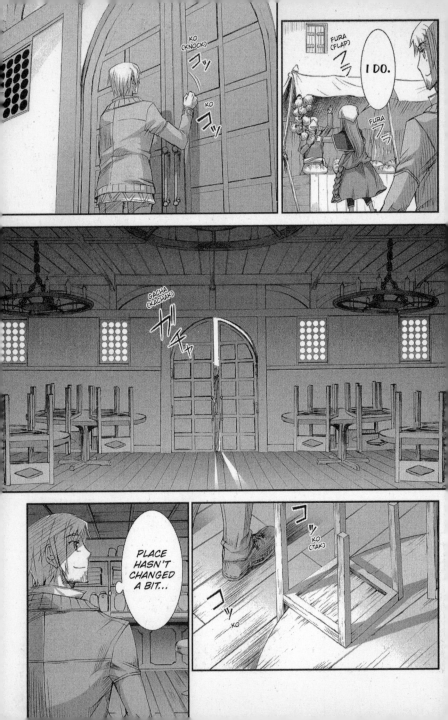

KO
(KNOCK)

KO

FURA
(FLAP)

I DO.

FURA

GACHA
(KACHAK)

PLACE
HASN'T
CHANGED
A BIT...

KO
(TAK)

KO

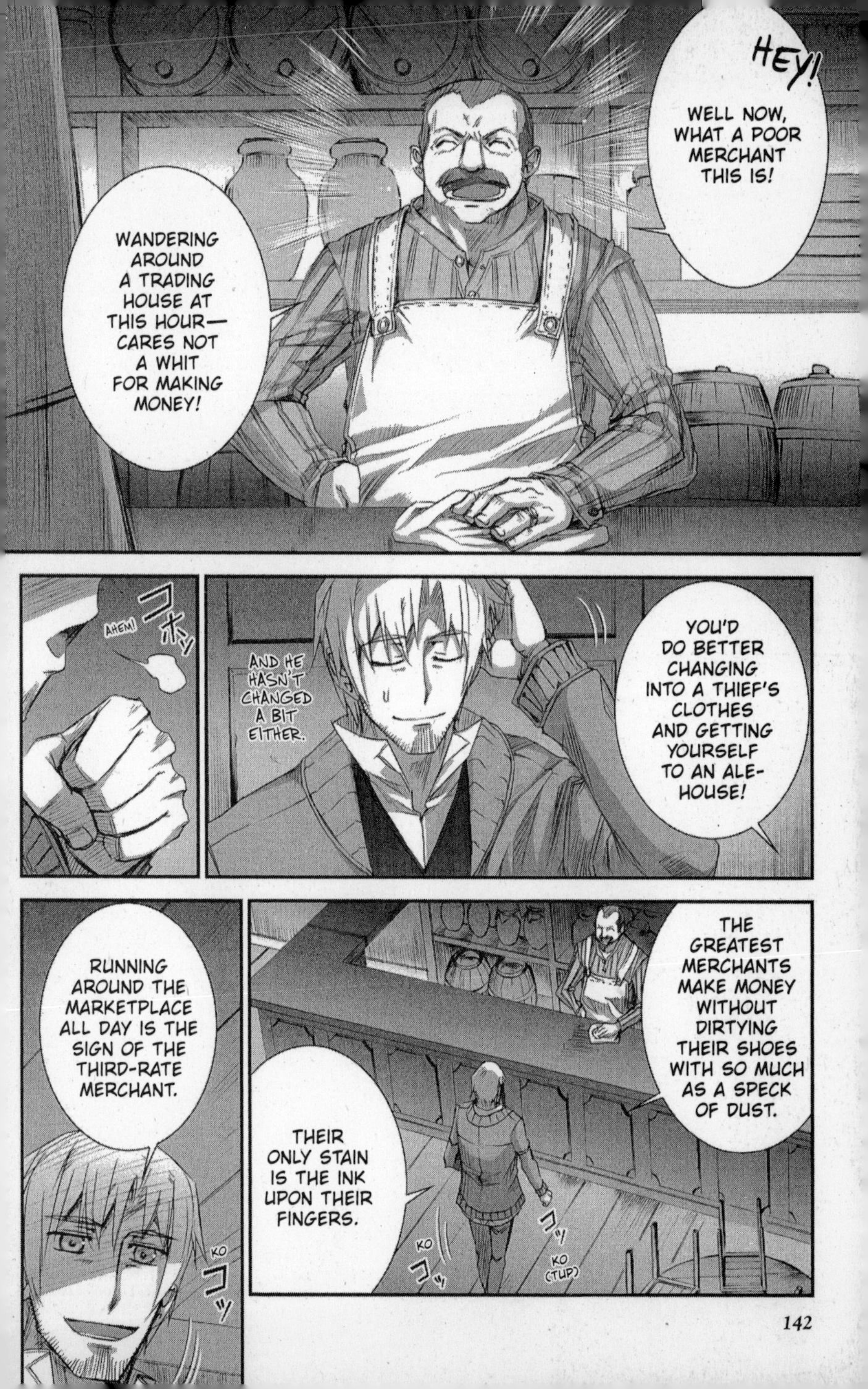
HEY!
WELL NOW, WHAT A POOR MERCHANT THIS IS!
WANDERING AROUND A TRADING HOUSE AT THIS HOUR—CARES NOT A WHIT FOR MAKING MONEY!
YOU'D DO BETTER CHANGING INTO A THIEF'S CLOTHES AND GETTING YOURSELF TO AN ALE-HOUSE!
AND HE HASN'T CHANGED A BIT EITHER.
AHEM!
コホッ
THE GREATEST MERCHANTS MAKE MONEY WITHOUT DIRTYING THEIR SHOES WITH SO MUCH AS A SPECK OF DUST.
THEIR ONLY STAIN IS THE INK UPON THEIR FINGERS.
KO
コッ
KO (TUP)
コッ
RUNNING AROUND THE MARKETPLACE ALL DAY IS THE SIGN OF THE THIRD-RATE MERCHANT.
KO
コッ

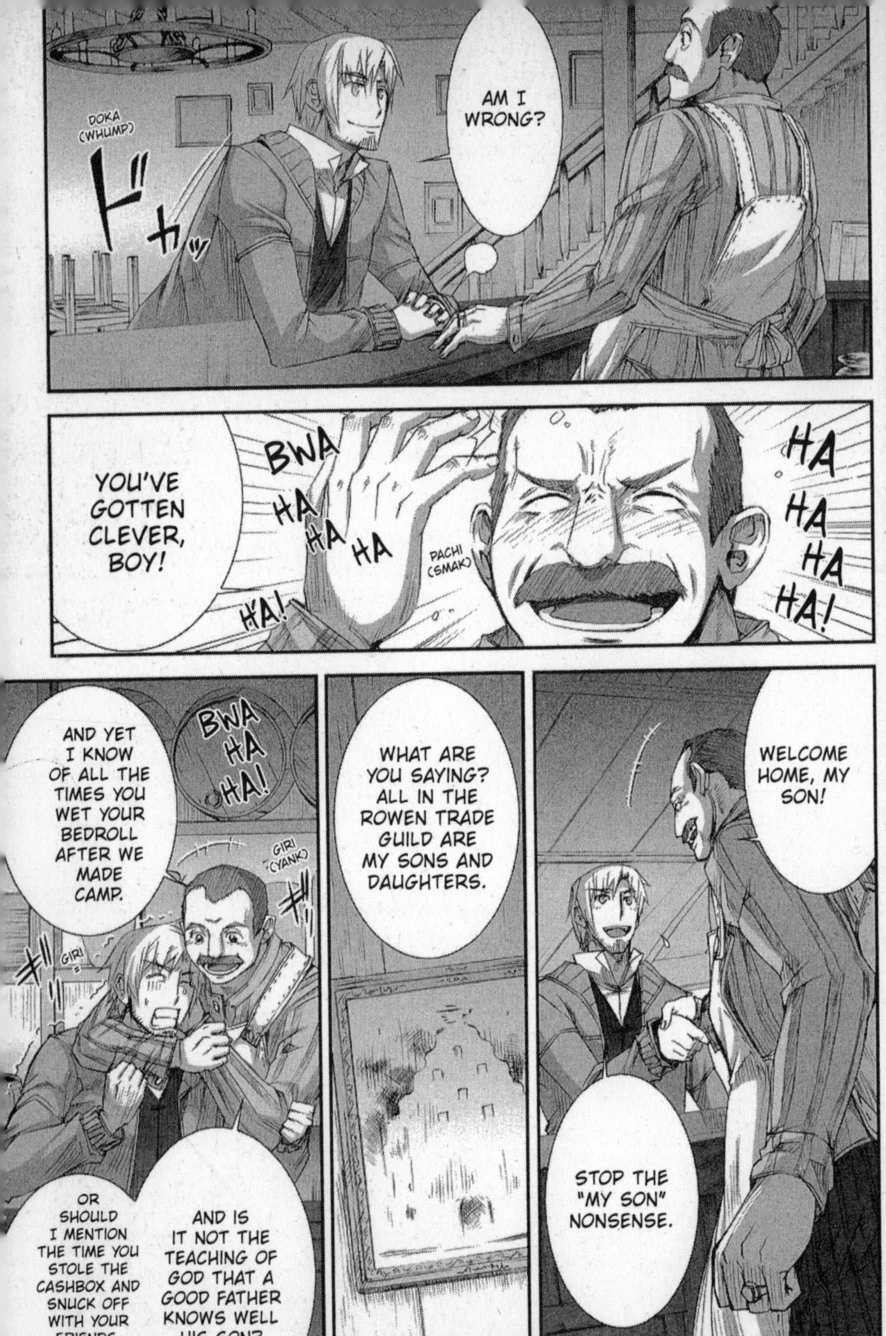
AM I WRONG?
DOKA (WHUMP)
HA HA HA HA!
PACHI (SMAK)
BWA HA HA HA HA!
YOU'VE GOTTEN CLEVER, BOY!
WELCOME HOME, MY SON!
STOP THE "MY SON" NONSENSE.
WHAT ARE YOU SAYING? ALL IN THE ROWEN TRADE GUILD ARE MY SONS AND DAUGHTERS.
BWA HA HA!
AND YET I KNOW OF ALL THE TIMES YOU WET YOUR BEDROLL AFTER WE MADE CAMP.
GIRI (YANK)
GIRI
AND IS IT NOT THE TEACHING OF GOD THAT A GOOD FATHER KNOWS WELL HIS SON?
OR SHOULD I MENTION THE TIME YOU STOLE THE CASHBOX AND SNUCK OFF WITH YOUR FRIENDS, TREMBLING, TO THE WHORE-HOUS—

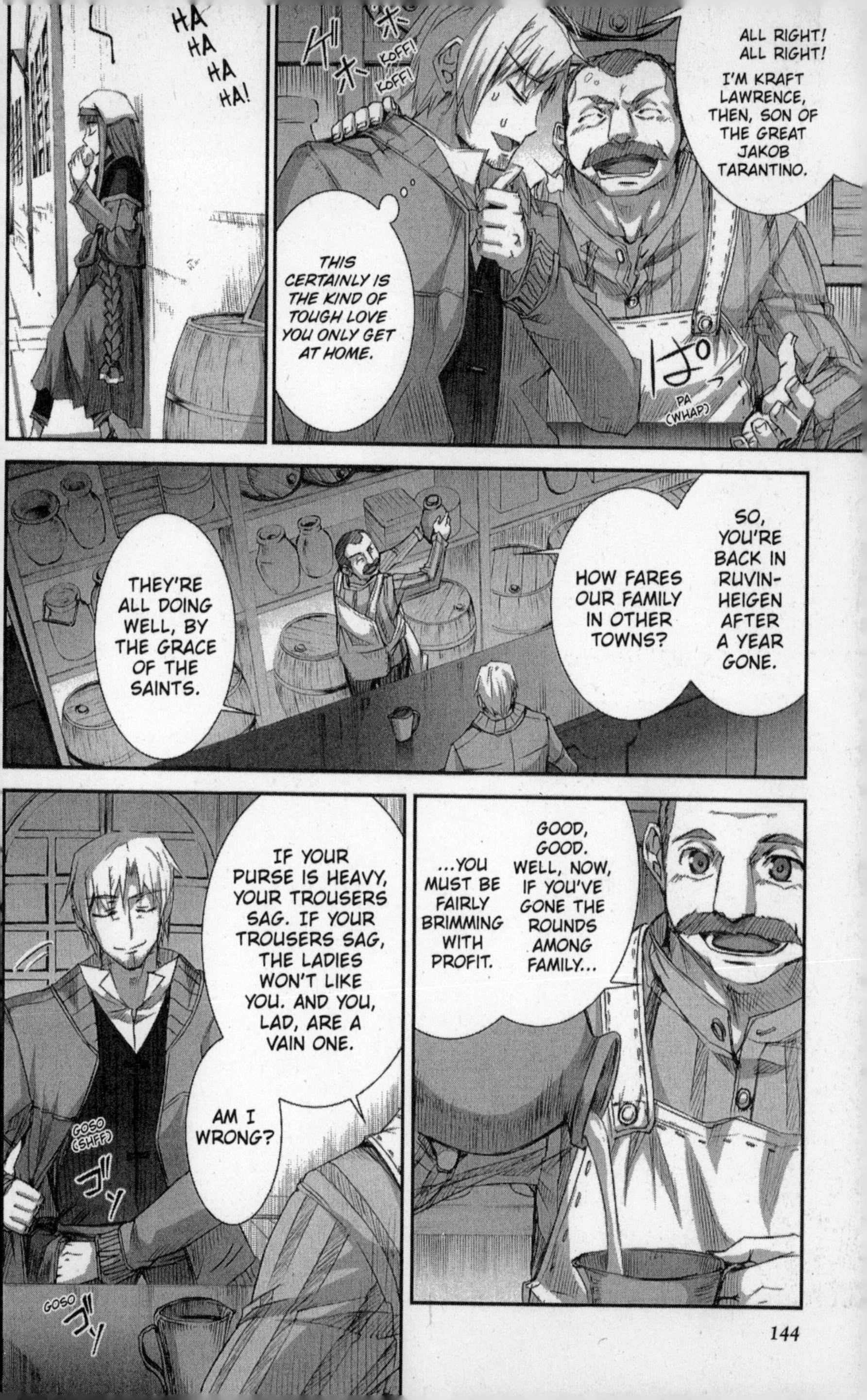
ALL RIGHT! ALL RIGHT!
I'M KRAFT LAWRENCE, THEN, SON OF THE GREAT JAKOB TARANTINO.
KOFF! KOFF!
THIS CERTAINLY IS THE KIND OF TOUGH LOVE YOU ONLY GET AT HOME.
PA (WHAP)
HA HA HA HA!
SO, YOU'RE BACK IN RUVINHEIGEN AFTER A YEAR GONE.
HOW FARES OUR FAMILY IN OTHER TOWNS?
THEY'RE ALL DOING WELL, BY THE GRACE OF THE SAINTS.
GOOD, GOOD. WELL, NOW, IF YOU'VE GONE THE ROUNDS AMONG FAMILY...
...YOU MUST BE FAIRLY BRIMMING WITH PROFIT.
IF YOUR PURSE IS HEAVY, YOUR TROUSERS SAG. IF YOUR TROUSERS SAG, THE LADIES WON'T LIKE YOU. AND YOU, LAD, ARE A VAIN ONE.
AM I WRONG?
GOSO (SHFF)
GOSO

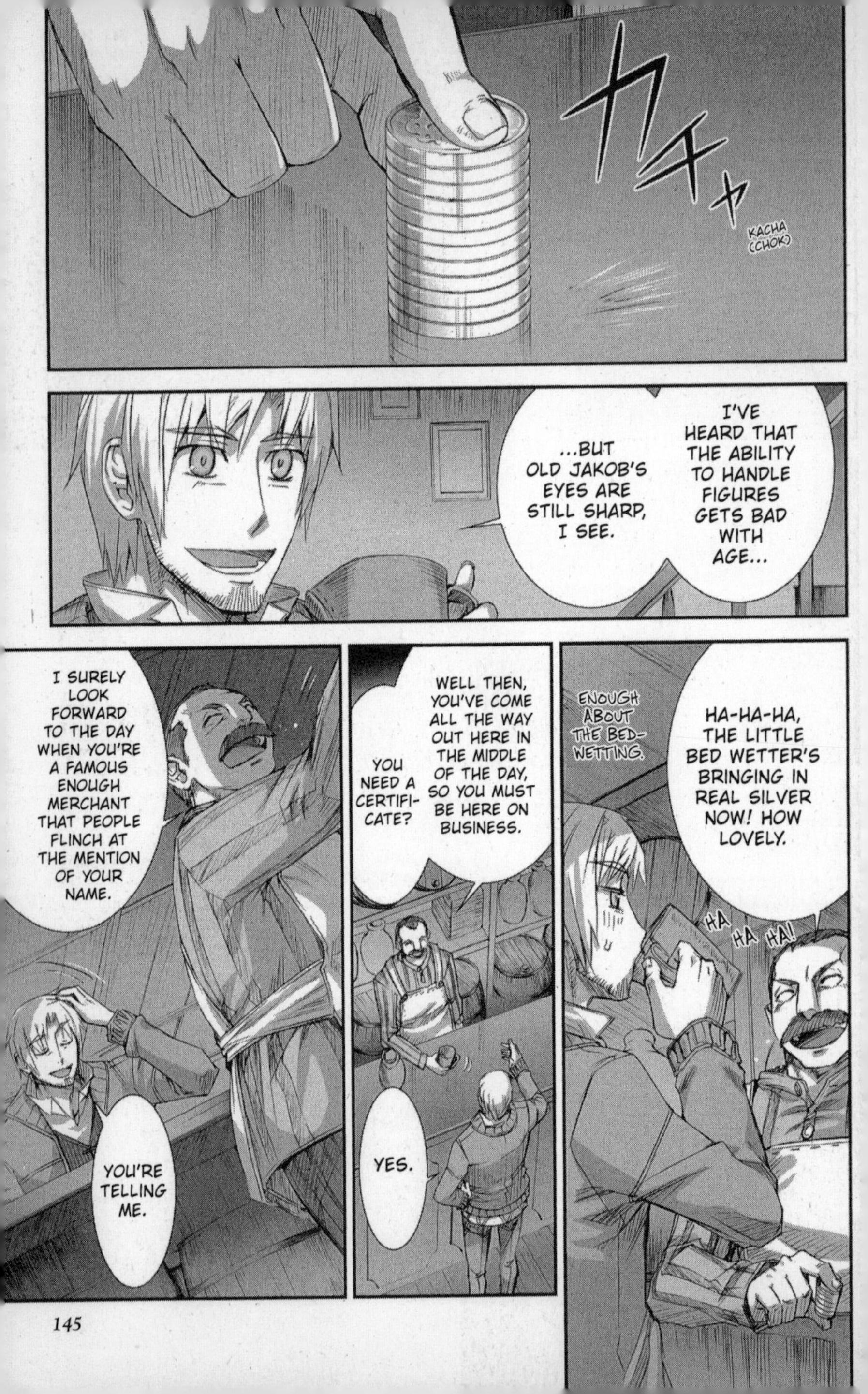
カチャ
KACHA (CHOK)
I'VE HEARD THAT THE ABILITY TO HANDLE FIGURES GETS BAD WITH AGE...
...BUT OLD JAKOB'S EYES ARE STILL SHARP, I SEE.
HA-HA-HA, THE LITTLE BED WETTER'S BRINGING IN REAL SILVER NOW! HOW LOVELY.
HA HA HA!
ENOUGH ABOUT THE BED-WETTING.
WELL THEN, YOU'VE COME ALL THE WAY OUT HERE IN THE MIDDLE OF THE DAY, SO YOU MUST BE HERE ON BUSINESS.
YOU NEED A CERTIFI-CATE?
YES.
I SURELY LOOK FORWARD TO THE DAY WHEN YOU'RE A FAMOUS ENOUGH MERCHANT THAT PEOPLE FLINCH AT THE MENTION OF YOUR NAME.
YOU'RE TELLING ME.

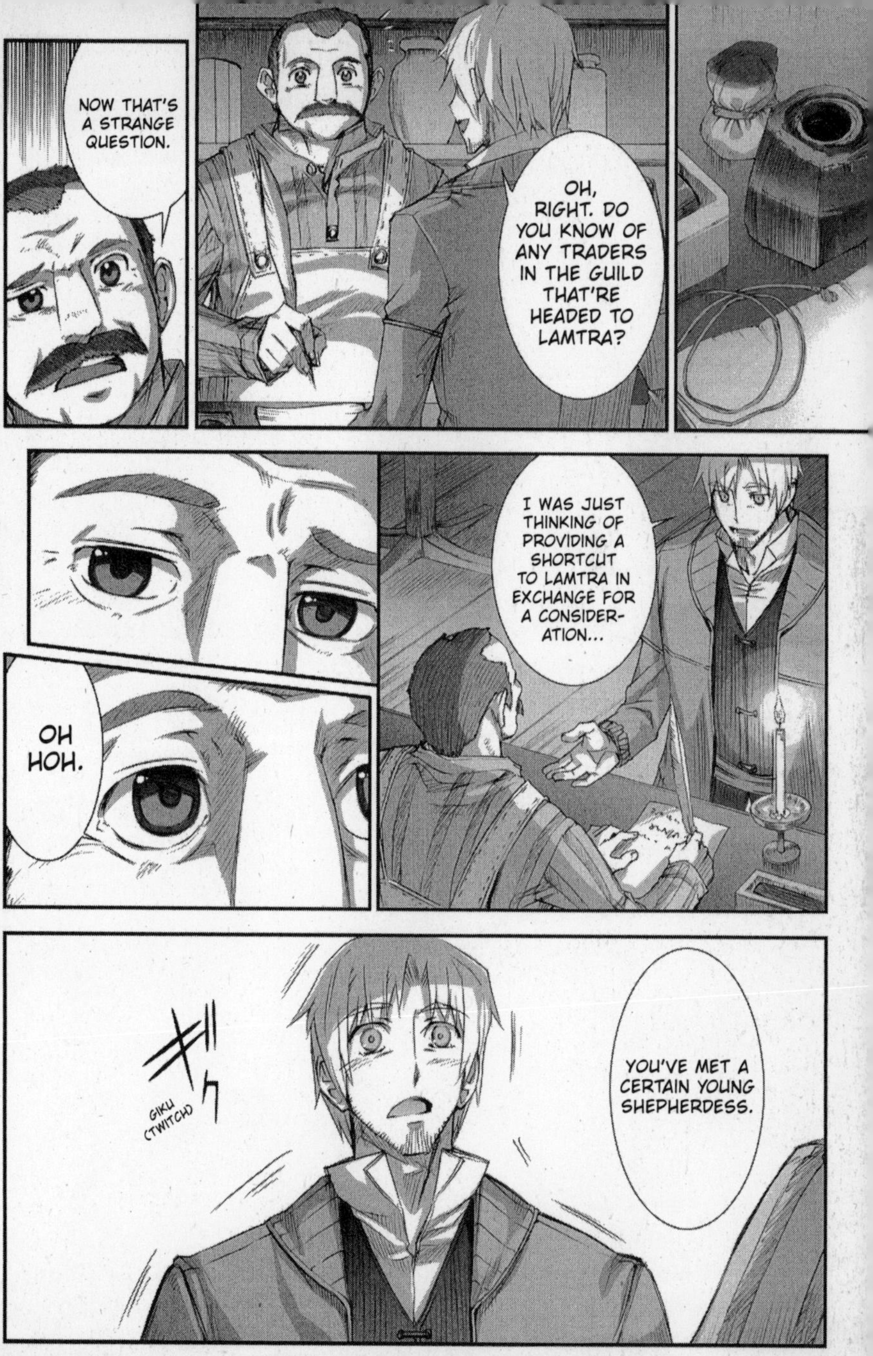
OH, RIGHT. DO YOU KNOW OF ANY TRADERS IN THE GUILD THAT'RE HEADED TO LAMTRA?
NOW THAT'S A STRANGE QUESTION.
I WAS JUST THINKING OF PROVIDING A SHORTCUT TO LAMTRA IN EXCHANGE FOR A CONSIDER-ATION...
OH HOH.
YOU'VE MET A CERTAIN YOUNG SHEPHERDESS.
GIKU (TWITCH)

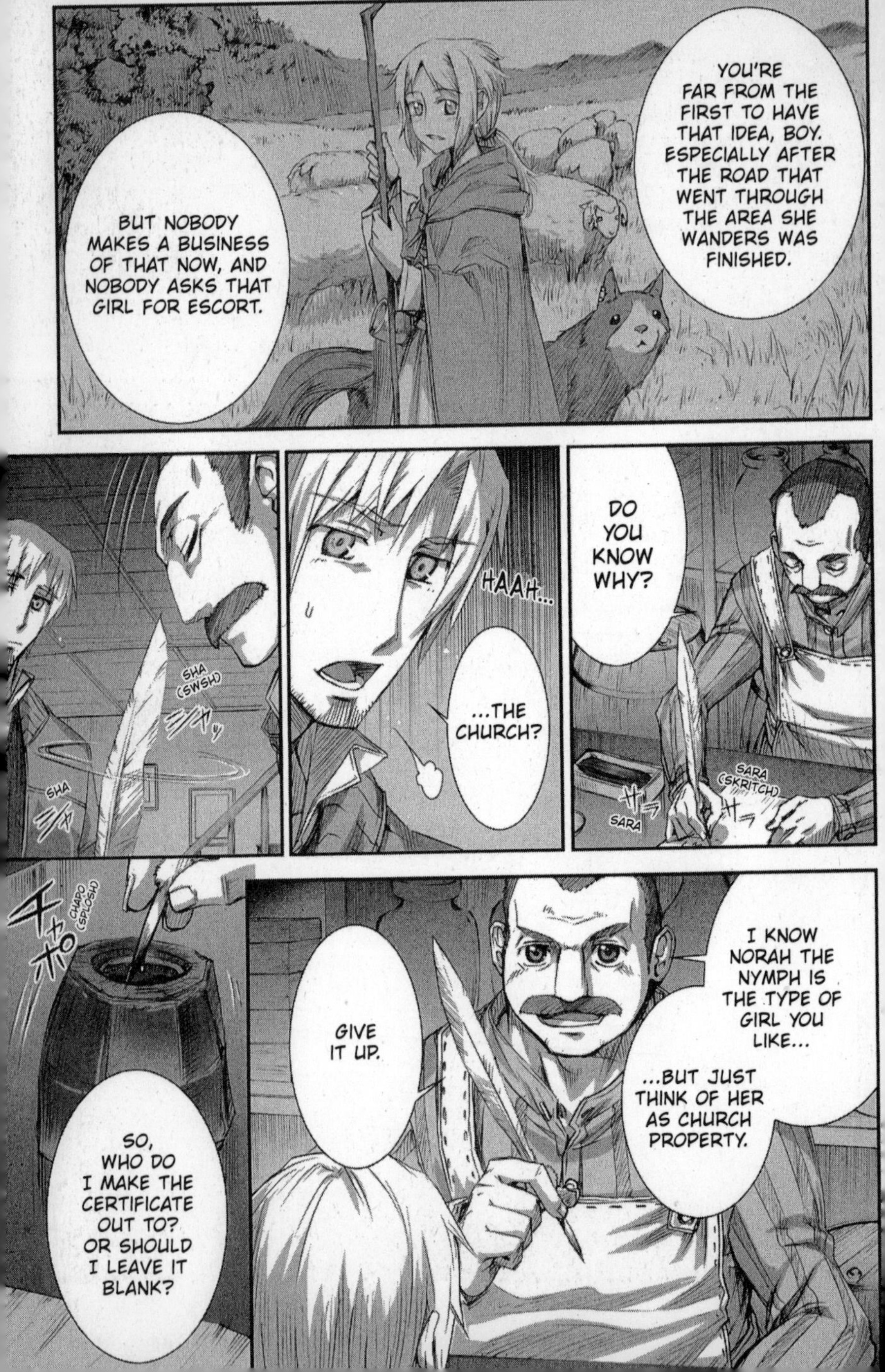
YOU'RE FAR FROM THE FIRST TO HAVE THAT IDEA, BOY. ESPECIALLY AFTER THE ROAD THAT WENT THROUGH THE AREA SHE WANDERS WAS FINISHED.
BUT NOBODY MAKES A BUSINESS OF THAT NOW, AND NOBODY ASKS THAT GIRL FOR ESCORT.
DO YOU KNOW WHY?
SARA (SKRITCH)
SARA
HAAH...
...THE CHURCH?
SHA (SWSH)
SHA
I KNOW NORAH THE NYMPH IS THE TYPE OF GIRL YOU LIKE...
...BUT JUST THINK OF HER AS CHURCH PROPERTY.
GIVE IT UP.
CHAPO (SPLOSH)
SO, WHO DO I MAKE THE CERTIFICATE OUT TO? OR SHOULD I LEAVE IT BLANK?

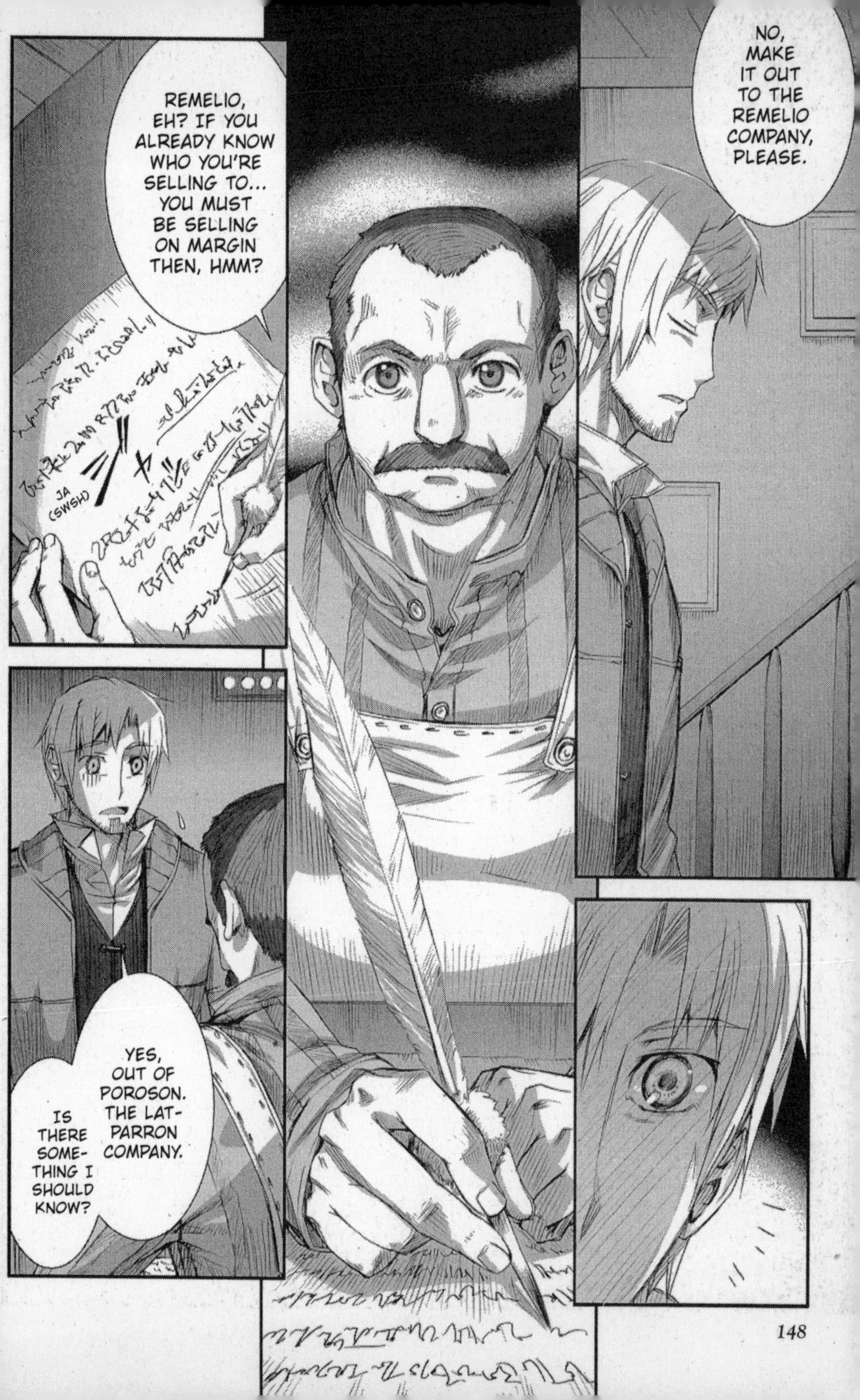
NO, MAKE IT OUT TO THE REMELIO COMPANY, PLEASE.
REMELIO, EH? IF YOU ALREADY KNOW WHO YOU'RE SELLING TO... YOU MUST BE SELLING ON MARGIN THEN, HMM?
JA (SWSH)
YES, OUT OF POROSON. THE LAT-PARRON COMPANY.
IS THERE SOME-THING I SHOULD KNOW?

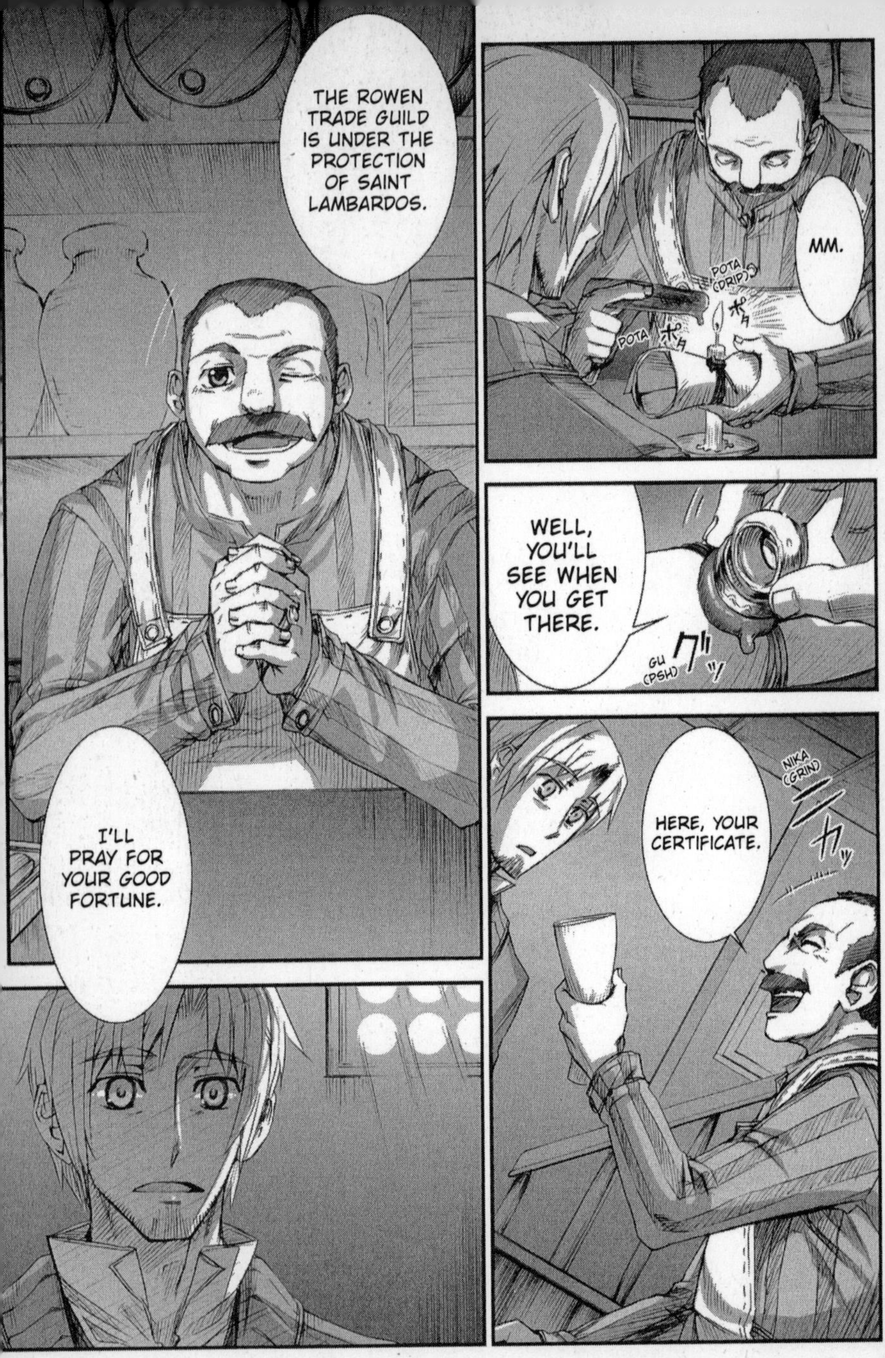
MM.
POTA (DRIP)
POTA
WELL, YOU'LL SEE WHEN YOU GET THERE.
GU (PSH)
THE ROWEN TRADE GUILD IS UNDER THE PROTECTION OF SAINT LAMBARDOS.
I'LL PRAY FOR YOUR GOOD FORTUNE.
HERE, YOUR CERTIFICATE.
NIKA (GRIN)

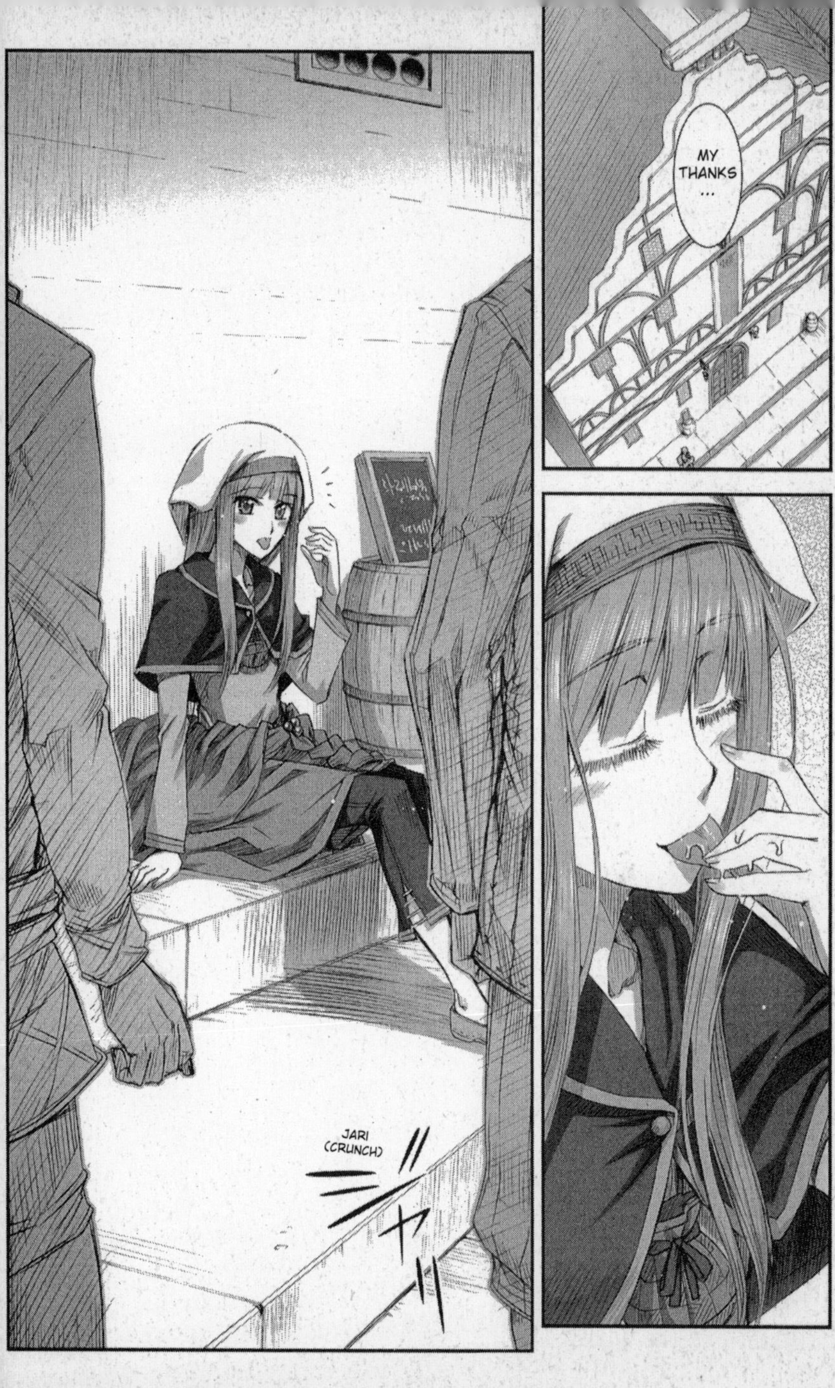
MY THANKS ...
JARI (CRUNCH)

SPICE & WOLF

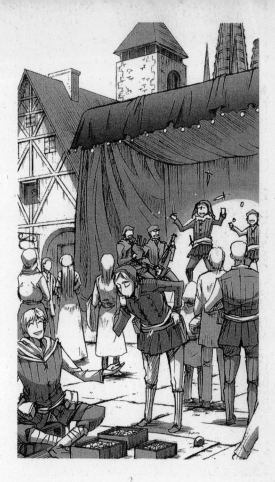

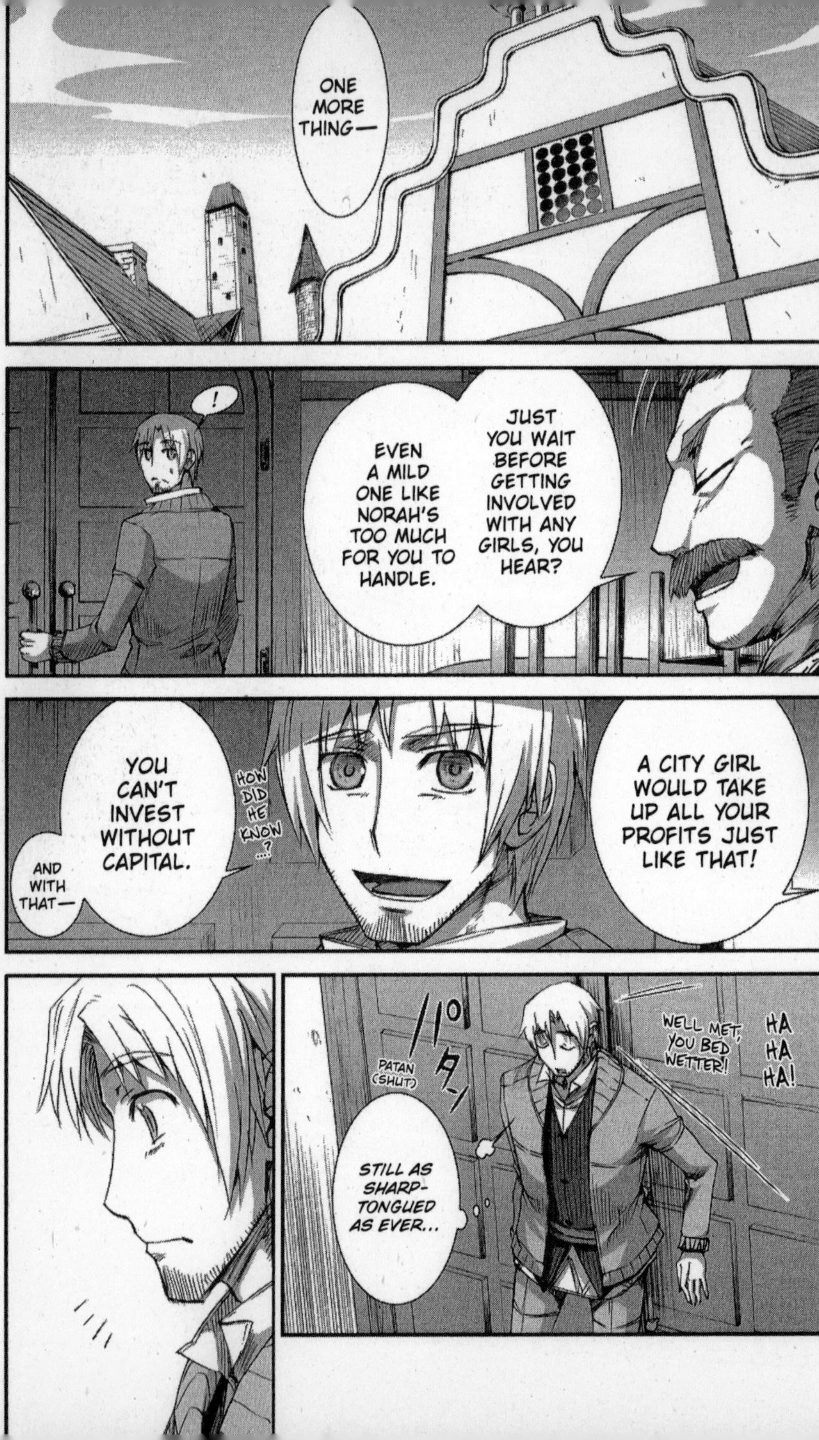
ONE MORE THING—
JUST YOU WAIT BEFORE GETTING INVOLVED WITH ANY GIRLS, YOU HEAR?
EVEN A MILD ONE LIKE NORAH'S TOO MUCH FOR YOU TO HANDLE.
!
A CITY GIRL WOULD TAKE UP ALL YOUR PROFITS JUST LIKE THAT!
HOW DID HE KNOW...?
YOU CAN'T INVEST WITHOUT CAPITAL.
AND WITH THAT—
HA HA HA!
WELL MET, YOU BED WETTER!
PATAN (SHUT)
STILL AS SHARP-TONGUED AS EVER...

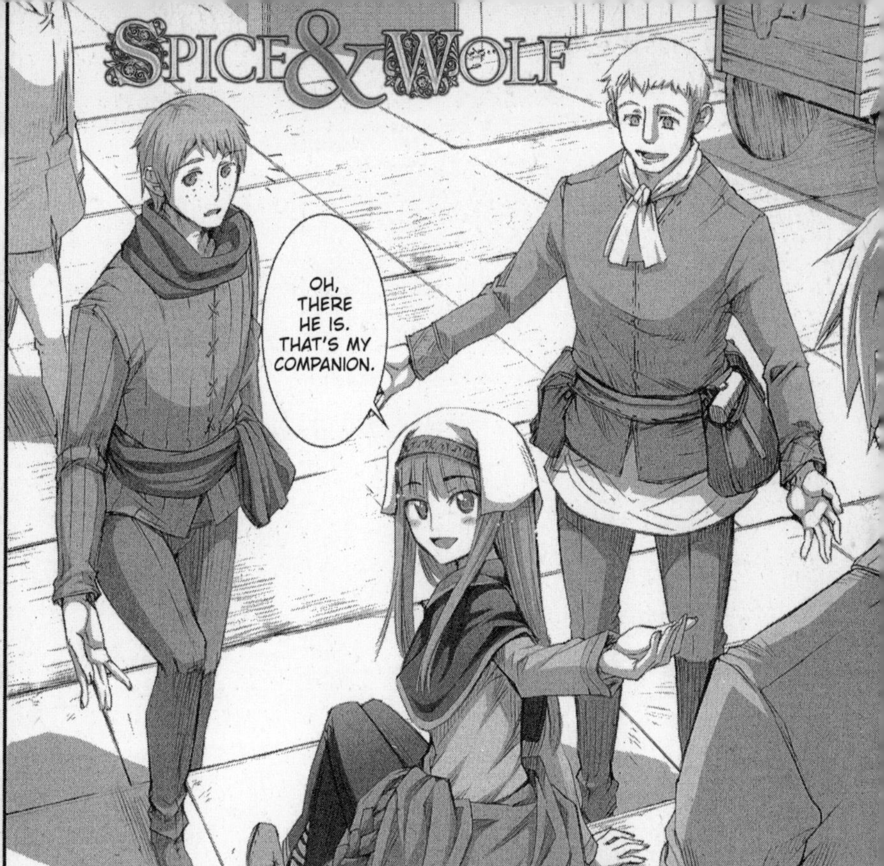
SPICE & WOLF
OH, THERE HE IS. THAT'S MY COMPANION.

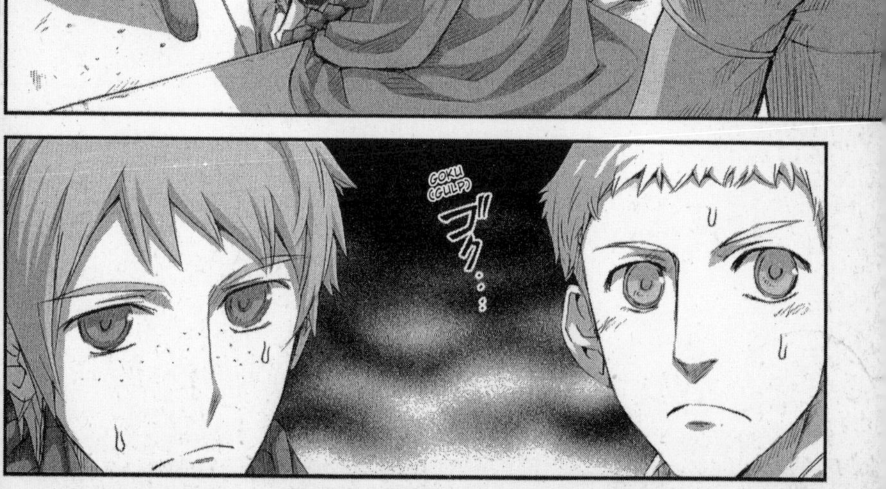
GOKU (GULP)

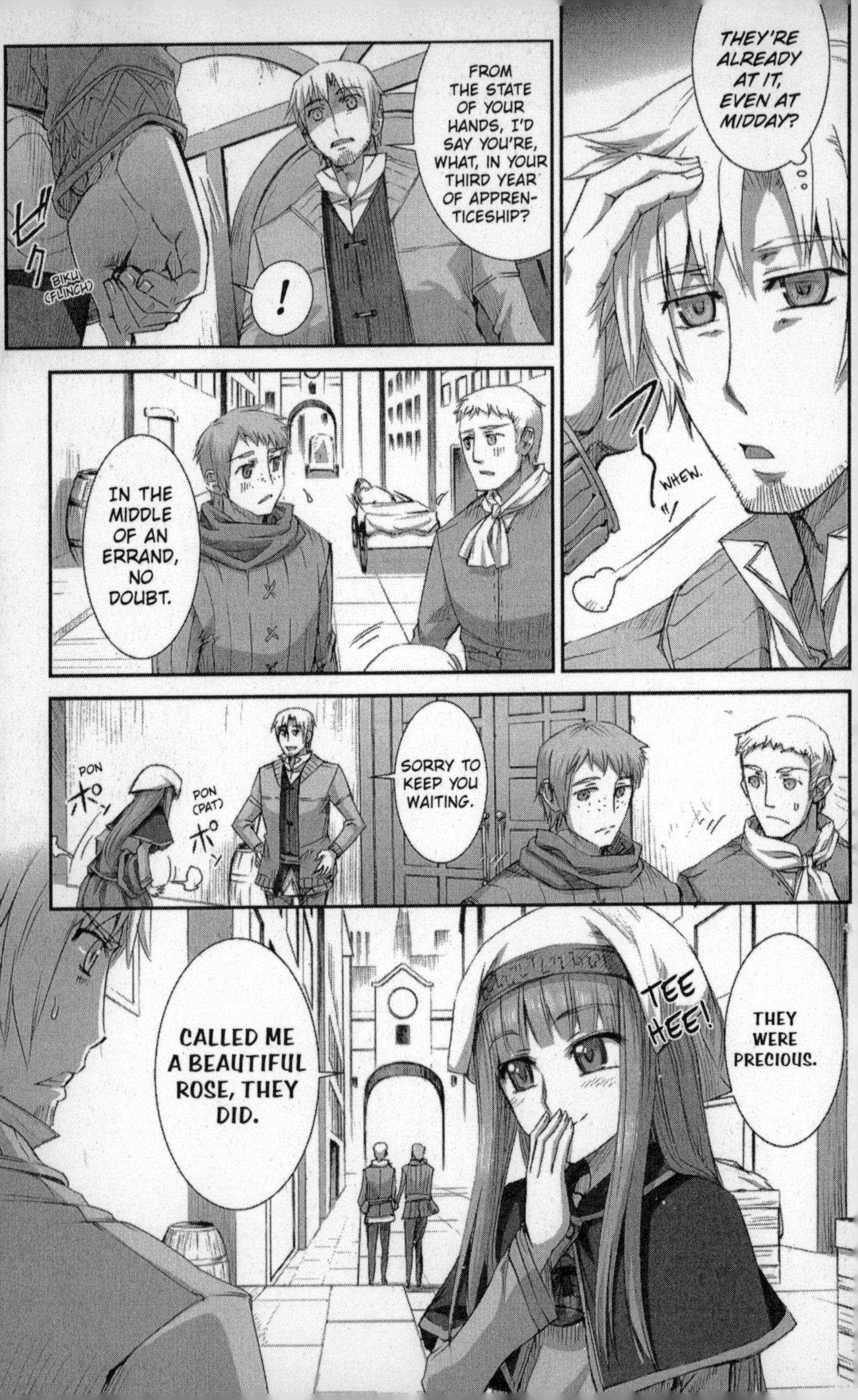
THEY'RE ALREADY AT IT, EVEN AT MIDDAY?
WHEW.
FROM THE STATE OF YOUR HANDS, I'D SAY YOU'RE, WHAT, IN YOUR THIRD YEAR OF APPREN-TICESHIP?
!
BIKU (FLINCH)
IN THE MIDDLE OF AN ERRAND, NO DOUBT.
SORRY TO KEEP YOU WAITING.
PON (PAT)
PON
THEY WERE PRECIOUS.
TEE HEE!
CALLED ME A BEAUTIFUL ROSE, THEY DID.

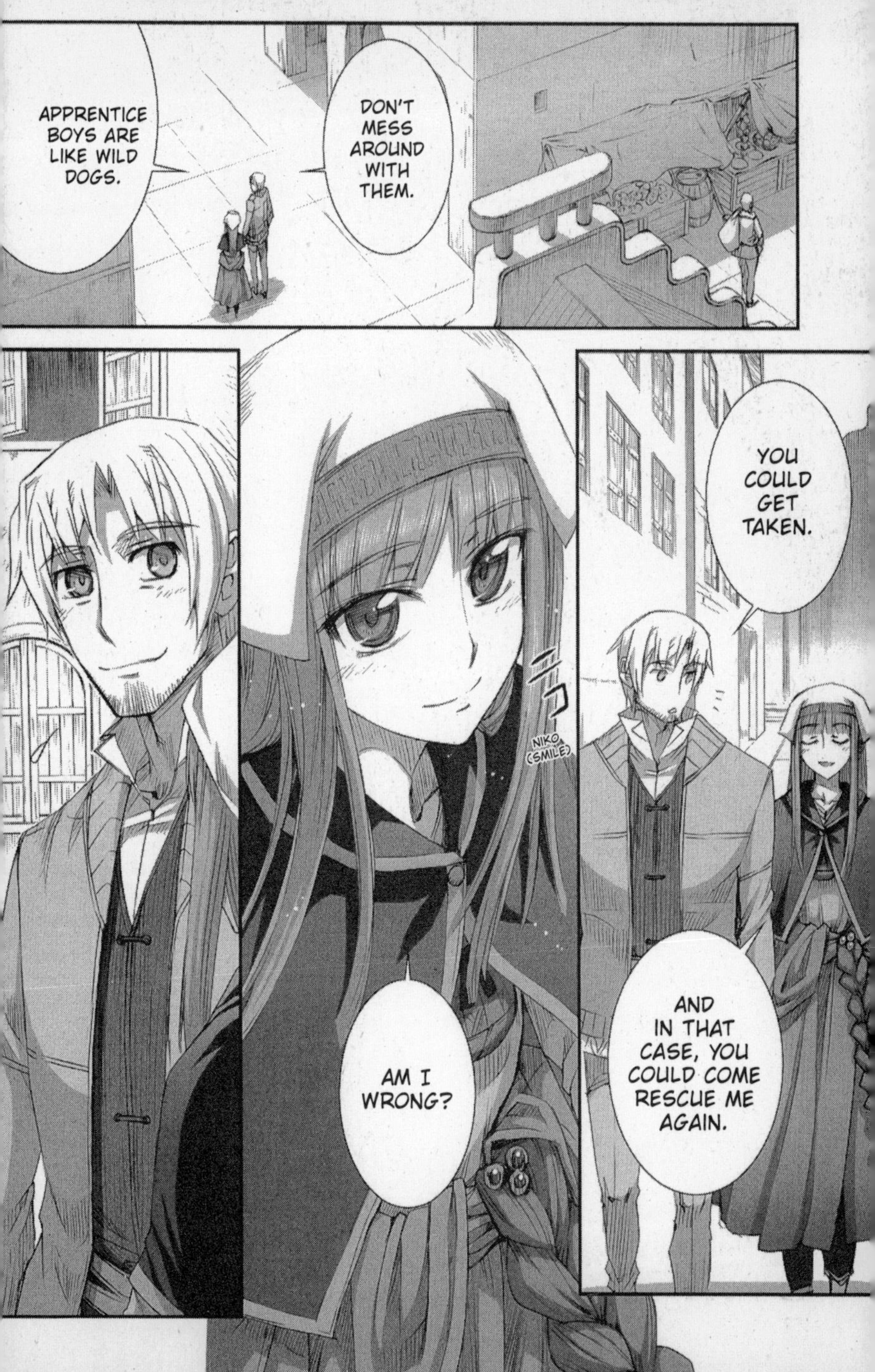
DON'T MESS AROUND WITH THEM.
APPRENTICE BOYS ARE LIKE WILD DOGS.
YOU COULD GET TAKEN.
AND IN THAT CASE, YOU COULD COME RESCUE ME AGAIN.
NIKO (SMILE)
AM I WRONG?

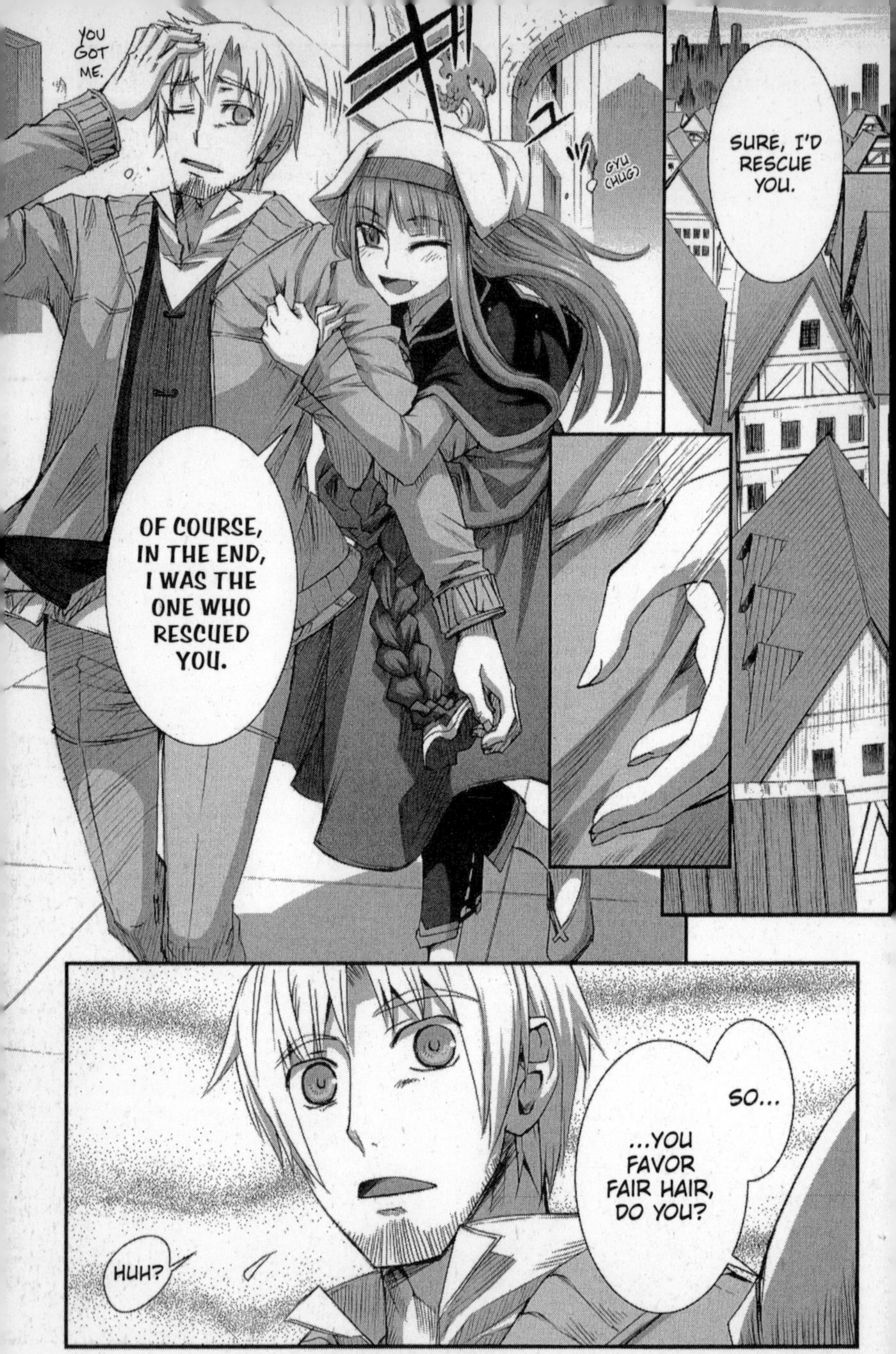
SURE, I'D RESCUE YOU.
GYU (HUG)
YOU GOT ME.
OF COURSE, IN THE END, I WAS THE ONE WHO RESCUED YOU.
SO...
...YOU FAVOR FAIR HAIR, DO YOU?
HUH?

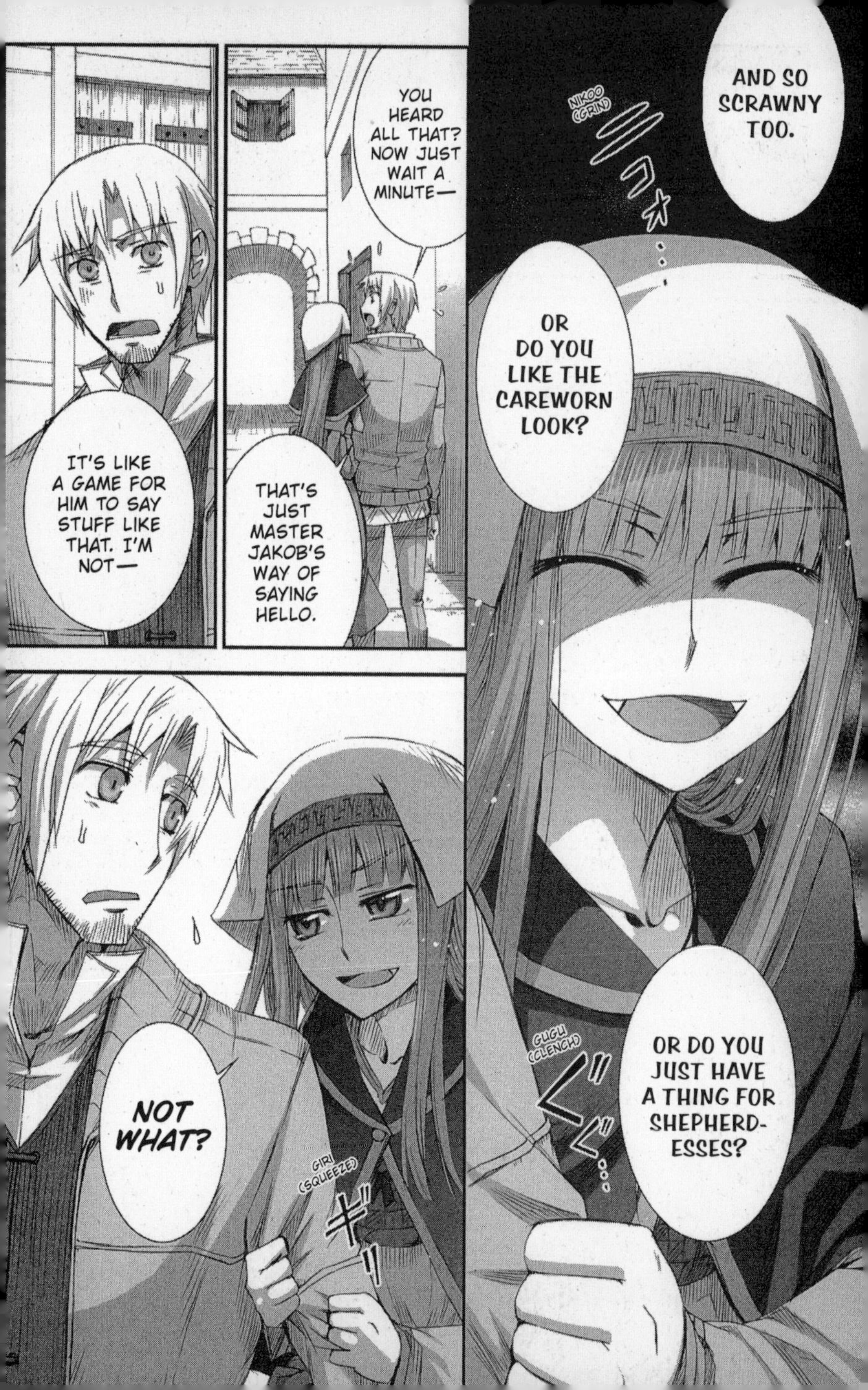
AND SO SCRAWNY TOO.
NIKOO (GRIN)
OR DO YOU LIKE THE CAREWORN LOOK?
GUGU (CLENCH)
OR DO YOU JUST HAVE A THING FOR SHEPHERD-ESSES?
YOU HEARD ALL THAT? NOW JUST WAIT A MINUTE—
THAT'S JUST MASTER JAKOB'S WAY OF SAYING HELLO.
IT'S LIKE A GAME FOR HIM TO SAY STUFF LIKE THAT. I'M NOT—
NOT WHAT?
GIRI (SQUEEZE)

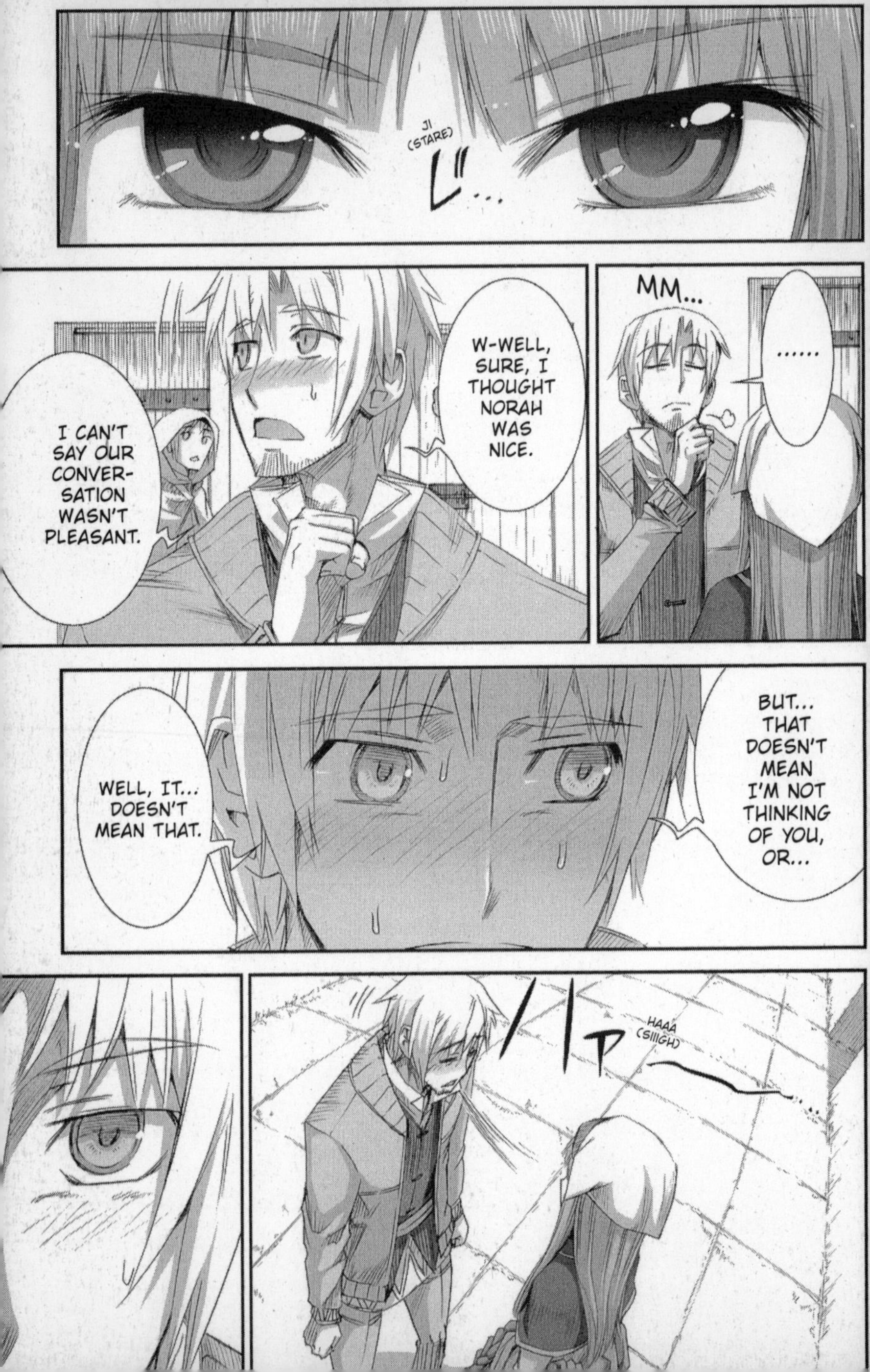
JI (STARE)
MM...
......
W-WELL, SURE, I THOUGHT NORAH WAS NICE.
I CAN'T SAY OUR CONVER-SATION WASN'T PLEASANT.
BUT... THAT DOESN'T MEAN I'M NOT THINKING OF YOU, OR...
WELL, IT... DOESN'T MEAN THAT.
HAAA (SIIIGH)

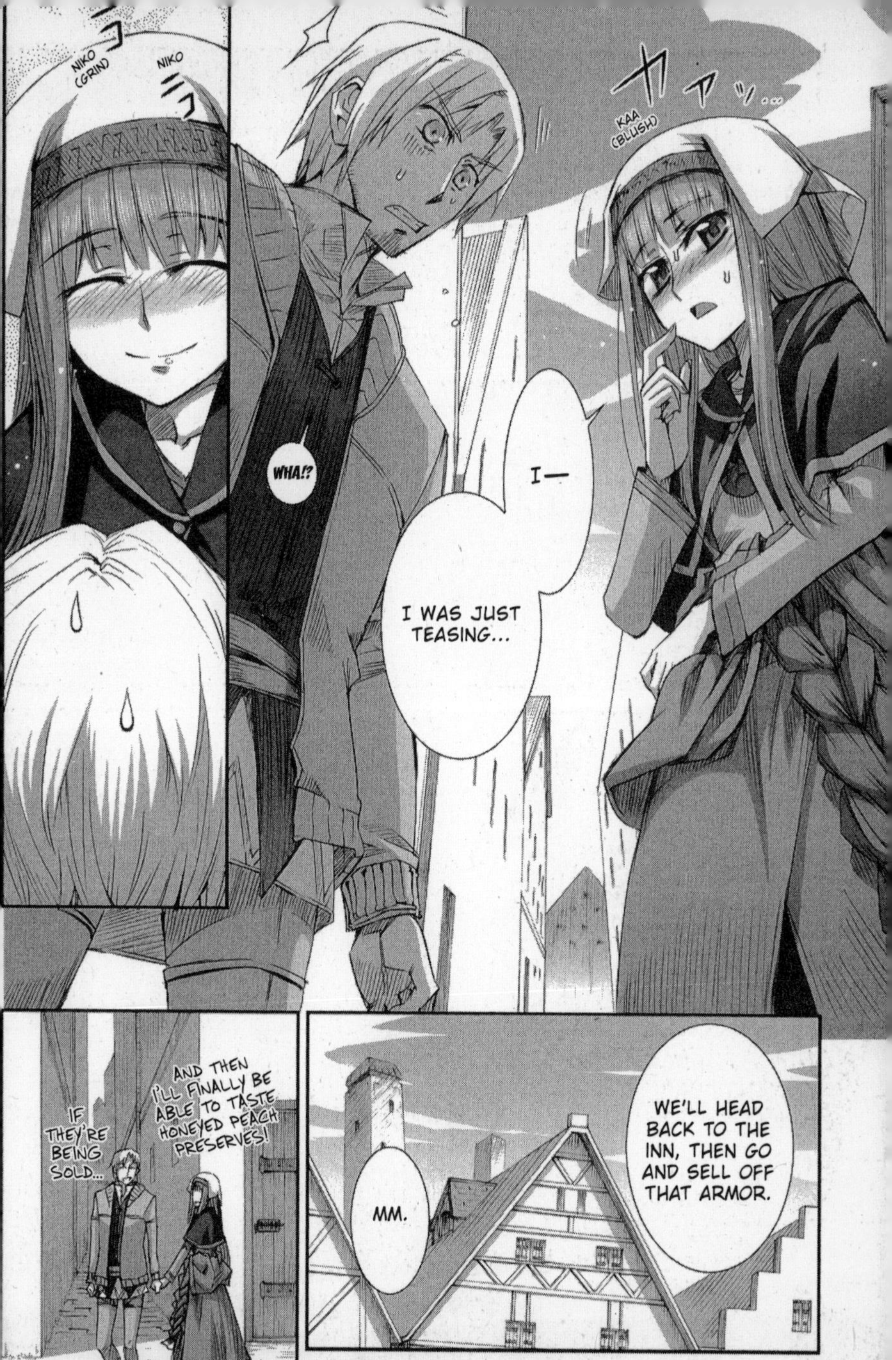
KAA (BLUSH)
I—
I WAS JUST TEASING...
WHA!?
NIKO (GRIN)
NIKO
WE'LL HEAD BACK TO THE INN, THEN GO AND SELL OFF THAT ARMOR.
MM.
IF THEY'RE BEING SOLD...
AND THEN I'LL FINALLY BE ABLE TO TASTE HONEYED PEACH PRESERVES!

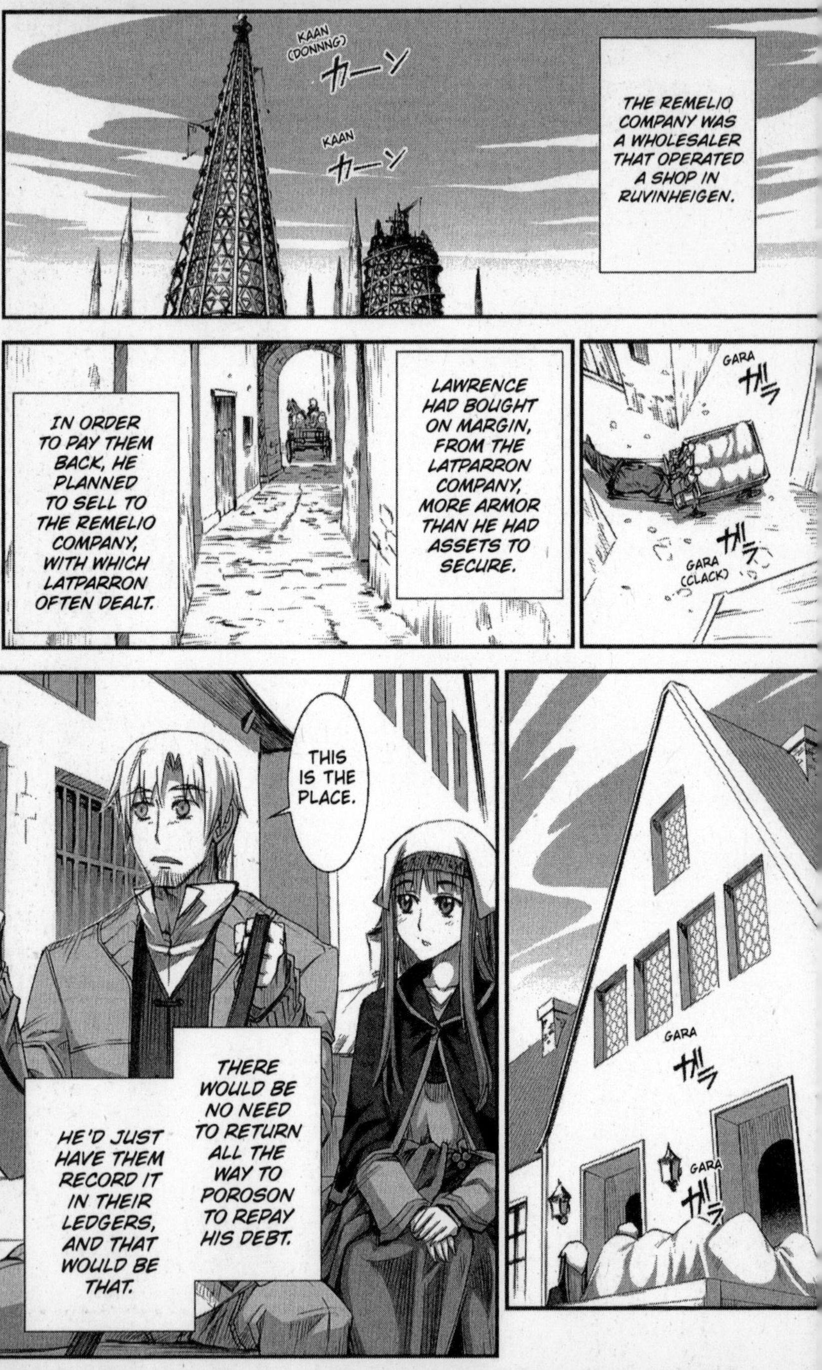

THE REMELIO COMPANY WAS A WHOLESALER THAT OPERATED A SHOP IN RUVINHEIGEN.
KAAN (DONNNG)
カーン
KAAN
カーン
GARA
ガラ
GARA (CLACK)
ガラ
LAWRENCE HAD BOUGHT ON MARGIN, FROM THE LATPARRON COMPANY, MORE ARMOR THAN HE HAD ASSETS TO SECURE.
IN ORDER TO PAY THEM BACK, HE PLANNED TO SELL TO THE REMELIO COMPANY, WITH WHICH LATPARRON OFTEN DEALT.
GARA
ガラ
GARA
ガラ
THIS IS THE PLACE.
THERE WOULD BE NO NEED TO RETURN ALL THE WAY TO POROSON TO REPAY HIS DEBT.
HE'D JUST HAVE THEM RECORD IT IN THEIR LEDGERS, AND THAT WOULD BE THAT.

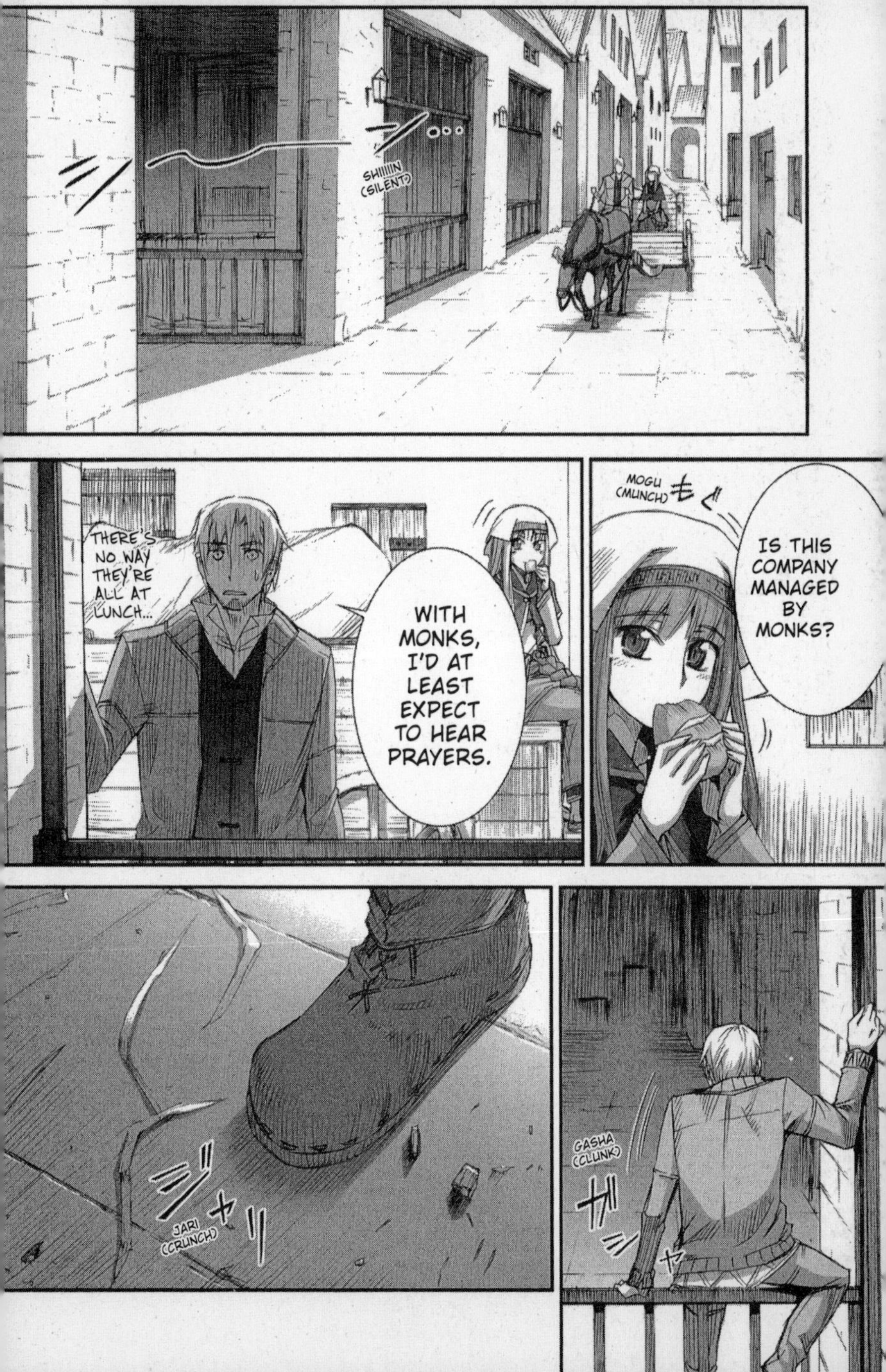

SHIIIIIN (SILENT)
MOGU (MUNCH)
IS THIS COMPANY MANAGED BY MONKS?
WITH MONKS, I'D AT LEAST EXPECT TO HEAR PRAYERS.
THERE'S NO WAY THEY'RE ALL AT LUNCH...
GASHA (CLUNK)
JARI (CRUNCH)

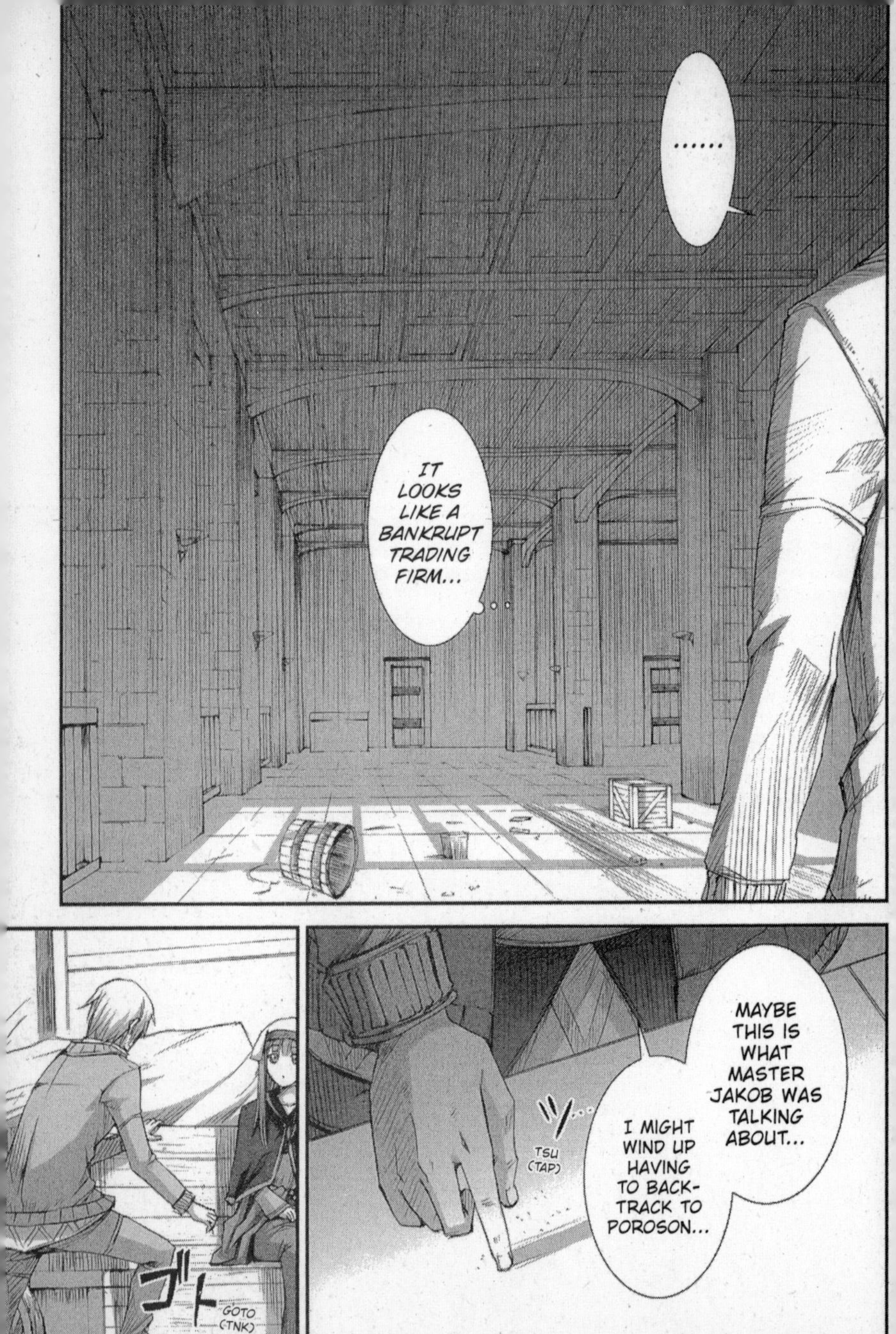
......
IT LOOKS LIKE A BANKRUPT TRADING FIRM...
MAYBE THIS IS WHAT MASTER JAKOB WAS TALKING ABOUT...
I MIGHT WIND UP HAVING TO BACK-TRACK TO POROSON...
ツ...
TSU (TAP)
ゴト
GOTO (TNK)

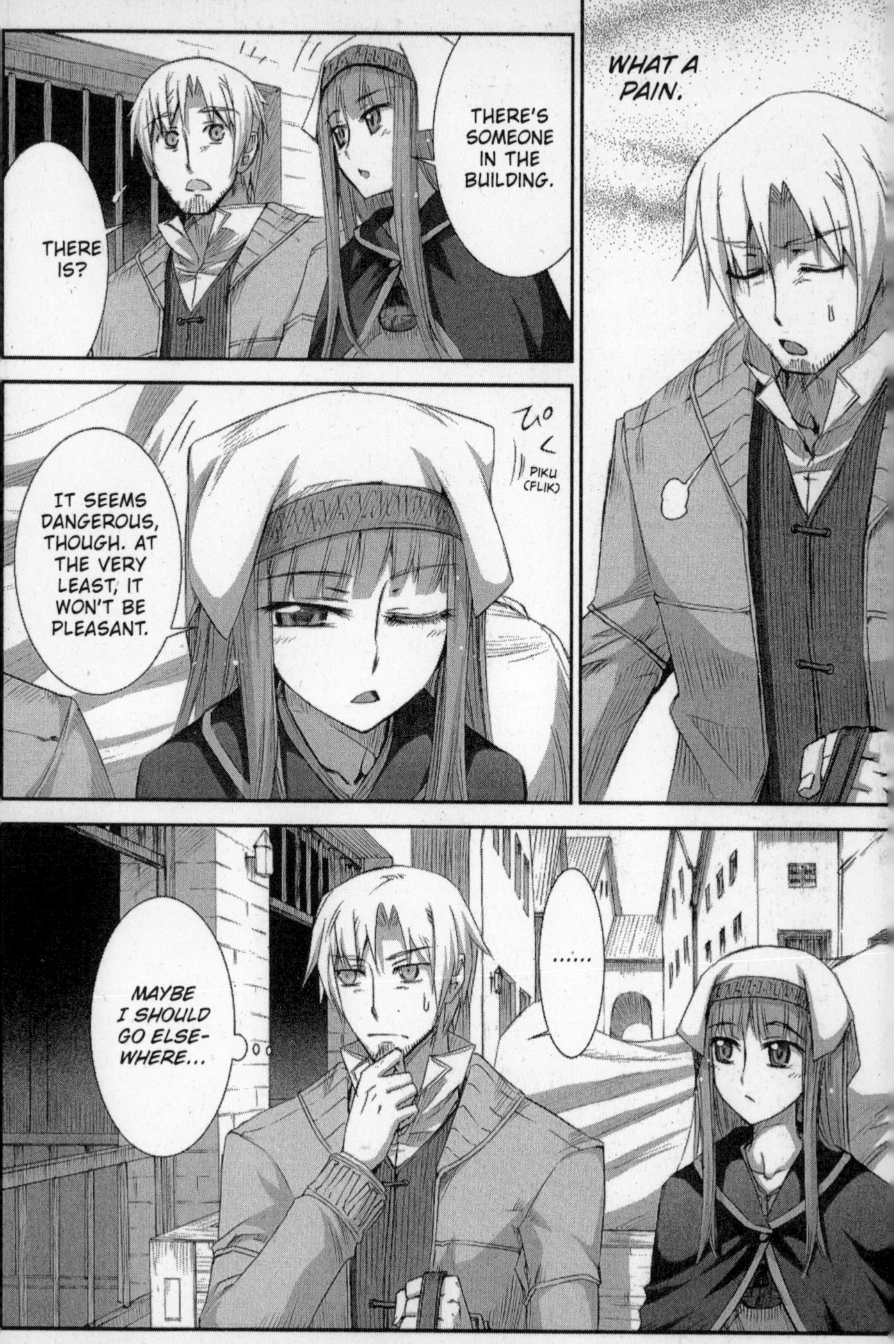
WHAT A PAIN.
THERE'S SOMEONE IN THE BUILDING.
THERE IS?
ぴく
PIKU (FLIK)
IT SEEMS DANGEROUS, THOUGH. AT THE VERY LEAST, IT WON'T BE PLEASANT.
......
MAYBE I SHOULD GO ELSE-WHERE...

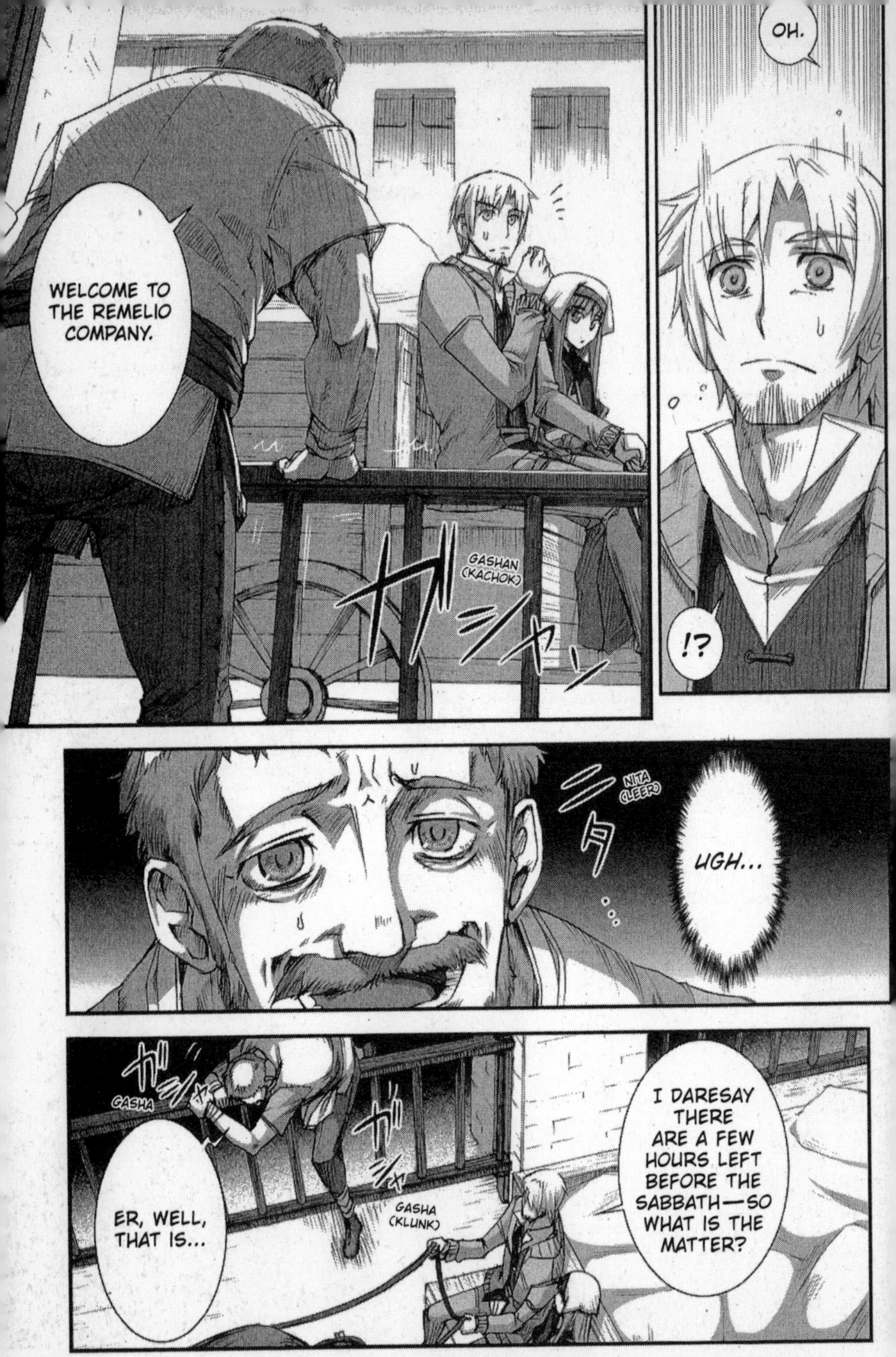
OH.
!?
WELCOME TO THE REMELIO COMPANY.
GASHAN (KACHOK)
NITA (LEER)
UGH...
I DARESAY THERE ARE A FEW HOURS LEFT BEFORE THE SABBATH—SO WHAT IS THE MATTER?
GASHA (KLUNK)
ER, WELL, THAT IS...
GASHA

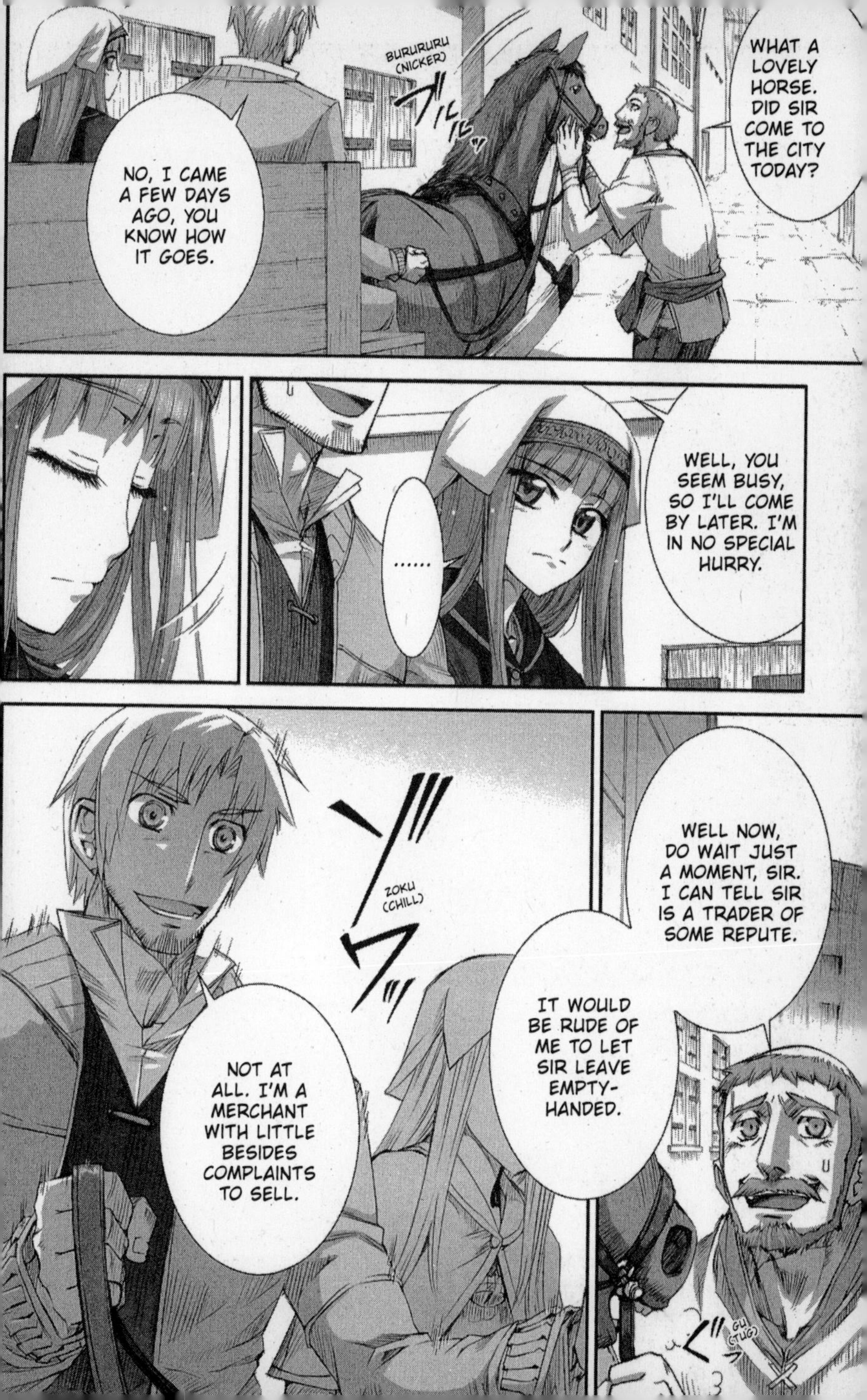
WHAT A LOVELY HORSE. DID SIR COME TO THE CITY TODAY?
BURURURU (NICKER)
NO, I CAME A FEW DAYS AGO, YOU KNOW HOW IT GOES.
WELL, YOU SEEM BUSY, SO I'LL COME BY LATER. I'M IN NO SPECIAL HURRY.
......
WELL NOW, DO WAIT JUST A MOMENT, SIR. I CAN TELL SIR IS A TRADER OF SOME REPUTE.
IT WOULD BE RUDE OF ME TO LET SIR LEAVE EMPTY-HANDED.
GU (TUG)
ZOKU (CHILL)
NOT AT ALL. I'M A MERCHANT WITH LITTLE BESIDES COMPLAINTS TO SELL.

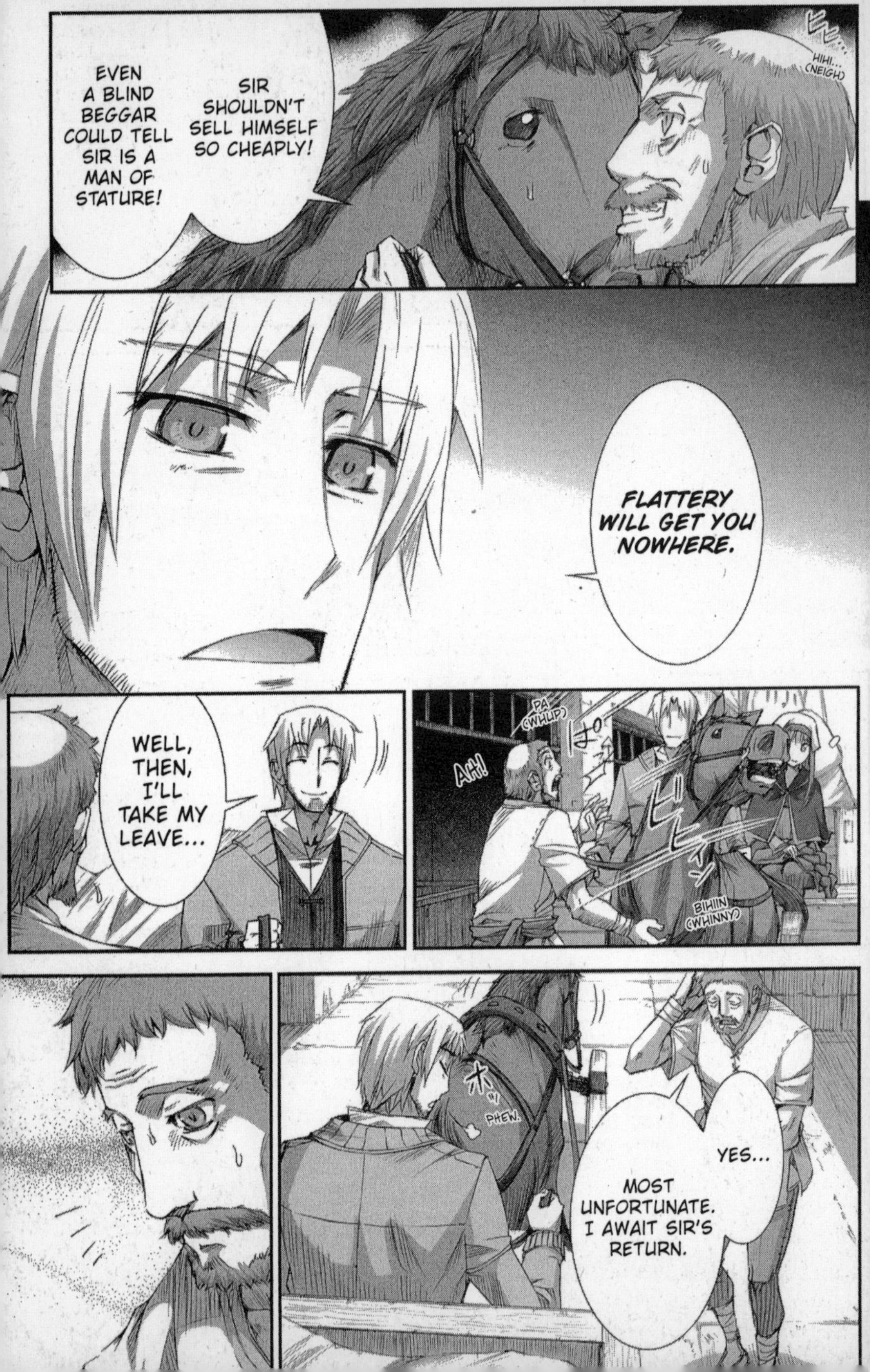
HIHI... (NEIGH)
SIR SHOULDN'T SELL HIMSELF SO CHEAPLY!
EVEN A BLIND BEGGAR COULD TELL SIR IS A MAN OF STATURE!
FLATTERY WILL GET YOU NOWHERE.
PA (WHIP)
AH!
BIHIIN (WHINNY)
WELL, THEN, I'LL TAKE MY LEAVE...
PHEW.
YES...
MOST UNFORTUNATE. I AWAIT SIR'S RETURN.

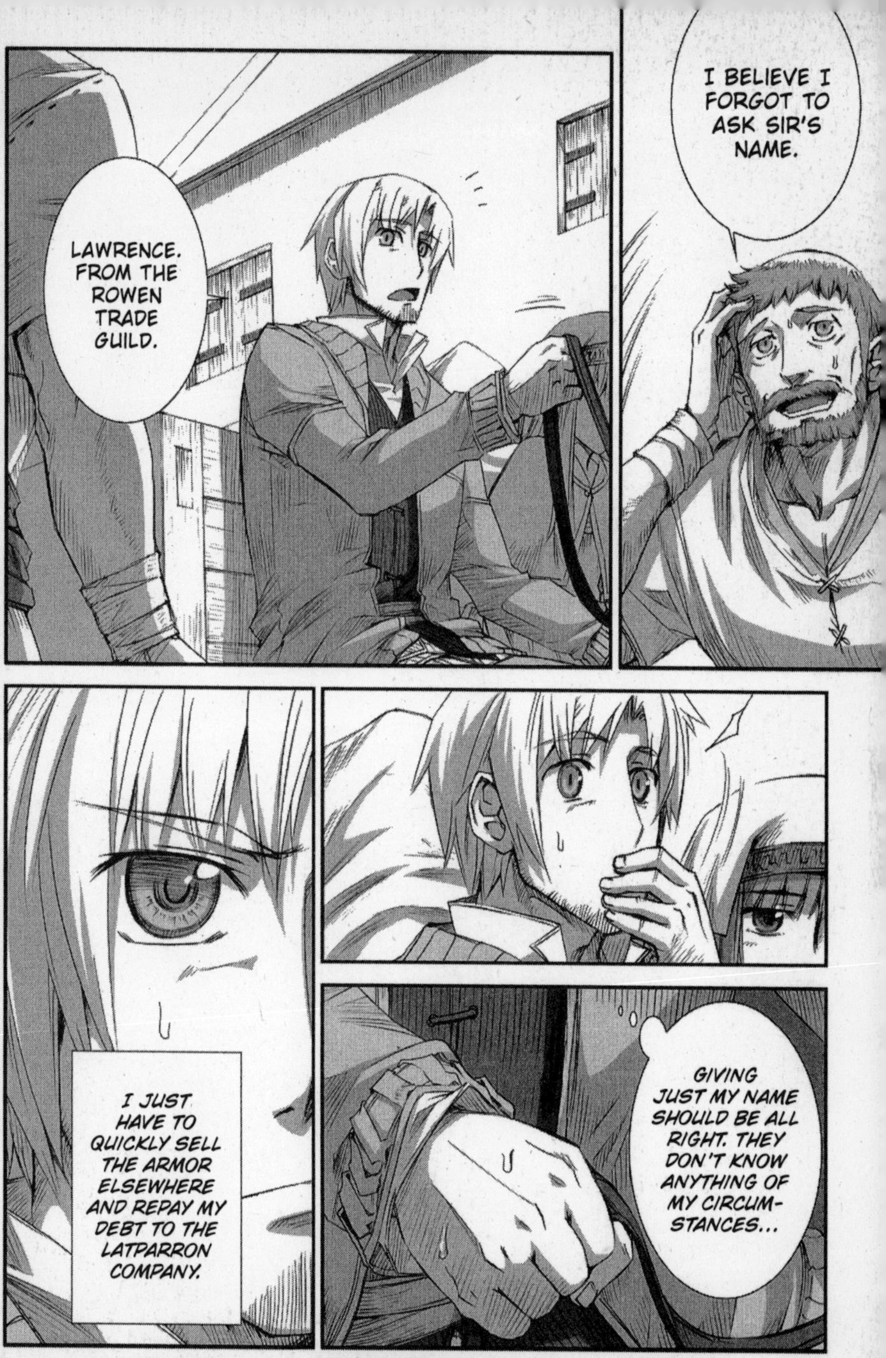
I BELIEVE I FORGOT TO ASK SIR'S NAME.
LAWRENCE. FROM THE ROWEN TRADE GUILD.
GIVING JUST MY NAME SHOULD BE ALL RIGHT. THEY DON'T KNOW ANYTHING OF MY CIRCUM-STANCES...
I JUST HAVE TO QUICKLY SELL THE ARMOR ELSEWHERE AND REPAY MY DEBT TO THE LATPARRON COMPANY.

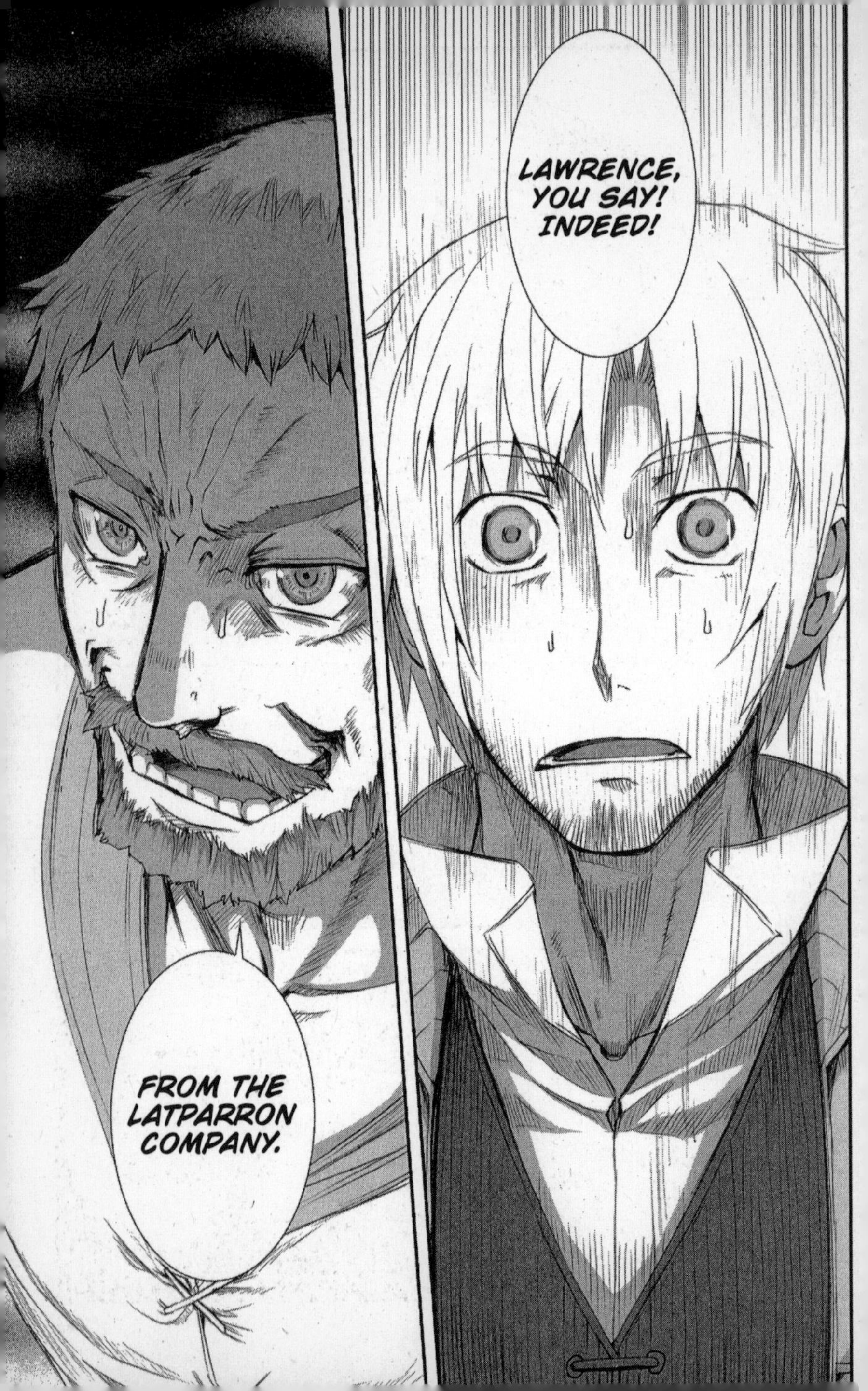
LAWRENCE, YOU SAY! INDEED!
FROM THE LATPARRON COMPANY.

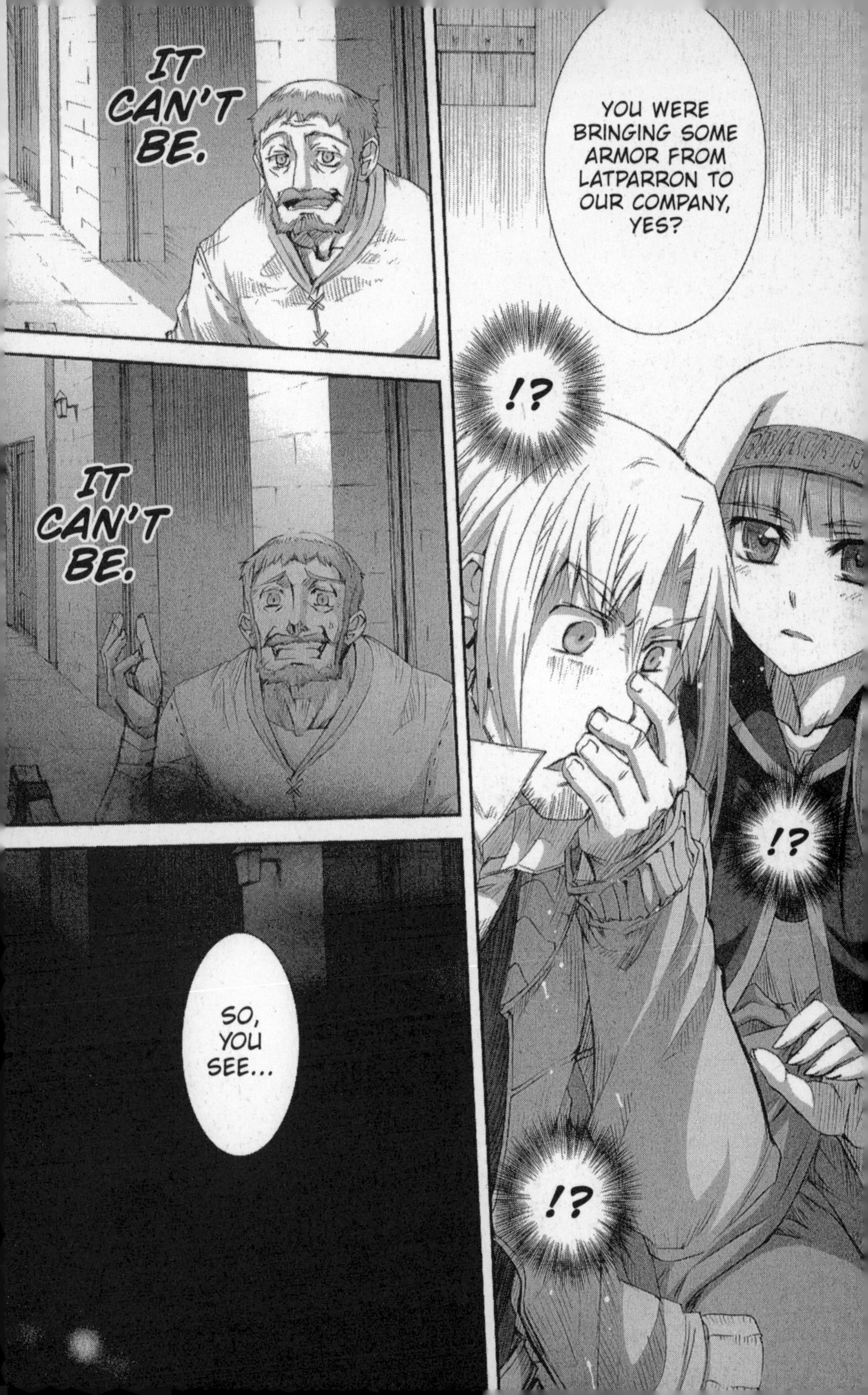
YOU WERE BRINGING SOME ARMOR FROM LATPARRON TO OUR COMPANY, YES?
!?
!?
!?
IT CAN'T BE.
IT CAN'T BE.
SO, YOU SEE...

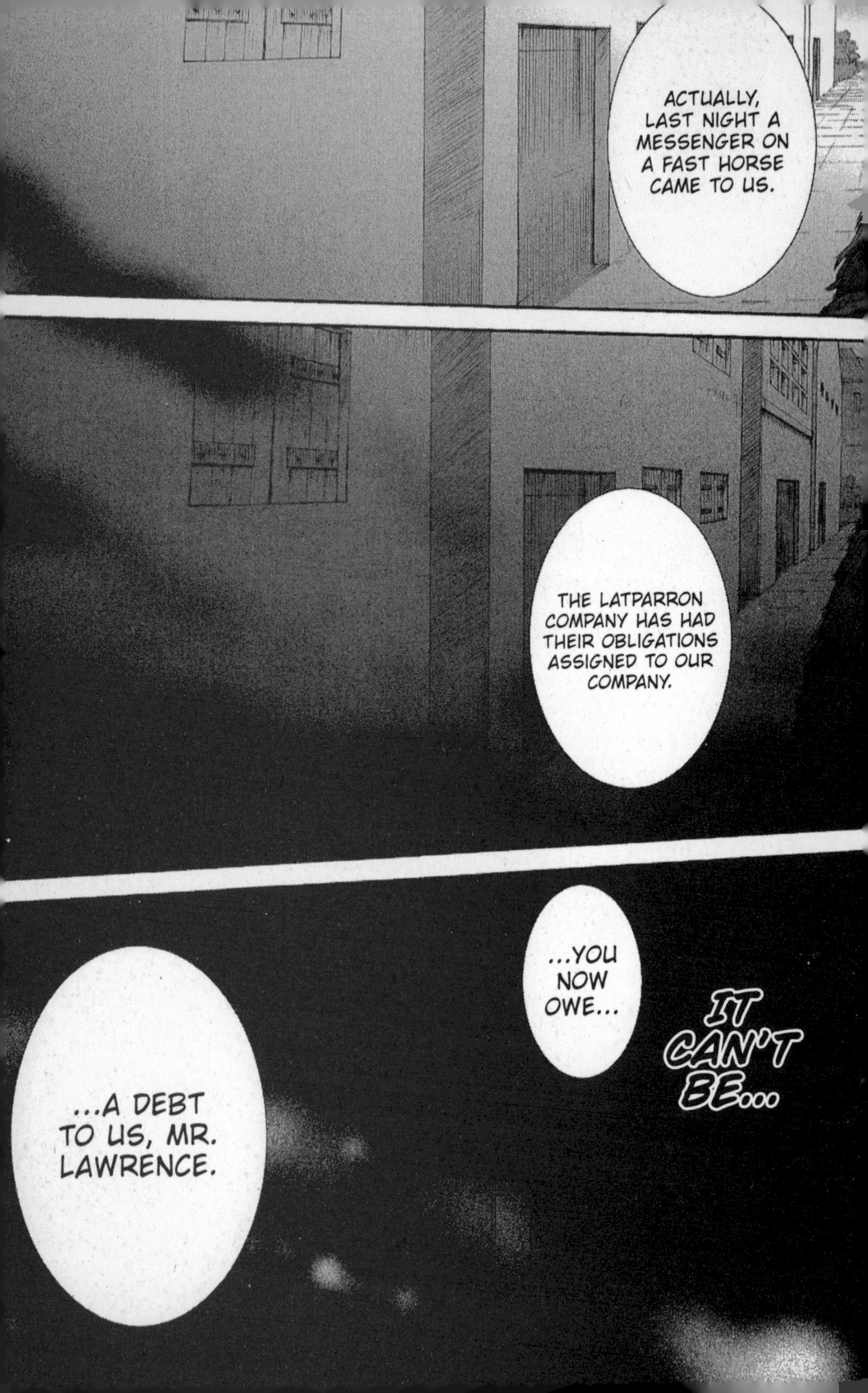
ACTUALLY, LAST NIGHT A MESSENGER ON A FAST HORSE CAME TO US.
THE LATPARRON COMPANY HAS HAD THEIR OBLIGATIONS ASSIGNED TO OUR COMPANY.
IT CAN'T BE...
...YOU NOW OWE...
...A DEBT TO US, MR. LAWRENCE.

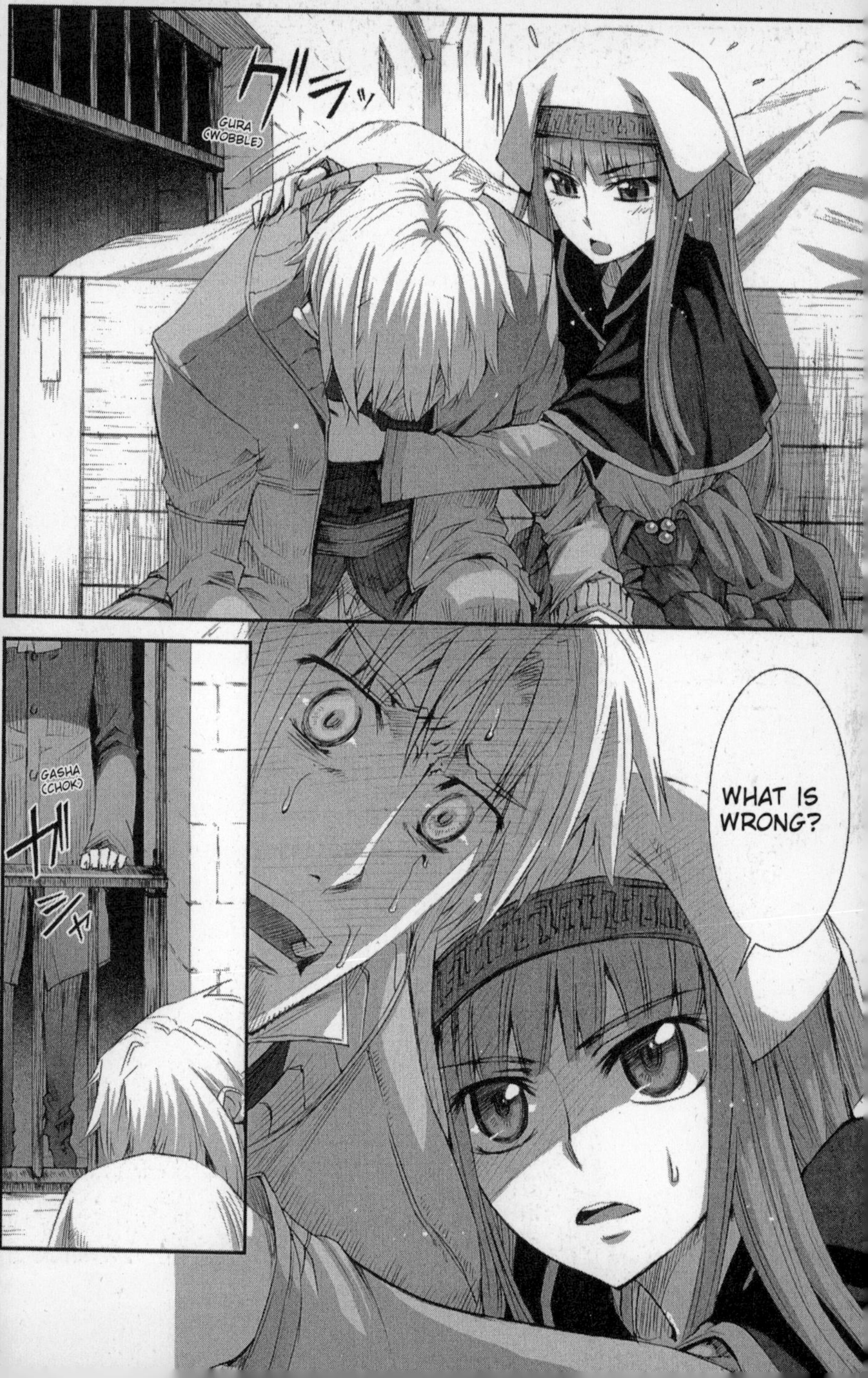
グラッ
GURA (WOBBLE)
WHAT IS WRONG?
ガシャ
GASHA (CHOK)

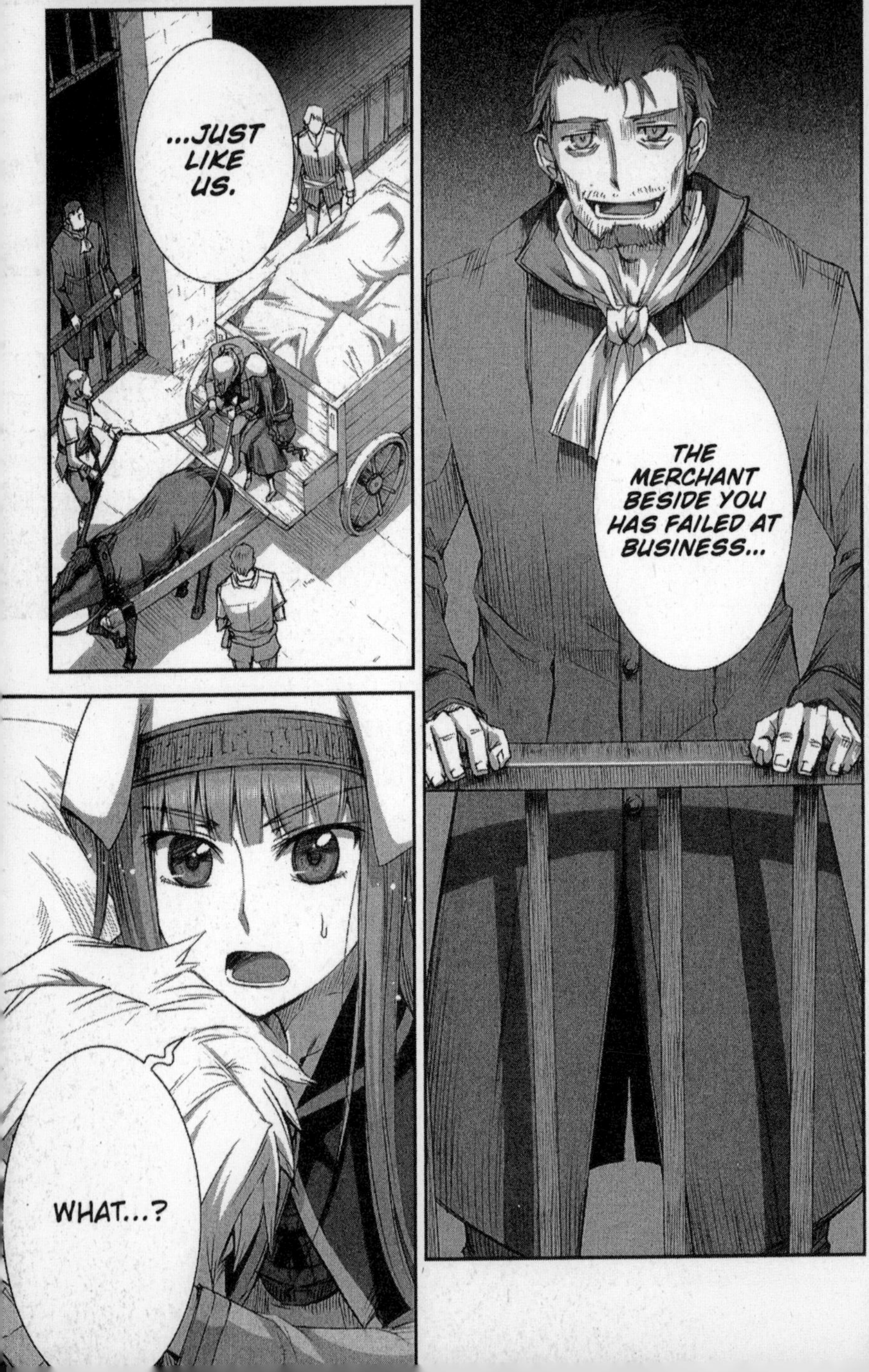
THE MERCHANT BESIDE YOU HAS FAILED AT BUSINESS...
...JUST LIKE US.
WHAT...?

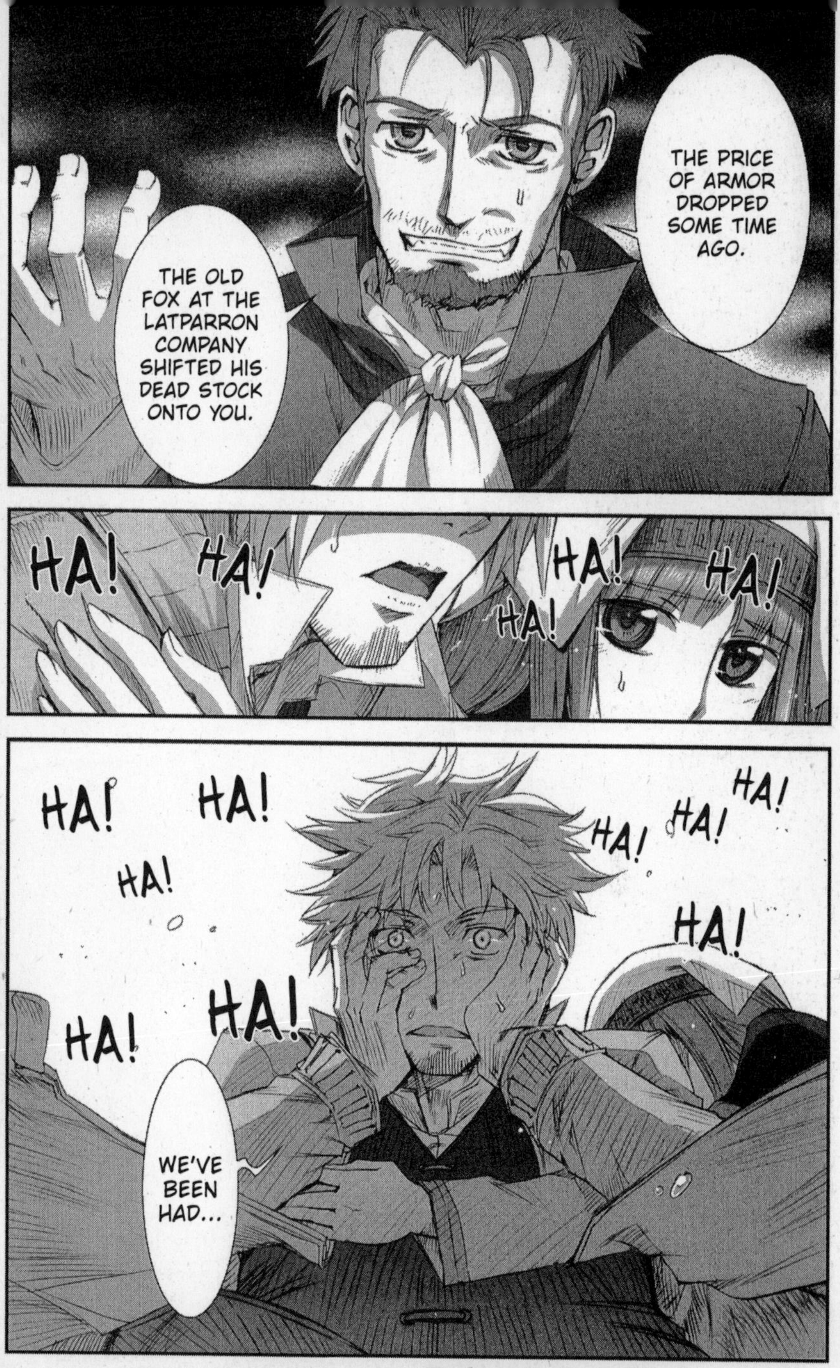
THE PRICE OF ARMOR DROPPED SOME TIME AGO.
THE OLD FOX AT THE LATPARRON COMPANY SHIFTED HIS DEAD STOCK ONTO YOU.
HA!
HA!
HA!
HA!
HA!
HA!
HA!
HA!
HA!
HA!
HA!
HA!
HA!
HA!
WE'VE BEEN HAD...

To be continued in Volume 5...

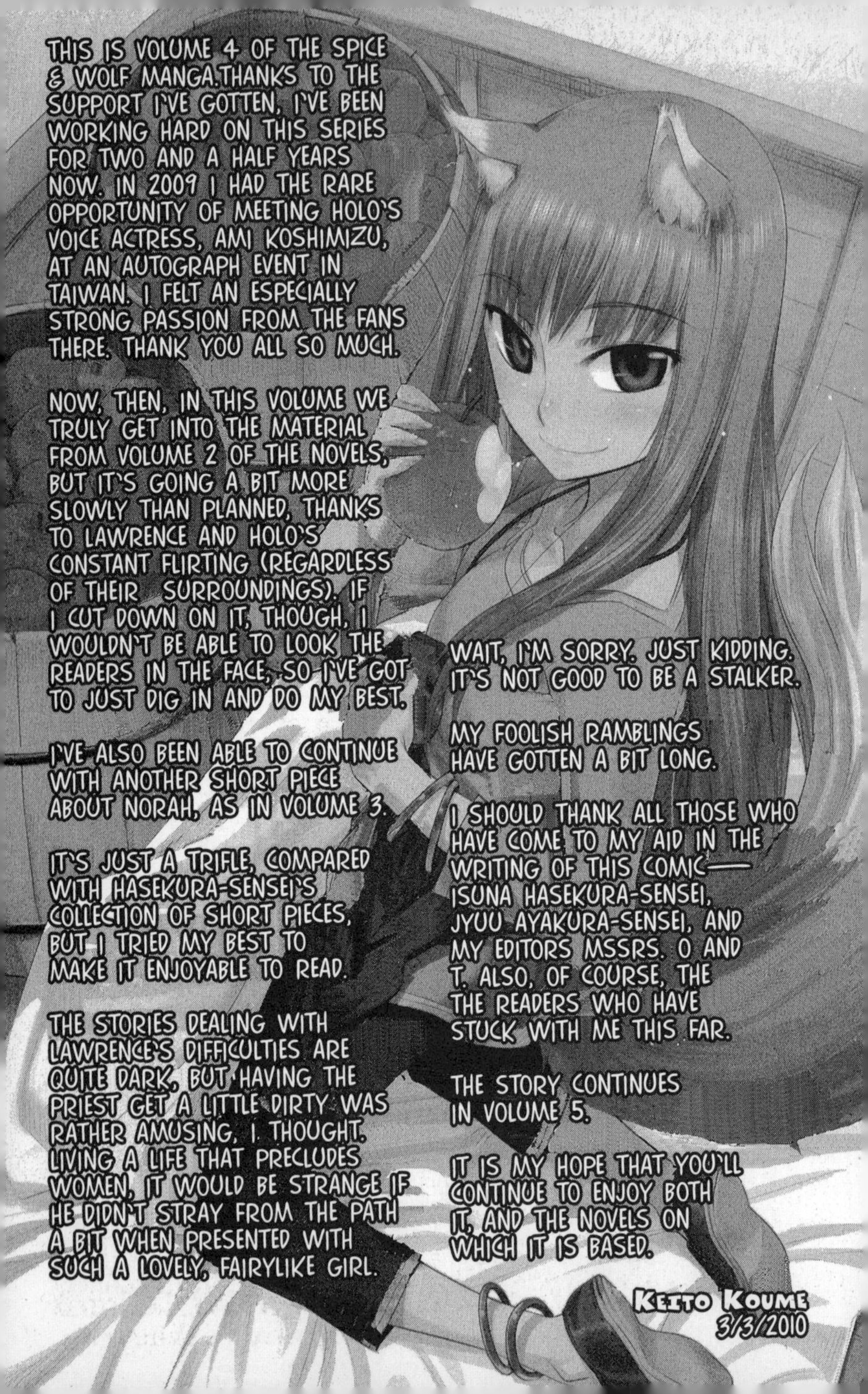

THIS IS VOLUME 4 OF THE SPICE & WOLF MANGA. THANKS TO THE SUPPORT I'VE GOTTEN, I'VE BEEN WORKING HARD ON THIS SERIES FOR TWO AND A HALF YEARS NOW. IN 2009 I HAD THE RARE OPPORTUNITY OF MEETING HOLO'S VOICE ACTRESS, AMI KOSHIMIZU, AT AN AUTOGRAPH EVENT IN TAIWAN. I FELT AN ESPECIALLY STRONG PASSION FROM THE FANS THERE. THANK YOU ALL SO MUCH.

NOW, THEN, IN THIS VOLUME WE TRULY GET INTO THE MATERIAL FROM VOLUME 2 OF THE NOVELS, BUT IT'S GOING A BIT MORE SLOWLY THAN PLANNED, THANKS TO LAWRENCE AND HOLO'S CONSTANT FLIRTING (REGARDLESS OF THEIR SURROUNDINGS). IF I CUT DOWN ON IT, THOUGH, I WOULDN'T BE ABLE TO LOOK THE READERS IN THE FACE, SO I'VE GOT TO JUST DIG IN AND DO MY BEST.

I'VE ALSO BEEN ABLE TO CONTINUE WITH ANOTHER SHORT PIECE ABOUT NORAH, AS IN VOLUME 3.

IT'S JUST A TRIFLE, COMPARED WITH HASEKURA-SENSEI'S COLLECTION OF SHORT PIECES, BUT I TRIED MY BEST TO MAKE IT ENJOYABLE TO READ.

THE STORIES DEALING WITH LAWRENCE'S DIFFICULTIES ARE QUITE DARK, BUT HAVING THE PRIEST GET A LITTLE DIRTY WAS RATHER AMUSING, I THOUGHT. LIVING A LIFE THAT PRECLUDES WOMEN, IT WOULD BE STRANGE IF HE DIDN'T STRAY FROM THE PATH A BIT WHEN PRESENTED WITH SUCH A LOVELY, FAIRYLIKE GIRL.

WAIT, I'M SORRY. JUST KIDDING. IT'S NOT GOOD TO BE A STALKER.

MY FOOLISH RAMBLINGS HAVE GOTTEN A BIT LONG.

I SHOULD THANK ALL THOSE WHO HAVE COME TO MY AID IN THE WRITING OF THIS COMIC— ISUNA HASEKURA-SENSEI, JYUU AYAKURA-SENSEI, AND MY EDITORS MSSRS. O AND T. ALSO, OF COURSE, THE THE READERS WHO HAVE STUCK WITH ME THIS FAR.

THE STORY CONTINUES IN VOLUME 5.

IT IS MY HOPE THAT YOU'LL CONTINUE TO ENJOY BOTH IT AND THE NOVELS ON WHICH IT IS BASED.

KEITO KOUME
3/3/2010

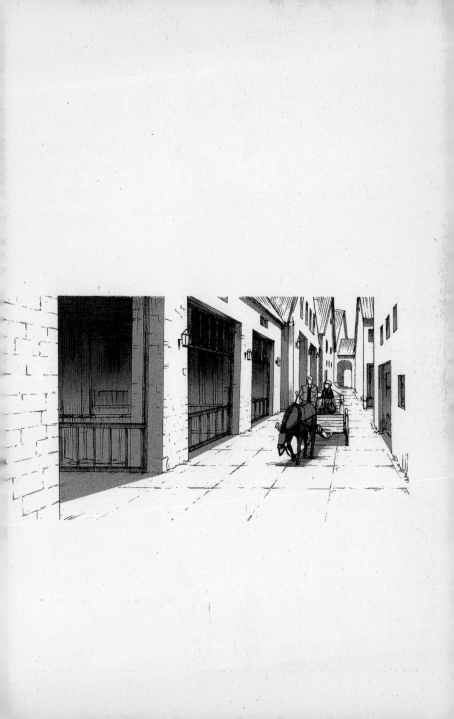

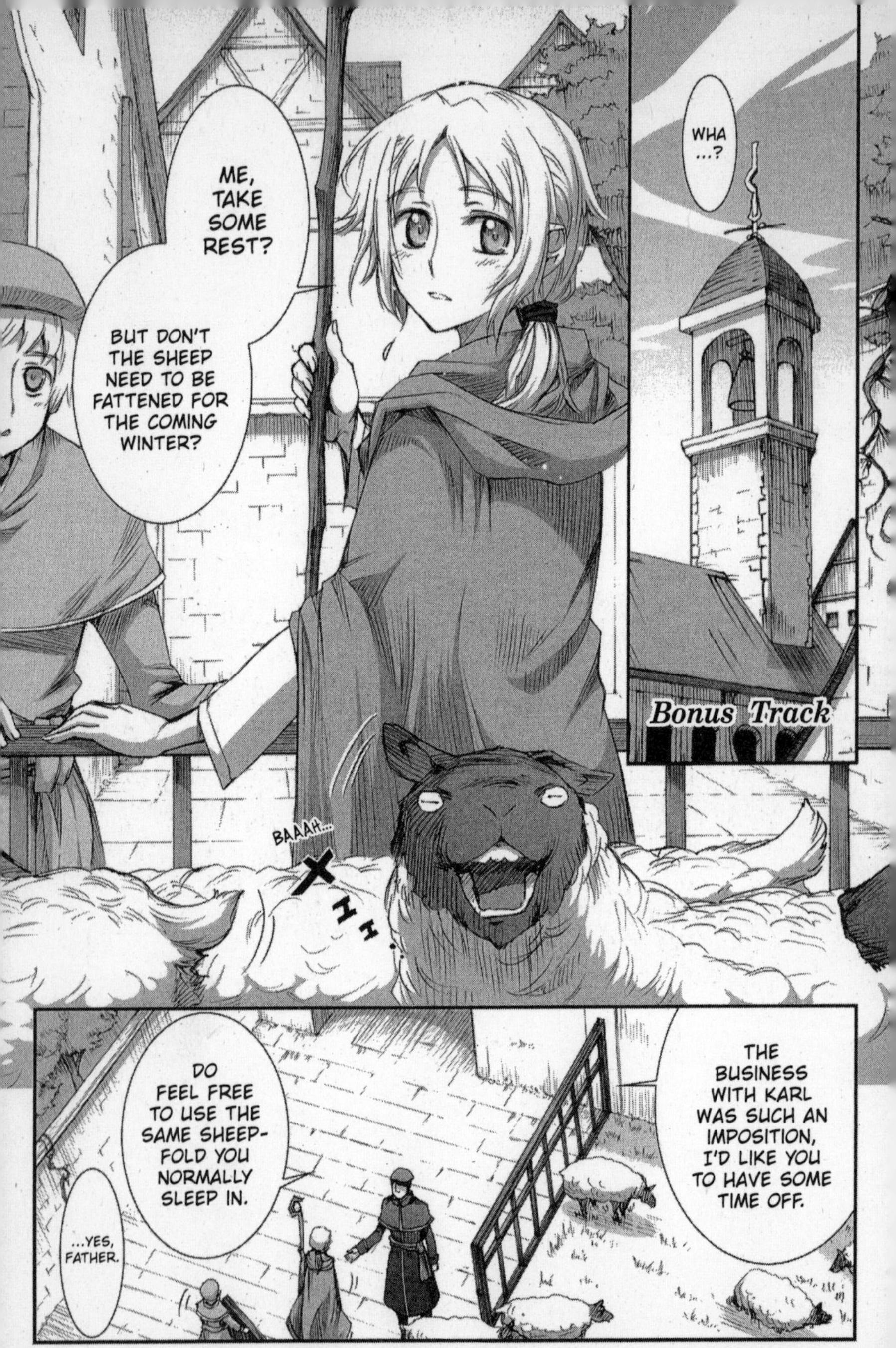
WHA ...?
Bonus Track
ME, TAKE SOME REST?
BUT DON'T THE SHEEP NEED TO BE FATTENED FOR THE COMING WINTER?
BAAAH...
THE BUSINESS WITH KARL WAS SUCH AN IMPOSITION, I'D LIKE YOU TO HAVE SOME TIME OFF.
DO FEEL FREE TO USE THE SAME SHEEP-FOLD YOU NORMALLY SLEEP IN.
...YES, FATHER.

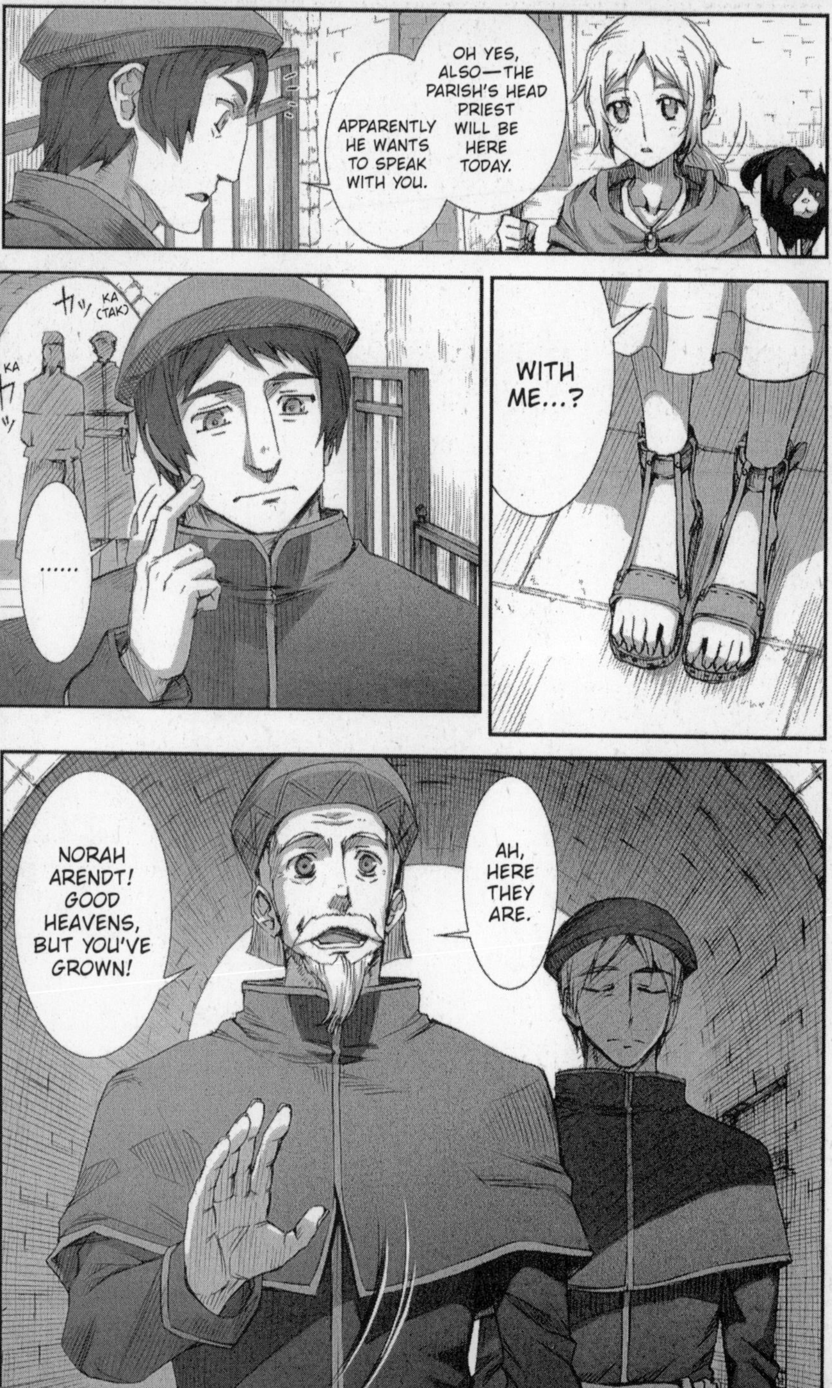
OH YES, ALSO—THE PARISH'S HEAD PRIEST WILL BE HERE TODAY.
APPARENTLY HE WANTS TO SPEAK WITH YOU.
WITH ME...?
カッ KA (TAK)
カッ KA
......
AH, HERE THEY ARE.
NORAH ARENDT! GOOD HEAVENS, BUT YOU'VE GROWN!

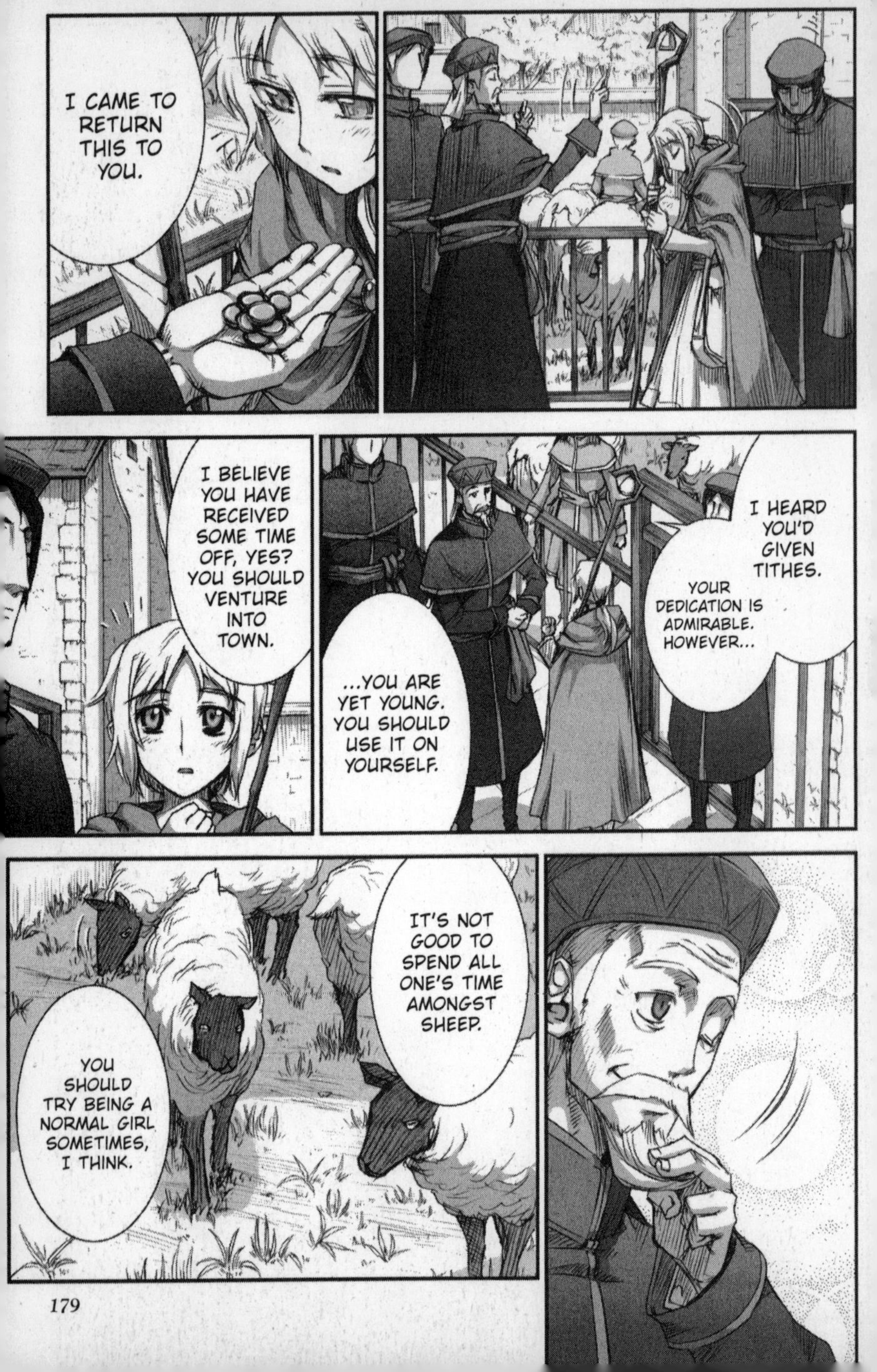
I CAME TO RETURN THIS TO YOU.
I HEARD YOU'D GIVEN TITHES.
YOUR DEDICATION IS ADMIRABLE. HOWEVER...
...YOU ARE YET YOUNG. YOU SHOULD USE IT ON YOURSELF.
I BELIEVE YOU HAVE RECEIVED SOME TIME OFF, YES? YOU SHOULD VENTURE INTO TOWN.
IT'S NOT GOOD TO SPEND ALL ONE'S TIME AMONGST SHEEP.
YOU SHOULD TRY BEING A NORMAL GIRL SOMETIMES, I THINK.

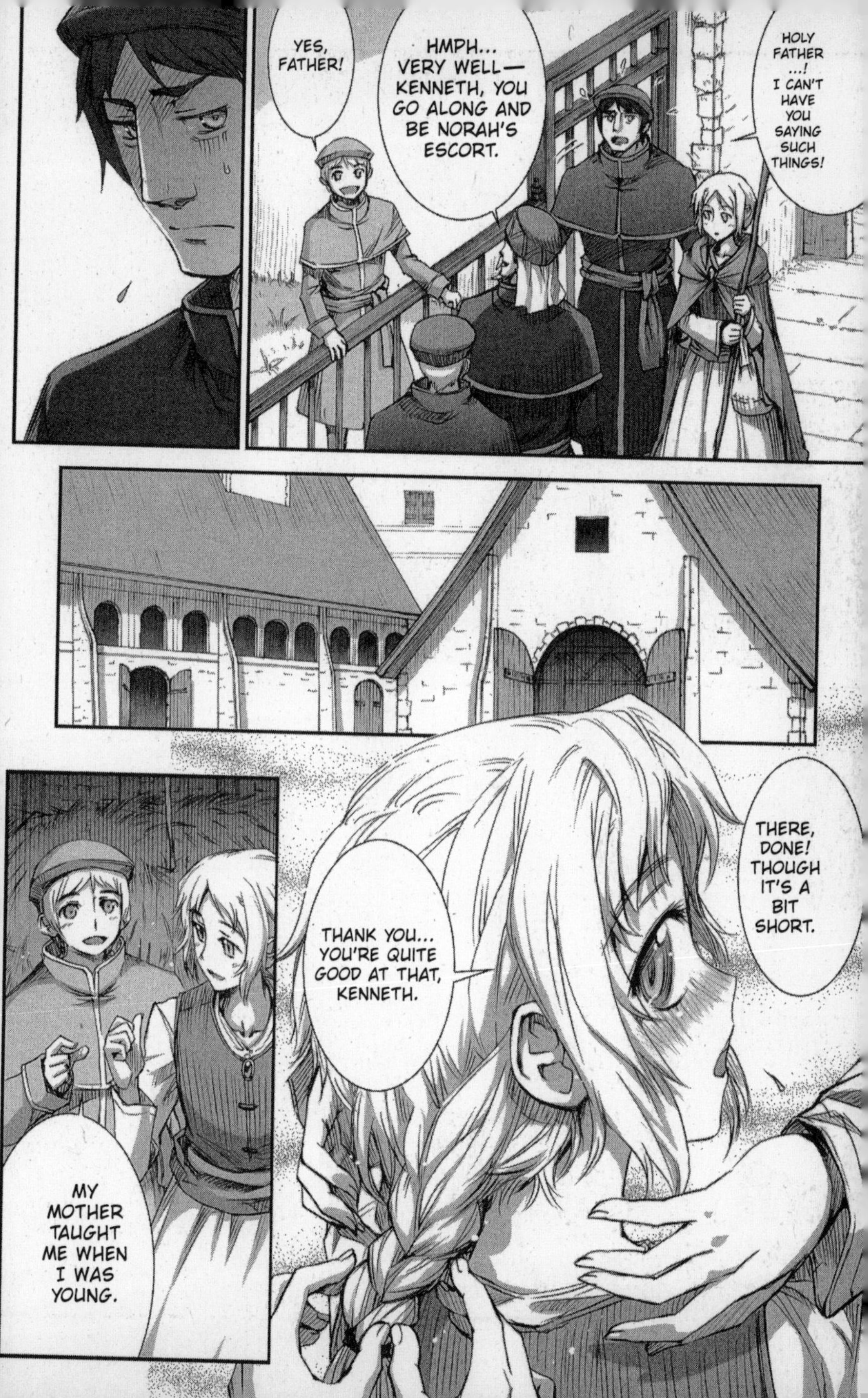
HOLY FATHER...! I CAN'T HAVE YOU SAYING SUCH THINGS!
HMPH... VERY WELL— KENNETH, YOU GO ALONG AND BE NORAH'S ESCORT.
YES, FATHER!
THERE, DONE! THOUGH IT'S A BIT SHORT.
THANK YOU... YOU'RE QUITE GOOD AT THAT, KENNETH.
MY MOTHER TAUGHT ME WHEN I WAS YOUNG.

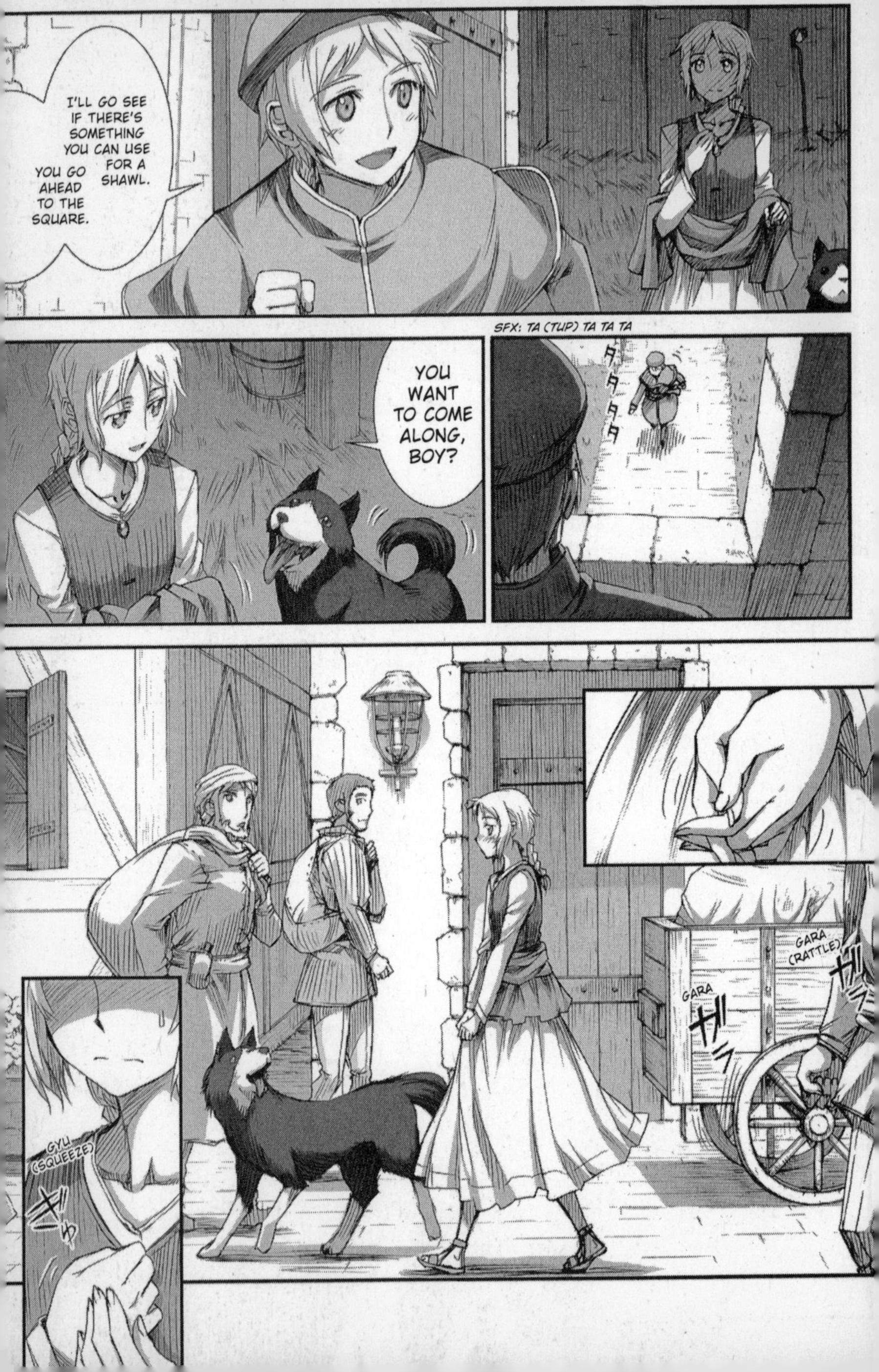
I'LL GO SEE IF THERE'S SOMETHING YOU CAN USE FOR A SHAWL.
YOU GO AHEAD TO THE SQUARE.
SFX: TA (TUP) TA TA TA
YOU WANT TO COME ALONG, BOY?
GARA GARA (RATTLE)
GYU (SQUEEZE)

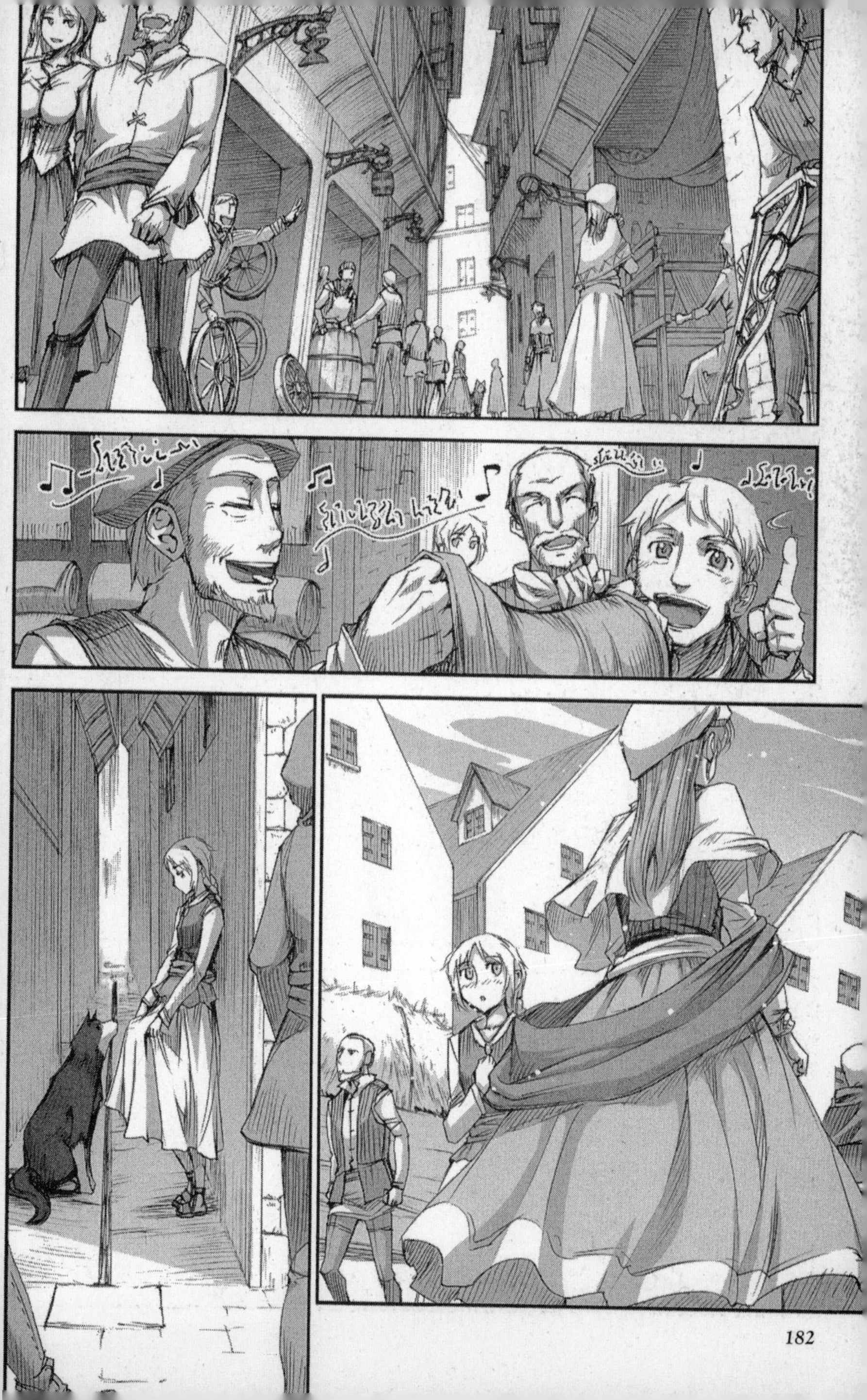

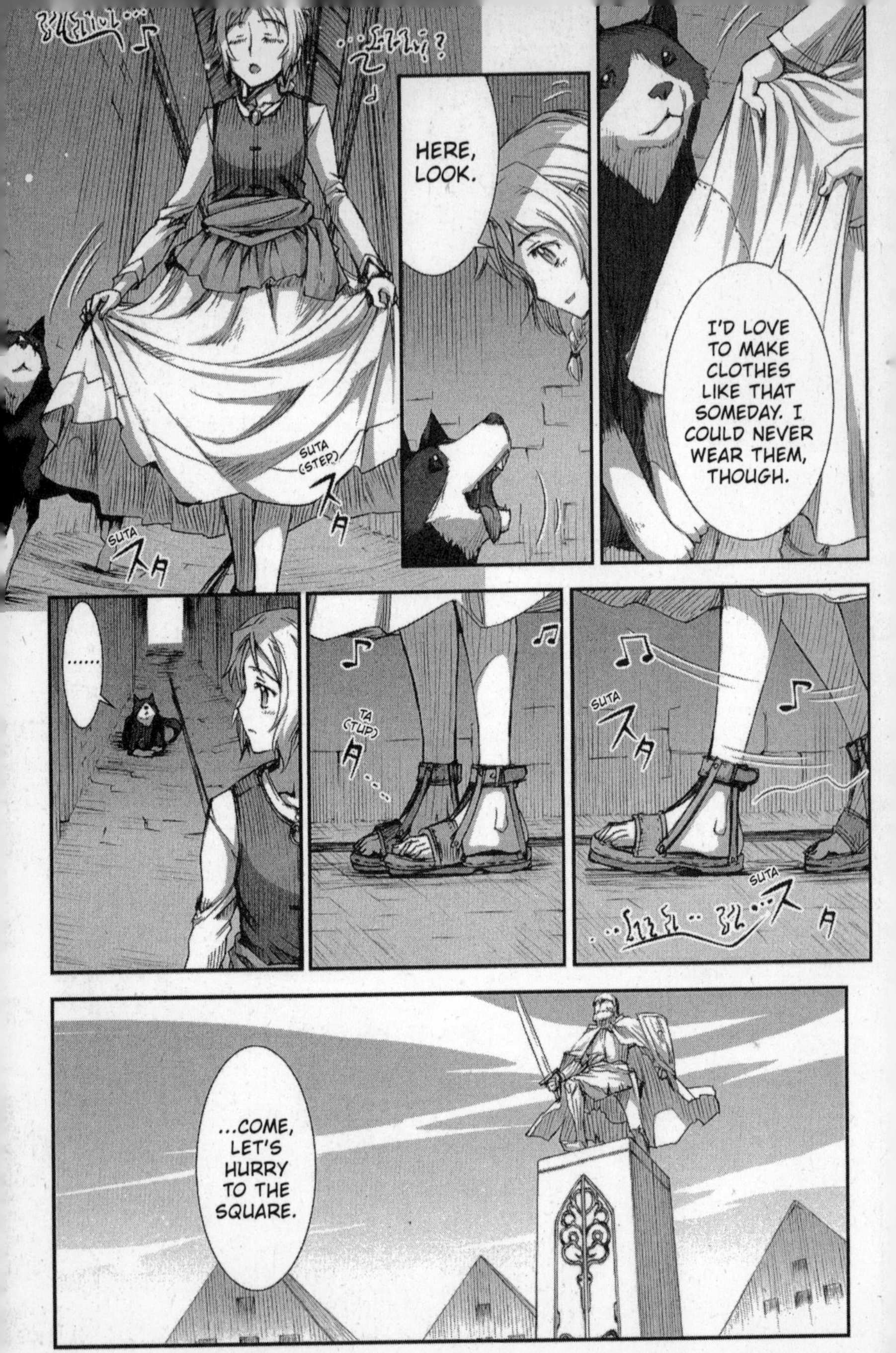
I'D LOVE TO MAKE CLOTHES LIKE THAT SOMEDAY. I COULD NEVER WEAR THEM, THOUGH.
HERE, LOOK.
SUTA (STEP) スタ
SUTA スタ
SUTA スタ
SUTA スタ
TA (TUP) タ...
......
...COME, LET'S HURRY TO THE SQUARE.

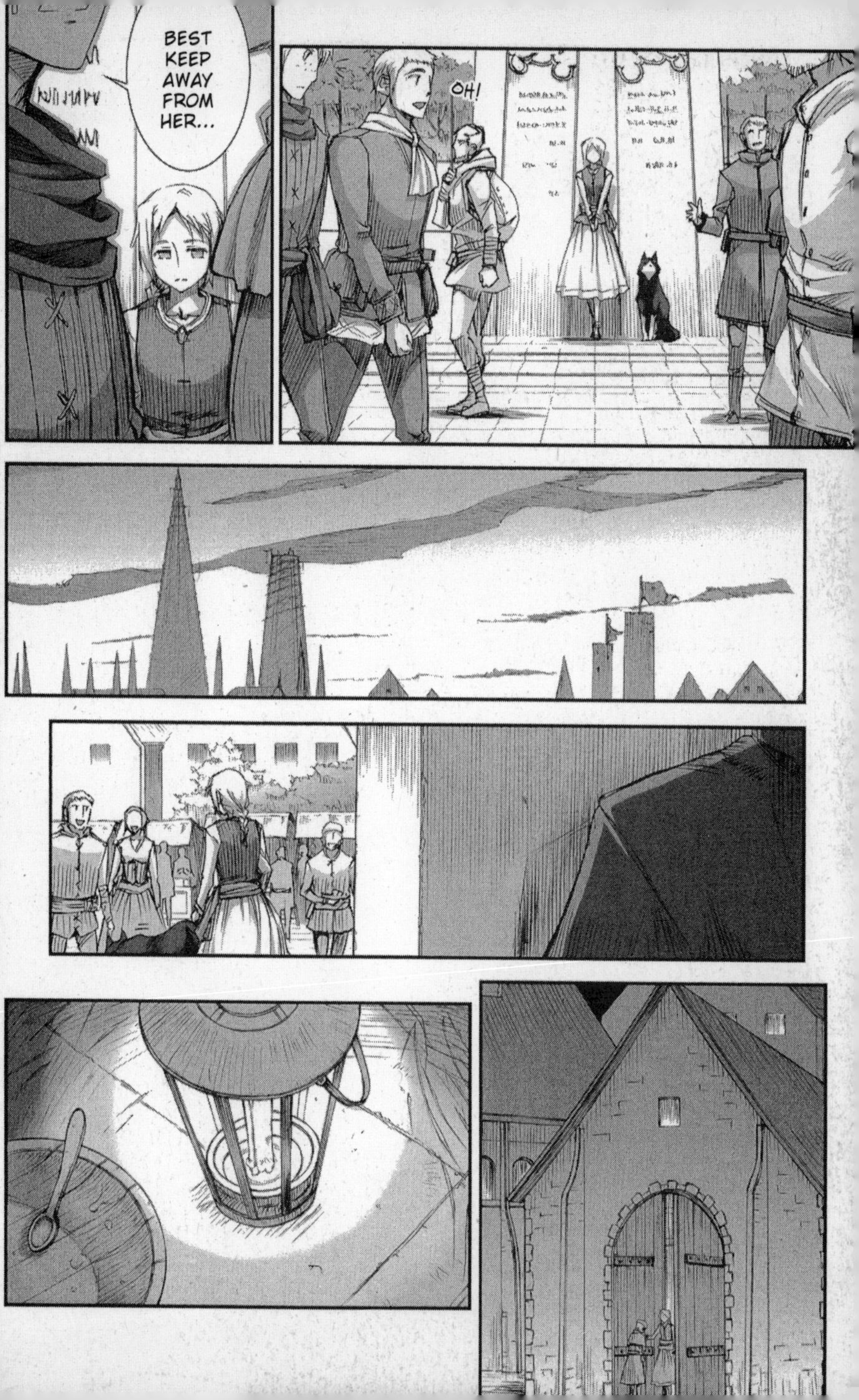
OH!
BEST KEEP AWAY FROM HER...

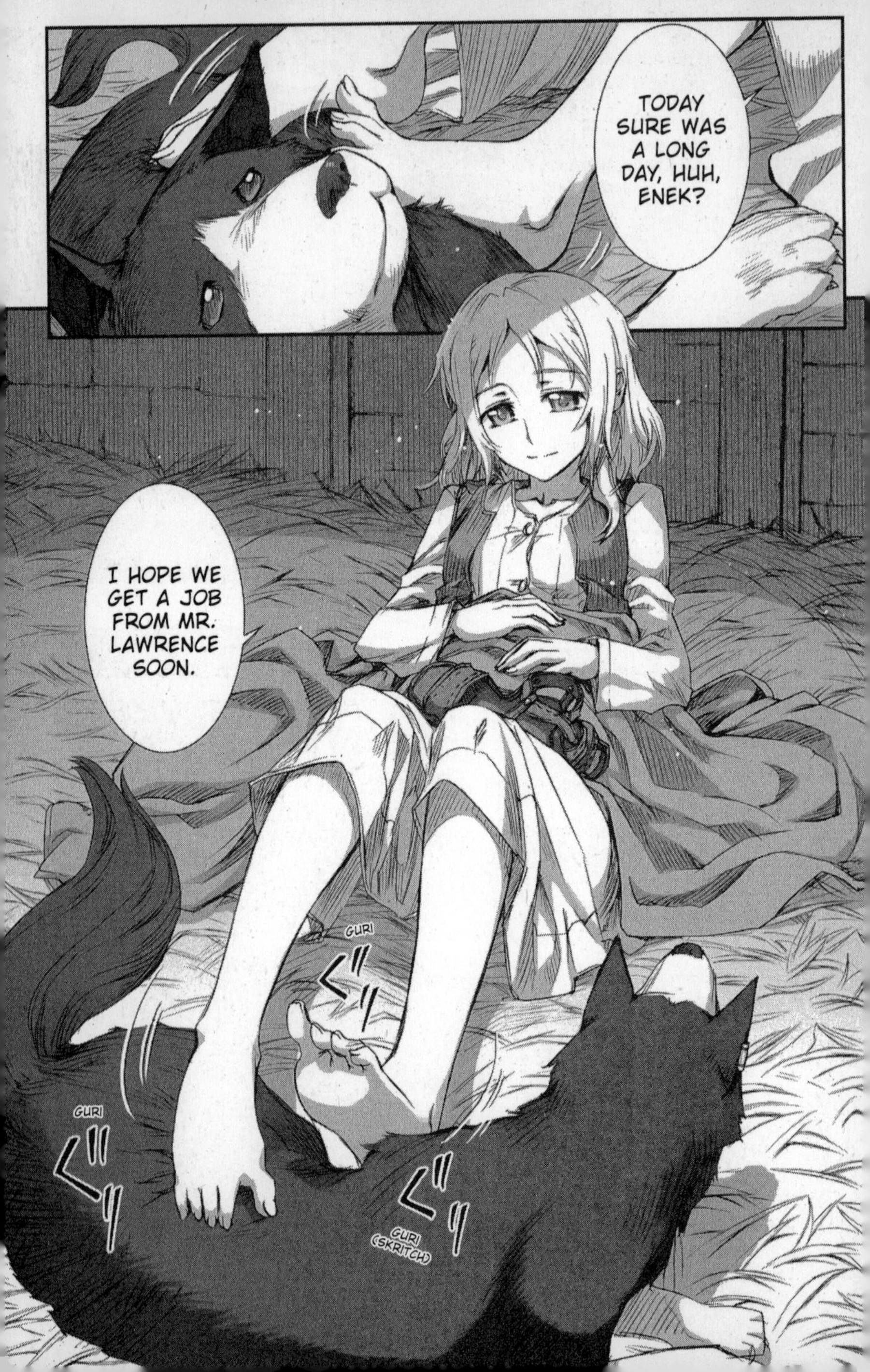
TODAY SURE WAS A LONG DAY, HUH, ENEK?
I HOPE WE GET A JOB FROM MR. LAWRENCE SOON.
GURI
ぐり
GURI
ぐり
ぐり
GURI (SKRITCH)

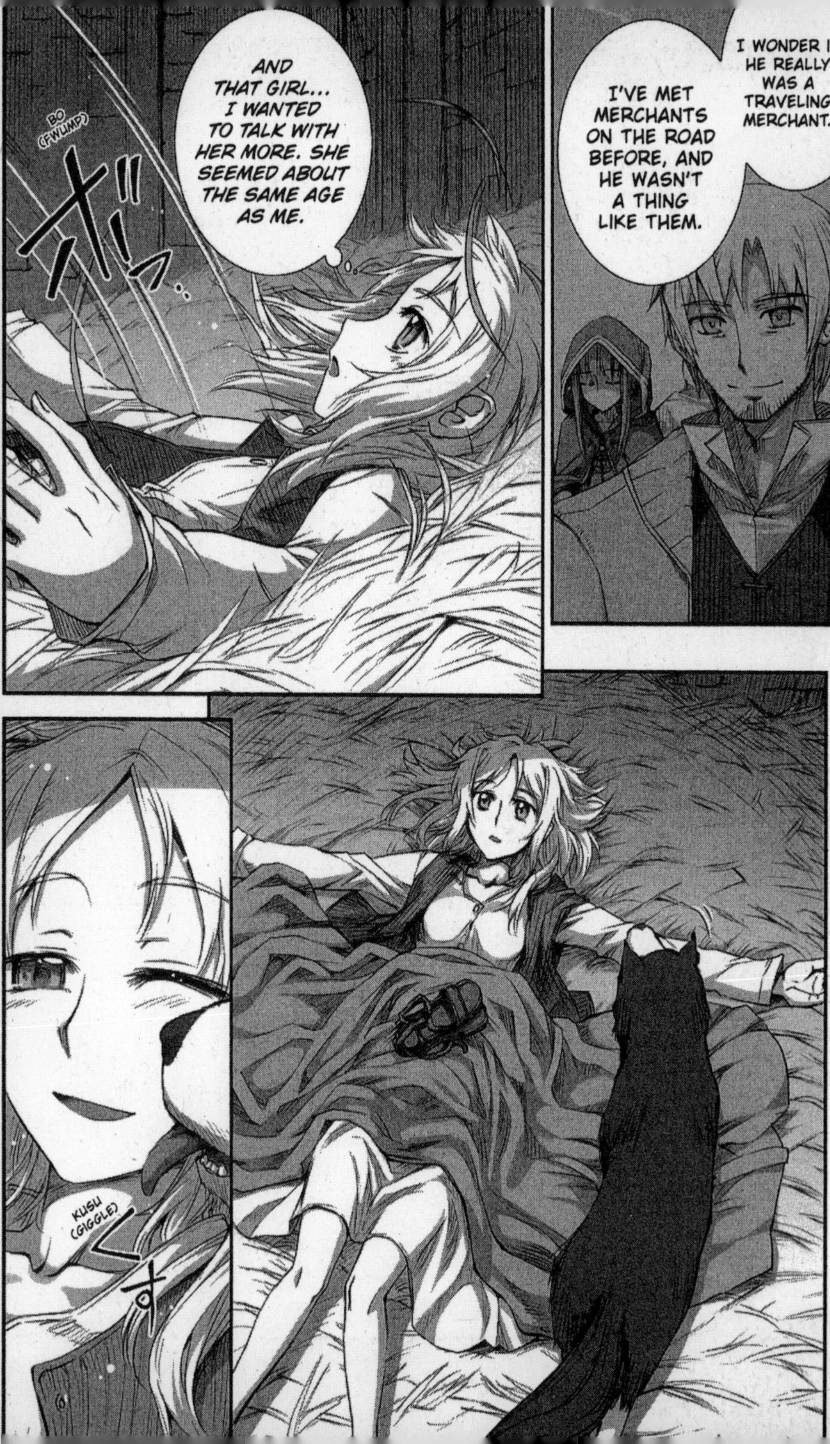
I WONDER IF HE REALLY WAS A TRAVELING MERCHANT.
I'VE MET MERCHANTS ON THE ROAD BEFORE, AND HE WASN'T A THING LIKE THEM.
AND THAT GIRL... I WANTED TO TALK WITH HER MORE. SHE SEEMED ABOUT THE SAME AGE AS ME.
BO (FWUMP)
KUSU (GIGGLE)

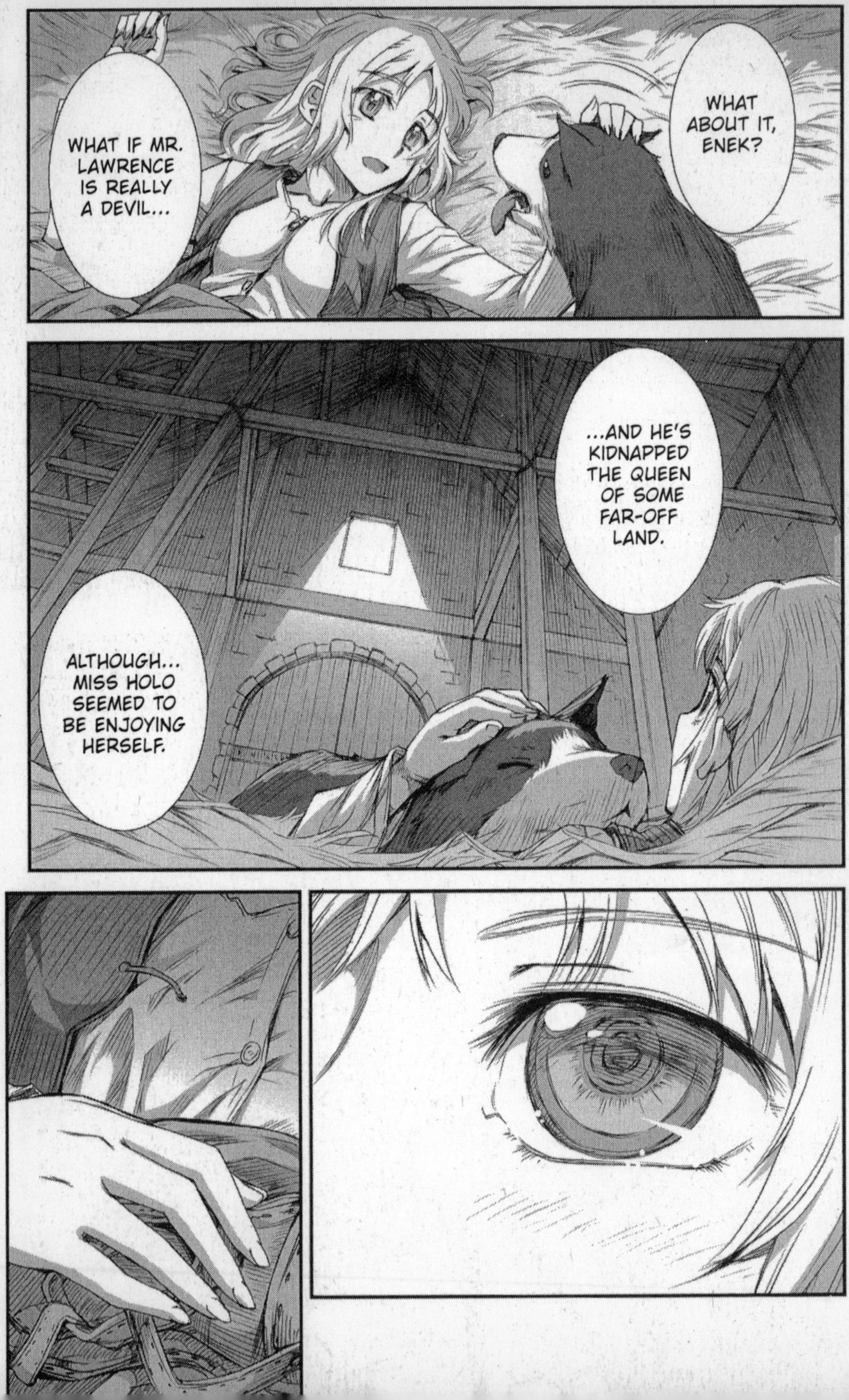
WHAT ABOUT IT, ENEK?
WHAT IF MR. LAWRENCE IS REALLY A DEVIL...
...AND HE'S KIDNAPPED THE QUEEN OF SOME FAR-OFF LAND.
ALTHOUGH... MISS HOLO SEEMED TO BE ENJOYING HERSELF.

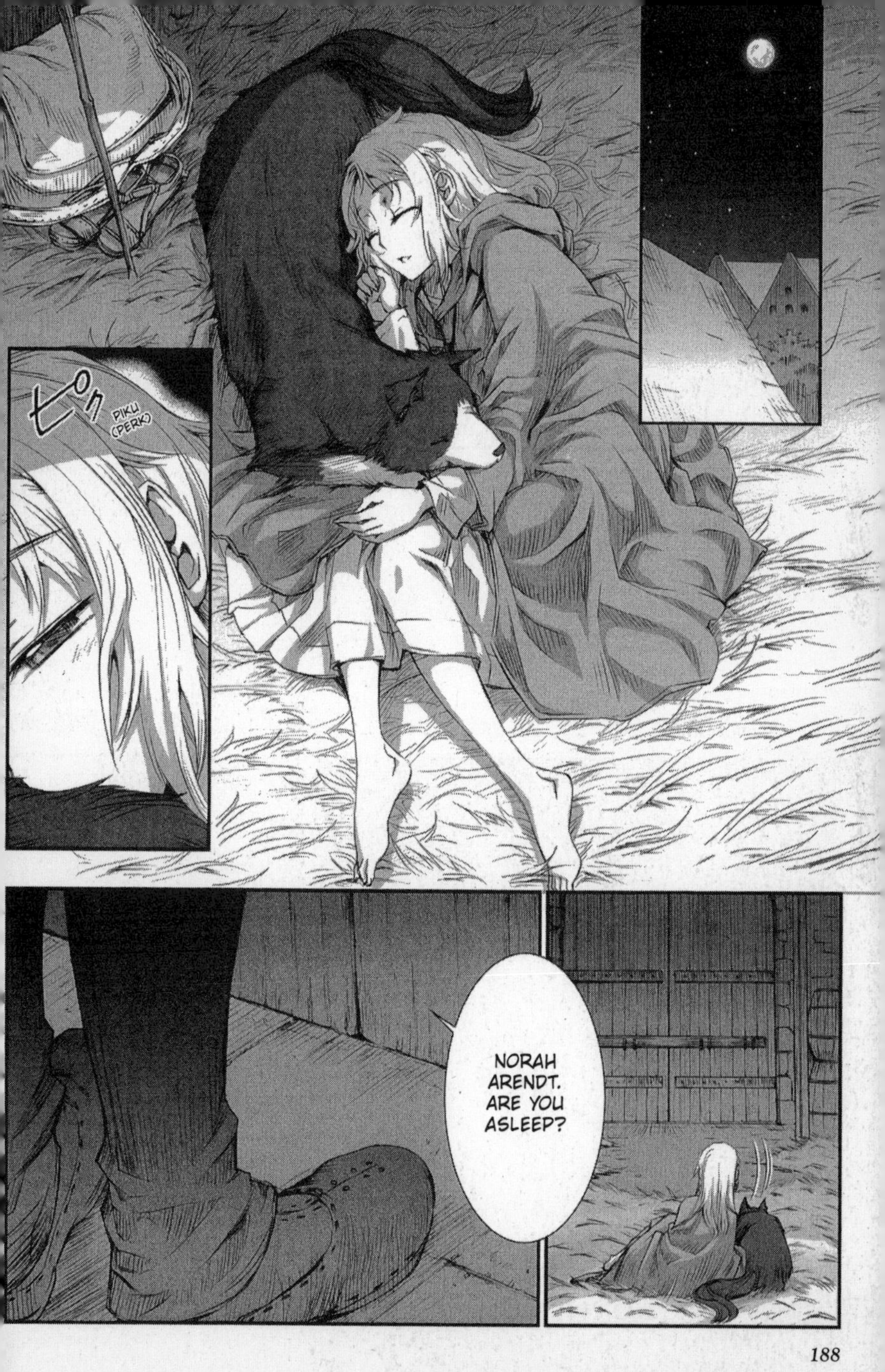
ピクッ
PIKU (PERK)
NORAH ARENDT. ARE YOU ASLEEP?

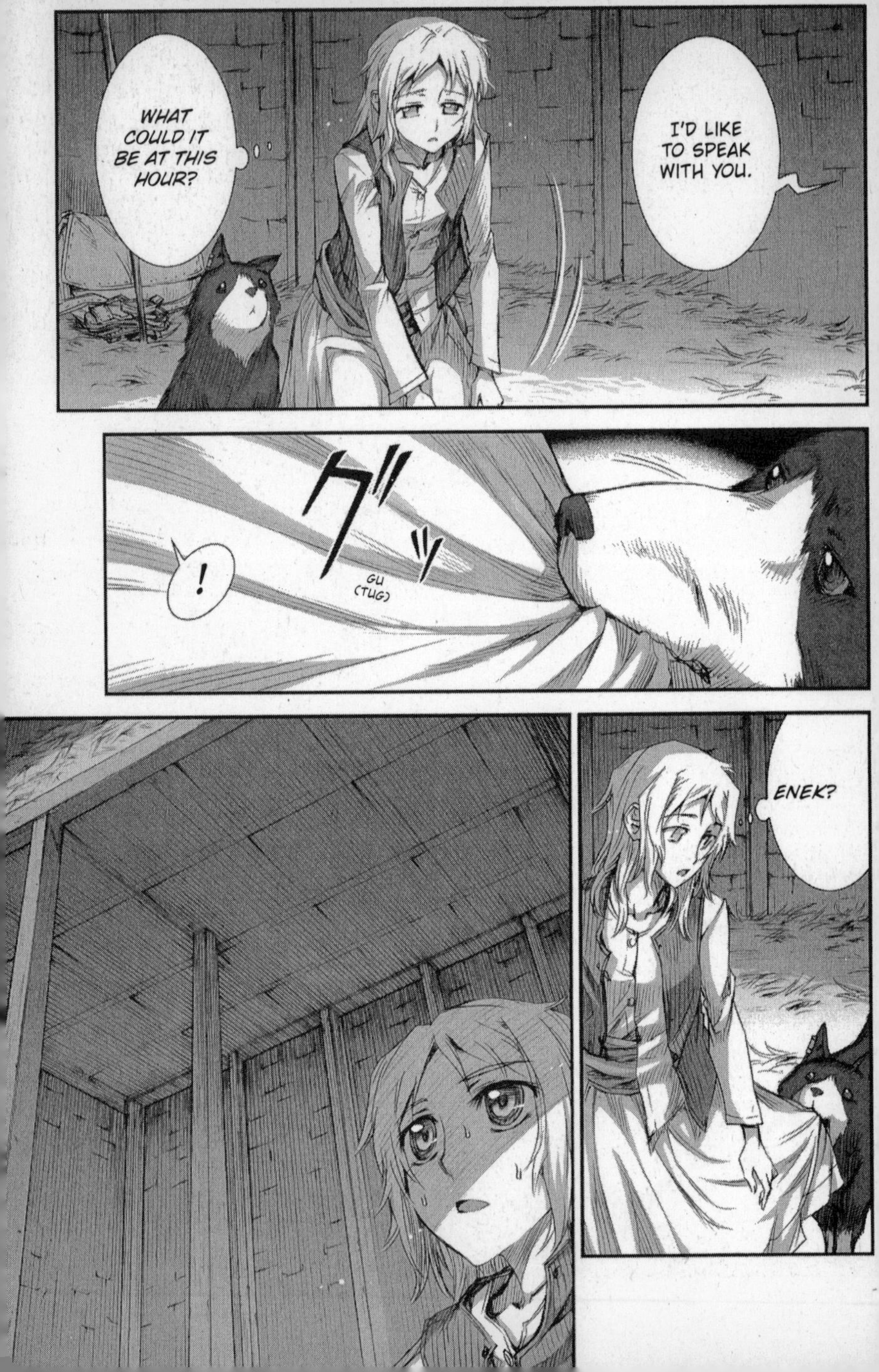
I'D LIKE TO SPEAK WITH YOU.
WHAT COULD IT BE AT THIS HOUR?
GU (TUG)
!
ENEK?

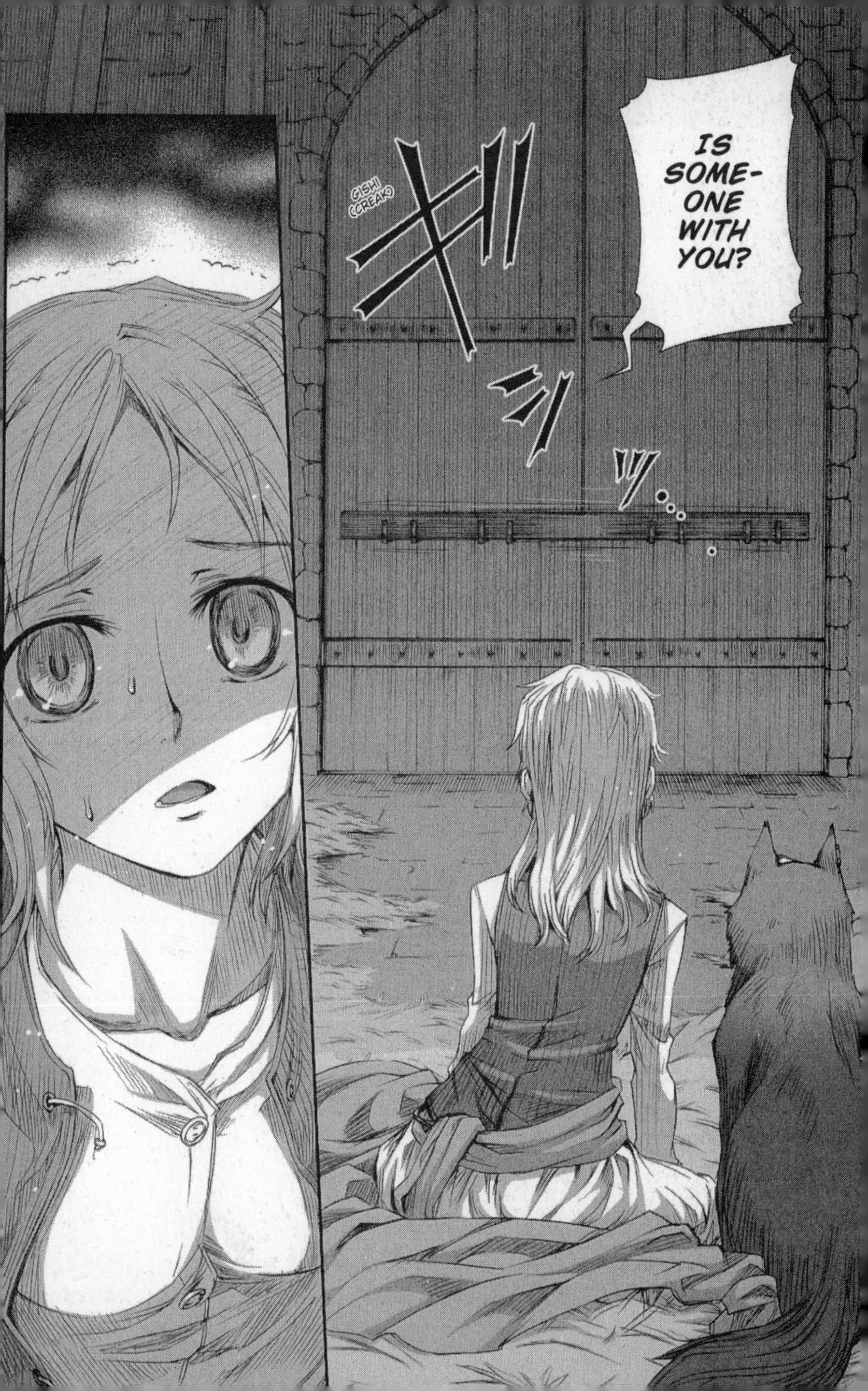
IS SOME-ONE WITH YOU?
GISHI (CREAK)

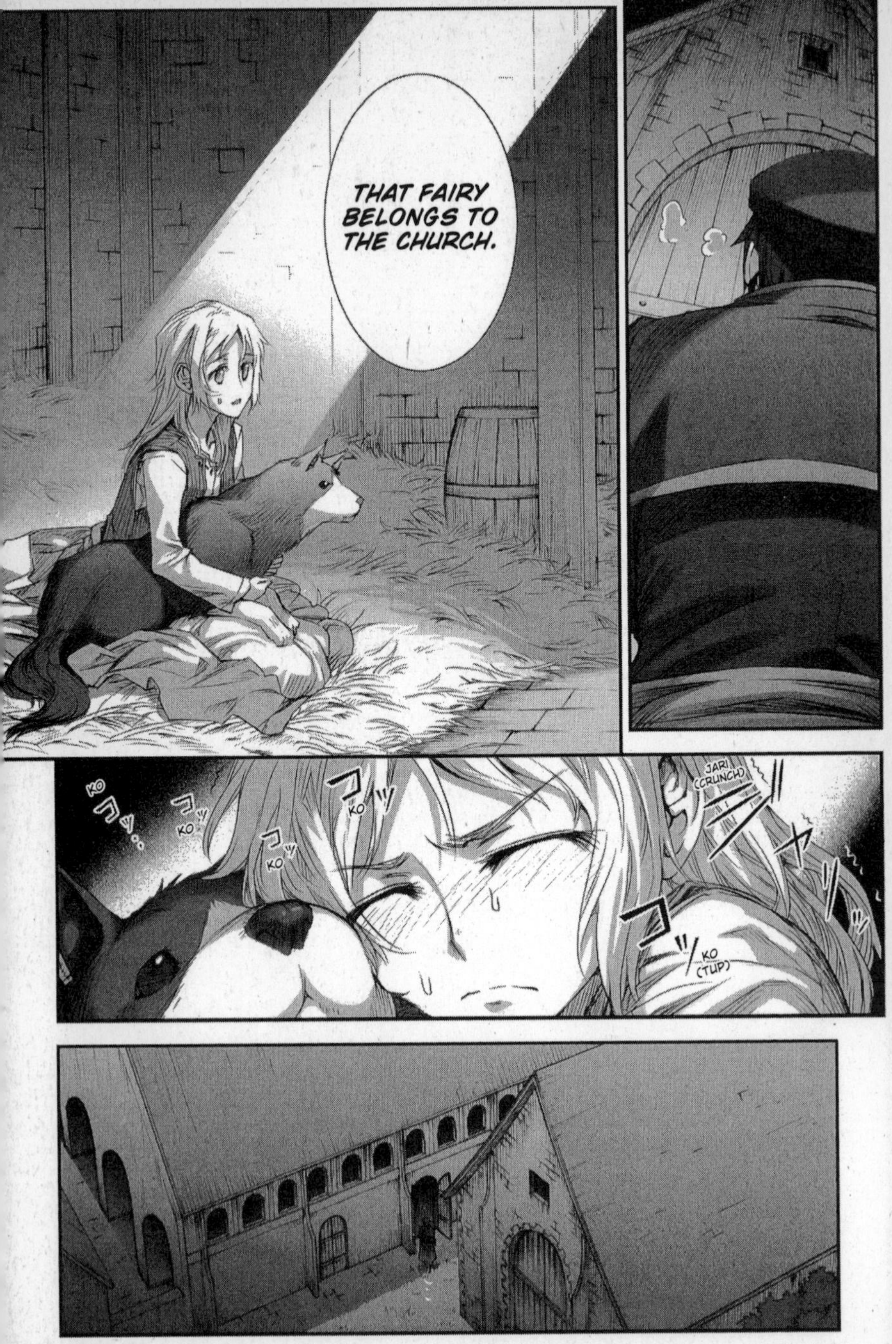
THAT FAIRY BELONGS TO THE CHURCH.
JARI (CRUNCH)
KO (TUP)
KO
KO
KO
KO

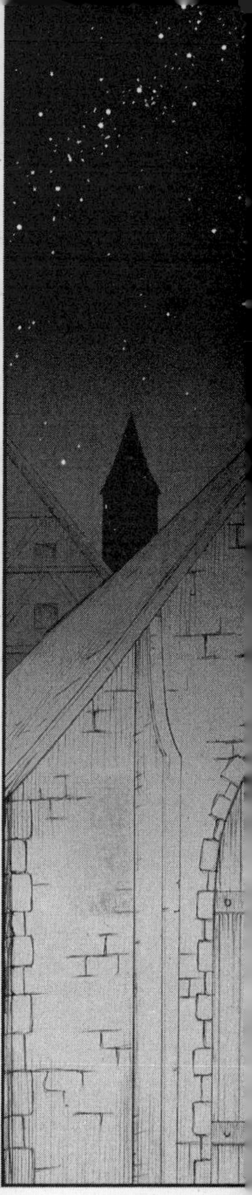

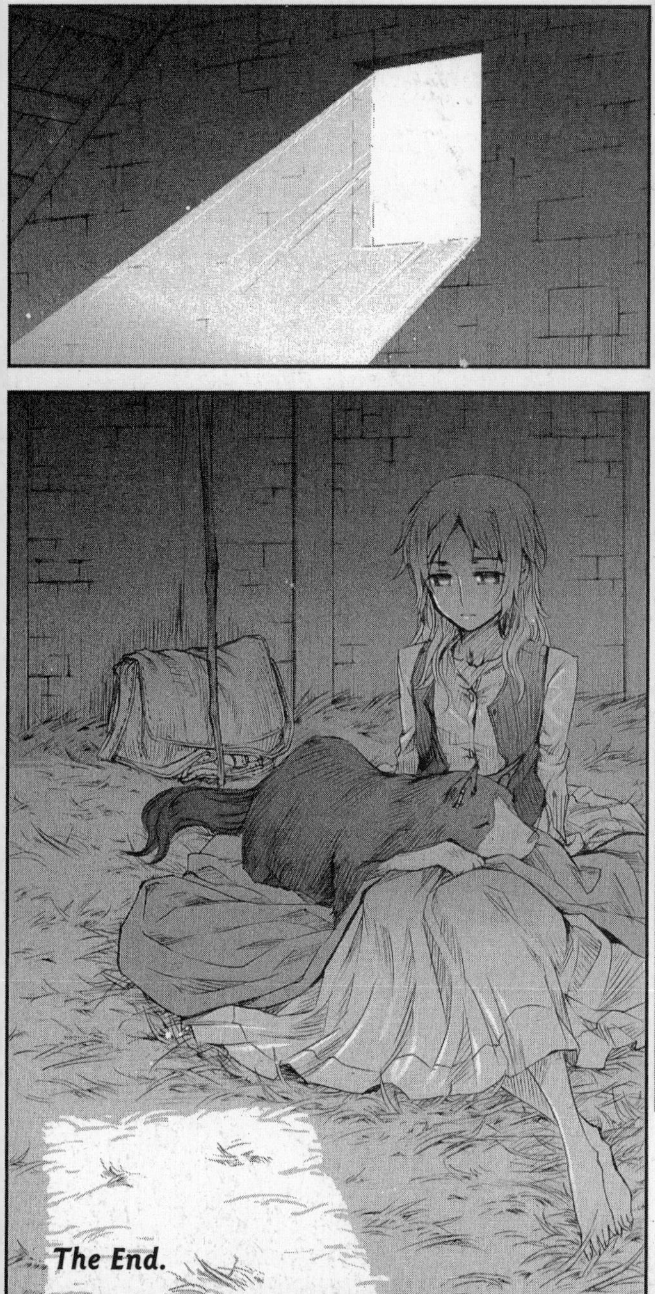
The End.

Special Thanks!
MR. OKAMOTO ITTOUHEI, MR. TENTSU TOI, MR. YAKKUN, MR. N-TA

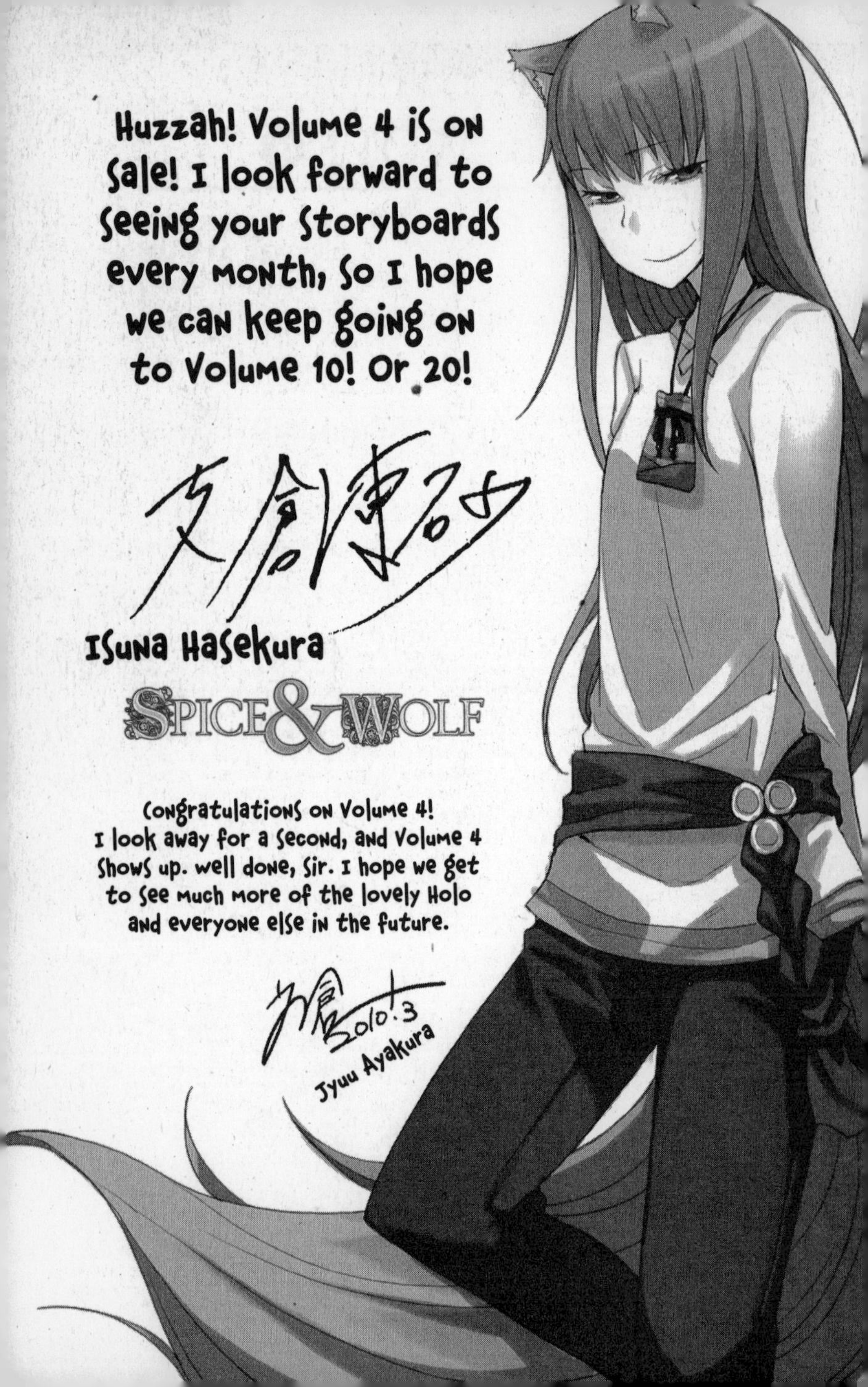

Huzzah! Volume 4 is on sale! I look forward to seeing your storyboards every month, so I hope we can keep going on to Volume 10! Or 20!

Isuna Hasekura

SPICE & WOLF

Congratulations on Volume 4!
I look away for a second, and Volume 4 shows up. well done, Sir. I hope we get to see much more of the lovely Holo and everyone else in the future.

2010.3
Jyuu Ayakura

SPICE & WO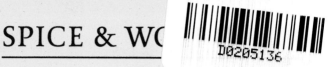

ISUNA H...

KEITO KOUME
CHARACTER DESIGN:
JYUU AYAKURA

TRANSLATION: PAUL STARR

LETTERING: TERRI DELGADO

OOKAMI TO KOUSHINRYOU VOL. 4 © ISUNA HASEKURA / ASCII
MEDIA WORKS 2010 © KEITO KOUME 2010. ALL RIGHTS RESERVED. FIRST
PUBLISHED IN JAPAN IN 2010 BY ASCII MEDIA WORKS INC., TOKYO.
ENGLISH TRANSLATION RIGHTS IN USA, CANADA, AND UK ARRANGED WITH
ASCII MEDIA WORKS INC. THROUGH TUTTLE-MORI AGENCY, INC., TOKYO.

TRANSLATION © 2011 BY HACHETTE BOOK GROUP

YEN PRESS
HACHETTE BOOK GROUP
237 PARK AVENUE, NEW YORK, NY 10017

WWW.HACHETTEBOOKGROUP.COM
WWW.YENPRESS.COM

YEN PRESS IS AN IMPRINT OF HACHETTE BOOK GROUP, INC. THE YEN PRESS
NAME AND LOGO ARE TRADEMARKS OF HACHETTE BOOK GROUP, INC.

FIRST YEN PRESS EDITION: MAY 2011

ISBN: 978-0-316-17826-6

10 9 8 7 6 5 4

BVG

PRINTED IN THE UNITED STATES OF AMERICA